International Law and the Global South

Perspectives from the Rest of the World

Series Editor

Leïla Choukroune, International Law and University Research, Portsmouth University, New Delhi, India

This book series aims to promote a complex vision of contemporary legal developments from the perspective of emerging or developing countries and/or authors integrating these elements into their approach. While focusing on today's law and international economic law in particular, it brings together contributions from, or influenced by, other social sciences disciplines. Written in both technical and non-technical language and addressing topics of contemporary importance to a general audience, the series will be of interest to legal researchers as well as non-lawyers. In referring to the "rest of the world", the book series puts forward new and alternative visions of today's law not only from emerging and developing countries, but also from authors who deliberately integrate this perspective into their thinking. The series approach is not only comparative, post-colonial or critical, but also truly universal in the sense that it places a plurality of well-informed visions at its center.

The Series

- Provides a truly global coverage of the world in reflecting cutting-edge developments and thinking in law and international law
- Focuses on the transformations of international and comparative law with an emphasis on international economic law (investment, trade and development)
- Welcomes contributions on comparative and/or domestic legal evolutions

More information about this series at http://www.springer.com/series/13447

Ajendra Srivastava

Modern Law of International Trade

Comparative Export Trade and International Harmonization

Springer

Ajendra Srivastava
Faculty of Law
Banaras Hindu University
Varanasi, India

ISSN 2510-1420 ISSN 2510-1439 (electronic)
International Law and the Global South
ISBN 978-981-15-5474-2 ISBN 978-981-15-5475-9 (eBook)
https://doi.org/10.1007/978-981-15-5475-9

This Springer imprint is published by the registered company Springer Nature Singapore Pte Ltd.
The registered company address is: 152 Beach Road, #21-01/04 Gateway East, Singapore 189721, Singapore

Preface

This book is primarily concerned with the modern developments in all principal areas of the law-governing trans-border (private) commercial transactions. As is the case with many other fields of law, the law under discussion has undergone substantial changes over a century or more. With the phenomenal increase in volume and speed of trans-border, commercial transactions spurred by the rapid economic growth and the advent of modern means of communications, a plethora of new and modern principles and rules have evolved over the years to cope with new challenges and concerns which undoubtedly need to be thoroughly examined and analyzed.

But the purpose of the book is not limited to providing a comprehensive and modern account of the law concerning the international trade transactions. Rather, a key feature of the book is that it employs the comparative law method of study and examines the similarities and differences in the laws of the two key common law jurisdictions. The primary motivation for undertaking a comparative law study is indeed the remarkable unity among the national trade laws of different countries. One of the most important reasons for the striking similarities between different national laws is that they are traditionally premised on the mercantile customs of medieval times commonly applied to merchants of different nationalities. Later, they found their way into the national systems governing private, commercial transactions and, in some instances, were assimilated into national laws with a little or no change.

In addition, the book, with the overarching aim of the law reform, attempts to provide an account of the various efforts devoted to bringing harmony in the national trade laws. It is important to devote our attention to the current movement toward international unification of private, substantive laws which is a remarkable legal achievement of our times. Interestingly, the comparative law method of study is linked to the international harmonization of laws in many significant ways and is unquestionably crucial for the success of the latter.

It remains to express my sincere gratitude to all of those who helped me with this project. First, I am very grateful to my esteemed colleagues and friends. I am especially thankful to Prof. R. P. Rai, Head and Dean for giving me a supporting environment, and Dr. Rajnish Kumar Singh and Prof. Sibaram Tripathy for their constant support and encouragement. But I owe a particular debt to Dr. Rajnish Kumar Singh who has been extremely helpful in giving suggestions and comments upon the draft chapters. I have greatly benefitted from his ideas and thoughts. I am also indebted to the anonymous reviewer whose comments and suggestions have proved extremely helpful in giving final shape to the book.

Some of my students and research scholars willingly rendered their assistance with typing and preparing the lists of cases and contents. I wish to express my thanks also to them. In particular, I am thankful to Ms. Sonal Singh, a research candidate for helping me in giving finishing touches to the manuscript.

I am also very grateful to the publishing team at Springer. I highly appreciate the generous support and encouragement I received from Ms. Sagarika Ghosh, Ms. Nupoor Singh and Mr. Daniel Joseph Glarance.

Last but not least, I owe special debts to my wife and children who showed tremendous patience in allowing me to work late at night but never complained.

Varanasi, India Ajendra Srivastava

Contents

About the Author

Ajendra Srivastava holds a doctoral degree in law from the University of Delhi. He specializes in international law, but is also interested in human rights, international environmental law, trade law, sale of goods law, international investment law, and property law. He authored the textbook *An Introduction to Transfer of Property Act, Second Edition*, (Jaipur: University Book House, 2017) and co-edited *Science, Technology and Law Reform* (New Delhi: Satyam Books, 2014), which includes contributions by **Supreme Court** and **High Court** judges, as well as leading academics from India and abroad. In addition, the author has published more than a dozen research papers in respected national and international journals. He has also been an occasional Op-Ed contributor to the leading national daily, The Statesman.

List of Cases

Chapter 1
Nature and Scope of the Law of International Trade

1.1 Characteristics and Sources

The law of international trade may be described as the law that governs the inter-jurisdictional, private (commercial) transactions. Much of this law, therefore, is private, domestic law as opposed to the public law of international trade. The latter is aimed at regulating the trading relations between states and therefore is beyond the scope of this book.[1] Another important characteristic of the law under discussion is that, unlike most of the branches of law such as the law of contract, tort, property and family law, it is not a distinct branch of law. It rather embraces a wide array of laws governing the delivery of goods and services across the national borders. These are as wide and different as the law of sale and carriage of goods, insurance, export finance, and dispute resolution. Evidently, the areas covered are too wide in scope and too different and fragmented that they can be hardly treated as a separate and distinct subject. However, the law of international trade is unique in at least one important respect. It places emphasis on a comparative method of study. It hardly needs to be said that, in recent years, the comparative method of study has assumed great significance.[2] This is particularly true in respect of international trade law where its potential uses in reconciling differences between domestic laws are widely acknowledged.

[1]The public law of international trade is mainly to be found in the World Trade Organization (WTO) law and the regional trade agreements. The former is a single body of law consisting of the WTO Agreement, i.e., the 1994 Marrakesh Agreement Establishing the World Trade Organization and the agreements—multilateral trade agreements (MTAs) and plurilateral trade agreements (PTAs) to be found in its various annexes. See Sect. 1.5.

[2]See Paton and Derham (eds.) (1972), p. 42.

A. Srivastava, *Modern Law of International Trade*, International Law and the Global South, https://doi.org/10.1007/978-981-15-5475-9_1

Furthermore, the law of international trade is a heterogeneous mass of legal rules. Put simply, the rules governing international trade are to be found in a variety of sources of law.[3] In addition to mercantile customs, statutes, international conventions, judicial decisions, and arbitral awards, these comprise sources like model laws, international restatements of law, and model clauses developed by international organizations such as the UNCITRAL and UNIDROIT; and the rules of practices developed by the various trade organizations such as the International Chamber of Commerce (ICC). Remarkably, in the field of trade law, the applicable law typically includes not just the legally binding law but also a kind of informal, living law. In contrast to the former, the latter derives their strength from the quality of the text itself.[4] Some of the striking examples in the context include the UNIDROIT Principles of International Commercial Contracts (UNIDROIT Principles) which were first published in 1994 as an international restatement of the contract law (see Chap. 2); and the International Rules for the Interpretation of Trade Terms (the INCOTERMS), promulgated by the ICC. It may be noted that the rules of practices, like Incoterms, being "transactional law" do not have the force of (true) law but become law for the parties by their incorporation into contracts (see Chap. 2, Sect. 2.4.3). This aspect will be explored more fully in the subsequent chapter, suffices it to state here that the modern, transnational commercial law rest on a variety of harmonization instruments promulgated by a variety of actors—states, international organizations, trade associations, and groups of the scholars.

1.2 Modern Law and *Lex Mercatoria*[5]

In fact, the significance of the informal law-making, in the field of modern law, cannot be overstated. Driven by the desire of making trade laws harmonized and truly international the international community has shown considerable interest in developing a set of non-positive norms, such as the rules of practices and standard-term contracts, as well as the international restatements both at international and regional levels which has resulted in an impressive number of uniform law instruments existing independently of the state. Interestingly, for many scholars these instruments exhibit the features of the *lex mercatoria*[6] and thus may deserve the label of a "new *lex*

---

[3]The term, sources of law is commonly understood as referring to the formal or authoritative source of law reflecting the will of state such as statutes, court decisions, and custom. However, here a broad approach to the meaning of the source is taken, which concerns not only the official sources as based on state-sanctioned positive norms but also the living law.

[4]Furmston (2012), p. 35.

[5]See Goody (2005), pp. 539–62; Volckart and Mangels (1999), pp. 427–50; Burdick (1902), pp. 470–85; Trakman (2003), pp. 265–304; Michaels (2007), pp. 447–468; Kerr (1929), pp. 350–367.

[6]Bonell (1992), p. 629. The UNIDROIT Principles expressly state: They [the Principles] may be applied when the parties have agreed that their contract be governed by "general principles of law", the "*lex mercatoria*" or the like. Preamble to the UNIDROIT Principles. See also Volckart and Mangels (1999), pp. 427–50.

mercatoria" or a "new new *lex mercatoria*" of the present day.[7] In order to enable us to better understand this relationship between the modern law of international trade and the *lex mercatoria,* we need to examine the matter in some more detail.

The phrase, "modern *lex mercatoria*" is usually identified with the existence of trade usages, model contracts, standard clauses, general legal principles, and international commercial arbitration.[8] A great part of this law is viewed as "developed autonomously" that is to say, developed by the business community with a little involvement of state agencies. Sometimes, the term, a "new new *lex mercatoria*" is also used to denote an established system of law with codified legal rules and strongly institutionalized international arbitration.[9] However, the modern *lex mercatoria,* though it displays the elements of its medieval counterpart, differs in some important respects from the latter. The (medieval) *lex mercatoria,*[10] as the term is traditionally understood, denotes a system of law which was evolved from the practices and usages of the medieval merchants of different countries. Although there is considerable debate about the true characteristics of the *lex mercatoria,* there seems to be the general agreement that it consisted of customs and usages observed by merchants across the borders and commonly recognized by the courts of the different parts of the world. Since the *lex mercatoria* was mainly administered by the merchant courts and was not created by the national statutes or decisions of the regular courts, it acquired a homogenous and distinct character.[11] Further, the *lex mercatoria,* unlike many modern instruments of harmonization, was not the product of a conscious decision-making; rather it was the product of the spontaneous dealings.[12] On the other hand, a great part of the modern trade law, in particular, the modern instruments of harmonization—rules of practices, model clauses, and standard terms are not the legally binding instruments and are quite different from the (medieval) *lex mercatoria.* In view of these significant differences between the early *lex mercatoria* and its modern counterpart, it is doubtful whether the modern instruments of harmonization that make up a bulk of (modern) trade law can rightly be labeled as part of the *lex mercatoria.*[13]

[7]For different conceptions of the *lex mercatoria,* see Michaels (2007), p. 448.

[8]Volckart and Mangels (1999), p. 430.

[9]Michaels (2007), p. 448.

[10]Although the existence of the *lex mercatoria* is traced back to the ancient times, it took a definite shape only during the medieval period.

[11]Burdick (1902), p. 478. Until the seventeenth century, the *lex mercatoria* was rarely referred to in the common law courts. See ibid. However, it is questionable whether the medieval law merchant ever existed as an autonomous system.

[12]However, as Burdick says, since the early sixteenth century the *lex moratoria* gradually lost its homogenous character and no longer recognized as a separate body of legal rules administered in certain courts. Burdick (1902), p. 480. As a result, in the subsequent period we witness an amalgamation of the *lex mercatoria* with common law. Ibid., p. 482.

[13]See Goody (2005), pp. 546–49.

1.3 International Trade: Distinctive Features

1.3.1 Nature of Trade Transactions

In a broad sense, a trade transaction concerns an exchange of goods or services. In other words, it involves the supply of goods or services for money or an exchange or barter of goods.[14] In an exchange or barter, the supply of goods from one side replaces money for the supply of goods from the other side.[15] Thus, where goods are exchanged for money the transaction is a sale transaction but where goods are exchanged for goods it is a barter or exchange.[16] It may be mentioned that an exchange transaction is a kind of "countertrade." In "countertrade," the exporter receives payment in terms of products from the importer. For example, where an Indian exporter of textile to the United States receives payment in an equivalent value of soft drinks the transaction in question is countertrade.[17] The products that form the subject-matter of an overseas trade are broadly of two kinds: goods or services, or both.[18] It needs emphasis that like the goods, services are also tradable

[14]"Trade" is generally understood as buying and selling of commodities for profit. See *Shorter Oxford English Dictionary on Historical Principles*, vol. 2, pp. 3312–13. According to *Black's Law Dictionary*, Eighth Edition, "trade" is the business of buying and selling or bartering goods or services. Garner (ed.) (2006) *Black's Law Dictionary*, p. 1529. Revised Fourth Edition of *Black's Law Dictionary* defines "trade" as "the business of buying and selling for money; traffic; barter." *Black's Law Dictionary* (2002), p. 1665.

[15]On distinction between sale and barter, see Chap. 5 infra.

[16]In a sale of goods transaction, consideration must be in the form of money. This requirement ordinarily distinguishes a sale from an exchange. See Guest AG (ed.) (2006), p. 33; Sale of Goods Act, 1930, s. 4 ("[a] contract of sale of goods is a contract whereby the seller transfers or agrees to transfer the property in goods to the buyer for a price."). For further discussion on the distinction between "sale" and "exchange," see infra, Chap. 5.

[17]According to the *Legal Guide on International Countertrade Transactions*, prepared by the UNCITRAL, "countertrade transactions" are "those transactions in which one party supplies goods, services, technology or other economic value to the second party, and, in return, the first party purchases from the second party an agreed amount of goods, services, technology or other economic value." In a countertrade, thus, the supplies in the two directions are linked in a manner that the conclusion of the supply contract in one direction depends on the conclusion of the supply contact in the other direction. See UNCITRAL *Legal Guide on International Countertrade Transactions* (New York: United Nations, 1993), A/CN.9/SER.B/3. Terms used for various types of "countertrade" or "barter" are: "counter-purchase," "buy-back," "direct offset," and "indirect offset." Id., p. 5. For further discussion, see Chap. 5. The distinction between a countertrade (counter-purchase or buy-back) and barter is that the latter is a "spot" transaction while the former connotes a long-standing contractual relationship. For example, in a buy-back transaction the seller is paid in the form of products produced by it for the buyer. Further, in an exchange of goods or barter, unlike the countertrade transactions, there is no "export price." See Howse (2010), p. 289.

[18]International commercial transactions, in addition to the goods and services-based transactions, embrace transactions involving transfer of technology. "Transfer of technology" has been defined as the transfer of "systematic knowledge for the manufacture of a product, for the application of a process or for the rendering of a service and does not extend to the transactions involving the mere sale or lease of goods." See the United Nations Conference on Trade and Development (UNCTAD)

commodity and as a matter of fact, in recent years, the services sector has undergone profound transformation. There has been phenomenal increase in international trade in services which represents an important contemporary development in the field of international trade law. In fact, traditional view that services cannot form the subject-matter of trade or commerce and their role is limited to "service the economy" no longer holds true and services are now treated as equivalent to durable goods.[19] Services include commercial services such as carriage of goods, construction works; financial services including banking and insurance services; health care and education; information and communications technology (ICT)-enabled services, such as software services, information services, engineering, research and development (R&D); and tourism (see infra, Chap. 5).[20] As a result of the growing importance of trade in services and the recognition of the need to liberalize and regulate it, international trade in services is now regulated under the legal framework established by the WTO Agreement. The General Agreement on Trade and Services (GATS) which applies to international trade in services is set out in Annex 1C of the WTO Agreement (see infra Sect. 1.5).

Although both—goods and services—have much in common and like the goods services can also be exported or supplied to a non-resident, there is the need to treat them separately from a purely legal perspective. Services, unlike goods, are not homogeneous in nature and can be delivered to an importer in a variety of ways. Modes of supply of services include: (a) "cross-border supply," such as supply of services through internet; (b) "consumption abroad," such as when services are rendered to a consumer temporarily present in the country of export including a traveler, student, or patient; (c) "commercial presence," such as when services are delivered in the country of importer through subsidiaries or branches; and (d) "presence of natural persons," such as when services are delivered through employees of an organization in the country of import.[21] In this way, drawing a distinction between trade in goods and services is important at least from a regulatory perspective. Regulating trade in services is more challenging than regulating merchandise trade. We will notice the

---

Draft International Code of Conduct on the Transfer of Technology, sixth session of Conference on June 5, 1985, Chapter 1, Paragraph 1.2, Doc. TD/CODE TOT/47 (New York: UNCTAD 1985). However, this work does not extend to international technology transfer arrangements or transactions. These transactions give rise to a host of issues pertaining to the international protection of intellectual property rights (IPRs). On the issues that arise in the context of international technology transfer, see generally Zaphiriou (1992), pp. 879–915. Trade-related aspects of IPRs are now addressed by the Agreement on the Trade Related Aspects of Intellectual Property Rights (TRIPS Agreement). The TRIPS Agreement as well as the General Agreement of Trade in Services (GATS) have resulted from the Uruguay Round negotiations and are an integral part of the WTO Agreement. See infra, Sect. 1.5.

[19]See Wiener (2005) p. 145.

[20]For different categories of services, see generally Hussain et al. (1999).

[21]See the General Agreement on Trade in Services (GATS), Article I: 2. See also *Implementing a Survey on Exports of ICT-enabled Services: Analytical report on the main findings and lessons learnt from survey implementation during 2017*, UNCTAD, ICT Policy Section, Technical Note No. 11, Unedited TN/UNCTAD/ICT4D/11, June 2018; *A Handbook on the GATS Agreement* (2005), p. 4.

distinction between goods and service in some more detail at the appropriate places in this book.

A substantial portion of international trade, indeed, consists of merchandize trade which takes place between all countries irrespective of their level of economic development. Since the middle of the last century overseas trade in goods has grown very fast. According to the statistics released by the United Nations Conference on Trade and Development (UNCTAD), international trade in goods grew from $61,811 million in 1950 to $3,516,772 million in 1991 (at current prices); and by the end of 2015, it had reached $16,551,591 million.[22] Significantly, international trade in services has also grown strikingly fast. According to the UNCTAD, international trade in services which stood $395,600 million in 1980, rose to $4,720,180 million in 2013.[23] In fact, the rise in per capita income in many countries is primarily attributable to the growth in service sector.[24]

1.3.2 International and Domestic Trade Distinguished

An overseas trade is very different from a trade on the domestic market. The former relates to an array of widely different but contextually related contractual transactions that take place between the residents of different countries or customs territories.[25] In an international trade the initial sale of goods contract is linked to many further contracts, for example, a shipping contract under which goods are to be transported to a buyer in a foreign country; contract of insurance for minimizing or avoiding the risks involved in the transactions; contracts with bankers; and distribution agreements. Therefore, when compared to a domestic transaction under which delivery of goods usually occurs at the seller's premises, it is a very complex transaction and exhibit many peculiar features.

First, in international trade the parties operate under the foreign laws; goods travel a long distance and are delivered across the national borders. This requires the services of a carrier to transport the goods to their destination; an insurer to

---

[22] Available at: http://unctadstat.unctad.org/wds/TableViewer/tableView.aspx?ReportId=101.

[23] Ibid.

[24] Raychaudhuri and De (2012), p. 1.

[25] A "customs territory," though not an independent state, has long been recognized as capable of establishing trading relations with another state or customs territory. Such territories are eligible to become member of WTO provided that they possess "full autonomy in the conduct of its external commercial relations." See the (Marrakesh) Agreement Establishing the World Trade Organization (the WTO Agreement), Article XII, adopted on April 15, 1994. For the text, see (1994) 33 ILM 1125. Examples include Hong Kong and Macao. See also Davey (2005), p. 73. In addition, there are customs unions (CU), free trade areas (FTAs), and common markets composed of a group of countries. For example, European Union as a customs union is the largest group comprising 28 member states and is, in its independent capacity, a member of the WTO as are each of its member states. The member states of a CU eliminate tariffs, other barriers to trade between them and adopt a common external trade policy. See Bagwell et al. (2016) p. 1128. For more information on the WTO membership, visit https://www.wto.org/english/thewto_e/whatis_e/tif_e/org3_e.htm#join.

cover the goods against any loss during transit since liability of a carrier is usually limited; and several intermediaries such as the forwarding agents, bankers, insurers, and brokers to facilitate an exporter's operations in a foreign environment. In the international trade transactions export intermediaries have an important role to play. Their functions range from finding markets for the new exporters to helping the exporters to enter new and unfamiliar markets.[26] Here, it may also be pointed out that an exporter may sell goods directly to a buyer abroad or may employ agents or establish branch offices or place of business in a foreign country. An exporter may also enter a joint venture[27] with an independent firm or enter into distribution agreement with a person in the foreign country or establish a distribution franchise to carry out export trade. Not infrequently, an exporter enters into a distributorship agreement with the importer wherein the latter is given the authority to represent the former.

Secondly, international trade contracts usually make use of certain standardized trade terms based on mercantile custom. When incorporated in a contract these trade terms are binding on parties unless specifically excluded by them. They are basically delivery terms defining the methods of performance of trade contracts; are helpful in minimizing the liabilities and additional risks involved in international trade transactions. However, as discussed in Chap. 3, interpretation of these terms is a major issue and for that reason attempts have been made to standardize them.

Thirdly, in international trade, modes of payment are materially different and involve modern means of payments and credits by a network of banks that operate on an international plane.

Fourthly, international contracts in question may be having "substantial connections" with more than one state raising the issues of jurisdiction and the applicable law. In order to avoid disputes concerning these, the parties wish to add a "choice of law" clause to avoid legal uncertainty and risks in case any dispute arises between them. Here, the insertion of the "choice of law" clause in such a contract assumes significance.

Fifthly, risks involved in an international trade are manifold in comparison to a domestic trade. Physical and financial risks involved in an international trade transaction are especially notable. More often than not, goods have to travel a long distance and a variety of modes of transport, such as carriage of goods by sea, rail, or road are involved. Such transactions are also exposed to great financial risks and a range of payment and collection issues arise. Where an export transaction is in the form of a credit transaction the seller remains unprotected till he realizes the purchase money. Before a seller obtains payment, the buyer may become insolvent or the buyer's country may prohibit payment in the agreed form of currency.

---

[26] See Peng and York (2001), p. 328.

[27] The term "joint venture" refers to a firm or a company jointly owned by two or more independent enterprizes. See Muchlinski (2007), pp. 66–68.

Finally, international commercial contracts are primarily governed by the domestic laws that remain largely un-harmonized. This raises the issue of international harmonization or standardization of the domestic trade laws in order to reduce the transaction costs of inter-state transfers of goods and services (see infra, Chap. 2).

1.3.3 Criteria of Internationality

Having noted the distinctive features of international trade, it is now proposed to identify relevant criteria for determining international trade transactions. From a legal perspective, this is a matter of considerable importance for we need to know precisely whether a given trade transaction is international one or not. But considerable difficulties arise in agreeing on the defining characteristics of international commercial transactions. First, international commercial transactions exhibit so diverse features that it is extremely difficult to devise a single formula to embrace all forms of transactions and activities commonly understood as international transactions. A further difficulty is that such transactions are governed by different set of legal rules—the domestic rules that remain largely un-harmonized as well as the rules contained in the uniform law instruments. Because the same transaction can be looked at in a variety of ways differences naturally arise. Since regulatory purposes differ, so also legal perspectives on international transactions and a definition arrived at for regulating international contracts of carriage may not be fit for regulating international sale of goods transactions. The legislative and non-legislative instruments, whether national, regional, or international, differ on the issue of defining international transactions because they differ in their approaches. What further adds to complication is that interpretations of the courts or tribunals on the issue are not the same. In the face of these difficulties, it would be unrealistic to expect to find a precise and accurate criterion or formulae to distinguish international transactions from domestic ones. Instead, our approach should be to find such criteria or criterion which is broad enough to cover as much transactions within its ambit as is needed in regulating international trade effectively. It is hoped that the insights gained from this inquiry will be helpful in understanding what is international trade and also subjecting to an in-depth analysis of the domestic and international law instruments dealing with international trade.

In attempting to identify international trade it is proposed here to proceed in an unconventional manner. Instead of looking at the definitional issues, here we would be directing our efforts to look at the provisions of the various national and international instruments laying down criteria for identifying international trade transactions.[28] There are several possible situations where a transaction may be considered as a

[28]This is not to suggest that definitions are not important. They are indeed important. "Beneath definitions are concepts" and if it is important to understand concepts so also definitions. See Rasmusen (2017), p. 1199.

transaction with an international element. Where goods are to be transported from one country to another or the contract of sale is concluded between parties located in two different countries or where they have different nationalities, the transaction in question acquires an international dimension and needs to be treated distinctly. Further, it may also happen that the trade in question is otherwise domestic but parties to the trade transaction deliberately choose a law as the "applicable law" which is different from domestic laws of the parties. In this case also, the trade in question has international character and, therefore, is an international trade transaction. All these factors are undoubtedly relevant determinants of an international transaction but their relative significance varies from case to case. Regulatory approaches adopted from a domestic or regional perspective differ from those adopted from purely an international perspective, and a contract which is judged international from a national law perspective may not be the same under the regulatory approach adopted at the international level.

As already indicated, national legislations and international uniform law instruments adopt different criteria in identifying international trade. They refer to criteria as different as the parties' "places of business" or "party's habitual residence" or the movement of goods from one country to another or substantial connection with a state. Here reference may be made to the UNIDROIT Principles of International Commercial Contracts (UNIDROIT Principles)[29] that do not lay down any criterion for defining international contracts and conceptualize the internationality of a contract in "the broadest possible manner" so that only those situations are excluded that are purely domestic.[30]

Let's begin with an examination of those instruments that relate to international sale of goods. It may be mentioned that under the 1980 UN Convention on Contracts for the International Sale of Goods (CISG)[31] adopted to harmonize the law relating to international sales worldwide, the key requirements for attracting the Convention are: (1) the location of the parties' places of business in different contracting states; and (2) the knowledge on their part of the fact that the parties have their "places of business in different states." All other requirements such as the shipment of goods from one country to another or the nationality of the parties are irrelevant in determining the applicability of the Convention. Article 1(1) of the CISG provides that the Convention only applies if the contract of sale of goods is concluded between parties whose places of business are in different states:

(a) when such states are Contracting States; or
(b) when the rules of private international law lead to the application of the law of a Contracting State.
(c) In respect of situation (a), there is a further requirement that the parties know that they have the places of business in different states on the basis of "either the

---

[29] The latest edition of the "UNIDROIT Principles" was published in 2016. The text of the UNIDROIT Principles can be accessed from: www.uniddroit.org.

[30] Bonell (ed.) (2006), p. 44.

[31] Adopted on April 11, 1980; **entry into force**: January 1, 1988. For the text, see 19 ILM 668–69 (1980).

contract or from any dealings between, or from, information disclosed by the parties at any time before or at the conclusion of the contract." (Article 1(2)).

Moreover, according to Article 1(3), "the nationality of the parties shall be disregarded in determining the applicability of the Convention." Thus, CISG does not take into account other elements of internationality such as the shipment of goods from one country to another or the acts constituting offer and acceptance taking place in different countries. It also ignores the nationality of the party or in the case of a company, place of incorporation in determining the applicability of the Convention. The Convention, rather, relies on the requirements of the location of places of business of the parties in different *contracting states* and knowledge on the part of the parties of the international character of the transaction in question. The result is that a transaction of sale of goods between a seller in state A and a buyer in state B shall fall within the scope of the application of CISG provided that both states are *contracting states* and the parties to the contract of sale of goods are aware of the international character of the transaction and have not excluded the applicability of the Convention. This will be the case even if the goods are not crossing the national borders. For example, an "ex works" contract will be governed by the CISG if parties' places of business are in different contracting states although goods are delivered at the seller's premises and all the exports arrangements are to be assumed only by the buyer.[32] But a contract between parties located in the same state will not attract the provisions of CISG even if the goods are transported from one state to another.[33]

In contrast, under the 1964 Uniform Law on the International Sale of Goods (ULIS)[34] the situation of the goods figured as an important indicator of the internationality. It provides that it will apply to the parties having places of business in different states and where the contract of sale satisfies *any* of the following requirements: (1) where the goods are to cross the national borders; or (2) where the offer and acceptance have been effected in different states; or (3) where delivery of the goods is to take place "in the territory of a State other than that within whose territory the acts constituting the offer and acceptance have been effected" (Article 1). Thus, applicability of the Uniform Law is based on satisfying the cross-border movement element, that is to say, either the goods are to move from one country to another or formation of the contract is effected in different states.[35] In other words, for the

---

[32]On "ex works" contract, see infra, Chap. 3.

[33]A broadly similar approach is adopted in Article 1(1) of the 2005 United Nations Convention on the Use of the Electronic Communications in International Contracts (see infra, Chap. 9, Sect. 9.3.4).

[34]Here, reference may be made to two conventions adopted at The Hague in April, 1964, which came into force in 1972, namely the Convention relating to a Uniform Law on the International Sale of Goods, with a Uniform Law as an appendix (the Sales Convention), 13 *American Journal of Comparative Law* 13, 453–56 (1964) [ULIS]; the Convention relating to a Uniform Law on the Formation of Contracts for the International Sale of Goods, with a Uniform Law as an appendix (the Formation Convention), *American Journal of Comparative Law* 13, 470–74 (1964) [ULF]. The "Uniform Law" is contained in the annexes of these two Conventions and the formal Conventions merely contain the procedural provisions concerning the application of the Uniform Law.

[35]See Bridge 2007, p. 510; Ndulo (1989), pp. 7–8.

Uniform Laws to apply, in addition to the requirement of the parties' residence in different states, the cross-border element must be present.

Significantly, the Unfair Contract Terms Act 1977, in order to exclude international commercial transactions from its purview, adopts an approach similar to that of the Uniform Law. It defines an international supply contract as a contract entered into by parties with places of business in different states if one of the following conditions are met: (a) where the goods are, at the time of the conclusion of the contract, "in the course of carriage or will be carried from one state to another"; or (b) where the acts constituting the offer and the acceptance have been effected in different states; or (c) where the goods are to be delivered in a state other than the place where the offer and acceptance were effected.

Among the conventions based on the cross-border movement approach are included the conventions on international carriage of goods by sea, rail, and road. The 1978 Convention on the International Carriage of Goods by Sea (the "Hamburg Rules") defines internationality of a contract of carriage solely in terms of the shipment of cargo from one state to another. In other words, they rely on cross-border movement of goods criterion. In order to attract the Convention, either the port of loading or the port of discharge must be located in two different countries, although it is not necessary that both ports are located in the contracting states.[36] It is sufficient if only one such port is in a contracting state. A similar approach is adopted in the more recent convention on the subject, namely the 2008 Convention on Contracts for the International Carriage of Goods Wholly or Partly by Sea (the "Rotterdam Rules"). According to Article 5(1) of the Convention, a contract of carriage will be governed by the Rotterdam Rules where the port of loading and the port of discharge are in two different states. Like the Hamburg Rules, there is no requirement that both ports are in the contracting states. Thus, for the applicability of international carriage conventions, goods in question must cross the national borders.

As will be seen below, the conventions on carriage of goods involving other modes of transport such as rail and road also rely on the cross-border movement perspective. The Uniform Rules Concerning the Contracts for the International Carriage of Goods by Rail (CIM Rules) appended to the 1999 Convention on International Carriage by Rail (COTIF) apply to a situation where the place for taking over the goods and the place for delivery are situated in different states, one of which is a member state, and the parties have agreed to rely on the CIM Rules.[37] Similarly, the 1956 Convention on the International Carriage of Goods by Road (CMR Rules), adopted to harmonizing the international carriage of goods by road applies to a contract of carriage of goods by road where the place of taking over and the place of delivery are situated in different states.[38]

---

[36] Hamburg Rules, Article 2(1).

[37] CIM Rules, Article 2(1).

[38] CMR Rules, Article 1(1).

1.4 International Trade and Investment Distinguished

It is also important to draw a distinction between export trade and international investment. They are two related but distinct concepts. They are related in the sense that both relate to inter-state business activities and foreign investment by a business organization facilitates its trading operations across the borders; different in the sense, the former denotes trading activities, that is to say, exporting and importing activities while the latter concerns international capital flows both outwards and inwards. In more concrete terms, international investment is about the foreign investment which occurs when an investor owns and manages an asset in a foreign country.[39] Further, the foreign investment may be of two types: portfolio and direct investment. The former provides an investing enterprise only the financial stake without any managerial control. In (foreign) direct investment (FDI), on the other hand, an investing enterprise obtains not only a financial stake but also managerial control over a foreign entity.[40] The principal vehicle for making (foreign) direct investment is a "multinational enterprise" (MNE) which may be defined as a business entity which owns and controls productive assets in more than one country.[41] Where an entity trades in goods or services without owning the facilities in a foreign country, its operation is limited to export trade only, but where an entity also owns assets and facilities it is engaged in both direct investment and trading activities. However, no clear boundary can be drawn between international trade and investment. Since direct investment in a foreign country facilitates trading operations of an entity, it may find it attractive to engage in both investment and trading activities. In fact, the extensive FDI in trade is now a common feature and in recent years a tendency has grown to view trade and investment as related subjects. The host state may impose certain investment measures such as local content, export, and trade balancing requirements impeding

---

[39]See Winham (2005), p. 20; Rivera-Batiz and Oliva (2003), p. 1; Muchlinski (2007), pp. 5–6.

[40]In recent years FDI has surpassed the increase in international trade. According to the UNCTAD, *World Investment Report 2016*, in 2015, total FDI flows reached US$1.76 trillion. UNCTAD, *World Investment Report 2016* (United Nations 2016), p. 2, also available at: http://unctad.org/en/pages/PublicationWebflyer.aspx?publicationid=1555. Despite the central importance of FDI in global commerce, there does not exist an international legal framework for such investment equivalent to that provided under the WTO Agreement in respect of international trade. Recent initiatives taken in this regard have not produced any significant result. See Muchlinski (2007), pp. 666–74. Thus, in the absence of multilateral legal rules like those set out in the WTO Agreement, foreign investment is governed mainly by bilateral investment treaties (BITs), regional free trade agreements (FTAs), and international investment agreements (IIAs).

[41]Rivera-Batiz and Oliva ibid; Muchlinski, ibid. There is no precise definition of an MNE. MNEs, defined broadly, are not limited to equity-based corporate groups but include non-equity-based business entities as well such as joint venture and those based on contracts. See Muchlinski, id., pp. 51–79. The Organization for the Economic Cooperation and Development, *OECD Guidelines on Multinational Enterprises* describe MNEs as usually comprising business entities located in more than one country and are so linked that they are able to "co-ordinate their operations in various ways." See Muchlinski, id., pp. 6–7. An updated version of the *OECD Guidelines for Multinational Enterprises 2011 Edition* (OECD 2011) has now appeared, which can be accessed from the official website of the OECD, http://www.oecd.org/daf/.../oecdguidelinesformultinationalenterprises.htm.

free flow of goods and services. The inclusion of trade-related investment measures (TRIMS) on the agenda of the WTO is a recognition of increasing importance of interplay of investment-related issues and international trade. The TRIMS related WTO provisions are aimed at removing restrictions on the foreign investments that are viewed as impediments to free trade.[42]

1.5 Regulating Inter-state Trade Relations

As already indicated, this book solely concerns the private law of international trade, that is to say, the law which applies to the private, commercial transactions entered into between the business people across borders. But there is another part of the law which is regulatory in nature and applies to states and the similar entities. The latter is mainly contained in the WTO agreements as well as other agreements that operate at regional level. Although the public law aspects are beyond the scope of this book, yet a brief discussion of the legal framework of the WTO seems justified.

The idea of free trade inspired many nations in 1940s to launch a series of negotiations to establish a regulatory framework for conducting trade on the multilateral basis and to form a multilateral trade organization to coordinate international actions in respect of international trade.[43] As a result, a multilateral trade agreement, namely the General Agreement on Tariffs and Trade (GATT) containing general principles of international trade came into existence in 1947. GATT 1947 established a rule-based system and was based on the principle of non-discrimination. But efforts to establish a multilateral trade organization under the name of the International Trade Organization (ITO) to serve as an institutional mechanism for the conduct of multilateral trade negations could not come to fruition due to the opposition of the US Congress.[44] Since the ITO could not see the light of the day, the GATT emerged as an ad hoc institution to work in place of the ITO.[45] In the absence of a permanent institutional mechanism for the conduct of trade negotiations, states turned to the GATT as a forum to seek solutions to their trade-related problems. Gradually, the GATT 1947 assumed the role of an institution to serve as a substitute to the ITO which was never born. As Jackson put it, "Through trial and error [GATT] has evolved some fairly elaborate procedure for conducting its business."[46] However, it would be wrong to

---

[42] See Muchlinski, id, pp. 258–59.

[43] Moens & Gillies (2006) p. 359. For a history of the GATT/WTO system, see Jackson (2012), pp. 31–43.

[44] Ironically the USA had taken an active part in finalizing the draft Charter of the ITO as well as the draft of the GATT 1947.

[45] See Moens & Gillies (2006), pp. 359–60; Matsushita et al. (2006), pp. 1–5; Jackson (2012), pp. 31–43.

[46] Jackson, id., p. 42.

suggest that the GATT was an organization. In fact, it was never intended to be so. It was at best, to use the phrase of Jackson, "a de facto international organization."[47]

The GATT 1947 continued to perform the dual role of a multilateral trade agreement and an institutional mechanism until it was replaced in 1995 by the new WTO/GATT system. Remarkably, under its auspicious eight successful "rounds" multilateral trade negotiations took place addressing a wide range of issues, including tariffs reduction, non-tariff barriers, and anti-dumping. Of these, the last one—the "Uruguay Round" (1986–1994) was the most significant. The "Uruguay Round" resulted in the adoption of the Marrakesh Agreement Establishing the World Trade Organization (the WTO Agreement) on 15 April 1994 and a new and full-fledged multilateral trade organization, the World Trade Organization (WTO) was born with the overarching goal of promoting free trade among the members.[48] It formally entered into force on 1 January 1995."[49] The WTO is endowed with full legal personality and legal capacity to enable it to act as an organization of states.[50] In that way it also has privileges and immunities as are necessary for the exercise of its functions.[51]

The WTO Agreement replaced the old GATT 1947 with a new agreement, namely GATT 1994. Although GATT 1994 under the treaty system of the WTO is a distinct agreement,[52] it nevertheless consists of the original GATT 1947, as substantially transformed. It is incorporated as GATT 1994 in Annex 1A of the WTO Agreement. The GATT 1994 consists of the GATT 1947 and decisions, protocols, and understandings adopted post 1947. Thus, the GATT 1947 is not old GATT. While the original GATT served both as a treaty as well as a *de facto* organization under the WTO, it is now *merely* a multilateral trade agreement.

It may be noted that the WTO Agreement contains four Annexes. Annexes 1, 2, and 3 set out "multilateral trade agreements" (MTAs) that are integral part of the WTO Agreement; are binding on all members.[53] Annex 4 sets out "plurilateral

[47] See also Mavroidis (2005), p. 5.

[48] Preamble to the WTO Agreement declares that its main objective, much like that of the GATT 1947, is the conduct of relations in the field of trade and economic endeavor "with a view to raising standards of living, ensuring full employment and a large and steadily income and effective demand, and expanding the production of trade in goods and services, while allowing for the optimal use of the world's resources in accordance with the objective of sustainable development….".

[49] By the end of July 2016, the WTO had 164 members including India. Information available at the official website of the WTO: https://www.wto.org/. Like its predecessor GATT, the organization is open to independent states as well as customs territories. Thus, Hong Kong, Macao, and Taipei are members of the WTO.

[50] WTO Agreement, Article VIII:1.

[51] Id., Article VIII:2.

[52] WTO Agreement, Article II(4): "the General Agreement on Tariffs and trade 1994 as specified in Annex 1A…is legally distinct from the General Agreement on Tariffs and trade, dated 30 October 1947, annexed to the Final Act Adopted at the Conclusion of the Second Session of the Preparatory Committee of the United Nations Conference on Trade and Employment, as subsequently rectified, amended or modified ….".

[53] WTO Agreement, Article II(2) provides that the "agreements and associated legal instruments included in Annexes 1, 2, and 3 (hereinafter referred to as the 'Multilateral Trade agreements') are integral parts of this agreement, binding on all members.".

trade agreements" (PTAs)[54] which are binding on those members who have accepted them.[55] Further, Annex 1 of the WTO Agreement consists of Annex 1A; Annex 1B; and Annex 1C. Annex 1A consists of GATT 1994 and agreements covering agriculture; the application of sanitary and phytosanitary measures; textiles and clothing; technical barriers to trade; trade-related investment measures; anti-dumping; customs valuation; pre-shipment inspection; "rules of origin"; import licensing procedures; subsidies and countervailing measures; and safeguards. Annex 1B consists of the General Agreement on Trade in Services (GATS) and Annex 1C consists of the Agreement on Trade-Related Aspects of Intellectual Property Rights (TRIPS Agreement). Further, Annex 2 consists of the rules on "settlement of disputes," known as the "Dispute Settlement Understanding" (DSU); Annex 3 consists of the Trade Policy Review Mechanism.

It may also be noted that the new trade law created by the WTO Agreement, unlike the GATT 1947, is not merely "a collection of ad hoc agreements, Panel reports and understandings of the parties." Rather, it embraces all trade-related obligations under a single system of the WTO.[56] The WTO law is a single body of law consisting of the WTO Agreement and the multilateral trade agreements (MTAs) annexed to it. Because of the "single package approach" parties to the WTO Agreement are referred to as the members of the organization. Member states have to accept the obligations contained in all the WTO agreements.

One of the most spectacular features of the WTO system is the "streamlining" of the dispute settlement mechanism.[57] Contrary to a fragmented or ad hoc system of dispute resolution under the GATT 1947 the WTO dispute settlement mechanism is "integrated" and resembles a third-party compulsory adjudication system. The jurisdiction of the dispute settlement body (DSB)[58] is compulsory; is rule based; and determinations of the dispute panels or the appellate body are binding on the parties.

---

[54]Plurilateral Trade Agreements (PTAs) include Agreement on Trade in Civil Aircraft; Agreement on Government Procurement; International Dairy Agreement; and International Bovine Meat Agreement. Of these the last two were terminated in 1997.

[55]WTO Agreement, Article II(2): "The agreements and associated legal rules instruments included in Annex 4 ...are also part of this agreement for those Members that have accepted them, and are binding on those Members. The Plurilateral Trade Agreements do not create either obligations or rights for Members that have not accepted them.".

[56]Cameron & Gray (2001), pp. 248–98, 248 (citing Petersmann 1997, p. 64).

[57]See generally, Pauwelyn (2005), pp. 1–65.

[58]The Dispute Settlement Body has "the authority to establish panels, adopt panel and Appellate Body reports, maintain surveillance of implementation of rulings and recommendations, and authorize suspension of concessions and other obligations under the covered agreements." See Understanding on Rules and Procedures Governing the Settlement of Disputes (Dispute Settlement Undertaking), 33 International Legal Material 1226 (1994), Article 2:1.

1.6 Scheme of the Study

This book is aimed at addressing some of the most important issues and dimensions of the (private) law of international trade from a modern perspective. After introducing the subject-matter in the opening chapter, it then divides into six parts dealing with all major areas of relevance: international harmonization; contract of sale; electronic communications; contracts of carriage of goods; insurance and export finance; and trade dispute resolution.

This Chapter draws attention to the characteristic features of the law; discusses the concept of the *lex mercatoria* and its place in the modern law; highlights the complexities of the international trade transactions; examines different criteria evolved for identifying an international trade transaction.

Chapters 2 and 3 (Part I) are devoted to the theme of international harmonization of domestic trade laws. Since harmonization of domestic laws is a central issue in international trade law, the issue needs to be examined in the beginning itself. Chapter 2, "International Unification of Trade Laws" deals with the core concepts in the context, distinguishes between various means for achieving unification of laws and provides an account of the efforts directed toward international unification of substantive as well as private international law rules. Chapter 3 deals with standard trade practices and usages which serve as the law for the parties to a trade contract. It also provides a brief account of the International Rules for the Interpretation of Trade Terms (INCOTERMS) developed by the International Chamber of Commerce (ICC).

Of the several trade contracts, perhaps the most important one is the sale of goods contract. Therefore, Chaps. 4, 5, 6, 7 and 8 (Part II) consider several legal issues arising in the context from a comparative law perspective. This Part begins with a discussion of the general principles of the law of contract as found in two key jurisdictions with common law background—India and England (Chap. 4).

Chapters 5 and 6 deal with the domestic laws of international sale of goods of these countries as contained in the Sale of Goods Act, 1930 and Sale of Goods Act 1979. Since this is not a work on the law of contract or sale of goods as such, these chapters focus only on those aspects of the law that have relevance in the context of international trade. Chapter 7 deals with the 1980 UN Convention on Contracts for the International Sale of Goods (CISG) which is one of the most important conventions in the field of international trade law. And Chap. 8 includes a discussion on the UNIDROIT Principles of International Commercial Contracts and the (Hague) Principles on Choice of Law in International Commercial Contracts (the Hague Principles). Unlike CISG, UNIDROIT Principles and the Hague Principles are the soft-law instruments; are not formally binding. However, their usefulness as the instruments of harmonization is widely acknowledged.

Chapter 9 (Part III) is devoted to the issue of the harmonization of laws aimed at facilitating electronic communications in international trade. The issue has generated considerable interest in recent decades leading to the emergence of a number of uniform law instruments and it seems justified to give an account of some of the most noteworthy instruments, in particular, those adopted by the UNCITRAL.

As already noted above, in international trade, a sale transaction is often followed by the contract of carriage of goods. Since goods may be transported from a place in one country to a place in a different country by sea, air, rail, or road, or by the combination of two or more of these modes of transport, called multimodal transport, the carriage of goods contracts are governed by different international conventions aimed to standardize rules in this regard. These international conventions are discussed in Part IV comprising Chaps. 10 through 12.

The contracts of marine insurance are a commonplace in international trade. Therefore, Chap. 13 (Part V) draws attention to the principles governing such contracts. And Chap. 14 (Part V) discusses the principles of law governing various payment methods which are commonly used in financing of the export trade transactions.

Finally, Chap. 15 (Part VI) turns to the issue of trade dispute settlement. It first examines the private international issues that arise in the context; secondly, deals with various rules and practices of alternative dispute resolution (ADR) procedures and arbitration. Emphasis is placed on those rules which are new and specially apply to international trade transactions.

References

A Handbook on the GATS Agreement. (2005). A WTO Secretariat Publication, Cambridge: Cambridge University Press.

Bagwell, K., Brown, C. P., & Staiger, R. W. (2016). Is the WTO passé? *Journal of Economic Literature, 54*(1125–1231), 1128.

Black's Law Dictionary. (2002). St. Paul Minn. West Publishing Co.

Black's Law Dictionary. (2006). St. Paul Minn. West Publishing Co.

Bonell, M. J. (Ed.). (2006). *The UNIDROIT principles in practice: Caselaw and bibliography on the UNIDROIT principles of International Commercial Contracts*. New York: Transnational Publishers.

Bridge, M. (2007). *International sale of goods: Law and practice*. Oxford, New York: Oxford University Press.

Burdick, F. M. (1902). What is the law merchant? *Columbia Law Review, 2*(7), 470–485.

Burton, F. N. (1985). *Contemporary trade*. New Delhi: Heritage Publishers.

Cameron, J., & Gray, K. R. (2001). Principles of international law in the WTO dispute settlement body. *International and Comparative Law Quarterly, 50*, 248–98.

Davey, W. J. (2005). Institutional framework. In P. Macrury, A. E. Appleton & M. Plummer (Eds.), *The World Trade Organization: Legal, economic and political analysis* (Vol. I). New York: Springer.

Furmston, M. (2012). *Chesire, Fifoot & Furmston's law of contract*. Oxford: Oxford University Press.

Goody, R. (2005). Rule, practice, and pragmatism in transnational commercial law. *International and Comperative Law Quarterly, 54*(3), 539–562.

Guest, A. G. (Ed.). (2006). *Benjamin's sale of goods*. London: Sweet & Maxwell.

Howse, R. (2010). Beyond the countertrade taboo: Why the WTO should take another look at barter and countertrade. *University of Toronto Law Journal, 60*(2), 289–314.

Hussain, M., Iyanatul, I., & Kibria, R. (1999). *South Asian economic development: Transformation, opportunities and challenges*. London, New York: Routledge.

Jackson, J. H. (2012). *The world trading system: Law and policy of international economic relations* (2nd Edn.). New Delhi: Satyam Books. First Indian Reprint 2012.

Kerr, C. (1929). The origin and development of the law merchant. *Virginia Law Review, 15*(4), 350–367.

Mavroidis, P. C. (2005). *The general agreement on tariffs and trade: A commentary*. Oxford: Oxford University Press.

Michaels, R. (2007). The true lex mercatoria: Law beyond the State. *Indiana Journal of Global Legal Studies, 14*(2), 447–468.

Matsushita, M., Schoenbaum, T. J., & Mavroidis Petros, C. (2006). *The World Trade Organization: Law, practice, and policy*. Oxford: Oxford University Press.

Moens, G., & Gillies, P. (2006). *International trade and business: Law, policy and ethics*. Routledge-Cavendish.

Muchlinski, P. T. (2007). *Multinational enterprises and the law* (pp. 66–68). Oxford: Oxford University Press.

Ndulo, M. (1989). The Vienna sales convention 1980 and the Hague uniform laws on international sale of goods 1964: A comparative analysis. *International and Comparative Law Quarterly, 38*(1–25), 7–8.

Paton, G. W., & Derham, D. P. (Eds.). (1972). *A textbook of jurisprudence*. Oxford: Oxford University Press.

Pauwelyn, J. (2005). The transformation of world trade. *Michigan Law Review, 104,* 1–65.

Peng, M. W., & York, A. S. (2001). Behind intermediary performance in export trade: Transactions, agents, and resources. *Journal of International Business Studies, 32*(327–46), 328.

Petersmann, E. U. (1997). *The GATT/WTO dispute settlement system*. London: Kluwer Law International.

Rasmusen, E. (2017). Law, coercion, and expression: A review essay on Frederick Schauer's *The Force of law* and Richard McAdams's *The Expressive Powers of Law*. *Journal of Economic Literature, 55*(1098–1121), 1199.

Raychaudhuri, A., & De, P. (2012) *International trade in service in India: Implications for growth & inequality in a globalizing world*. New Delhi: Oxford University Press.

Rivera-Batiz, L. A., &. Oliva, M.-A. (2003). *International trade: Theory, strategies, and evidence*. Oxford: Oxford University Press.

Shorter Oxford English dictionary on historical principle. (2007). (Vol. 2, pp. 3312–3313). Oxford: Oxford University Press.

Trakman, L. E. (2003). From the medieval law merchant to E-merchant law. *University of Toronto Law Journal, 53*(3), 265–304.

UNCITRAL *legal guide on international countertrade transactions*. (1993). New York: United Nations. A/CN.9/SER.B/3.

United Nations Conference on Trade and Development (UNCTAD). Draft International Code of Conduct on the Transfer of Technology (1985). Chapter 1, Paragraph 1.2. New York, UNCTAD, Doc. TD/CODE TOT/47.

Volckart and Mangels. (1999). Are the roots of the modern Lex Mercatoria really medieval? *Southern Economic Journal, 65*(3), 427–450.

Wiener, J. (2005). GATS and the politics of trade in services. In D. Kelly & W. Grant (Eds.), *The politics of international trade in the twenty-first century: Actor, issues and regional dynamics*. Hampshire, New York: Palgrave Macmillan.

Winham, G. R. (2005). An interpretative history of the Uruguay round negotiation. In P. Macrury, A. E. Appleton & M. Plummer (Eds.), *The World Trade Organization: Legal, economic and political analysis* (Vol. I). New York: Springer.

Zaphiriou, G. A. (1992). Transnational technology protection. *American Journal of Comparative Law, 40,* 879–915.

Reports, Official Texts and Online Resources

International Institute for the Unification of Private Law (UNIDROIT). www.uniddroit.org.
Organization for Economic Cooperation and Development (OECD), http://www.oecd.org/daf/.../oecdguidelinesformultinationalenterprises.htm
United Nations Conference on Trade and Development (UNCTAD). (2016). *World investment report 2016*. http://unctad.org/en/pages/PublicationWebflyer.aspx?publicationid=1555.
UNCTAD. http://unctadstat.unctad.org/wds/TableViewer/tableView.aspx?ReportId=101.
World Trade Organization (WTO). https://www.wto.org/english/thewto_e/whatis_e/tif_e/org3_e.htm#join.

Part I
International Harmonization

Chapter 2
International Unification of Trade Laws

2.1 Desirability of Uniform Regulation of International Contracts

Achieving harmony between the laws of various countries is a central issue in overseas trade. As will be seen below, numerous problems arise due to the substantial differences in the domestic laws governing international commercial relations which have considerable negative impact on the growth of international trade. Concerned about this, states have long pursued the alternative of harmonizing or modernizing their laws (see Sect. 2.4). Today, harmonization of substantive laws as a tool of reconciling differences between different legal systems is widely favored by the international community and considered a precondition for international trade.[1] Two

---

[1]Harmonization of the international trade laws has generated considerable interest in the academic circles and a voluminous literature is available supporting it. See, for example Loh (2015), pp. 13–18; Goode (2005), pp. 539–62; David (1968), pp. 13–27; Kamba (1974), pp. 485–519; Rosett (1992), pp. 683–697; Bamodu (1994), pp. 125–43, 125 (1994); *Report of the Secretary General*, Sixth Committee, A/6396 in Official Records of the General Assembly, Twenty-first Session (Agenda Item 88), Sixth Committee, New York: 1966, at: http://www.uncitral.org/uncitral/en/commission/sessions/pre.html [hereinafter *Report of the Secretary General*]; General Assembly Resolution 2205 (XXI) of December 17, 1966 establishing the United Nations Commission on International Trade Law which, in its Preamble, reaffirms [the] "conviction" that differences in domestic laws governing international trade transactions are "one of the obstacles to the development of world trade." http://www.uncitral.org/uncitral/en/commission/sessions/pre.html; Recommendation of the Sixth Committee of the General Assembly on the Report of the United Nations Commission on International Trade Law on the Work of its Fiftieth session, October 26, 2017, which reiterates the need for a unified law on international trade suggesting that "progressive modernization and harmonization of international trade law" will reduce or remove legal obstacles to the flow of international trade, and thereby "would contribute significantly to universal economic cooperation among all States...." http://www.uncitral.org/uncitral/en/GA/6thcommittee_reports.html. But see Jacobson (1954), pp. 659–73, 661–62; Fox (1991), pp. 593–98, 596; Boodman (1991), pp. 699–724; Pistor (2002), pp. 97–130.

A. Srivastava, *Modern Law of International Trade*, International Law and the Global South, https://doi.org/10.1007/978-981-15-5475-9_2

principal techniques are employed to achieve harmonization: unification and harmonization.[2] In the context of the regulation of cross-border, private trade transactions, the former denotes a process of arriving at a set of unified rules which are directly applicable to such transactions in preference to the concerned domestic law. Since the rules resulting from the process of unification are to be the same or identical everywhere, there will not be any difficulty if they take precedence over domestic laws. Harmonization is a similar process which results in harmonized rather than unified (or uniform) rules.[3] As this Chapter shall show, with a massive increase in international trade, efforts toward harmonization of domestic trade laws have intensified in recent decades.[4]

For many reasons a unified approach to the regulation of international, private transactions is preferable to a variety of approaches. First, it can address the problem of legal uncertainty and unpredictability which is not uncommon in overseas trade. As already noted in the previous chapter, international trade transactions, being private in nature, are generally regulated under domestic (or national) laws. But national laws vary across jurisdictions. Notable differences exist, for example, in regard to international aspects of a contract such as, passing of property and risks; formation, terms and performance of the contract; and remedies. Since conflict of laws rules of various countries also differ from one another, this is not unlikely that the law to apply a transnational trade dispute remains unpredictable until determined by the court.[5] Particularly problematical are the disparities in the "choice of law" and the "choice of court" rules.[6] In the absence of a choice of law clause in an international contract

---

[2]Unification and harmonization of laws are the labels used to denote a varying degree of harmonization and it is possible that all kinds or techniques of harmonization do not precisely fit into these two categories. Hence, the issue of harmonization of national laws needs to be approached flexibly. As will be noticed below, the reason for using a wide range of harmonization techniques is that the same level of harmonization is not always desirable—in some situations a lesser degree of harmonization suffices (see infra, Sect. 2.2).

[3]In practice, however, a strict distinction between unification and harmonization is not generally maintained and the two terms are often used interchangeably. In this chapter also, unless the context otherwise requires, the two terms have been used interchangeably (see Sect. 2.2).

[4]While this book is primarily concerned with harmonization of substantive, national laws governing private, commercial transactions, a brief account of the efforts at unification of private international law rules may be found in Sect. 2.3. In deciding a dispute which contains a "foreign element" a domestic court is aided by private international law or conflict of laws rules. On the basis of these rules it has to determine first, whether it has jurisdiction; and secondly, if it has jurisdiction, what system of law shall govern such a case (see Sect. 2.3). The need for harmonization of private international laws of various countries is felt because these laws, like substantive laws, vary country by country which gives rise to the problem of uncertainty in the application of substantive laws.

[5]See Fawcett and Carruthers (2008), p. 9.

[6]The "choice of law" rules indicate the law by reference to which a dispute under an international contract is to be resolved. The law so identified is called "the applicable law." For the purpose of determining the applicable law, the parties normally insert a choice of law clause in their contract. But in the absence of any such choice, the "applicable law" is determined on the basis of the law of the forum, called the *lex fori*. The choice of law rules needs to be distinguished from the choice of court rules. The latter is a set of rules to determine the forum (see infra, Chap. 15).

the parties remain clueless about the applicable law.[7] Even in cases in which the applicable law is determined in accordance with the choice of law rules, the problem continues to arise because it is not unlikely that the parties are not familiar with the law so determined. This adds to woes of a trader who wants certainty in the application of laws.[8] Obviously, if domestic or internal trade laws are codified on identical or similar lines, not only the difficulties that arise as a result of applying a variety of substantive rules to international contracts can be avoided but the difficulties resulting from the application of divergent conflict of law rules can also be avoided or considerably reduced.[9] It may also be noted that unification of substantive laws will reduce the need for unifying conflict of law rules of different countries.[10] In fact, it is out of desire to escape from the problems encountered in finding solutions to the conflicting private international law rules that states turned to explore the option of unifying substantive laws.[11]

Secondly, the domestic legal systems are not, in general, created to suit the needs of modern-day business transactions which are truly global and need to be modernized to remain relevant.[12] The phenomenal increase in the scale of cross-border trade has brought about increasingly complex and sophisticated techniques of conducting business necessitating the modernization or standardization of legal rules.[13] In other words, given the complexities involved in the regulation of cross-border trade transactions, domestic regulations prove to be inadequate for the purpose.

Thirdly, the globally harmonized rules can facilitate trade between states by addressing the problem of externalities in international trade and by reducing "unnecessary transaction costs" resulting from disparities between national laws.[14] It has been suggested that diversity of the legal norms increases "the cost of compliance with law," thereby making the traders hesitant to enter into such transactions.[15] It is not hard to see that the cost of compliance with diverse set of rules will be higher than the cost of compliance with a uniform law. This is particularly true in a world which has increasingly become interdependent.[16] Finally, as unification is aimed at achieving conformity in the contents and quality of law across jurisdictions,[17] it may substantially improve the quality of the law supplanting the country-specific standards by the international standards.

---

[7]On the utility of "choice of law" and "choice of forum" clauses in international contracts, see Becker (1989), pp. 168–75.

[8]See Szászy (1934), pp. 156–77; Tunc (1965), pp. 1411–12, 1409–14.

[9]See Fawcett and Carruthers (2008), pp. 5–6; Haywod (2006), p. 2; Goode (2005), p. 555.

[10] See Goode (2005), 541.

[11]See Goode ibid; Bridge (2007), p. 507.

[12]Loh (2015), p. 13; General Assembly Resolution 2205 (XXI) of December 17, 1966.

[13]See Viejobueno (1995), pp. 200, 200–207; Suy (1981), pp. 141, 139–47.

[14]Loh (2015), p. 13; Goode (2005), p. 555.

[15]See Fox (1991), p. 593; Mckendrick (2000), p. 11.

[16]See Fox, ibid.

[17]Pistor (2002), p. 107.

International unification of (substantive) laws, thus, may be viewed as "virtue in itself"; "an ideal solution" to the problem of conflicting national laws from the perspectives of the parties to a contract as well as the contracting states.[18] The efforts so far made in this regard reveal that unification or harmonization of trade laws is, indeed, obtainable. It is attainable because, as has been suggested, trade laws have no religious sanction[19] and differences exist not because of the rigidity of a particular legal system but because of a lack of willingness to accommodate them.[20] Moreover, as explained by a noted scholar, when it comes to regulating the private commercial activities involving interests of the foreign nationals states tend to think differently and seem to be less determined about their sovereignty.[21]

However, there are many who think that international harmonization of laws is a "myth," though desirable, is certainly not feasible.[22] Several reasons are advanced to support this view. First, it is based on the "erroneous" belief that there is a "right" law which is the same for all countries."[23] Secondly, it ignores the significance of diversity among national laws. Thirdly, in the absence of a court having authority to adjudicate private, commercial disputes between various states, the proposed uniform law is likely to be interpreted differently in various jurisdictions. This result also follows because uniform laws tend to be general rather than specific in nature.[24] Fourthly, there is no consensus that the harmonization effort leads to economic efficiency[25] and finally, harmonization, in particular, a large-scale harmonization, is a very expensive and time-consuming project.

These are indeed serious criticisms to the current harmonization efforts which merit a detailed examination. But experience for over a century suggests that harmonization as an attempt to reconcile the essential differences between different legal systems is indeed possible and fruitful especially if undertaken through persuasion and is confined to a particular field, such as, commercial law and private international law. Critics of harmonization are in general not opposed to the various alternative forms of unification such as drawing up restatements of law by scholars and (voluntary) codes of practice. In fact, as will be seen below, harmonization of laws in the form of recommendations to achieve a general consistency in the law-governing cross-border transactions has been well received by the international community. For example, the UNIDROIT Principles of International Commercial Contracts (the UNIDROIT Principles), adopted by the International Institute for the Unification of

---

[18]Nadelmann (1965), p. 450; Goode (2005), p. 554.

[19]Jacabson (1954), p. 663.

[20]Graveson (1968), p. 10.

[21]Goode (2005), p. 554.

[22]Jacobson (1954), p. 662. For the view that international harmonization is not even desirable, see in particular, Kamba (1974), p. 502; Pistor (2002), p. 107; Fox (1991), p. 596.

[23]Fox, ibid. There may be some force behind the argument that there is no "right" law which is the same across the world but as noted in the previous chapter an underlying unity is clearly noticeable in the commercial laws of different countries which is a major force behind the current unification drive.

[24]Pistor (2002), id., p. 103.

[25]See ibid, note 14 and the authorities cited therein.

Private Law (UNIDROIT),[26] which are a major accomplishment of the unification efforts through persuasion. Other successful examples, as will be noticed below, include the Uniform Customs and Practice for Documentary Credits (UCP 600)[27] and International Rules for the Interpretation of Trade Terms, popularly known as the INCOTERMS[28] prepared by the International Chamber of Commerce (ICC) and the Rules of Arbitration prepared by the UNCITRAL and the ICC (see Sect. 2.4).

2.2 Concept and Methods of Unification

2.2.1 Unification and Harmonization Distinguished

The term, "unification" has no fixed meaning and is used in different senses depending on the context. It generally denotes a process of developing a set of international standards to serve as a model for the national laws so that all such transactions that have international dimension may be uniformly regulated.[29] This can be done either by reaching compromises taking into account diverse legal, economic, and social backgrounds of the participating states or agreeing on an "ideal solution" with the aim to adapting diverse regulatory systems to this ideal solution.[30]

In the context of international trading relationships between private persons with which we are mainly concerned, unification is commonly understood as a process of reconciling the differences between various national standards. For this purpose, a

---

[26]UNIDROIT Principles, the current version of which appeared in 2016, were first published in 1994. The text is available at: www.unidroit.org.

[27]The most recent revision of the UCP is the 2007 Revision of Uniform Customs and Practice of Documentary Credits, USP 600 (ICC Publication No. 600). Text is available at: iccwbo.org.

[28]INCOTERMS were first published in 1936 by International Chamber of Commerce (ICC). The texts of different editions of INCOTERMS are available at: https://iccwbo.org/resources-for-business/incoterms-rules/.

[29]For an insightful discussion of different approaches to harmonization, see generally Boodman (1991), pp. 699–724; Pistor (2002), pp. 97–130; Fox (1991), pp. 593–98; David (1968), pp. 13–27; Zaphiriou (1990), pp. 71–97. See also: Bridge (2007), pp. 506–07; Kamba (1974), p. 501; Rosett (1992), pp. 683–94.

[30]In the context of the laws to govern purely private relationships, such as contract law, it is the former approach to harmonization which is commonly preferred. Instead of adopting a particular country's law as a model law, the efforts have been directed toward finding a common solution taking into account common elements of different legal systems. It must also be said that harmonization or unification may have a quite different meaning in other contexts, such as setting international standards for the protection of human rights, environment, intellectual property rights (IPRs), and promotion of international trade. Many of the multilateral trade agreements (MTAs), environmental agreements (MEAs), and human rights instruments signed by states are examples of harmonization of a kind different from harmonization of domestic contract laws. While in the case of the former, efforts at standardization of the domestic norms or standards are driven by the necessity of ensuring minimum standards, in the latter case, harmonization is seen as a driver to economic development.

variety of methods may be employed—harmonization, modernization, standardization, internationalization, and codification—depending on the context but the overarching aim of all such procedures is indeed the removal of the existing differences in the domestic legislations or to rationalize those distinctions. In other words, these are the methods of reducing differences between the national laws by reconciling the existence of one national system with another. However, usage has not been uniform and these terms are often used interchangeably.

Turning to the most commonly used terms, unification and harmonization, it may be stated that they refer to broadly similar yet distinguishable processes. By the "unification" of (national) laws, we mean a process of unifying the substantive or conflict of law rules of different countries. In other words, it refers to a process whereby different legal systems are "supplanted" by a single system.[31] The object is to create an identical, unified legal system. Unification, thus, is the strictest form of harmonization and if accomplished may result in truly international legal rules. Since unification is aimed at producing the uniform or unified rules, it contemplates the drawing up of a binding international convention.

The 1980 UN Convention on Contracts for the International Sale of Goods (the CISG, also known as the "Vienna Convention"),[32] which provides for unified rules for the international sale of goods, may be cited as a striking example in this regard. Notably, the CISG, unless the parties show a preference for a different law, is directly applicable to a contract of sale between the parties of the ratifying states ignoring substantive and conflict of laws rules.[33] In other words, once the conditions of the applicability of the Convention are met, the concerned domestic law—the substantive as well as conflict of laws rules—is overridden by the CISG.[34] Since the CISG contains the uniform law as opposed to the law selected by the parties or determined

---

[31] Kamba (1974), p. 501.

[32] Adopted on April 11, 1980; entered into force on January 1, 1988; 90 states parties. India is not a party. For the text, see 19 ILM 668-69 (1980), the text can also be accessed from the official website of the United Nations Commission on International Trade Law (UNCITRAL): www.uncitral.org. The text of the Convention together with explanatory note is available at: http://www.uncitral.org/pdf/english/texts/sales/cisg/V1056997-CISG-e-book.pdf [hereinafter referred to as the "CISG"]. Conventions linked to the CISG are: the (New York) Convention on the Limitation Period in the International Sale of Goods, adopted on June 14, 1974, entry into force August 1, 1988. The New York Convention sets out uniform rules on the period of time within which a party to an international sale contract must commence legal action against another party to the contract; and the Geneva Convention on the Agency in the International Sale of Goods, 1983. The texts are available at: http://www.uncitral.org/uncitral/en/uncitral_texts/sale_goods/1974Convention_limitation_period.html.

[33] See *Report of the Secretary General*, supra note 1; Nadelmann (1965), p. 454; Bridge (2007), pp. 5–6; Liu and Ren (2017). CISG in Chinese courts: The issue of Applicability. *American Journal of Comparative Law*, LXV, 898, 873–918.

[34] The position may be compared to the law of a supra national organization, like the European Union (EU). The EU Regulations as well as the decisions of the European Court of Justice (ECJ) take precedence over the laws of the member countries. The EU was created by the Treaty of Maastricht signed on February 7, 1992 by the members of the European Community (EC). But the position regarding an EU Directive seems to be different. Directives often give a certain degree of flexibility in implementing them resulting into harmonized law, rather than uniform law.

on the basis of the choice of law rules, the widespread adoption of the Convention by states can successfully address the problem of the conflicting domestic rules including private international law rules. This is the true importance of a uniform law that it obviates the need for resorting to private international law rules (see Sect. 2.3). Some of the other notable conventions falling in this category are: the 1958 New York Convention on the Recognition and Enforcement of Foreign Arbitral Awards,[35] the 1978 Convention on the International Carriage of Goods by Sea (the "Hamburg Rules"),[36] the 2005 United Nations Convention on the Use of Electronic Communications in International Contracts[37] and the 2008 UN Convention on Contracts for the International Carriage of Goods Wholly or Partially by Sea (the "Rotterdam Rules").[38]

"Harmonization" of laws, on the other hand, as one scholar puts it, is "short of unification"; denotes a process of approximation or coordination of different legal systems by eliminating major differences and creating minimum requirements or standards.[39] It may also be noted that harmonization provides a varying degree of freedom in adopting these standards or requirements into national law. The purpose is to encourage the states to enact domestic laws on the lines similar to internationally agreed standards. In other words, harmonized or harmonious rules, unlike uniform rules, are optional as they do not impose legally binding obligations on states. Given this difference between harmonization and unification, the former does not result in the identical law but similar or broadly similar law. Simply put, through harmonization attempt is made to achieve the goal (of unification) through persuasion and not through imposing binding rules under a treaty or international convention. In particular, where a proposed set of rules is to apply to purely contractual relationships, harmonization is considered as preferable to unification.[40] Since harmonization of law gives considerable degree of flexibility to states, they are more willing to join the process of harmonizing the law than unifying it and, as a matter of fact, in recent years, harmonization has become more popular especially where parties resort to international arbitration instead of litigation through a court of law.[41]

---

[35] Adopted on June 10, 1958, entered into force on June 7, 1959 (159 parties including India).

[36] Entry into force: November 1, 1992, 34 State Parties.

[37] Entry into force: March 1, 2013, 11 State Parties.

[38] Adopted on December 11, 2008. Not yet in force.

[39] Zaphiriou (1990), p. 71; Kamba (1974) p. 501.

[40] See UNIDROIT: History and overview. www.unidroit.org/about-unidroit/overview.

[41] It is worth noting that unification efforts through international conventions in general have fallen short of expectations. Only a limited number of conventions have been widely ratified by states, for example, the CISG which has 90 states parties, and the 1958 Convention on the Recognition and Enforcement of Foreign Arbitral Awards, entered into force on June 7, 1959, which has 159 states parties including India. However, a significant number of conventions have not been ratified by sufficient number of states and some of these have not entered into force yet. The 1974 Convention on the Limitation Period in the International Sale of Goods, entered into force on August 1, 1988, has been ratified only by 23 states; the UN Convention on Contracts for the International Carriage of Goods Wholly or Partly by Sea ("Rotterdam Convention"), adopted on December 11, 2008, has not entered into force yet and has so far received only four ratifications; the 1978 UN Convention on the

As will be noticed below, harmonization as opposed to unification can be achieved by various means—model laws, uniform trade usages, and practice, known as uniform rules of practice, and the restatements of law. Some of the important harmonization instruments include: the UNIDROIT Principles, and the 2015 Hague Principles on the Choice of Law for International Commercial Contracts (international restatements of laws); the various model laws promulgated by the UNCITRAL, such as UNCITRAL Model Law on International Commercial Arbitration (1985) as amended in 2006, the 2002 UNCITRAL Model Law on International Commercial Conciliation, the 1996 Model Law on Electronic Commerce, the 2001 UNCITRAL Model Law on Electronic Signatures, and the 2017 UNCITRAL Model Law on Electronic Transferable Records (the model laws); and the UNCITRAL Arbitration Rules, 1976 as revised in 2010 and the UNCITRAL Conciliation Rules, 1980 (the uniform clauses, known as rules of practice intended to be incorporated into a contract).[42] It is not hard to see that the instruments of harmonization are commonly non-binding, soft-law instruments.

To sum up, the difference between the "unification" of law and the "harmonization" of law is this: in the former case, a multilateral convention is adopted setting out legal rules to be incorporated into domestic laws with little change. Since the contracting states are required to enact the law in terms identical to those contained in the relevant convention, the outcome is *uniform* or unified (substantive) law. Whereas in the case of the latter, states voluntarily adopt a model law, for example, the UNCITRAL Model Law on Electronic Commerce. As stated above, since the extent of the adoption of a model law by states will not be the same harmonization does not result in unified or identical law. A similar result will follow where rules of practice, such as the UNCITRAL's Arbitration Rules are incorporated into an international contract. It also needs emphasis that the issue of unification of laws has to be approached flexibly and no precise boundaries can be drawn between different methods of unification. Even where a high degree of harmony is needed, a convention may allow reservations. Furthermore, some instruments of unification may be less precise to provide sufficient flexibility in drafting national laws.[43] It has been rightly suggested that the difference between the unification and harmonization is of emphasis only; while unification falls high on the spectrum harmonization occupies a lower position.[44]

Carriage of Goods by Sea ("Hamburg Rules"), entered into force on November 1, 1992, has only 34 parties; the 2005 Convention on the Use of Electronic Communications in International Contracts, entered into force 1 March 2013, has been ratified only by 11 states; the 1988 UN Convention on International Bills of Exchange and International Promissory Notes, not yet in force; the 1995 UN Convention on Independent Guarantees and Stand-by Letters of Credit, entered into force on January 1, 2000 between eights states only.

[42]For the texts of the UNCITRAL's model laws and uniform clauses, visit: www.uncitral.org.

[43]See David (1968), pp. 20–21.

[44]See Bridge (2007), p. 506.

2.2.2 *International and Regional Harmonization*

It may be noted that unification or harmonization can occur on the national, regional, and international scales. Furthermore, it can take place within a single system or family such as the civil law system or between the countries of two or more legal traditions. The 1980 CISG is a good example of an attempt to unify national laws of all countries irrespective of their legal background.

Within a nation, there may be several sets of rules to govern a commercial transaction, and the problem of inconsistency can be addressed through enactment of a national or federal law replacing local law of states or provinces. There are many examples of unification of local or state laws. United States of America has achieved unification in several areas of laws through adoption of a federal law. Here, the Uniform Commercial Code (UCC) may be cited as an example of a uniform set of rules which is part of each state's and jurisdiction's law.[45] A kind of unification in the field of indirect taxes was recently achieved in India when a uniform goods and services tax (GST) to be levied for the supply of goods and services was introduced across the country except the state of Jammu and Kashmir to replace multiple indirect tax rates previously existed at center and state levels.[46] A uniform indirect tax rate to apply throughout the country, it is believed, will ensure a tax neutral market and reduce transaction costs.

Similarly, several attempts have been made that are aimed at ameliorating the problems connected with the diversity of laws among the member states of EU, African, Latin American, and Scandinavian countries. The regional unification has a long and inspiring history and has survived the test of time. In fact, the unification of laws at the regional scale or between groups of countries having similar economic interests is usual and has better prospects of success than unification at international scale.[47] As we are mainly concerned with international unification of domestic trade laws, only a brief reference to some of the recent initiatives aimed at achieving unity of the contract law at regional will suffice. These include the non-political initiatives, such as the European restatements or codes of contract law, namely the Principles of European Contract Law (PECL)[48] and the Draft Common Frame of Reference (DCFR)[49] as well as the uniform laws that are directly applicable to member countries of a regional organization. The PECL and the DCFR are promulgated as the soft-law

[45]See generally Zaphiriou (1990), pp. 71–72.

[46]On April 12, 2017, the Central Goods and Services Tax Act, Integrated Goods and Services Tax Act, Union Territory Goods and Services Tax Act and Good and Services Tax (Compensation to States) Act were passed by the Parliament to implement a uniform indirect taxes regime in the country.

[47]Notably, many of the arguments against unification noted above do not apply to the regional unification of laws.

[48]See Lando (2005), pp. 379–401; Jansen and Zimmermann (2011), pp. 625–662; Bonell (2008), pp. 1–28.

[49]See Eidenmüller et al. (2008), pp. 659–708; Jansen and Zimmermann (2010), pp. 98–112; Antoniolli et al. (2010), pp. 343–58. For an account of the differing views on the true nature of the DCFR, see Jansen and Zimmermann. ibid.

instruments by a group of distinguished scholars and for that reason, as will be noted below, they may be useful in multiple ways and may be used by multiple agencies—legislators, arbitrators, and business community.[50] As examples of uniform laws we may refer to several uniform acts promulgated by the Organization for the Harmonization of Business Law in Africa (OHDHA).[51] These include: the Uniform Acts on General Commercial Law[52]; on Contracts for the Carriage of Goods by Road[53]; on Arbitration Law.[54] Aimed to promote economic integration between the member countries, these acts are directly applicable to the member countries.[55]

2.3 Unification of Private International Law

2.3.1 Reducing Conflicts Through Unification

As stated above, private international law addresses the issues of jurisdiction, choice of law, and recognition of foreign judgments in cases in which a "foreign element" is involved.[56] However, the rules of private international law, being part of the domestic law, vary from one country to another. One way to address the problem of uncertainty as to jurisdiction and the applicable law resulting from the conflicting private international law rules is to unify or harmonize them.

Unification of private international law rules, thus, provides an alternative to the unification of substantive laws. It is widely recognized that the hardships caused by the presence of diverse national laws may be reduced to a considerable degree by unifying private international law rules.[57] The unification of these rules ensures that a case involving the foreign element results in the same decision no matter where the case is tried.[58] In fact, both the processes of the standardization of private laws—the unification of the substantive and private international laws—may be viewed as "complementary to each other."[59] Where agreement on the substantive rules cannot

---

[50]The two instruments will be discussed in some detail in Chap. 4 (Sect. 4.6) dealing with the nature of a contract in general.

[51]OHADA was established by the 2008 Treaty on the Harmonization of Business Law in Africa (OHADA), at: https://www.ohada.org/index.php/en/au-droit-commercial-general-presentation-en/audcg-presentation-and-innovations.

[52]Adopted on December 15, 2010, entry into force May 15, 2011. Web address: www.ohada.org.

[53]Adopted on March 22, 2003, entry into force, January 1, 2004. Web address: www.ohada.org.

[54]Adopted on November 23, 2017, entry into force, March 15, 2018. Web address: www.ohada.org.

[55]See Nelson (2007), pp. 95–116.

[56]Foreign element means a contact with the law of a different country. See Collins (ed.) (2006), pp. 3–4.

[57]*Report of the Secretary General*, supra note 1; Fawcett and Carruthers (eds.) (2008), pp. 10–11; Haywod (2006), p. 2.

[58]Fawcett and Carruthers, id., p. 11.

[59]*Report of the Secretary General*, supra note 1.

be expected, the unification of the private international law may be undertaken as the "next best solution" as states seem to be more willing to join the process of harmonization of the conflict rules than reaching agreement on the substantive law.[60] Furthermore, harmonization of the conflict rules also seems necessary for the reason that unification of the substantive law is unlikely to cover all topics.[61]

Since unification of the substantive law and the unification of private international law rules have more or less similar objectives, the efforts directed at the unification in two domains are going hand-in-hand. This is recognized by the *Report of the Secretary General*, cited above, which refers to the unification efforts in two areas of law as the "conflict avoidance techniques" or the "legal techniques used to reduce conflicts and divergences." According to the *Report*, the method of unification of conflict of laws rules is aimed to establish the [uniform] rules governing the conflict of laws issues that include the rules determining "competing substantive law" in a particular transaction and the rules determining jurisdiction of a court or tribunal in a particular dispute. The unification of substantive law, on the other hand, is about reducing the conflicts between the laws of different countries, referred to as harmonization or unification of substantive laws.[62]

2.3.2 European Union Initiatives

Among the EU countries the progress in regard to the unification of private international law rules concerning the international contracts has been quite impressive (see Chap. 15). Some of the most important legal instruments on the subject include: the Council Regulation (EC) No. 44/2001 on jurisdiction and the recognition and enforcement of judgments in civil and commercial matters as updated by Regulation No. 1215/2012[63] replacing the 1968 Brussels Convention on jurisdiction and enforcement of judgments in civil and commercial matters[64]; the 2007 Lugano Conventions on jurisdiction and the enforcement of judgments in civil and commercial matters[65] replacing the 1988 Lugano Convention; and the Regulation (EC) No. 593/2008 on the law applicable to contractual obligations (Rome I)[66] replacing the 1980 Rome

---

[60]Nadelmann (1965), supra note 18, p. 450.

[61]Ibid.

[62]*Report of the Secretary General*, supra note 1.

[63]See Fawcett and Carruthers (2008), pp. 480–81. The Brussels Convention was implemented in UK law by the Civil Jurisdiction and Judgments Act, 1982.

[64]The Brussels Convention still applies to the territories of the Contracting States, such as the French overseas territories and Aruba in relation to the Netherlands. See Fawcett and Carruthers (2008), p. 342.

[65]The new Lugano Convention is binding on the EU member states and the European free Trade Association (EFTA) states. See Fawcett and Carruthers (2008), pp. 342–43.

[66]June 17, 2008. The Rome I Regulation was implemented in UK by the Law Applicable to Contractual Obligations (England and Wales and Northern Ireland) Regulations 2009.

Convention on the Law applicable to contractual obligations.[67] In addition, there exist a number of EU directives and regulations that contain conflict of law provisions specially designed for particular types of contract such as those related to the protection of consumers[68] and posted workers.[69]

2.3.3 Hague Conference on Private International Law

The Hague Conference on Private International Law (HCCH), which is an intergovernmental organization with 83 members including the European Union, has played an admirable role in unifying the rules of private international law.[70] Since 1893 when it began its work, the HCCH has produced a number of instruments of harmonization on different aspects relevant to international trade.[71] However, in the initial years, the focus was mainly on unifying the rules related to family law matters. The first four Hague Conferences (1893, 1894, 1900, and 1904) which resulted in the conclusion of six international conventions covering various important aspects of family law did not touch the issue of the conflict of laws problems arising in international trade.[72] Work of the Conference was interrupted due to the outbreak of the First World War and could be assumed only in 1925 at the Fifth Hague Conference. It is only after this period that the Conference paid its attention to the issue of international trade. The matter was placed on the agenda of the Sixth Hague Conference (1928) which established a special committee for preparing a draft Convention on the conflict of laws related to international sale of goods and the same was then adopted in 1931. Subsequently, the Seventh Hague Conference (1951), having deliberated on the 1931 draft, finally adopted a Convention on the Law Applicable to International Sale of Goods which was later signed by five European states.[73] The Convention, known as the 1955 Convention on the Law Applicable to International Sale of Goods, entered into force in 1964.[74]

---

[67]The Rome Convention was implemented by the Contracts (Applicable Law) Act 1990 largely replacing the common law rules on the subject. On the Rome Convention and the Rome I Regulation, see Chap. 15 infra.

[68]Directive 93/13/EEC on Unfair Terms in Consumer Contracts (1993) OJ L95/29.

[69]Directive 96/71/EC on the posting of workers in the framework of the provision of services (1997) O.J. L18/1. For a discussion of the impact of these special conflicts provisions on the normal choice of law rules provided for by the Rome Convention, see Knofel (1998), pp. 439–45.

[70]HCCH was given a permanent character following the Second World War.

[71]Information is available at the website of the HCCH. See, in addition, Lipstein (1993), pp. 553–653, 558; Fawcett and Carruthers (2008), pp. 11–12.

[72]Lipstein, ibid.

[73]For the text of the Draft Convention on the Law Applicable to International Sale of Goods, see 1(3) *American Journal of Comparative Law* 275–77 (1952).

[74]On the adoption of the 1955 Convention and subsequent developments, see, in particular, Nadelmann (1965), pp. 448–49. On the Convention, see generally Jacobson (1954) supra note 1, pp. 663–71; Lipstein (1993), pp. 616–19.

The 1955 Convention was followed by several instruments dealing with the particular and general aspects of contract, most notably, the 1986 Convention on the Law Applicable to Contracts for the International Sale of Goods, the 2005 Convention on the Choice of Court Agreements, and the 2015 Hague Principles on Choice of Law for International Commercial Contracts ("The Hague Principles").[75] The 1986 Convention, aimed to removing inconsistency in the choice of law rules related to sale of goods, was adopted as a substitute to the earlier 1955 Convention.[76] As will be noted in Chap. 15, the Choice of Court Agreements Convention is intended to establish a regime which is parallel to that of the New York Convention on Recognition and Enforcement of Foreign Awards. Notably, the Convention concerns only the exclusive choice of court agreements and in this way, it adopts an approach similar to the Brussels I Regulation cited above. As far as The Hague Principles are concerned, as will be seen below, they are a soft-law instrument and set forth "general rules for international commercial contracts." According to their Preamble, they may be useful as "a model for national, regional, supranational or international instruments" in developing the rules of private international law (see Sect. 2.4).

2.4 Toward Unification of Substantive Laws

2.4.1 Unification Efforts by UNIDROIT

In a sense, the history of uniform laws is traceable to the ancient times and the Roman law may indeed be cited as a conspicuous example of a legal system that grew by the process of assimilation of various national legal systems. In fact, unification of laws by voluntary adoption of a foreign law is old and continuous process.[77] Here reference may also be made to the law merchant or the lex mercatoria as an example of a kind of harmonized law that existed until the middle of the nineteenth century with a striking success. It consisted of usages or custom of merchants from varied legal backgrounds. Notably, the lex mercatoria was applied by the courts of different states to cross-border commercial transactions even in the absence of the state sanction.[78] But these early examples of harmonized law cannot be viewed as part of the modern movements toward harmonization for the obvious reasons that they did not emerge

[75]The texts of the various uniform law instruments including The Hague principles adopted under the auspices of the HCCH can be accessed from the official website of the Conference: https://www.hcch.net/en/home.

[76]The 1986 Convention has now paled into insignificance in view of the success of the CISG laying down substantive law on the international sale of goods which can be applied uniformly in disregard to the rules enacted by the former.

[77]See Graveson (1968), pp. 4–12.

[78]Rosett (1992), p. 685.

to address the needs of the modern trade and were not the product of the modern methods of unification—international conventions, model laws, and so on.[79]

In fact, the modern movement toward harmonization of private laws dates back to the late nineteenth century.[80] The growing interest in comparative law studies in those years contributed to various (modern) movements of harmonization.[81] Significantly, the first International Congress of Comparative Law held in Paris in 1900 underlined the need of employing comparative law methods in mobilizing the efforts at the unification of similar systems of law.[82] As will be seen below, the efforts toward harmonization intensified in the subsequent years resulting in an impressive number of legislative and non-legislative instruments with varying degree of success.

Some early measures for unification of substantive laws in certain key areas include the adoption of the 1912 Convention Relating to Bills of Exchange and Promissory Notes with an attached Uniform Law, which though failed to enter into force became basis for adoption of the 1930 Convention providing a Uniform Law for Bills of exchange and Promissory Notes and the 1931 Convention providing a Uniform Law for Cheques (the Geneva system),[83] the 1924 International Convention for the Unification of Certain Rules relating to Bills of Lading, and the 1929 Warsaw Convention on the Carriage of Goods by Air, as subsequently amended and updated.[84]

Unification efforts got a major push with the establishment of the International Institute for the Unification of Private Law (UNIDROIT), on September 3, 1926 in Rome as an auxiliary organ of the League of Nations.[85] UNIDROIT is an intergovernmental organization devoted "to study needs and methods for modernizing,

[79]The reception of Roman and common law in different countries was not prompted by any general desire to unify different legal systems and was indeed for reasons essentially different from those that explain the rise of uniform laws over the course of a century. See Graveson (1968), p. 7. Regarding the lex mercatoria, it may be stated that it was essentially a kind of (informal) law which developed out of mercantile custom and was not a product of any formal process of law-making or conscious decision-making. Notably, the modern efforts toward harmonization, in contrast, represent concerted and organized endeavors which are founded on the drawing up of a variety of instruments of harmonization by a variety of actors—states, various international organizations, trade associations and scholars.

[80]Bergsten (2015). Thirty-five years of the United Nations Convention on Contracts for the International Sale of Goods: expectations and deliveries. In *Thirty-five Years of Uniform Sales Law*, supra note 1, p. 8.

[81]Kamba (1974), pp. 501–502. On the contribution of comparative law in nurturing the concept of harmonization of inter-jurisdictional, private laws, see, in addition, Boodman (1991), pp. 702–05.

[82]Kamba, ibid.

[83]Geneva System applies to civil law countries while in common law jurisdictions it is the Anglo-American system that applies. As will be seen in Chap. 14, there now exists the UNCITRAL's 1988 Convention on International Bills of Exchange and Promissory Notes which is intended to harmonize the bill of exchange rules of two systems.

[84]For a discussion on the first attempts at unification, see Bergsten (2015), p. 8; Fawcett and Carruthers (2008), p. 10.

[85]The UNIDROIT was reestablished in 1940 following the demise of the League of Nations. For a more detailed account of the work of the UNIDROIT, visit the official website of the Organization: www.unidroit.org.

harmonizing and coordinating private and in particular commercial law between states" and also to formulate uniform law instruments. Since its establishment, the organization has been a major force in directing our efforts toward these objectives.[86]

UNIDROIT's efforts at unification have taken a variety of forms—international conventions, model laws, legislative guides, and restatements. Some of the most recent examples include the UNIDROIT Model Law on Leasing (2008) and A Guide to International Master Franchise Agreements (2007). UNIDROIT's work in preparing (non-binding) restatements is particularly notable. As already noted, the UNIDROIT's Principles as a restatement of law are a major achievement in this regard. As will be seen below, they are useful in multiple ways and, as a matter of fact, are widely used by the parties to an international contract, and arbitrators. Since a more fully discussion of the model laws and restatements prepared by the UNIDROIT, in particular, the UNIDROIT Principles will be found in Chap. 8 of this book, we shall now draw our attention to the 1964 Hague Conventions which were the first to establish a uniform (substantive) law regime for international sale of goods.

On April 29, 1930, a committee consisting of the representatives from different legal systems was formed by UNIDROIT to prepare a draft of a unified sales law.[87] This led the first draft of a uniform sales law coming out in 1935 which was adopted by UNIDROIT, in 1939, as the Draft Uniform Law on International Sale of Goods. After the Second World War when the work on unification was resumed in 1951, a diplomatic conference on unification of sales law was convened in The Hague by the Dutch government to deliberate on the 1939 Draft.[88] After successive revisions the Draft Uniform Law on the International Sale of Goods and a Draft of the Uniform Law on the Formation of Contracts for the International Sale of Gods, which in the meantime had been prepared by UNIDROIT, were submitted to a diplomatic conference convened at The Hague in April 1964.[89] After weeks of deliberations they were finalized as two distinct but related international conventions: (1) the Convention relating to a Uniform Law on the International Sale of Goods[90]; and (2) the Convention relating to a Uniform Law on the Formation of Contracts for the

---

[86] UNIDROIT's work is devoted to harmonizing substantive law. It touches private international law rules only incidentally, at www.unidroit.org/about-unidroit/overview.

[87] For a brief historical account of the attempts to unify international sales law, see Schwenzar and Hachem (2009), p. 459; Lando (2005), pp. 379–80; Jacobson (1954), p. 660; Reczei (1981), p. 522; Ndulo (1989), pp. 1–4; Honnold (1964), pp. 451–53; Honnold (1979), pp. 223–24, 223–30; Nadelmann (1965), p. 449.

[88] In fact, the Seventh Hague Conference on Private International Law (1951) and the (Seventh) Hague Conference on substantive law were held in the same year in The Hague. While the former took place in the month of October resulting in the 1951 Draft Convention (see Sect. 2.3), the latter (The Hague Conference on the unification of Sales Law) took place in November resulting in the draft of the substantive law aspects of international sale of goods which became basis for the adoption in 1964 of the twin international conventions establishing uniform rules for international sale of goods by the UNIDROIT.

[89] Ndulo (1989), p. 2; Schwenzar and Hachem (2009), id., p. 459.

[90] For the text, see 13 *American Journal of Comparative Law* 453–56 (1964).

International Sale of Goods[91] including the "Uniform Law for International Sale of Goods" (ULIS) and the "Uniform Law on the Formation of Contracts for International Sale of Goods" (ULF), respectively, as annexes.[92] The two conventions, namely the ULIS and ULF, entered into force on August 18, 1972 and August 23, 1972, respectively.

Significantly, the ULIS and ULF (sometimes referred to as the Uniform Laws) mark the first attempts toward international harmonization of sales laws involving both civil and common law systems.[93] The ULIS, annexed to the first Convention, sets forth basic obligations of the parties to the international sales contracts while the ULF, annexed to the second Convention, contains rules on the formation of contract, that is, the rules on offer and acceptance and related issues. Notably, the Uniform Laws contain only substantive law on international sales and are not concerned with conflict of laws rules. Regarding the scope of application, it may be noted that they only dealt with the rights and obligations of seller and buyer inter se and left the issues concerning the rights of third parties and validity unaddressed. Moreover, they applied to commercial sales only and excluded from there purview consumer sales (see Chap. 7).

In order to bring about uniformity in the application of laws, the Uniform Laws adopted a "novel" approach. They forbade recourse to private international law rules once requirements of their applicability were fulfilled subject to the reservation referred to below.[94] In other words, once the conditions of the applicability were met, the ULIS applied without more. The effect of this rule was to open the door of the Convention wide enough to make it apply to all sales transactions including those which were entered into between the parties of signatory states; between the parties of a signatory and non-signatory state; and also between the parties of non-signatory states provided that the court of a signatory state was seized of the matter. Had the recourse to private international law rules were not excluded, the ULIS would have applied only when the forum selected the law of a signatory state. This "open door" approach, according to which the ULIS applied even to a non-signatory state, was adopted apparently to make it a truly universal Convention. It is worth noting that prior to the 1964 Uniform Laws the law to govern a sale transaction was determined solely by reference to private international law rules which could be either the rules of the forum or based on an international conflict convention.[95] For example, under the Convention on the Law Applicable to International Sales of Goods, cited earlier, uniform sales laws were applicable only when private international law rules would require the application of the law of a contracting state. Since the rule was difficult to

---

[91]For the text, see 13 *American Journal of Comparative Law* 470–74 (1964).

[92]In fact, the formal Conventions merely contain the procedural matters and the (uniform) substantive laws, namely the ULIS and ULF, collectively referred to as the "Uniform Laws" are contained in the annexes of the 1964 Conventions.

[93]Szakats (1966), p. 751; Bridge (2007), p. 511.

[94]ULIS, Article 2. See Reczei (1981), p. 515.

[95]Reczei (1981), id, p. 514.

apply during deliberations at The Hague, it was decided that for the sake of simplicity the Uniform Laws should be applied without recourse to private international law rules.[96]

However, the formula of precluding the conflict of law rules adopted under the ULIS, though novel, proved to be unworkable. This solution failed to garner support of international community. Notably, under the CISG—successor of Uniform laws—position is different. The CISG provides that the Convention will be applicable only when a contract of sale is concluded between the parties of the contracting states or when the rules of private international law "lead to the application of the law of a Contracting State" (see infra, Chap. 7).

Another change relates to the applicability requirements. Article 1 of the ULIS provided that it "shall apply" to any contract of sale of goods entered into by the parties whose places of business are in *different states* as opposed to different contracting states in each of the following cases: (a) where the goods were required to be carried from one country to another; (b) where the offer and acceptance had been effected in different countries; (c) where delivery of the goods was to be made in the territory of a state other than that within which the offer and the acceptance had been effected. Thus, the sphere of application of the Uniform Laws was considerably wide.[97] In order to trigger their application, in addition to the above said three conditions, it suffices that the parties' places of business is located in different states as opposed to different contracting states. It follows then even in a situation in which there was no contract between a sale transaction and the forum, the Uniform Laws could be applied by the latter.[98] The condition of its applicability was satisfied when a dispute was submitted before the forum of a contracting state. However, as will be noted in Chap. 7, this "universalist" or "no contact" approach was not retained in the CISG. The CISG applies to the parties of different contracting states and not simply different states.

The ULIS allowed certain reservations which considerably diminished its uniform character.[99] First, a contracting state could invoke Article III to limit the application of the Uniform Laws to the contracting states only. Secondly, state parties were allowed under Article IV to declare the applicability of the Uniform Law conditional. The effect of this reservation was that the Uniform Law could be applied only when a previously adopted conflict convention itself required the application of the Uniform Law. This seemed necessary for the reason that at that time many states had already adopted conventions on uniform conflict rules from which they declined to withdraw.[100] Thirdly, under Article V of the ULIS, a state party was allowed to adopt it subject to the condition that the Uniform Law shall apply only when the parties

---

[96]Ibid.

[97]See Bridge (2007), p. 514; Reczei (1981), p. 515; Ndulo (1989) pp. 7–8.

[98]Honnold (1979), p. 227; Bridge (2007), pp. 514–15.

[99]See Reczei (1981), p. 515.

[100]Ibid.

to a contract positively choose it as the law of the contract.[101] Finally, two or more states parties could declare that they did not consider themselves as different states for the purposes of the Uniform Law. This also seemed necessary for the reason that some states, especially the Scandinavian countries, have the same or very similar sales laws.[102]

Hague Conventions, however, failed to fulfil the expectations of the most of the countries. Only nine countries including United Kingdom ratified these Conventions.[103] In particular, developing and socialist countries were generally opposed to the Hague Conventions. For them, the Conventions did not meet the needs of modern trade and tended to favor the sellers of the manufactured goods in the industrialized countries.[104]

Notwithstanding their failure, the Hague Conventions were not without significance. In fact, their successor—the CISG—which is considered a better convention and is widely regarded "a success" is based on the experience learnt from the failure of these conventions.[105] UNCITRAL in preparing the draft of CISG took Hague Conventions of 1964 as "the starting point" and as a matter of fact the draft as finally agreed upon by UNCITRAL is based on the modifications made in the texts of the two uniform laws to make it more acceptable.[106] It may be recalled that soon after the establishment of UNCITRAL, a Working Group was set up to ascertain what modifications were required to make the text of Hague Conventions capable of wider acceptance by countries of different legal, social, and economic backgrounds.[107] However, the Working Group while making a number of changes in the texts of the Uniform Laws recommended that UNCITRAL should adopt them as its own conventions.[108]

2.4.2 Unification Efforts by UNCITRAL

Establishment of UNCITRAL on December 17, 1966, marks a most important step forward toward the unification of trade laws. As is evident from the discussion below, the current unification efforts are strongly influenced by the UNCITRAL, which is rightly regarded a "key organization" for developing the legal framework

[101] This reservation was proposed by United Kingdom (UK) which ratified the Convention subject to the condition that the contracting parties would be bound by the ULIS only when they chose it as the applicable law. See Nadelmann (1965), p. 455.

[102] Nadelmann, id., p. 455.

[103] Of the nine states parties, seven were European states: Belgium, Federal Republic of Germany, Italy, Luxembourg, San Marino, The Netherlands, and UK.

[104] Lando (2005), p. 379; Schwenzar and Hachem (2009), p. 460; Strub (1989), pp. 475–76.

[105] Lando, id., p. 380.

[106] Bridge (2007), pp. 510–11.

[107] See Farnsworth (1972), p. 317.

[108] Ibid.

for facilitating international trade.[109] The organization was created by the UN General Assembly through Resolution 2205 (XXI) of December 17, 1966 with a view to "the promotion of the progressive harmonization and unification of the law of international trade."[110] The Resolution specifies the following main activities of UNCITRAL—(1) preparation of the instruments of harmonization; (2) ensuring wide participation of states in the process of harmonization; (3) collecting and disseminating information about legal developments concerning the law of international trade; and (4) coordinating the work of organizations having similar objectives. It may be noted that UNCITRAL is the only organization created by the UN for the unification of private law.[111] Further, UNCITRAL represents all geographical regions and the principal legal systems of the world.[112] The membership of the UNCITRAL now stands at 60. The members are elected by the General Assembly for terms of six years from amongst the members of the UN representing all principal regions. The member states include 14 African states, 14 Asian states, 8 Eastern European states, 10 Latin American and Caribbean states, and 14 Western European and other states.[113]

Significantly, UNCITRAL's instruments of harmonization cover all key areas of the commercial law including the sale of goods, international transport, insolvency, electronic commerce, and international payments, procurement of goods, and infrastructure development, as well as dispute resolution.[114] Moreover, they embrace a variety of forms or means—international conventions, model laws, legislative guides, uniform rules, or clauses to be adopted into a contract, and legal and practice guides. While international conventions, model laws, and legislative guides and model provisions fall into the category of legislative means, the non-legislative means category includes instruments like uniform rules of practice and legal guides.[115]

Here it is important to understand the difference between an international convention and other legislative instruments. As already noted, the former is legally binding on the contracting states and for that reason it results in unification of law. In contrast, a model law and other similar legislative instruments are recommendatory in nature. Being the non-treaty harmonization instruments, they allow departures from their texts and thus produce harmonized law rather than uniform law. Examples of model

---

[109] See Martonyi (2015), p. 3. For more information, see *A Guide to UNCITRAL: Basic facts about the United Nations Commission on International Trade Law* (2013), Vienna, at: http://www.uncitral.org/uncitral/en/about/origin.html [hereinafter referred to as the *Guide to UNCIRAL*]. It may be noted that the UNCITRAL is one of the two core international legal bodies created by the United Nations for the purpose of codification. The other is the International Law Commission (ILC). The difference between the two organizations is that the mandate of UNCITRAL is the unification and harmonization of private or domestic law while the ILC is engaged in "the progressive development of international law and its codification" in pursuance of Article 13(a) of the UN Charter.

[110] Resolution 2205 (XXI), December 17, 1966, supra note 1, sect. II, para. 8.

[111] Other organizations tasked to the unification of private law such as The Hague Conference on Private International Law (HCCH), and the UNIDROIT are not created by the UN.

[112] Sono (1984), p. 8.

[113] A *Guide to UNCITRAL*, supra note 109.

[114] Ibid.

[115] Ibid.

laws include: the UNCITRAL Model Law on International Commercial Arbitration (1985) as amended in 2006, the 2002 UNCITRAL Model Law on International Commercial Conciliation, the 2016 UNCITRAL Model Law on Secured Transactions, the 1997 UNCITRAL Model Law on Cross-Border Insolvency, the 1992 UNCITRAL Model Law on International credit Transfers, the 2017 UNCITRAL Model Law on Electronic Transferable Records, the 1996 Model Law on Electronic Commerce, and the 2001 UNCITRAL Model Law on Electronic Signatures. Furthermore, legislative guides and model legislative provisions have similar effects and are intended to provide possible legislative solutions in the form of recommendations.[116]

Turning to the non-legislative means of harmonization employed by UNCITRAL, it may be stated that they are used to standardize mercantile usage and practice in order to assist the business people in drawing up contracts. The model clauses or rules of practice resulting from the use of the non-legislative techniques, like the non-treaty legislative instruments, referred to above, are non-binding (uniform) rules. The UNCITRAL Arbitration Rules, 1976 as revised in 2010 and UNCITRAL Conciliation rules, 1980 are good examples of the uniform clauses or rules of practice to be incorporated in a contract (see Sect. 2.4.3). These rules are intended to assist the parties to an international contract to amicably settle a dispute through arbitration or conciliation. It may further be noted that as an alternative to the model or uniform contract clauses, the UNCITRAL has adopted the legal guides or notes explaining various issues that arise in the context of a particular type of a contract. In situations where it is not possible to develop the uniform contract clauses, because of the peculiar circumstances, it is better to adopt a legal guide to assist the parties. Examples of the legal guides include the UNCITRAL legal guide on International countertrade transactions, 1992 and the UNCITRAL Notes on Organizing Arbitral Proceedings.

Finally, we may also briefly refer to the system established by UNCITRAL for the uniform interpretation of legislative texts, known as the Case Law on UNCITRAL Texts (CLOUT). The system collects and disseminates court decisions and awards related to the legislative texts to promote uniformity in the interpretation of these texts. It is intended to be used by courts, arbitral tribunals, lawyers, and academics throughout the world.[117]

2.4.3 *Soft-Law Instruments: Codes of Practice and Restatements of Law*

In view of the growing importance of the soft-law instruments in harmonization of trade laws, a separate treatment of such instruments, especially codes of practice and restatements, seems justified. As already stated, the modern movement

---

[116]For example, UNCITRAL in 2003 adopted the Model Legislative Provisions on Privately Financed Infrastructure Projects to supplement its legislative guide on the same subject.

[117]Information available at: www.uncitral.org/uncitral/en/about/origin.html.

toward international harmonization is profoundly influenced by the soft-law, non-binding instruments representing the living law which challenges some old-fashioned assumptions about law.[118] At the cost of repetition it may also be stated that in situations, where a high degree of harmonization is not considered desirable or where it cannot be achieved, harmonization through standardization or codification of trade practices and restatements of laws are commonly resorted to by the international community. Furthermore, the non-binding nature of these instruments provides the business community and states a greater scope for cooperating in the process of internationalization of the law of contract.[119]

As already noted, trade associations, such as ICC with the aim to encourage the use of standard trade terms by their members very often promulgate codes of practice or model rules of practice. More commonly referred to as the standard trade terms or model clauses, these are intended to be voluntarily adopted into international commercial contracts.[120] However, they need to be distinguished from the usages or customs that are part of the *lex mercatoria*. It may be noted that rules of practice referred to here are *not* rules of law in true sense of the term as they are not promulgated by legislatures and, as already stated, they acquire legal effect only after their incorporation into a contract.[121] The codes of practice, just referred to above, include the Uniform Customs and Practice for Documentary Credits (or letters of credit), referred to as the UCP, current version of which is the UCP 600, the UNCITRAL Arbitration Rules, and the ICC's International Rules for the Interpretation of Trade Terms, popularly known as the Incoterms, the current version of which is the Incoterms 2020.

Turning to the restatements of law, such as the UNIDROIT Principles, it may be stated that while the codes of practice are "essentially rules of practice," restatements are designed as "rules of law."[122] However, as it is the case with the phrase, "rules of practice," just referred to above, the term, "rules of law" is also not used here in the sense of the true law or the law of a state as contained in legislations and case law but in the sense of non-state (or advisory) norms created by international trade associations or bodies of experts, such as the UNCITRAL, UNIDROIT, ICC, and the American Bar Association (ABA).[123] Though restatements are not legally binding instrument as not endorsed by states, they have significant persuasive authority as they embody the consensus of scholars from all leading national systems. They are

---

[118]See further Kozolchyk (1998). The UNIDROIT Principles as a model for the unification of the best contractual practices in the Americas, pp. 151–179.

[119]Pistor (2002), supra note 1, pp. 101–02. See also *Model Clauses for the Use of the UNIDROIT Principles of International Commercial Contracts*, UNIDROIT Principles Model Clause No. 1. 29 (a), International Institute for the Unification of Private Law (UNIDROIT), Rome (2013). The text can be accessed from: www.uniddroit.org. [Hereinafter referred to as the "Model Clauses].".

[120]Goode (2005) note 1, p. 547. See further Sect. 2.4.4.

[121]Id., p. 550.

[122]Ibid. See also Symeonides (2013), p. 892.

[123]See Commentary to the Principles on Choice of Law in International Commercial Contracts, p. 24 at: www.hcch.net; Goode, supra note 1, p. 553; Symeonides (2013) ibid; Model Clauses, supra note 119.

intended to be adopted by the parties to a contract, legislators and arbitrators across the countries to bring about consistency in the law on the subject.

While a more fully discussion of the UNIDROIT Principles and the Hague Principles, referred to above, is to be found in Chap. 8, which is devoted to a discussion of the role of the soft-law instruments in international trade, here a brief reference to these instruments will not be out of place. The UNIDROIT Principles are a codification or restatement of "the general part of international contract law" and are envisaged to be applied across the countries irrespective of the legal background of a country.[124] They were first published in 1994, with successive editions appearing in 2004, 2010, and 2016.

The UNIDROIT Principles are not intended to be unification of national laws but to offer solutions that are "best adapted" to the special requirements of international contracts.[125] It is worth stressing that these Principles are useful in multiple ways.[126] First, they are intended to serve as a model for drawing up national, supra-national instruments as well as international commercial contracts. Secondly, as stated in the text of the Model Clauses, they can well be chosen as the applicable law or incorporated as terms of the contract by the parties to a contract as well as the arbitral tribunals. Here, they may provide a useful alternative to the choice of the law of a third country as a "neutral" law. Thirdly, as Preamble to these principles state, they may also apply where the parties have agreed that their contract be governed by "general principles of law," or the "*lex mercatoria*" or the like or even "when the parties have not chosen any law to govern their contract." Thus, these Principles can be freely used by arbitrators for they are not bound to apply domestic law (see Chap. 15). Fourthly, Preamble to the UNIDROIT Principles and Model Clauses states that the UNIDROIT Principles may be used to interpret or supplement international uniform law instruments as well as domestic law. Finally, although these principles are conceived for international commercial contracts, they can also be used to apply to purely domestic contracts. As already stated, the UNIDROIT Principles—largely because they are non-binding and universal in application—are valuable resource for the business community, legislatures, judges, and arbitrators and, as a matter of fact, has been much more successful than the uniform law instruments.[127]

Regarded as "the first normative soft-law instrument" developed by the HCCH, the Hague Principles were adopted in 2015.[128] These Principles while affirming the principle of party autonomy aim to harmonize the choice of law rules in international commercial contracts. The Hague Principles, being a restatement of law, are

---

[124]Preamble to the UNIDROIT Principles, Article 1.1. See also 'Introduction' to the UNIDROIT Principles of International Commercial Contracts 2016, International Institute for the Unification of Private Law (UNIDROIT), Rome, at: www.uniddroit.org.

[125]Bonell (1992), p. 622.

[126]See generally ibid; Model Clauses, supra note 119.

[127]See Michael Joachim Bonell (ed.), *The UNIDROIT Principles in Practice: Case law and Bibliography on the UNIDROIT Principles of International Commercial Contracts*, Second Edition (NY: Transnational Publishers, 2006), Preface to the Second Edition, xi.

[128]Foreword to (The Hague) Principles on Choice of Law, approved on 19 March, 2015. The text can be accessed from the official web site of the HCCH.

intended for the use "as a model" by the legislatures across the countries to draft the law on the similar lines and to be a valuable resource for the courts and the tribunals.[129] In addition, according to the Preamble, these Principles are intended to be used "to interpret, supplement and develop rules of private international law."[130] Although termed as "Principles," they are the soft-law rules intended to be incorporated into the domestic legal regimes relating to the choice of law.[131] According to the HCCH's Commentary to the Principles on Choice of Law in International Commercial Contracts, the Principles adopt "current best practice" regarding the recognition of the party autonomy in choice of law in international contracts while making certain appropriate innovations.

The main objective of the Hague Principles is to promote the principle of party autonomy for choice of law. These Principles were promulgated by the HCCH in the hope that the states which have not yet adopted the principle of party autonomy will be encouraged to do so.[132] As already stated, except the Latin American countries, the support for this principle is almost universal. The Principles are thus quite helpful in promoting the principle of party autonomy in these countries.[133]

2.4.4 *Role of Non-Governmental Organizations: International Chamber of Commerce*

Apart from inter-governmental organizations, there are a number of professional bodies and associations whose efforts have had significant effect on the process of harmonization of trade laws. Some of these organizations are: ICC, the International Federation of Consulting Engineers (FIDIC), the Grain and Feed Trade Association (GAFTA), the Federation of Oils, Seeds and Fats Associations (FOSFA), and International Bar Association (ABA).

Established in 1920 and rightly described as the "world business organization," ICC is the world's largest business organization integrating 1200 chambers of commerce and their communities across the world with a view to facilitating free trade and investment.[134] It is a private, "voluntary body" of traders to suggest reforms in laws and customs regulating international commerce, in addition to guiding the business men across the world.[135]

---

129 See Symeonides (2013), p. 876.

130 See Preamble to the (The Hague) Principles on Choice of Law, approved on 19 March, 2015. Text can be accessed from the official web site of the HCCH.

131 Commentary to the Principles on Choice of Law in International Commercial Contracts (The Hague: HCCH, 2015), p. 24, at: www.hcch.net.

132 Id., p. 27.

133 Symeonides (2013), p. 876.

134 Information is available at: www.icc.org.

135 See Fahey (1921), p. 128.

ICC's initiatives toward codifying trade usages and encouraging their use by traders worldwide have been admirable and deserve special mention. It has established codes of voluntary rules in order to facilitate international trade in goods. Notable among these are the INCOTERMS and the Uniform Customs and Practice (UCP) for Documentary Credits. The rules of practice contained therein are widely used across the world and are quite familiar in business circles. These rules of practice have played an admirable role in streamlining business practices across the world.

The INCOTERMS, the current version of which was published in 2019, are to be voluntarily adopted rules of practice or standard trade terms especially designed for use in overseas commodity trades. Often referred to by their abbreviations, they are basically the shipping terms finding their source in mercantile customs. They mainly standardize the obligations of the sellers and buyers in respect of the overseas delivery of the goods. As will be seen in the next chapter which is devoted to a discussion of standard trade terms, the effect of these (standardized) trade terms is to substitute the obligations of the parties arising under domestic law in a number of respects (see Chap. 3).

The UCP for Documentary Credits (or letters of credit) is also a collection or code of voluntary rules of practice. These rules standardize banking practice in regard to international letters of credit and other kinds of documentary collections and are widely used in international commerce (see Chap. 14). Also noteworthy is the ICC's initiatives in the field of electronic commerce. A brief discussion of some of these initiatives will be found in Chap. 9 that is devoted to the harmonization of rules for electronic commerce.

Significantly, ICC has also been instrumental in promoting international commercial arbitration and providing arbitration services to private parties in cases involving business disputes of an international character.[136] The ICC has a permanent arbitral body—the ICC-International Court of Arbitration (ICA)—which was established in 1923.[137] The ICA administers the cases submitted for settlement by arbitration in accordance with the rules laid down under the Arbitration Rules framed by the ICC.[138] The ICC's arbitration rules were last revised in 1997, which entered into force on January 1, 1998.[139] The statutes of the ICA are set forth in the Appendix I of the Arbitration Rules. The ICC has also drawn the rules for optional conciliation. The present ICC Rules of Conciliation entered into force on January 1, 1988 (see Chap. 15).

Among the specialized trade or professional organizations, mention should be made of the FIDIC which is the "global representative body for the national associations of the consulting engineers" that publishes international standard form contracts

---

[136]ICC's Rules of Arbitration of, Article 1.

[137]Ibid. Article 1 provides that the International Court of Arbitration of the International Chamber of Commerce "is the arbitration body attached to the ICC.".

[138]The ICA does not itself settle a dispute. It monitors the application of the arbitration rules of the ICC.

[139]For the text, see 36 *International Legal Material* 1604 (1997).

for construction works to be used by consulting engineers.[140] They, like Incoterms, are essentially rules of practice widely recognized and used in many countries. GAFTA is an international trade association with members from 95 countries. Aimed to promote commodities trade worldwide, it issues standard forms of contracts for the use by traders and also renders arbitration service for the parties who use those contracts. Similarly, FOSFA, which is concerned with trade in oilseeds, oils, and fats with members from 89 countries, issues a wide range of standard forms contracts and act as an arbitral body. According to the information available on its website, currently 85% of global trade in oils and fats takes place using contracts issued by FOSFA.

References

2007 Revision of Uniform Customs and Practice of Documentary Credits, USP 600 (ICC Publication No. 600). Text is available at: iccwbo.org.

A Guide to UNCITRAL: Basic facts about the United Nations Commission on International Trade Law (2013). United Nations. http://www.uncitral.org/uncitral/en/about/origin.html Resolution 2205 (XXI), 17 December 1966, supra note 1, sect. II, para. 8.

Antoniolli, L., Fiorentini, F., & Gordley, J. (2010). A case-based assessment of the Draft Common Frame of Reference. *American Journal of Comparative Law, 58*(2), 343–358.

Bamodu, G. (1994). Transnational law, unification and harmonization of international commercial law in Africa. *Journal of African Law, 38*(2), 125–143.

Becker, J. D. (1989). Choice-of-law and choice-of-forum clauses in New York. *International and Comparative Law Quarterly, 38*(1), 168–175.

Bergsten, E. E. (2015). Thirty-five years of the United Nations Convention on Contracts for the International Sale of Goods: Expectations and deliveries. In *Thirty-five Years of Uniform Sales Law: Trends and Perspectives*, New York: United Nations.

Bonell, M. J. (2008). The CISG, European contract law and the development of a world contract law. *American Journal of Comparative Law, 56*(1), 1–28.

Bonell, M. J. (Ed.). (2006). *The UNIDROIT principles in practice: Case law and bibliography on the UNIDROIT principles of international commercial contracts*, 2nd edn, Preface to the Second Edition (p. xi). NY: Transnational Publishers.

Bonell, M. J. (1992). Unification of law by non-legislative means: The UNIDROIT draft principles for international commercial contracts. *American Journal of Comparative Law, 40*(3), 617–633.

Boodman, M. (1991). The myth of harmonization of law. *American Journal of Comparative Law, 39*(4), 699–724.

Bridge, M. (2007). *The international sale of goods: Law and practice.* Oxford: Oxford University Press.

Collins, S. L. (Ed.). (2006). *Dicey, Morris and Collins on the conflict of laws* (Vol. I). London: Sweet & Maxwell.

Commentary to the Principles on Choice of Law in International Commercial Contracts. (2015). HCCH, The Hague. www.hcch.net.

David, R. (1968). The methods of unification. *American Journal of Comparative Law, 16*(1/2), 13–27.

de Szászy, S. (1934). Choice of law by the parties to a contract with principal reference to the English and American law. *Transactions of the Grotius Society, 20*, 156–177.

[140] Web address: http://fidic.org/.

Eidenmüller, H., Faus, F., Grigoleit, H. C., Jansen, N., Wagner, G., & Zimmermann, R. (2008). The Common Frame of Reference for European private law: Policy choices and codification problems. *Oxford Journal of Legal Studies, 28*(4), 659–708.
Fahey, J. H. (1921). The International Chamber of Commerce. *The Annals of the American Academy of Political and Social Science, 94,* 126–130.
Farnsworth, E. Allan. (1972). Uncitral—Why? What? How? When? *American Journal of Comparative Law, 20*(2), 314–322.
Fawcett, J. J., & Carruthers J. M. (2008). *Chesire, North and Fawcett: Private international Law.* Oxford: Oxford University Press.
Foreword to (The Hague) Principles on Choice of Law, approved on 19 March, 2015. The text can be accessed from the official web site of the HCCH.
Fox, E. M. (1991). Harmonization of law and procedures in a globalized world: Why, what, and how? *Antitrust Law Journal, 60*(2), 593–598.
Goode, R. (2005). Rule, practice, and pragmatism in transnational commercial law. *International and Comparative Law Quarterly, 54*(3), 539–562.
Graveson, R. H. (1968). The international unification of law. *American Journal of Comparative Law, 16*(1/2), 1–12.
Haywod, R. (2006). *Conflict of laws.* Sydney: Cavendish Publishing.
Honnold, J. (1964). The 1964 Hague conventions on uniform laws on the international sale of goods. *American Journal of Comparative Law, 13,* 451–453.
Honnold, J. (1979). The draft convention on contracts for the international sale of goods: An overview. *American Journal of Comparative Law, 27*(2/3), 223–230.
ICC's Rules of Arbitration. www.icc.org.
Jacabson, D. (1954). International sale of goods. *International and Comparative Law Quarterly, 3*(4), 659–673.
Jansen, N., & Zimmermann, R. (2010). "A European Civil Code in all but name": Discussing the nature and purposes of the Draft Common Frame of Reference. *Cambridge Law Journal, 69*(1), 98–112.
Jansen, N., & Zimmermann, R. (2011). Contract formation and mistake in European contract law: A genetic comparison of transnational model rules. *Oxford Journal of Legal Studies, 31*(4), 625–662.
Kamba, W. J. (1974). Comparative law: A theoretical network. *International and Comparative Law Quarterly, 23*(3), 485–519.
Knofel, S. (1998). EC legislation on conflict of law: Interactions and incompatibilities between conflicts rules. *International and Comparative Law Quarterly, 47*(2), 439–445.
Kozolchyk, B. (1998). The UNIDROIT principles as a model for the unification of the best contractual practices in the Americas. *American Journal of Comparative law, 46*(1), 151–179.
Lando, O. (2005). CISG and its followers: A proposal to adopt some international principles of contract law. *American Journal of Comparative Law, 53*(2), 379–401.
Lipstein, K. (1993). One hundred years of Hague conferences on private international law. *International & Comparative Law Quarterly, 42*(3), 553–653.
Liu, Q., & Ren, X. (2017). CISG in Chinese courts: The issue of Applicability. *American Journal of Comparative Law, LXV*, 873–918.
Loh, Q. (2015). Perspectives on harmonizing transnational commercial law. In *Thirty-Five Years of Uniform Sales Law: Trends and Perspectives.* New York: United Nations.
Martonyi, J. (2015) Introduction. In *Thirty-Five Years of Uniform Sales Law: Trends and Perspectives.* New York: United Nations.
Mckendrick, E. (2000). *Contract law.* London: Macmillan Press Ltd.
Model Clauses for the Use of the UNIDROIT Principles of International Commercial Contracts. UNIDROIT Principles Model Clause No. 1. 29 (a), International Institute for the Unification of Private Law (UNIDROIT), Rome (2013). The text can be accessed from www.uniddroit.org.
Nadelmann, K. H. (1965). The Uniform law on the international sale of goods: A conflict of laws imbroglio. *Yale Law Journal, 74*(3), 449–464.
Ndulo, M. (1989). The Vienna Sales Convention 1980 and the Hague Uniform Laws on international sale of goods: A comparative analysis. *International & Comparative Law Quarterly, 38*(1), 1–4, 1–25.

Nelson, E. (2007). The Harmonization of business law in Africa: Is Article 42 of the OHADA treaty a problem. *Journal of African Law, 51*(1), 95–116.

Pistor, K. (2002). The standardization of law and its effects on developing economies. *American Journal of Comparative Law, 50*(1), 97–130.

Reczei, L. (1981). The area of operation of the international sales conventions. *American Journal of Comparative Law, 29,* 513–522.

Rosett, A. (1992). Unification, harmonization, restatement, codification, and reform in international commercial law. *American Journal of Comparative Law, 40*(3), 683–697.

Schwenzar, I., & Hachem, P. (2009). The CISG—Successes and pitfalls. *American Journal of Comparative Law, 57*(2), 457–478.

Sono, K. (1984). UNCITRAL and the Vienna sales convention. *International Lawyer, 18*(1), 7–15.

Strub, M. G. (1989). The Convention on the international sale of goods: Anticipatory repudiation provisions and developing Countries. *International and Comparative Law Quarterly, 38*(3), 475–501 (1989).

Suy, E. (1981). Achievements of the United Nations Commission on International Trade Law. *International Lawyer, 15*(1), 139–147.

Symeonides, S. C. (2013). The Hague principles on choice of law for international contracts: Some preliminary comment. *American Journal of Comparative Law, 61*(4), 873–899.

Szakats, A. (1966). The influence of the common law principles on the uniform law on the international sale of goods. *International & Comparative Law Quarterly, 15*(751), 749–779.

Thirty-Five Years of Uniform Sales Law, supra note 1.

Tunc, A. (1965). The uniform law on the international sale of goods: A reply to Professor Nadelmann. *Yale Law Journal, 74,* 1409–1414.

UNIDROIT Principles of International Commercial Contracts 2016, International Institute for the Unification of Private Law (UNIDROIT), Rome. www.uniddroit.org.

UNIDROIT: History and overview. www.unidroit.org/about-unidroit/overview.

Viejobueno, S. (1995). Progress through compromise: The 1980 United Nations convention on contracts for the international sale of goods. *Comparative & International Law Journal of South Africa, 28*(2), 200–207.

Zaphiriou, G. A. (1990). Harmonization of private rules between civil and common law jurisdictions. *American Journal of Comparative Law, 38*(Supplement), 71–97.

Reports, Official Texts and Online Resources

General Assembly Resolution 2205 (XXI) of 17 December 1966 establishing the United Nations Commission on International Trade Law. http://www.uncitral.org/uncitral/en/commission/sessions/pre.html.

Recommendation of the Sixth Committee of the General Assembly on the Report of the United Nations Commission on International Trade Law on the Work of its Fiftieth session, 26 October 2017. http://www.uncitral.org/uncitral/en/GA/6thcommittee_reports.html.

Report of the Secretary General, Sixth Committee, A/6396 in Official Records of the General Assembly, Twenty-first Session (Agenda Item 88), Sixth Committee, New York: 1966. http://www.uncitral.org/uncitral/en/commission/sessions/pre.html.

Hague Conference on Private International Law. www.hcch.net.

INCOTERMS. www.incoterms.org.

International Chamber of Commerce. www.icc.org.

International Federation of Consulting Engineers (FIDIC). http://fidic.org/.

International Institute for the Unification of Private Law (UNIDROIT). www.uniddroit.org.

OHADA. www.ohada.org/.

United Nations Commission on International Trade Law (UNCITRAL). www.uncitral.org.

Chapter 3
Standard Trade Terms

3.1 Unification Through Trade Practices

As pointed out in the introductory Chapter, a distinguishing feature of international sales contracts is that they often employ various trade terms, such as "free on board" (FOB), and "cost, insurance and freight" (CIF), especially designed to indicate the obligations of the parties in respect of the overseas delivery of the goods. These trade terms have evolved over the years and are especially relevant in cases of overseas sales. Often referred to by their abbreviations, they are basically the shipping terms finding their source in the mercantile customs and usages. Put differently, the effect of these trade terms is to substitute the obligations of the parties arising under domestic law in a number of respects. For example, in a CIF sale, the seller is subject to various documentary obligations which are in addition to his obligations under domestic law applicable to export sales. Notably, in this type of a sale contract, a seller is under obligations to ship the goods to a named destination; to enter into contract of carriage; to take out insurance; and to tender shipping documents to the buyer. This is in contrast to the FOB sale in which a seller's delivery obligations are complete once the goods in question are loaded on to a ship free on board. Further, since trade terms differ substantially in setting out the delivery obligations, they can serve as basis for distinguishing one type of export sale from another.

The international trade terms having the same or similar names carry different meanings in different jurisdictions which is a source of confusion and ambiguities. In view of this, the trade terms have been standardized at international level to avoid or reduce to a considerable degree any doubt regarding their true meanings. Here mention may be made of the "Incoterms" (International Commercial Terms) rules—a set of common trade rules or practices—drafted by the International Chamber of Commerce (ICC).[1] The different versions of the Incoterms define the responsibilities of sellers and buyers in respect of the cross-border delivery of goods. Incoterms are aimed "to provide a set of international rules for the interpretation of the most

[1]Information is available at the official website of ICC: www.iccwborg.

A. Srivastava, *Modern Law of International Trade*, International Law and the Global South, https://doi.org/10.1007/978-981-15-5475-9_3

commonly used trade terms in foreign trade."[2] These terms contain internationally accepted rules of interpretations and are used in international and domestic transactions involving sale of goods. As already stated in the previous chapter, Incoterms are the non-binding rules, and are meant for providing guidance to the business people. In other words, they are "a useful accomplishment of unification" by defining the meaning attached by traders across the countries to certain common terms of trade employed by them in the business contracts.[3] A brief overview of Incoterms is provided in Sect. 3.3.

3.2 Common Trade Terms[4]

3.2.1 EXW "Ex Works"

"Ex Works" export sale is "the most favorable" trade arrangement and also the most convenient one from a seller-exporter's point of view. Under this type of a sale contract, the seller's obligation is limited to making available the goods for collection by the buyer at the seller's premises including his factory, warehouse, works, and so on. It is the buyer's duty to collect the goods from the seller's workplace and to make all other arrangements related to cross-border movement of goods including carriage of goods, obtaining insurance, and export and import licenses. Since under the domestic law of the sale of goods, as a general rule, the delivery is required to be made at the seller's premises, and that it is the buyer's duty to take delivery at the works, an "ex works" sale contract closely resembles an ordinary domestic sale of goods transaction.[5]

Although, in "ex works" contract, the seller's only obligation is to make the goods available at his workplace, it does not relieve him of other obligations which ordinarily apply to a seller. For example, the goods should conform to the description; the seller must supply the sale invoice and other documents; pay any costs incurred in placing the goods at the buyer's disposal. Similarly, a buyer is under obligations to take delivery and pay for goods; obtain export and import licenses; make arrangements for the transport of the goods; pay any costs incidental to the transportation of the goods. It may also be noted that it is the buyer who has to bear the risks of loss or damage to the goods once goods are delivered to him.

---

[2]Ibid.

[3]David (1968), p. 16.

[4]See D'Arcy et al. (2000), p. 7–51; Guest (ed.) (2006), pp. 1457–1787; Atiyah et al. (2010), pp. 407–21; Chuah (2009), pp. 28–79; Carr (2014), pp. 6–58; Bridge (2007), pp. 69–224; Moens & Gillies (2006), pp. 131–59; Schnitzer (2006), pp. 13–37; Kouladis (2006), pp. 201–11.

[5]See D'Arcy et al. (2000), id., p. 11; Atiyah et al. (2010), id., p. 408.

3.2.2 FAS "Free Alongside Ship"

In the FAS contract, the seller has to deliver the goods alongside the ship. Once goods are so placed, the seller's delivery obligations are fulfilled. At this point the buyer's risks begin and now it is his duty to insure the goods against risks of loss or damage to the goods. Further, in this type of contract, the buyer also has to arrange for the carriage of the goods and that once the goods are delivered alongside the ship the loading of the goods is the responsibility of the buyer.[6]

As far as the obligations of the seller are concerned, they extend to supply the goods of contract description and of right quality; deliver the goods alongside the ship and give the buyer notice of that; pay handling and transportation costs up to the point when the goods are placed alongside the ship; provide assistance to the seller in obtaining export license by the buyer[7]; and obtain export license or other documents required for the purpose if so agreed between the parties. It may be noted that although a seller is not responsible for the carriage of the goods and for obtaining export license, there does exist a duty on the part of the seller to assist a buyer in obtaining export license if so requested.[8]

Obligations of the buyer include duty to nominate the ship,[9] giving notice to the seller of the name of the ship, and the delivery date to enable the seller to comply with the contract; making arrangement for carriage of the goods; and to bear the costs and risks in that respect. Once the goods are delivered alongside the ship, the risks pass to the buyer.

In the FAS contract, goods are taken as appropriated when they are placed alongside the ship. Therefore, if the placing of the goods alongside the ship is unconditional, property in the goods and risks pass to the buyer at that point. But if the seller has reserved the right of disposal the property will not pass to the buyer.[10]

3.2.3 "Ex Ship"

Under an Ex Ship contract of sale, the seller is under duty to deliver the goods at the named port or destination. As will be seen below, despite this similarity between the Ex Ship and the CIF contract, they considerably differ from each other. While a CIF contract is performed by tender of shipping documents to the buyer and actual delivery of the goods to the buyer is not important, in an Ex Ship contract delivery of actual goods is essential. In this contract the seller's duty is to deliver the goods on arrival at the port of destination.[11] An Ex ship contract cannot be performed by

---

[6] D'Arcy et al. (2000), id., p. 12.

[7] *Anglo Russian Merchant Traders Ltd v Batt* [1917] 2 KB 679.

[8] Ibid.

[9] See *MW Hardy & Co. v AV Pound & Co. Ltd.* [1956] AC 588.

[10] *Transpacific Eternity SA v Knematsu Corpn (The Antares III)* [2002] 1 Lloyd's Rep 233.

[11] *Yangtsze Insurance Association v Lukmanjee* [1918] AC 585.

mere delivery of the shipping documents to the buyer.[12] As it was stated in *Yangtsze Insurance Association v Lukmanjee*,[13] the seller's duty is to deliver the goods to the buyer from a ship which has arrived at the port of delivery and has reached a placed therein usual for the delivery of the goods of the kind in question. It was also pointed out in *Yangtsze Insurance Association* that in an Ex Ship contract, the provision like "ex ship, payment against documents" cannot be construed in the same manner as it is construed in a CIF contract and that the provision for payment against documents did not oblige the CIF seller to tender to the buyer the policy of insurance.

Under the Ex Ship contract, property in the goods (if the goods are specific or ascertained) passes to the buyer at the time of delivery of the goods. A similar rule applies to the passing of risks, which too, pass to the buyer when the goods are delivered to the buyer.[14] This result follows because in an Ex Ship contract, as opposed to a CIF contract, as was pointed out in *Yangtsze Insurance Association* case, property cannot pass by delivery of shipping documents only. In that case, the buyer attempted to claim under the policy taken out by the seller. But it was held by the Privy Council that the buyers could not do so because property in the goods had not passed to them. It was pointed out that in an Ex Ship contract, property in the goods passes upon delivery of the goods to the buyer.

3.2.4 FOB "Free on Board"

3.2.4.1 Nature of FOB Contract

In the FOB contract, the seller's obligation is to deliver the goods "free on board," that is to say, the seller undertakes the duty to place the goods free on board a ship nominated by the buyer.[15] The FOB contract of sale differs from the FAS contract in that in the latter a seller's duty is limited to delivering the goods alongside the ship and does not extend to loading the goods on board a ship. But under the FOB terms, a seller's duty extends to deliver the goods on board a ship.

In a contract under the FOB terms, once the goods are delivered on board the ship, the seller's delivery obligation is fulfilled.[16] As was pointed out in the leading case

---

[12]Guest (ed.) (2006), p. 1772; Carr (2010), p. 31; Chuah (2009), p. 32. See also *Comptoir d' Achat et de Vente v Luis de Ridder Lda* (*The Julia* Case) [1949] AC 293.

[13][1918] AC 585.

[14]See Guest (ed.) (2006), pp. 1774–75.

[15]See *Pyrene and Co. Ltd. v Scindia Navigation Co. Ltd.* [1954] 2 QB 402; *Ian Stach Ltd v Baker Bosley Ltd* [1958] 2 QB 130; *Wimble, Sons & Co. Ltd. v Rosenberg & Sons* [1913] 3 KB 743; *Contship Container Lines Limited v D. K. Lall and Others* AIR 2010 SC 1704.

of *Wimble v Rosenberg*,[17] an FOB contract is generally understood as a contract in which "goods are not sent by sea by the vendor, but are delivered by him at the rail of the ship and are taken over by the shipowner nominated by the buyer, and conveyed by him across the sea." In *Wimble*, Hamilton J quoted Brett M. R. in *Stock v. Inglis*[18] as suggesting:

> …the words 'free on board,' according to the general understanding of merchants, would mean more than merely that the shipper was to put them on board at his expense; they would mean that he was to put them on board at his expense on account of the person for whom they were shipped; and in that case the goods so put on board under such a contract would be at the risk of the buyer whether they were lost or not on the voyage. Now that is the meaning of those words 'free on board' in a contract with regard to specific goods, and in that case the goods are at the purchaser's risk, even though the payment is not to be made on the delivery of the goods on board, but at some other time, and although the bill of lading is sent forward by the seller with documents attached in order that the goods shall not be finally delivered to the purchaser until he has either accepted bills or paid cash.[19]

Thus, in the FOB contract, the seller is generally under no obligation to arrange for carriage of goods nor is under any duty to insure the goods, although he has to obtain export clearance. As noted above, in this type of contract, the seller must put the goods on board a ship nominated by the buyer. Significantly, the seller is under no obligation to bear any expense toward shipment after the goods are put on board the ship.[20] As will be seen below, in this classic FOB contract; and also in a FOB contract "with additional services," the seller is party to the contract of carriage.[21] But in the third type of FOB contract, that is to say, a "simple" FOB contract, the contract for carriage is entered into between the buyer and the ship-owner. A seller has to incur all the expenses up to this point and it is the buyer's duty to make further arrangements and bear all subsequent expenses toward the shipment of goods.[22] However, it may happen that a seller may find it convenient to arrange for shipment of goods and enter into a contract of carriage. If this happens, the price of goods includes the costs of carriage of goods. As will be seen presently, this is normally the case with a classic type of FOB contract wherein it is the seller who arranges for the carriage of goods also.

The nature of FOB contract of sale was in issue in *Wimble v Rosenberg* (cited above). In *Wimble*, by a contract of June 27, 1912, Messrs. Rosenberg & Sons, the defendants, bought 200 bags of rice. The rice was to be shipped within three months. It was bought f.o.b. Antwerp. Defendants-buyers sent the plaintiffs instructions to ship the rice to Odessa and to pay freight. No ship was nominated by the defendants. Instead, they left it to the plaintiffs-seller to select the ship. The instructions to ship

---

[16]See *Stock v. Inglis* (1885) 10 AC 263 at pp. 271–273.
[17][1913] 3 KB 743.
[18]Supra note 16.
[19][1913] 3 KB 743, pp. 759–60.
[20]Guest (ed.) (2006), p. 1654.
[21]See Bridge (2007), pp. 77–80.
[22]See *Ian Stach*, supra note 15; *Pyrene and Co.*, supra note 15.

rice were given in writing omitting the customary request according to which the seller was to inform the buyer about the name of the ship and the date of the proposed shipment. The rice was shipped on board a steamer called the *Egyptian* on August 24, 1912. The *Egyptian* sailed from Antwerp on the 25th of August. But on the 26th the steamer stranded and the rice was lost. The defendants came to know about it only on 29th of August, when an invoice and bill of lading reached them, and they were requested to pay against documents in accordance with the terms of the contract. They immediately on receipt of the bill of lading attempted to insure the bags of rice, but their attempt failed. The buyers thereupon refused to take up the shipping documents and to pay for the rice.

In an action for the price, it was argued by the defendants that the plaintiffs, under s. 32(3) of the (English) Sale of Goods Act, 1893,[23] were under duty to give notice to the buyers enabling them to insure the goods and since the same was not given the sea transit was at the risk of the plaintiffs (sellers). While taking the position that s. 32(3) [of the 1893 Act] applied to an FOB contract, the Court ruled that since in the present case, the buyers had sufficient knowledge to enable them to insure the goods, "there was no obligation upon the plaintiffs, under s. 32(3), to give notice to the defendants of the shipment on a particular ship."

Taking the view that the natural meaning of the words of sub-s. 3 of s. 32 of the Sale of Goods Act [the 1893 Act] covers a f.o.b. contract, Vaughan Williams LJ stated:

> I construe the word "send," both in sub-s. 1 and in sub-s. 3, in the sense of "forward" or "dispatch," and in my opinion the word "send" covers every obligation of the seller in reference to effecting or securing the arrival of the goods the subject of sale at the destination intended. It is not true in fact to say that the purchased goods are being sent to the ship on which they are placed for the purpose of delivery at the port of destination. The purchased goods are not the less being sent to the buyer at the port of destination because delivery f.o.b. is prima facie delivery to the buyer, or because the property has passed to the buyer. Sub-s. 3, in my opinion, casts a duty on the seller forwarding the goods to the buyer by a route involving sea transit, under circumstances in which it is usual to insure, to give such notice as may enable the buyer (to whom be it observed the property in the purchased goods has passed), to insure them during their sea transit. The penalty for not performing this duty is that goods, though the goods of the buyer, shall be at the risk of the seller during such sea transit. Moreover the same result is arrived at if the words "where goods are sent by the seller to the buyer," at the beginning of sub-s. 3, are construed as describing the whole transaction.[24]

It may be noted that in a FOB contract, the property in the goods and risks pass to the buyer once the goods are placed on board a ship.[25] A ship's rail at the port

---

[23]The corresponding provision is contained in s. 39(3) of the Indian legislation on the subject, namely the Sale of Goods Act, 1930. S. 39(3) reads as follows: "Unless otherwise agreed, where goods are sent by the seller to the buyer by a route involving sea transit, in circumstances in which it is usual to insure, the seller shall give such notice to the buyer as may enable him to ensure them during their sea transit, and if the seller fails so to do, the goods shall be deemed to be at his risk during such sea transit.".

[24] *Wimble v Rosenberg*, supra note 17, pp. 750–51.

[25]*Pyrene and Co*, supra note 15; *Colonial Insurance Co. of New Zeeland v Adelaide Marine Insurance Co.* (1886) 1 AC 128; *Contship Container Lines Limited v D. K. Lall and Others*, supra note 16.

of shipment is considered the "equivalent of frontier" which divides the countries of export and import.[26] Obviously, the seller is not responsible for any damage to the goods once they pass over the rail. But till the goods are placed on board the vessel, subject to the terms of the contract, it is the supplier who has to undertake the responsibility to arrange for coverage of risk.[27] As stated by the Supreme Court in *Contship Container Lines Limited v D. K. Lall and Others*[28]: "[I]n the case of FOB contracts, the goods are delivered free on board the ship. Once the seller has placed the goods safely on board at his cost and thereby handed over the possession of the goods to the ship in terms of the Bill of Lading or other documents, the responsibility of the seller ceases and the delivery of the goods to the buyer is complete. The goods are from that stage onwards at the risk of the buyer."[29]

The question of passing of the property is decided on the basis of the applicable law. As has already been noted, under the domestic laws of India and England property passes when the parties to a contract of sale so intend. The FOB contract implies that parties intend that property in goods should pass when they are placed on board the ship. However, this rule will not apply where a seller obtains bill of lading in his own name. In that situation he is acting as a principal and not as an agent of the buyer.

3.2.4.2 Kinds of FOB Contracts

FOB contracts are flexible in nature[30] and may take any of the three forms—"simple," "classic," and FOB contract "with additional services." In a simple FOB contract, carriage of goods is the responsibility of the buyer and it is he who enters into a contract of carriage with the carrier either through himself or an agent.[31] The seller places the goods on board the ship and obtains a mate's receipts to be transmitted to the buyer who exchanges the same for the bill of lading. Further, the shipping arrangements and insurance cover for the goods are the responsibility of the buyer. Since the bill of lading is obtained by the buyer and not the seller, property and risks pass to the buyer the moment goods are put on board the ship.

---

[26] Moens & Gillies (2006), p. 143.

[27] *VST Tillers Tractors Limited, Bangalore v National Insurance Company Limited* 2010 (2) Kar LJ 502.

[28] AIR 2010 SC 1704.

[29] See also *VST Tillers Tractors Limited*, supra note 27.

[30] See *Pyrene Co. Ltd. v Scindia Navigation Co. Ltd.*, supra note 15; *Mckay Massey Harris Pvt Ltd v Imperial Chemical Industries of Australia & New Zealand Ltd.* [1960] 1 Lloyd's Rep. 191.

[31] See *The EL Amria and The El Minia* [1982] 2 Lloyd's Rep. 28; See also Atiyah et al. (2010), p. 409.

In a classic type of FOB contract, it is the seller who enters into a contract of carriage with the carrier and puts the goods on board a ship.[32] The bill of lading is obtained by the seller to be transferred to the buyer. Since the bill of lading is in the name of the seller, property in the goods does not pass from the seller to the buyer upon merely placing the goods on board the ship.

In FOB contract "with additional services," making shipping and insurance arrangements and also nominating the ship are the responsibilities of the seller. Costs of carriage and insurance are to be borne by the buyer. A practical implication of this is that risks associated with price fluctuations are borne by the buyer.[33] In this type of contract of sale, the seller places the goods on board a ship; enters into the contract of carriage; obtains the bill of lading in his own name; and transfers the same to the buyer.

Here mention may be made of *The El Amira case* (cited above) in which the three kinds of FOB contracts dealt with by Devlin J in *Pyrene Co. Ltd.* (cited below) were defined in the following manner. In the first or classic type, the buyer nominates the ship and the seller puts the goods on board for the account of the buyer, procuring a bill of lading. The seller is a party to the contract of carriage. In the second type of an FOB contract (FOB with additional services), "which is a variant of the first, the seller arranges for the ship to come on birth, but the legal incidents are the same." And in the third type (simple FOB contract) "the seller puts the goods on board, takes a mate's receipt and gives this to the buyer or his agent who takes a bill of lading." Here, the "buyer is a party to the contract of carriage *ab initio*."[34]

Here reference may also be made to the following passage in the judgment by Devlin J in *Pyrene Co. Ltd. v Scindia Navigation Co. Ltd.*[35] which is often quoted as dealing with the different kinds of an FOB contract:

> The fob contract has become a flexible instrument. In what counsel called the classic type-…the buyer's duty is to nominate the ship, and the seller's to put the goods on board for account of the buyer and procure a bill of lading in terms usual in the trade. In such a case the seller is directly a party to the contract of carriage at least until he takes out the bill of lading in the buyer's name. Probably the classic type is based on the assumption that the ship nominated will be willing to load any goods brought down to the berth or at least those of which she is notified. Under present conditions, when space often has to be booked well in advance, the contract of carriage comes into existence at an earlier point of time. Sometimes the seller is asked to make the necessary arrangements; and the contract may then provide for his taking the bill of lading in his own name and obtaing payment against the transfer as in a cif contract. Sometimes the buyer engages his own forwarding agent at the port of loading to book space and to procure the bill of lading; if freight has to be paid in advance this method may be the most convenient. In such a case the seller discharges his duty by putting the goods on board, getting the mate's receipt and handling it to the forwarding agent to enable him to obtain the bill of lading. The present case belongs to this third type...[36]

[32] See *Brown (AR), McFarlane & Co. v Shaw (c), Lovell & Sons* [1921] 7 Lloyd's L Rep. 36.

[33] See Bridge (2007), p. 79.

[34] [1982] 2 Lloyd's Rep. 28 at p. 32.

[35] [1954] 2 QB 402.

[36] Id., p. 424.

3.2.4.3 Obligations of Seller and Buyer

In the first place, the FOB seller, like a seller under an ordinary contract for the sale of goods, is under the obligation to ship the goods of contract description and the provisions contained in ss. 15–17 of Sale of Goods Act (SoGA) 1930 [ss. 13–15, Sale of Goods Act (SoGA) 1979] which deal with the implied conditions as to description, quality, and fitness for any particular purpose apply to the FOB sale.[37]

A second obligation of an FOB seller is to deliver the goods in the specified period and at the specified port of shipment. Since it is the buyer's duty to make shipping arrangements the seller acts on the instructions of the buyer. But where, fixing the time of shipment is left to the seller, the seller is under duty to notify the buyer of the date of shipment so that he can make arrangement for shipment and insurance of the goods during transit. The seller is also under obligation to pay handling and transportation costs up to the point when the goods cross the ship's rail.

In the FOB contract of sale, as already indicated, the shipment of the goods is the responsibility of the buyer. Therefore, he is under obligation to nominate a ship or to secure shipping space to effect a carriage, and inform the seller about this in time. As has been noted above, this happens in the case of a classic FOB contract. The buyer must inform about the name of the ship and the port of shipment.[38] However, in some cases, it is the seller who is required to nominate the ship. As has already been noted that an FOB contract is a flexible instrument and a seller, under the contract, may be required to arrange carriage and insurance for the account of the buyer.[39]

The second duty of the buyer is to pay the price of the goods. It may be stated that where the goods have been put on board a ship and the bill of lading has been obtained by the seller who tenders the same to the buyer, the price normally becomes payable.[40] Unless otherwise agreed, time and place of payment are the time and place of tender of documents.[41]

3.2.4.4 Passing of Property and Risks

As stated above, in an FOB contract the property in the goods generally passes once goods are put on the ship's rail.[42] Similar is the case with the passing of risks. Risks too pass from the seller to the buyer at the point the goods pass the ship's rail at the port of shipment. This effect follows from the rule that property and risks, prima

---

[37] On the implied terms under a contract of sale, see Chap. 6, Sect. 6.1.4 infra.

[38] See *David T Boyd and Co. Ltd. v Luis Louca* [1973] 1 Lloyd's Rep 209.

[39] See also Bridge (2007), pp. 78–79.

[40] Guest (ed.), pp. 1699–1700.

[41] Ibid.

[42] *Contship Container Lines Limited v D. K. Lall and Others* supra note 15; *Pyrene Co. Ltd. v Scindia Navigation Co. Ltd.*, supra note 15.

facie, pass together.[43] Further, since in an FOB contract a seller's duty is limited to putting the goods on the ship's rail, property in the goods and risks pass as soon as the goods are placed on board a ship provided that the seller does not reserve the right of disposal of the goods by taking out the bill of lading in his own name.[44] S. 19 of the SoGA 1930 and S. 17 of the (English) SoGA 1979 also enact a similar rule. According to s. 19(1) of the Act of 1930, "where there is a contract for the sale of *specific or ascertained goods* the property in them is transferred to the buyer at such time as the parties to the contract intend it to be transferred."[45] But this result will follow only when the goods in question are specific or ascertained.[46] Where the goods are unascertained the property will not pass until they are ascertained.[47] The meaning is that unless the goods are appropriated by the seller property in the goods shall not pass to the buyer.[48] But delivery of the goods to a carrier may amount to an act of appropriation.

In an old case, *Inglis v Stock*,[49] 200 tons of sugar was to be delivered "f.o.b. Hamburg" and payment was to be made by cash in London in exchange for bill of lading. When sugar was sold it was unascertained. The sugar was subsequently lost. In an action on the insurance policy, the House of Lords, affirming the decision of the Court of Appeal, held that although property in the goods did not pass to the buyer, the risks did pass. In that case, the Court of Appeal had held that the sale being FOB Hamburg, the sugar was at the buyer-respondent's risk after shipment, that he had an insurable interest in it, and that the underwriters were liable. In the context of international sales, where the goods are delivered to the carrier for transmission to the buyer and the right of disposal is not reserved by the seller it will be taken that the goods have been unconditionally appropriated to the contract.[50]

S. 19 of SoGA 1930 further provides in subsection (2) that in ascertaining the intention of the parties "regard shall be had to the terms of the contract, the conduct of the parties and the circumstances of the case." It follows, then, where a seller obtains the bill of lading in his own name, it will be taken that the seller has reserved the right to transfer the property in the goods at a time later than that of shipment of the goods. Retaining of title documents shows that the seller has not intended to transfer

---

[43]See S. 26 of the Sale of Goods Act, 1930 ("Unless otherwise agreed, the goods remain at the seller's risk until the property therein is transferred to the buyer, but when the property therein is transferred to the buyer, the goods are at the buyer's risk whether delivery has been made or not."). For further discussion see Chap. 6 infra.

[44]Bridge (2007), p. 339.

[45]Emphasis is supplied. See *Carlos v Charles Twigg* [1957] 1 Lloyd's Rep 240.

[46]On the meaning of specific or ascertained goods, see infra, Chap. 5.

[47]*Inglis v Stock* [1885] 10 AC 263; *Jute and Gunny Brokers Limited and Another v Union of India and Others* AIR 1961 SC 1214.

[48]*Laurie & Morewood v Dudin & Sons* [1926] 1 K.B. 223 (where 200 quarters of maize, as part of 618 quarters of maize were sold, but which had never been separated from the bulk, it was held that property did not pass to the buyer).

[49][1885] 10 AC 263.

[50]Chuah (2009), p. 141; *The Seven Pioneer* [2001] 2 Lloyd's Rep. 57.

property in the goods. In *The Seven Pioneer* case,[51] the bill of lading was never sent by the seller to the buyer. It was held that the claimants had not acquired sufficient interests in the goods to enable them to successfully bring a claim on negligence.

But where, though the bill of lading is taken in the name of the seller, the seller endorses it in favor of the buyer and sends the same to the buyer together with sale invoice stating that the goods are shipped "on account and risk of buyers" the seller has not reserved the right of disposal.[52]

3.2.5 CIF Cost, Insurance, and Freight

3.2.5.1 Nature of a CIF Contract

Simply put, the term "CIF" denotes that the price is to include not only the cost of goods but also the cost of insurance and freight. In describing a CIF contract, the Supreme Court's decision in *Phulchand Exports Ltd v Ooo Patriot*[53] cites the following passage in Kennedy's *C.I.F. Contracts* (ed., Dennis C. Thompson), Third Edition, p. 1:

> It is a contract which contemplates the carriage of goods by sea, and is the most common form of shipping contract in use today. It is known as a c.i.f. contract, for the price which the buyer has to pay is the cost of the goods, together with the insurance of the goods during transit and the freight to the port of destination.

It may be noted that in comparison to a FOB contract, the seller of a CIF contract assumes additional duties, such as shipping the goods of contract description at the port of shipment, entering into contract of carriage and arranging for insurance of the goods during the voyage, and tendering to the buyers all shipping documents, including the bill of lading, the policy of insurance, and the sale invoice. Thus, the term, "CIF Chennai" suggests that the goods shall be delivered to the purchaser at the port of Chennai and the seller undertakes the duty to either ship the goods at the port of shipment or to buy goods afloat and bear the costs of freight and insurance, obtain the bill of lading and insurance policy, and tender these documents to the buyer against payment. The bill of lading represents the goods in transit and transfer of the same to the buyer enables him to obtain possession of the goods at the port of destination, and a policy of marine insurance protects the buyer's interest if the goods are lost in transit. The buyer, in turn, is under obligation to pay the cost of the goods, the freight, and the cost of insurance.[54]

---

[51] Ibid.

[52] Kannan (ed.) (2012), p. 71.

[53] (2011) 10 SCC 300.

[54] *Arnhold Karberg & Co. v Blythe, Green, Jourdon & Co.*, [1916] 1 KB 495, at p. 512.

The nature of a CIF contract is well settled, and there is a long line of decisions of the English courts dealing with the true nature of such a contract.[55] In *Arnhold Karberg & Co.*,[56] Warrington LJ described an ordinary CIF contract as "a bargain made by sellers of goods abroad for their shipment, for providing for their carriage to the port of destination and for insuring the goods during the voyage, the buyer having to pay the cost of goods, the freight, and the cost of insurance."[57] And to quote Bankes LJ in the same case, the [CIF] contract "is a contract for the sale of goods whereby the sellers also undertake inter alia, to enter into a contract of affreightment to the appointed destination, which contract will be evidenced by the bill of lading, and secondly to take out a policy of insurance upon the terms current in the trade."[58] The legal position was succinctly dealt with in *Smyth & Co.* by the House of Lords. In that case, it was stated that the seller's duty, in a CIF contract, is to ship the goods and to transfer to the buyer the bill of lading and the policies of insurance. To quote Lord Wright in *TD Bailey, Son & Co. v Ross T Smyth & Co.*[59]:

> The initials [CIF] indicate that the price is to include cost, insurance and freight....The seller has to ship or acquire after that shipment the contract goods, as to which, if unascertained, he is generally required to give a notice of appropriation. On or after shipment, he has to obtain proper bills of lading and proper policies of insurance. He fulfils his contract by transferring the bills of lading and the policies to the buyer. As a general rule, he does so only against payment of the price, less the freight which the buyer has to pay. In the invoice which accompanies the tender of the documents on the "prompt"—that is, the date fixed for payment—the freight is deducted, for this reason. In this course of business, the general property remains in the seller until he transfers the bill of lading....

And to quote the following passage in the judgment of Hamilton J in *Biddell Brothers v E Clemens Horst Co.*[60] which has been cited by many authorities as a classic exposition of the CIF contract:

> ...A seller under a contract of sale containing such terms[as to be found in a CIF contract] has firstly to ship at the port of shipment goods of the description contained in the contract; secondly to procure a contract of affreightment under which the goods will be delivered at the destination contemplated by the contract; thirdly to arrange for an insurance under the terms current in the trade which will be available for the benefit of the buyer; fourthly to make out an invoice... and finally to tender these documents to the buyer so that he may know what freight he has to pay and obtain delivery of the goods, if they arrive or recover for

---

[55] See, in particular, *James Finley & Co. v NV Kwik Hoo Tong Handel Maatschappij* (1928) 31 Ll LR 220 ("The c.i.f. seller is bound to procure and tender to the buyer shipping documents, that is, in particular, a bill of lading, which will, among other things, show the date of shipment, that being a condition of the contract." at p. 225), affirmed by the Court of Appeal, [1929] 1 KB 400; *Arnhold Karberg & Co.*, ibid; *Biddell Brothers v E Clemens Horst Co.*, [1911] 1 KB 214; *Johnson v Taylor Bros*, [1920] AC 144; *State Trading Corporation of India Ltd v M. Golodetz Ltd* [1988] 2 Lloyd's Rep. 182; *Manbre Saccharine Company v Corn Products Company* [1919] 1 KB 198; *Hindley and Co. Ltd. v East Indian Produce Co. Ltd.* [1973] 2 Lloyd's Rep. 515.

[56] [1916] 1 KB 495.

[57] Id., p. 512.

[58] Id., p. 509.

[59] (1940) 67 Ll. L R 147, at p. 156.

[60] [1911] 1 KB 214.

> their loss if they are lost on the voyage. Such terms constitute an agreement that the delivery of the goods, provided they are in conformity with the contract, shall be delivery on board ship at the port of shipment. It follows that against tender of these documents, the bill of lading, invoice, and policy of insurance, which completes delivery in accordance with that agreement, the buyer must be ready and willing to pay the price.[61]

In the Court of Appeal, Kennedy LJ provided the following description of the CIF contract:

> At the port of shipment...the vendor ships the goods intended for the purchaser under the contract. Under the Sale of Goods Act, 1893, s. 18, by such shipment the goods are appropriated by the vendor to the fulfil-ment of the contract, and by virtue of s. 32 the delivery of the goods to the carrier—whether named by the purchaser or not—for the purpose of transmission to the purchaser is prima facie to be deemed to be a delivery of the goods to the purchaser. Two further legal results arise out of the shipment. The goods are at the risk of the purchaser, against which he has protected himself by the stipulation in his c. i. f. contract that the vendor shall, at his own cost, provide him with a proper policy of marine insurance intended to protect the buyer's interest, and available for his use, if the goods should be lost in transit; and the property in the goods has passed to the purchaser, either conditionally or unconditionally..[62]

Mention may also be made of the case of *James Finlay & Co. v NV Kwick Hoo Tong Handel Maatscchappij*,[63] wherein the following description of a CIF contract is to be found:

> A c.i.f. contract...is a contract for the sale and delivery of goods which must be shipped as called for by the contract description, but it is also a sale of documented goods. The c.i.f. seller is bound to procure and tender to the buyer shipping documents, that is, in particular, a bill of lading, which will, among other things, show the date of shipment, that being a condition of the contract. In my judgment it is an implied condition of the contract that the bill of lading so to be tendered shall be a true and accurate document and correctly state the date of shipment.[64]

It needs to be emphasized that in the CIF contract, the delivery of shipping documents is of crucial importance in determining the issues related to the performance of the contract. As already noted, a CIF contract of sale, in many cases, involves string transactions under which goods are sold several times during transit through the tender of the shipping documents including the bill of lading and insurance policy and a seller discharges his obligations as regards delivery by tendering a bill of lading relating to the goods in question without actually shipping the goods.[65] Similar opinion was expressed in *Hindley and Co. Ltd. v East Indian Produce Co.*

---

[61] Id. p. 220. The judgment of Hamilton J. in *Biddell Brothers* case, though reversed in the Court of Appeal [1911] 1 KB 934, was finally approved by the House of Lords. See *E.Clemens Horst Company v Biddell Brothers* [1912] AC 18.

[62] [1911] 1 KB 934, at pp. 955–56.

[63] Ll L R 220.

[64] Id., at p. 225.

[65] *Gardano and Giampieri v Greek Petroleum George Mamidakis & Co.* [1962] 1 WLR 40 at p. 52 (per McNair J., "the seller discharges his obligations as regards delivery by tendering a bill of lading covering the goods.").

Ltd.,[66] wherein it was stated that a CIF contract is a contract for sale of goods to be performed by the delivery of documents. To quote from the judgment in *Hindley and Co.*:

> …that a C&F or CIF contract is to be performed by the tender of documents covering goods which have been shipped either by the seller or by the seller or by someone else in accordance with the terms of the contract. If no goods have in fact been shipped the sellers have not performed their obligation. I cannot see any basis for the distinction which the sellers here seek to draw between a seller who is the shipper and a seller who is not the shipper. At the date of the contract it may well be unknown which means of performance the particular seller will employ, and in an ordinary CIF or C&F contract, as in the present case, there will be nothing in the contract which restricts his choice between the alternative methods of performance.[67]

Manbre Saccharine Company v Corn Products Company[68] is particularly instructive as underscoring the great significance attached to the sale of documents in the CIF contracts. In that case, the King's Bench ruled that where a seller has shipped the goods of contract description "under a contract of carriage and obtained the proper documents, can effectively tender those documents to the purchaser notwithstanding that he knew at the time of such tender of the loss of the goods." As stated by the Supreme Court in the case of *State of Travancore-Cochin and Others v Shanmugha Vilas Cashew Nut Factory*,[69] the reason for attaching so much importance to the tender of proper shipping documents lies in the exigencies of the foreign trade. "The exigencies of foreign trade require that he [the seller] must be permitted to sell the goods by delivering the shipping documents and realise his money and to again invest it in fresh imports. This is how foreign trade is done." The Court went on to quote the following passage from *Halsbury's Law of England*:

> The commercial reason for the evolution of the 'c.i.f.' contract lies in the length of the time taken in the carriage of goods by sea. It is to the advantage of neither seller nor buyer that the goods, the subject matter of the contract should remain en dehors commerce while they are in course of shipment. It is to the seller's interest to receive the money equivalent to the goods as soon as possible after the date of the contract of sale, and until he has received actual payment of the price he normally desires to be able, if he wishes, to obtain credit upon the security of the transaction. The buyer, on the other hand, normally desires to be able to deal with the goods, for resale or finance, as soon as possible. To meet these business necessities on the part of both buyer and seller, the 'c.i.f.' contract was evolved.

While judicial opinion clearly supports the view that the delivery of shipping documents plays a key role in the performance of a CIF contract, the opinion is divided on the issue whether a CIF contract is to be treated as *merely* a sale of documents or it should be treated as a sale of goods as it is normally the case. Taking the view that a CIF contract is a sale of goods and not a sale of documents, contrary to what had been stated by Scrutton J in the King's Bench Division in *Arnhold karberg*

---

[66] [1973] 2 Lloyd's Rep. 515.

[67] Id., p. 518.

[68] [1919] 1 KB 198.

[69] AIR 1953 SC 333.

v Blythe, Green, Jourdain and Co.,[70] the Court of Appeal stated that a CIF contract is a contract of sale of goods which is to be performed by the delivery of the documents. "I prefer to look upon it as a contract for the sale of goods to be performed by the delivery of documents and what those documents are must depend upon the terms of the contract itself," said Bankkes LJ in the Court of Appeal.[71] In *Arnhold*, a question arose about the effect of the outbreak of war upon certain c.i.f. contracts entered into before the outbreak of war. While agreeing to the position taken by Scrutton J that the buyers were entitled to refuse the tender, inasmuch as at the date of tender the documents had become void as to carry out their original obligations after the outbreak of war would involve entering into contractual relations with the enemy country, the opinion expressed by Scrutton J that a CIF contract for sale is not a sale of goods, but a sale of documents relating to goods was clearly rejected by Bankes LJ and Warrington LJ.[72]

The issue was specifically addressed in *Hindley and Co.* (cited above), wherein the King's Bench Division took the firm view that notwithstanding the duality of obligations of a seller in a CIF contract—namely obligations in respect of goods which are the subject matter of the contract and tender of documents covering the goods—a CIF contract is a contract for the sale of goods to be performed by the delivery of the documents.

In *Hindley and Co. Ltd.*, certain quantity of jute was sold on C&F terms. The sellers having bought the goods from a third party, tendered the bill of lading to the buyers. The buyers paid the contract price but on arrival of the ship on the port of destination, it was found that no goods had actually been shipped by the sellers. In an action brought against the sellers it was, however, contended that they were not liable to the buyers for the reason that a contract for sale of goods on C&F or CIF terms was in reality a sale of documents and not a sale of goods. In these facts of the case, the issue presented before the Court was whether the buyers were entitled to the return of the price of the goods and/or damages for breach of contract by the sellers?

Kerr J held that the sellers were clearly in breach of the obligations. According to him, under the C&F [or CIF] terms the sellers were under obligation to ship or procure the shipment of goods of the contract description. He further held that in a contract on C&F terms it was implied that the bill of lading tendered should be a proper one, that is to say, it should not only appear to be true and accurate in the material statements, but that such statements should in fact be true and accurate. But the bill of lading which was tendered was not a proper one, and therefore the sellers were in breach on that ground also.

According to Kerr J, a seller under the C&F (or CIF) terms has "duality of obligations relating respectively to the goods which are the subject-matter of the contract

[70] In *Arnhold*, [1915] 2 KB 379, Scrutton J expressed the opinion that "the key to many of difficulties arising in a c.i.f. contract is to keep firmly in mind that the cardinal distinction that a c.i.f. sale is not a sale of goods, but a sale of documents relating to goods.".

[71] [1916] 1 KB 495, at p. 510.

[72] Ibid.

and the documents covering the goods which have to be tendered to the buyer."[73] Dealing with the seller's obligations in respect of the goods, he said that the obligation of the seller under that type of contract was "either to ship or to procure the shipment of goods of the contract description under a proper contract of affreightment...."[74] Kerr J went on to hold, "alternatively, the seller's obligation, if he does not himself ship or procure the shipment, is to procure documents—and in this connection one is referring to a bill of lading or a number of bills of lading—which cover such goods so shipped. In either event the obligation of the seller is therefore to deliver such documents to the buyer."[75]

Referring to the passage in the judgment of Mr Justice Hamilton in *Biddel Brothers* (cited above) on the seller's obligations in respect of goods and similar passages in other judgments, Kerr J remarked that "it is an oversimplification to say that a c.i.f. contract is merely a contract for the sale of documents." He also quoted Lord Justice Bankes in *Arnold Karberg & Co.* as stating that it is "a contract for the sale of goods to be performed by the delivery of documents." Kerr J further quoted the following passage of Kennedy J in vol. 5 of the *British Shipping Laws*,[76] which provides a description of the seller's obligations in a CIF contract:

> [U]nder this form of contract the seller performs his obligations by shipping, at the time specified in the contract or, in default of express provision in the contract within a reasonable time, goods of the contractual description in a ship bound for the destination named in the contract, or by purchasing documents in respect of such goods already afloat and by tendering to the buyer as soon as possible after the goods have been destined to him, the shipping documents.

In *Biddell Brothers case*, the contracts in question were about sale of 100 bales of hops to be shipped by the defendants, the sellers, from the Pacific Coast to Sunderland provided that the plaintiffs-purchasers, should pay "at the rate of 90 shelling sterling per 112 lbs, cif to London, Liverpool or Hull, terms net cash." The contracts contained no terms expressly providing for payment against shipping documents. The issue raised was whether a contract for foreign hops "cif to London, terms net cash," but without the words "against documents" means that the price is to be paid against documents, or after the buyer has had the opportunity of inspecting the goods? In other words, the issue related to the seller's right to receive payment before the arrival of the goods at the port of destination?

It was contended that the purchaser was not bound to pay for the hops until their arrival at the destination and a reasonable opportunity had been allowed to him for examining the said hops to know if they were in conformity with the contract description. But Hamilton J in the King's Bench Division held that the sellers were entitled to payment against shipping documents upon delivery of the hops on board the ship at the port of the shipment. According to him, a seller's right to receive the payment in such cases had nothing to do with the buyer's right to reject the goods

[73] [1973] 2 Lloyd's Rep. 515, at p. 517.

[74] Ibid.

[75] Ibid.

[76] Id. p. 518.

which remained unimpaired if upon arrival they were found not to be in conformity with the contract. Regarding the argument that under S. 34 of the Sale of Goods Act, 1893, for delivery of goods to be valid, the seller must afford the buyer a reasonable opportunity of examining the goods for the purpose of ascertaining whether they are in conformity with the contract, Hamilton J expressed the view that the buyers were under duty to pay the price in exchange of for the shipping documents even if payment was not expressed to be against documents. To quote Hamilton J:

> It is well settled law… that where, either by the express terms of the contract or by implication from the letters cif in the contract, payment has to be made against documents, the buyer's right to examine the goods and reject them if they are not in conformity with the contract still remains unimpaired.[77]

Referring to s. 28 of the Sale of Goods Act, 1893 [s. 32 of SoGA 1930], according to which "unless otherwise agreed, delivery of the goods and payment of the price are concurrent conditions" Justice Hamilton expressed the opinion that the fact that "the buyer cannot see the goods until their arrival" does not make the contract inconsistent with the provisions of S. 28 of the Act. He went on to state:

> I certainly cannot infer that, where the parties have dealt on c.i.f. terms, the buyer is not afforded a reasonable opportunity of examining the goods, though he may be bound to pay the price against tender of the documents and have no opportunity of seeing the goods until arrival at their destination. Nor does the fact that the buyer cannot see the goods until their arrival make the contract inconsistent with the provisions of s. 8 of the Sale of goods Act, 1893, which provides that "unless otherwise agreed, delivery of the goods and payment of the price are concurrent conditions, that is to say, the seller must be ready and willing to give possession of the goods to the buyer in exchange for the price, and the buyer must be ready and willing to give possession of the goods to the buyer in exchange for the price, and the buyer must be ready and willing to pay the price in exchange for possession of the goods."[78]

However, in the Court of Appeal (Kennedy LJ dissenting) the decision of Hamilton J was reversed. Vaughan Williams LJ and Farwell LJ found that the buyers were not bound to pay for the hops on tender of the shipping documents; were entitled to refuse payment until, upon the arrival of the hops, they had been given an opportunity for seeing the goods for the purpose of ascertaining whether they meet the contract description or not.

Kennedy LJ, however, dissented. In his opinion, the plaintiffs' contention that a buyer's duty to pay arises only on the actual delivery of goods to the buyer was clearly erroneous in view of the peculiar nature of a CIF contract.[79] As has already been pointed out that on appeal, Kennedy LJ's opinion was affirmed by the House of Lords.[80]

---

[77] [1911] 1 KB 214, at p. 221.

[78] Ibid.

[79] [1911] 1 KB 934.

[80] See *Clemens Horst Company v Biddel Brothers* [1912] AC 18 (reversing the decision of the Court of Appeal [1911] 1 KB 934).

3.2.5.2 Seller's Obligations

A seller's obligations under a CIF contract broadly include obligations to ship the goods of the contract description at the port of shipment or to procure the goods already afloat; to enter into a contract of carriage and to secure a bill of lading which is accurate and genuine; to procure a contract of insurance which is available for the use of the purchaser; to append a sale invoice which conforms to the contract description of the goods; and finally to tender these documents to the purchaser.[81] These obligations are broadly of two types: obligations about goods and obligations about documents. To quote a passage from the judgment in *Johnson v Taylor Bros*[82]: "He (the CIF seller) is bound, in the first place, to ship goods of the contract description on board a ship bound to the contract destination. He is bound, in the second place, to tender to the purchaser within a reasonable time after shipment the shipping documents e.g. the Bill or Bills of Lading, and a policy of insurance."[83] The following passage in the judgment of McCardie J. in *Manbre Saccharine Co. v Corn Products Co.* vividly summarizes the extent of the seller's duty and the buyer's right in a CIF contract of sale:

> I conceive that the essential feature of an ordinary c.i.f. contract as compared with an ordinary contract for the sale of goods rests in the fact that performance of the bargain is to be fulfilled by delivery of documents and not by the actual physical delivery of goods by the vendor. All that the buyer can call for is delivery of the customary documents. This represents the measure of the buyer's right and the extent of the vendor's duty. *The buyer cannot refuse the documents and ask for the actual goods, nor can the vendor withhold the documents and tender the goods they represent.*[84]

And in *Phulchand Exports Ltd v Ooo Patriot*, the Supreme Court described the obligations of a seller in similar terms. It cited the following passage in Kennedy's *C.I.F. Contracts* (Third Edition) revised by Dennis C. Thompson (p. 1):

> Under this form of contract the seller performs his obligations by shipping, at the time specified in the contract or, in default of express provision in the contract, within a reasonable time, goods of the contractual description in a ship bound for the destination named in the contract, or by purchasing documents in respect of such goods already afloat, and by tendering to the buyer, as soon as possible after the goods have been destined to him, the shipping documents, i.e., a bill of lading for carriage of goods, a policy of insurance covering the reasonable value of the goods, together with an invoice showing the amount due from the buyer.

Obligations as to Goods

Obligation to ship the goods of contract description is treated as a condition under a CIF contract a breach of which gives rise to the right to reject the goods and to

[81] See Carr (2010), pp. 11–24; Chuah (2009), pp. 51–79; D'Arcy et al. (2000), pp. 38–47; Atiyah et al. (2010), pp. 218–21.

[82] [1920] AC 144.

[83] Id., p. 184.

[84] [1919] 1 KB 198, at p. 202 [emphasis added].

claim damages by the buyer. To quote McCardie J in *Manbre Saccharine Co.*: "A vendor must supply goods in accordance with the contract description, and he is not entitled to say that another description of goods will suffice for the purposes of the purchaser."[85] Referring to stipulation as to packaging, McCardie J further observed that the size of bags was a material part of the contract because "[t]he size of bags may be important to a purchaser in view of sub contracts or otherwise."

In *Manbre Saccharine Co.*, the goods in question (starch) were to be shipped in 280 lb bags, whereas the goods shipped by the sellers were partly in 220 lb bags and partly in 140 lb bags. It was contended that the words "280 lb. bags" were not a material part of the bargain. But McCardie J thought otherwise and replied:

> But, in my opinion, it is clear that such words were an essential part of the contract requirements. They constitute a portion of the description of the goods. The size of bags may be important to a purchaser in view of sub contracts or otherwise. A man may prefer to receive starch either in small or large or medium bags. If the size of the bags was immaterial I fail to see why it should have been so clearly specified in the contract. A vendor must supply goods in accordance with the contract description, and he is not entitled to say that another description of goods will suffice for the purposes of the purchaser...The tender by the defendants of starch in bags other than 280 lb. bags was a failure to comply with their contract.[86]

In elucidating a buyer's duty to supply goods of contract description, in *Edmund Bowes v Charles Shand*,[87] Lord Blackburn adopted an illustration used by Lord Abinger as stating: "...if you contract to sell peas, you cannot oblige a party to take beans. If the description of the article tendered is different in any respect it is not the article bargained for, and the other party is not bound to take it."[88]

It may further be noted that terms as to time and place of shipment is also regarded as essence of a CIF contract especially where it is stipulated that the shipping of a cargo shall take place at a particular time. If it is stipulated that the goods shall be put on board at a particular time or in a particular month or months, then buyer is entitled to repudiate the contract if the cargo was not loaded in proper time. The principle is well settled that on a sale of goods a condition as to the time of shipment is vital and is taken as an essence of the contract. "Accordingly, if a person has contracted to sell a September shipment, it is useless for him to tender an October shipment and say that the difference is very little."[89] *Edmund Bowes v Charles Shand* (cited above), decided by the House of Lords, is instructive on this point. In that case, it was stipulated that the goods (rice) will be shipped during the months of March and/or April of 1874. But most part of the cargo was shipped in the month of February, 1874. Reversing the decision of the Court of Appeal, the House of Lords held that the sellers were in breach of their obligation. According to the House of Lords, in the circumstances of the case, rice shipped in February was not the same rice that was stipulated to be shipped in March or April. It held:

---

[85] Id., p. 207.

[86] Ibid.

[87] [1877] 2 AC 455.

[88] Id., at 488.

[89] *James Finlay & Co.* [1929] 1 KB 400, p. 408.

> …[I]t is not the article rice only that is sold, but the thing that is sold is the article rice shipped in March or April, and that the article rice shipped in February is not the article which has been purchased by the Defendants.[90]

Lord Cairns offered the following explanations in bringing home the point:

> It is quite obvious that merchants making contracts for the purchase of rice, contracts which oblige them to pay in a certain manner for the rice purchased, and to be ready with the funds for making that payment, may well be desirous both that the rice should be forthcoming to them not later than a certain time, and also that the rice shall not be forthcoming to them at a time earlier than it suits them to be ready with funds for its payment. Therefore it may well be that a merchant making a number of rice contracts, ranging over several months of the year, will be desirous of expressing that the rice shall come forward at such times, and at such intervals of time, as that it will be convenient for him to make the payments, and it may well be that a merchant will consider that he has obtained that end if he provides for the shipment of the rice during a particular month, or during particular months, and that he will know that provided he has made that stipulation the rice will not be forthcoming at a time when it will be inconvenient for him to provide the money for the payment. My Lords, there is still another explanation… that these contracts were made for the purpose of satisfying and fulfilling other contracts which Messrs. *Bowes, Martin, & Kent*, had made with other persons…[91]

The principle that time of shipment is an essence of a CIF contract was reiterated in many decisions including *James Finley v Kwik Hoo Tong* (cited above) and *Foreman & Ellams Ltd v Blackburn.*[92] In *Foreman & Ellams Ltd*, discussed more fully below, some part of the goods in question (frozen rabbits) had already been shipped before the contract was concluded. The goods were actually shipped in the month of June, 1926 but the bill of lading was issued on August 17, 1926. The Court found:

> In the first place it appears from the freezing certificate, which is a material document, that before the date of the contract either the goods or some part of the goods had been already shipped. Whether that is true of all or only some of the goods is immaterial, because on a sale of goods all goods tendered must correspond with the contract description, and the fact that some do correspond whereas others do not does not make the tender good. I consider that the word "shipment" in the contract must be understood as referring to shipment in the future and that it is entirely inapt as referring to a shipment which at the date of the contract, namely July 2, 1926, had already, in whole or in part, taken place.[93]

Mention may also be made of a recent decision of the Supreme Court in *Phulchand Exports Ltd v Ooo Patriot*[94] which considers the issue of late shipment of goods. In the opinion of the Supreme Court, "if there is a late shipment or the seller has put goods on board a ship not bound to the contract destination as stipulated, in our view …the seller has not put on board goods conforming to a contract destination." The Court said:

---

[90] [1877] 2 AC 455, at 475.

[91] Id., at 463.

[92] [1928] 2 KB 60.

[93] Id., p. 64.

[94] (2011) 10 SCC 300.

> The sellers breached the terms of the contract at the very threshold by late shipment of goods and by loading on board the vessel which was no longer to reach the port of Novorossiysk as the first port of discharge.…In a case such as this one, the sellers" failure to discharge the primary obligation under the contract regarding the shipment of goods can be held to have resulted in postponement of transfer of title in goods to the buyers.

Obligations as to Documents

In a CIF contract certain shipping documents including bill of lading and insurance policy play a key role for property in the goods pass only when shipping documents are tendered.[95] As stated above, a seller in a CIF contract fulfils his obligations not only by shipping the goods of contract description and shipping them at the proper time but also by obtaining proper documents for tender to the buyer.[96] He is under an obligation to procure and tender a proper bill of lading. And as stated by Scrutton LJ in *James Finley v Kwik Hoo Tong*, a CIF seller is under obligation not only to ship goods but also to furnish buyers with certain documents which include among others:

> (1.) a contract for the carriage of the goods, so that if they are lost during the voyage, in circumstances for which the ship is responsible, the buyers can recover their loss from the shipowner; and (2.) a policy of insurance covering the contract goods, so that if they are lost during the voyage by a risk covered by the policy the buyers can recover from the underwriters.[97]

A similar view was expressed by the Supreme Court in the *National Insurance Company Limited v Sky Gem.*[98] The Court cited the following passage in the judgment of Lord Porter in *Comptoir d' Achat vs. Luis de Ridder, The Julia* [1949] A.C. 293 at 309:

> The obligations imposed on a seller under a c.i.f. contract are well known, and in the ordinary case, include the tender of a bill of lading covering the goods contracted to be sold and no others, coupled with an insurance policy in the normal form and accompanied by an invoice which shows the price and, as in this case, usually contains a deduction of the freight which the buyer pays before delivery at the port of discharge. Against tender of these documents the purchaser must pay the price.[99]

The bill of lading and the insurance policy are intended to provide continuous cover from the port of shipment to the port of discharge, "so that the c.i.f. buyer, whatever happens to the goods, will have either a cause of action on the bill of lading against the ship or a cause of action against the underwriters on the policy."[100] As

---

[95] See *Mitsui & Co. Ltd. v Flota Mercante Grancolumbiana SA* [1989] 1 All ER 951.

[96] *Manbre Saccharine Co. v Corn Products Co*, supra note [1919] 1 KB 198.

[97] *James Finley v Kwik Hoo Tong* [1929] 1 K.B. 400, p. 408. See also *Phulchand Exports Ltd v Ooo Patriot* (2011) SCC 300 (In a C.I.F. contract "delivery is satisfied by delivery of documents and not by actual physical delivery of the goods").

[98] (2002) 2 SCC 273.

[99] See also *Phulchand Exports Ltd v Ooo Patriot* (2011) SCC 300; *SIAT v Tradax* [1980] 1 Lloyd's Rep. 53.

[100] *Margarine Union GmbH v Cambay Prince Steamship Co. Ltd.* [1969] 1 QB 219.

will be noted in Chap. 10 dealing with the contract of carriage by sea, a bill of lading is the receipt for the goods and is the evidence of the fact that the carrier is in possession of goods. It also serves the purpose of a document of title. A person who is in possession of a bill of lading has constructive possession of the goods, while actual possession is with the carrier of the goods.[101] Further, the bill of lading should conform to the contract of sale and should not be defective on the face of it.

Further, the bill of lading must be clean, genuine and must accurately state the date of shipment. A clean bill of lading means a bill which clearly admits that the goods in question are shipped in good condition.[102] A qualification to the effect that the goods in question are not in good order and condition renders the bill unclean. However, if the bill of lading clearly states that the goods in question are shipped in good order and condition, then any statement in the bill of lading made subsequently that the goods were damaged and hence the "bill of lading has been discharged" would not render the bill unclean.[103]

A further requirement is that a genuine bill of lading should be tendered showing the right date of shipment.[104] Incorrect dating of a bill of lading is the breach of a CIF contract.[105] As Sankey LJ observed in *Finley v Kwik Hoo Tong*:

> A c.i.f. contract is a contract for the sale of goods, but, as every one knows, there are certain specific documents which are part of that contract, one of them being a bill of lading, as to which there is an implied obligation that it shall be dated accurately. In this case, by some unfortunate circumstance, the bill of lading given was inaccurately dated. It was dated September 30, whereas the sugar was not shipped till October. No fraud is imputed to the appellants, and I assume that they are blameless in the matter; but it is admitted that they broke one of the fundamental conditions of the contract - namely, the condition or obligation to give an accurately dated bill of lading. As a result the respondents took the sugar, but they did not get what the defendants had contracted to give them.[106]

Regarding the policy of insurance, it may be stated that a CIF seller is under duty to procure and tender to the buyer the marine insurance policy which provides protection to the buyer in the event of any damage to the property in the goods. To quote Lord Denning MR: "That is what CIF means: *cost of the goods, insurance of the goods; and freight of the goods right through to their destination.*"[107] What is important to note is that the insurance policy should cover the goods from the port of shipment to their destination. *Lindon Tricotagefabrik v White* is instructive on this point. In *Lindon*, sellers agreed to supply pullovers to buyers under a CIF contract with carriage through to buyers' warehouse. The goods which should have been delivered to the buyers' warehouse were delivered by the sellers' agents to the

---

[101] D'Arcy et al. (2000), p. 289. See also *Sanders Brothers v Maclean & Co.* (1883) 11 QBD 327.

[102] D'Arcy et al. (2000), p. 33; Carr (2010), p. 15.

[103] See *M. Golodetz & Co. v Czarnikow-Rionda Co. (The Galatia)*, [1980] 1 All ER 501.

[104] Id., p. 410. See also *The Almak* [1985] Lloyd's Rep. 21.

[105] A bill of lading is correctly dated when it is dated after all the goods or parcels of goods are loaded. See *Mendala III Transport v Todd Transport Corp: The Wiloma Tanana* [1993] 2 Lloyd's Rep. 41.

[106] [1929] 1 KB 400, at p. 417.

[107] *Lindon Tricotagefabrik v White and Mecham* [1975] 1 Lloyd's Rep. 384, at p. 385.

buyers' office when there was no one of the buyers' office to receive the goods. The goods were left outside and sellers' agents promised to collect and deliver the goods at the correct address. But before the goods could be collected the goods were stolen. Lord Denning MR (to whom Orr LJ and Browne LJ concurred) observed that in a CIF sale, the sellers are under duty to put the goods aboard a ship; to get the bill of lading; and to obtain a policy of insurance so as to cover the goods right through to their destination. He went to state:

> In this case, the policy should cover the goods, not merely as far as the Port of London; it should cover the goods right through to the customer's warehouse. The seller has to pay the freight, that is the carriage cost, right through; that is the carriage cost right through to destination. That is what c.i.f. means....[108]

Further, the insurance policy must specify the risks insured against.[109] In *Malmberg v Evans*,[110] it was stated that since the policy in question did not specify clearly the risks insured against, it was not a valid policy. Uncertainty about the protection of the buyer's interests in the goods would render the policy invalid.

3.2.5.3 Buyer's Obligations

Duty to Pay Upon Tender of Documents

Since in a CIF contract of sale, documents represent the goods, the buyer is bound to pay for the goods upon tender of the shipping documents. The principle is well settled and is supported by many authorities. Where the terms of the contract of sale provide that payment is to be made in exchange for bills of lading the buyer is bound to pay when a duly indorsed bill of lading is tendered to him, although the bill of lading be drawn in triplicate, and all the three are not then tendered or accounted for.[111] Cotton LJ held in *Sanders Brothers v Maclean & Co.*:

> There is no stipulation in this contract except that the payment shall be made in exchange for bills of lading, which I understand to be that, when a tender is made to the purchaser of a duly indorsed bill of lading which will effectually pass the property in the goods, then payment is to be made in cash by the purchaser to the vendor.[112]

In *Sanders Brothers v Maclean & Co.*,[113] on July 17, 1880, a contract was entered into between the sellers and the defendants for the sale of certain quantities of iron rails. The cargo was to be paid for in London in cash in exchange for bills of lading. The contract provided: "Payment to be made in London in cash in exchange for bills of lading and policies of insurance." Two sets of the bill of lading of the cargo were tendered to the defendants on the 3rd of August, but were rejected

---

108 Ibid.

109 *Malmberg v Evans* (1924) 29 Com. Cas. 235.

110 Ibid.

111 *Sanders Brothers v Maclean & Co.* (1883) 11 QBD 327.

112 Id., p. 339.

113 Ibid.

by the buyer on the ground that the bill of lading had been drawn in three parts, and only two were tendered to them. In fact, the third part of the bill of lading was still with the person in Russia to whom this cargo had originally belonged. However, the third part of the bill of lading which was retained by the original shipper was never in any way dealt with. The plaintiff thereupon wrote the original shipper for the third part of the bill of lading, and having received it, they tendered all the three bills of lading to the defendants on August 9, 1880. But the defendants refused again to pay.

The Court found that the third part of the bill of lading had not been in any way dealt with; the two parts of the bill of lading which were tendered were effective to pass the property in this cargo to the defendants, and to enable them to receive the cargo.[114] Rejecting the argument of the defendant that the third part being still outstanding, the defendants were not secure, Cotton LJ in the Court of Appeal stated that though it did expose the defendants to some risk, "but the question is whether what was done by the tender of the 3rd of August did comply with the terms of the contract." He then went on to observe:

Therefore, in my opinion, the tender on the 3rd of August was one which ought to have been accepted by the defendants, and that decides this case, there being no question at all as to the tender on the 3rd of August having been made within ample and sufficient time.[115]

In the opinion of Brett MR, in the circumstances of the case, the seller did everything what was reasonably expected of him:

> I quite agree that he has no right to keep the bill of lading in his pocket, and when it is said that he should do what is reasonable it is obvious the reasonable thing is that he should make every reasonable exertion to send forward the bill of lading as soon as possible after he has destined the cargo to the particular vendee or consignee. If that be so, the question of whether he has used such reasonable exertion will depend upon the particular circumstances of each case.[116]

And further:

> They were bound to use all reasonable exertion to get the bill of lading from St. Petersburgh and to offer it in London as soon as under the circumstances it was reasonable for them to do so. Whether they did use such reasonable exertion, and whether what they did was under the circumstances done within a reasonable time, was a question for the jury, and in this case it seems to me that substantially the jury found that they had done all that was reasonable, and therefore even if the first tender had been bad I should have thought that the second tender was good.[117]

---

[114] Id., p. 338.

[115] Ibid.

[116] Id., p. 337.

[117] Id., p. 338.

To quote Bowen LJ:

> It appears to me, accordingly, that a tender is at all events in compliance with the present contract, by which all the effective bills of lading in existence are tendered. If, indeed, the absent original had been misused so as to defeat the title of the indorsees of the tendered residue of the set, the tender would have been bad. But the vendee was not entitled to reject the tender of the only effective documents on the bare chance that a third effective bill of lading might possibly have been dealt with when in fact it had not. The person who rejects effective and adequate documents of title on the ground that another document may possibly be outstanding, does so at his own.[118]

Duty to Take Delivery of Goods

The CIF buyer is under duty to take delivery of the goods at the port of destination. Where a CIF contract mentions more than one destination, the buyer is under duty to notify the seller of his choice of destination.[119] It may also be noted that if any import license is required it is the duty of the buyer to obtain the license, unless otherwise agreed upon by the parties.[120]

3.2.5.4 Passing of Property and Risks

In a CIF sale, the rule that property and risks pass simultaneously does not apply. While risks pass upon shipment of the goods, property in the goods passes at a later stage, in particular when shipping documents are tendered and paid for since a CIF contract is "a contract for the sale of goods to be performed by the delivery of the documents."[121] To put it differently, as a general rule property in the goods pass only when shipping documents are tendered. And in most cases indeed, property passes upon delivery of shipping documents. But this rule will not apply where the goods remained unascertained for s. 18 of the Sale of Goods Act, 1930 clearly provides that property in the goods cannot pass "unless and until the goods are ascertained."[122] Further, it is also possible that property passes on shipment but where the seller has retained the shipping documents, property may not pass on shipment.

Further, although risks pass to the buyer upon shipment the buyer is not at the disadvantage even if the goods are damaged before he takes up the documents. The buyer can claim insurance money. "The policy must be tendered even if the goods

---

[118] Id., p. 343.

[119] Guest (ed.) (2006), p. 1529.

[120] Carr (2010), p. 28.

[121] See *Hindley and Co. Ltd. v East Indian Produce Co. Ltd.*, [1973] 2 Lloyd's Rep. 515; *Mitsui & Co. Ltd. v Flota Mercante Grancolumbiana SA*, [1989] 1 ALL ER 951.

[122] See discussion on S. 18 of the Sale of the Goods Act, 1930 Chap. 6.

have safely arrived at the time of tender."[123] As has already been noted, in *Manbre Saccharine Company* case,[124] it was held by the King's Bench that in a CIF contract, the seller is bound to tender to the buyer a policy of insurance and the buyer is entitled to demand a policy of insurance covering the goods in question. To quote McCardie J: "In my opinion a purchaser under a c.i.f. contract is entitled to demand, as a matter of law, a policy of insurance which covers only the goods mentioned in the bills of lading and invoices."[125] It was ruled in *Manbre* case, if the goods are lost during transit the buyer is still bound to make payment because risks pass to the buyer upon shipment.

Finally, some reference may also be made of certain common variants of the CIF contract, such as C&F (Cost and Freight), CIF&C (Cost, Insurance, Freight, and Commission), and CIF&E (Cost, Insurance, Freight, and Exchange).[126] It may be noted that under the C&F terms, the seller, like a CIF seller, delivers the goods on board the ship or procures the goods already so delivered; undertakes to pay the costs and freight necessary to bring the goods to the named port of destination. But he, unlike a CIF seller, is not under duty to arrange insurance of the goods during transit. The risks associated with loss of or damage to the goods is passed on to the buyer when the goods are placed on board the vessel. Further, as it happens in the case of a CIF contract, the price is payable on tender of shipping documents. Under CIF&C terms, the price of the goods includes the exporter's commission also; and in CIF&E, the letter "E" refers to "exchange." CIF&E indicates that price includes the banker's commission.[127]

3.3 Incoterms[128]

The Incoterms are periodically revised to reflect current practice regarding matters they cover. Since 1936 when Incoterms were first published, they were revised in 1953, 1967, 1976, 1980, 1990, 2000, 2010, and 2019. Recently, the ICC has published the latest version of Incoterms—*Incoterms 2020* which update the existing trade practices to make them "more accessible and easier to use."[129] They are to take effect from January 1, 2020. However, the earlier version—*Incoterms 2010* rules which came into effect on January 1, 2011 will remain in force. Although traders are

---

[123] *Manbre Saccharine Company* case [1919] 1 KB 198, p. 203.

[124] Ibid.

[125] Id., p. 203.

[126] See Carr (2010), pp. 35–36; D'Arcy et al. (2000), pp. 47–48.

[127] D'Arcy (2000), p. 48.

[128] This description of the Incoterms terms of trade is based on the material accessed from http://www.iccwbo.org/products-and-services/trade-facilitation/incoterms-2010/the-incoterms-rules/. The full official text of the rules can be obtained from the ICC BusinessBookstore.

[129] Incoterms 2020 is available in as many as 29 languages on ICC's e-commerce platform ICC Knowledge 2 Go from where they can be purchased. Web address: www.iccwbo.org.

recommended to use the latest version of the Incoterms, there is nothing to prevent them from using previous versions of the Incoterms.[130] Thus, all contracts which incorporate earlier versions like Incoterms 2000 or Incoterms 2010 remain valid even after coming into force of the Incoterms 2020.

There exist 11 terms of trade in Incoterms 2010 and Incoterms 2020 placed in two groups.[131] Under Incoterms 2010, the first category includes the seven trade rules that apply to any mode or modes of transport. Included among these are:

EXW "Ex works"
FCA "Free Carrier"
CPT "Carriage Paid To"
CIP "Carriage and Insurance Paid To"
DAT "Delivered at Terminal"
DAP "Delivered at Place"
DDP "Delivered Duty Paid"

The second group includes the four Incoterms rules which carry the title "sea and inland waterway transport" rules since they apply to situations where "the point of delivery and the place to which the goods are carried to the buyer are both ports." Included in this category are:

FAS "Free Alongside Ship"
FOB "Free on Board"
CFR "Cost and Freight"
CIF "Cost, Insurance and Freight"

Under the last three Incoterms 2010 rules, goods are taken as delivered when they are "on board" the ship. Further, in 2010 edition, two new rules, DAT (Delivered at Terminal) and DAP (Delivered at Place) were added. They replace the Incoterms 2000 terms—DAF (Delivered at Frontier), DES (Delivered Ex Ship), DEQ (Delivered Ex Quay), and DDU (Delivered Duty Unpaid).[132]

It may also be noted that under Incoterms 2010 terms—CPT, CIP, CFR, CIF, DAT, DAP, and DDP—it is the seller who arranges for the carriage of goods to the agreed destination and while the freight is paid by the seller it is included in the price of the goods.

Significantly, Incoterms 2020 cover the carriage of goods with own means of transport in FCA (Free Carrier), DAP (Delivered at Place), DPU (Delivered at Place Unloaded), and DDP (Delivered Duty Paid). Further, in the latest edition of Incoterms there is a change in the name for DAT (Delivered at Terminal) to DPU (Delivered at Place).[133]

---

[130]Ibid.

[131]The 2000 version of Incoterms contains 14 Incoterms rules.

[132]Information is available at: https://iccwbo.org/resources-for-business/incoterms-rules/incoterms-rules-2010/.

[133]Information is available at: https://iccwbo.org/resources-for-business/incoterms-rules/incoterms-2020/.

References

Atiyah, P. S., Adams, J. N., & Macqueen, H. (2010). *Atiyah's sale of goods*. New Delhi: Dorling Kindersley.

Bridge, M. (2007). *The international sale of goods: Law and practice*. Oxford: Oxford University Press.

Carr, I. (2010). *International trade law*. London, New York: Routledge-Cavendish.

Carr, I. (2014). *International trade law*. London, New York: Routledge-Cavendish.

Chuah, J. C. T. (2009). *Law of international trade: Cross-border commercial transactions*. London: Sweet & Maxwell (South Asian Edition, 2011).

D' Arcy, L., Murray, C., & Cleave, B. (Eds.). (2000). *Schmitthoff's export trade: The Law and practice of international trade*. London: Stevens.

David, R. (1968). The methods of unification. *American Journal of Comparative Law, 16*(1/2), 13–27.

Guest, A. G. (Ed.). (2006). *Benjamin's sale of goods*. London: Sweet & Maxwell.

Kannan (Ed.). (2012). *Mulla: The sale of goods act and The Indian partnership act*. New Delhi: LexisNexis.

Kouladis, N. (2006). *Principles of law relating to international trade*. New York: Springer.

Moens, G., & Gillies, P. (2006). *International trade & business: Law, policy and ethics*. Oxon, New York: Routledge-Cavendish.

Schnitzer, S. (2006). *Understanding international trade law*. UK: Law Matters Publishing.

Online Resource

International Chamber of Commerce (ICC). http://www.iccwbo.org.

Part II
Contract of Sale

Chapter 4
Nature and Formation of Contract

4.1 Growth of Modern Contract Law

Historically, though the law of contract dates from the medieval times or even earlier,[1] the early developments do not have any direct bearing on the law as it exists today. A great bulk of the rules which figure prominently in the present-day law only took shape around the eighteenth and nineteenth centuries.[2] In fact, it is not until the early sixteenth century that we begin to see certain key changes in the medieval law which eventually led to the growth of the law with which we are familiar today. Interestingly, the very idea that an agreement is enforceable by law did not emerge until the sixteenth century as the earlier cases show no action would lie at common law unless some wrong was done to the plaintiff or he furnished the consideration.[3] Although agreements under seal (covenants) were actionable by action of *assumpsit*, no action was maintainable for the breach of something merely a promise; only formal contracts were recognized by the law; treated as enforceable not because of their substance but of their form. Informal agreements as such were not actionable; required to be supported by *causa* in order to be enforceable. The obligations created by contracts under seal derived their validity not from the fact of agreement but from

---

[1] See Simpson (1975), pp. 3–5; James (1979), pp. 272–73; Atiyah (1961), p. 2; Applebey (2001), p. 8.

[2] The will theory of contract, the rules of offer and acceptance and expectation damages, the requirement of an intention to create legal relations and principles of interpretation represent as some of the most striking developments of the nineteenth century. See Horwitz (1974), p. 918; Atiyah (1961), pp. 1–3; Beatson et al. (2010), p. 1; Furmston (2017), pp. 13–14.

[3] See Barton (1969), p. 376. It may also be noted that in those days, unlike today, an ordinary action in contract was not recognized and the remedy solely depended on an appropriate form of action. The only form of action, however, known to law which could provide relief to the promisee without more was the action of *assumpsit*. Furmston, ibid. It appears that an action for breach of a promise was not maintainable until the early sixteenth century when the doctrine of nonfeasance, in the case of a promise supported by a consideration, was abandoned. See Barton (1969), pp. 373–74; Simpson (1975), pp. 249.

A. Srivastava, *Modern Law of International Trade*, International Law and the Global South, https://doi.org/10.1007/978-981-15-5475-9_4

their "form."[4] The position had continued to exist until the early sixteenth century when the rule that no action of *assumpsit* would lie for a misfeasance was finally abandoned.

Some of the most significant gains of the sixteenth and seventeenth centuries providing the basis for the modern law may briefly be referred to here. The first is the action of *assumpsit* to provide remedy for the breach of informal agreements.[5] Although the action arose as back as the fourteenth century, for a quite long time the action of *assumpsit* would not lie for a nonfeasance. This was a major restraint on the growth of the contract law. It is only in the early sixteenth century when the courts in England came to recognize that the action of *assumpsit* could lie for a pure nonfeasance, the action emerged as a substitute for the action of covenant and came to be established as regular action in the early seventeenth century.[6] It scarcely needs the saying that the abandonment of the "shadowy" distinction between nonfeasance and misfeasance was a development of great significance.[7] Other significant achievements of the sixteenth and seventeenth centuries include the doctrine of consideration,[8] the law of quasi-contracts,[9] and the Statute of Frauds 1677[10] which introduced the requirement of writing for certain specified contracts.

Although the impact of these developments was profound, the process of development of the modern contract law during this period was far from complete. In fact, as Professor Horwitz has shown that as late as the eighteenth century the contract law was still dominated by the old legal thought which conceived contract merely as creating a proprietary interest in specific goods.[11] The subordination of contract to the law of property continued until the emergence of the (modern) will theory of contract in the late eighteenth and the early nineteenth century which asserted that the source of the contractual obligations was the wills of the contracting parties.[12]

The subject came into prominence only from the early nineteenth century mainly as a result of the greatly increased commercial and industrial activities. The industrial revolution and a transition to the capital economy in the nineteenth century led to the substantial changes in the economic and social conditions. The rapid growth of industries and a transition from the agrarian to capital economy, from traditional rural to modern urban societies created the need for a law which could provide protection to the parties to a contract[13]; enable them to engage in calculated economic risks.[14]

---

[4] James (1979), p. 271.

[5] Simpson (1975), p. 3. The action of assumpsit dates from the fourteenth century. However, it became a regular action of common law only in the seventeenth century. Ibid.

[6] Ibid., p. 249.

[7] Barton (1969), p. 374; Furmston (2017), p. 6.

[8] Simpson (1975), p. 322.

[9] Id., p. 489.

[10] Id., p. 599.

[11] Horwitz (1974), p. 920.

[12] Id., p. 917. On will theory, see infra, Sect. 4.2.1.

[13] Atiyah (1961), p. 2.

[14] Friedman (1972), p. 121.

Earlier, commercial transactions were mostly instantaneous; therefore, no need was felt for a law to support an instrument creating future obligations. As Atiyah put it, a well-developed law of contract became inevitable for at least two reasons: the division of labor and the emergence of the institution of credit.[15] While the former created increased demand for the transfer of property and the performance of service, the latter required an ability to rely on others. These were not possible without a well-developed law of contract.[16] Admittedly, these changes were influenced by the laisez faire and individual rights philosophy of the eighteenth and nineteenth centuries. The general sentiment of the period was in favor of granting the parties unlimited freedom of contracting that found expression in the principle of freedom of contract.[17] Around this period the support for the principle was overwhelming. The theory generated the belief that contracts entered into voluntarily and freely were sacred; the parties had full freedom to enter into contract and decide its terms; and the role of the law was restricted to merely enforce such contracts.[18] It scarcely needs saying that the theory of freedom of contract has played a vital role in encouraging the everyday commercial transactions based on mutual promises. A major accomplishment of that period was the Indian Contract Act, 1872 which was the first major effort to codify the English contract law with minor modifications.[19] The Contract Act gave statutory recognition to the most of the rules of the English contract law which had developed by that time and introduced certain new concepts upon which the bulk of the classical law of contract is based.

The development of the law continued to accelerate in the twentieth century. Life became more complex and changes in economic and social conditions were taking place more rapidly necessitating a fresh look at certain key principles and rules evolved earlier. A marked shift in thinking away from individualism and the philosophy of laisez faire; the advent of the welfare state, consumer-orientated society and the notion of human rights; as well as the forces of globalization led to the significant changes in the sphere of contract law which run counter to the theory of freedom of contract.[20] The theory which was at the peak in the nineteenth century came under constant attack in the twentieth century and experienced a gradual decline.[21] However, it would not be correct to say that the freedom of contract theory has totally lost its influence. In fact, its significance in international trade transactions is well recognized.[22] The UNIDROIT Principles of International Commercial Contracts

---

[15]Atiyah (1961), p. 2. See also Paton & Derham (1972), p. 437.

[16]Ibid.

[17]Atiyah (1961), p. 3.

[18]Ibid., p. 2; Beatson et al. (2010), p. 4. As will be noted below, the theory has never been treated as conferring absolute power to the parties in respect of agreeing on the terms of contract.

[19]Beatson et al. (2010), p. 18; Diamond (1968), p. 362.

[20]Pretorius (2004b); p. 100; Pretorius (2004a), p. 229.

[21]See Atiyah (1961); Pretorius (2004a), p. 227.

[22]Some of the most important modern cases supporting the theory of contract include *Photo Production Ltd. v Securicor transport Ltd* [1980] AC 827; *Suisse Atlantique Societe d'Armement maritime SA v NV Rotterdamsche Kolen Centrale* [1967] 1 AC 361.

(UNIDROIT Principles), the latest edition of which appeared in 2016 clearly supports the theory as it provides: "The parties are free to enter into a contract and to determine its content" (Article 1.1).[23]

The most important change we now notice is the unprecedented legislative and judicial interventions in the freedom of the parties. This is in contrast to the policy of the minimal regulation of contract terms of the previous centuries. Differently put, the increasing statutory controls over contracts is one of the most important features of the modern law. There is a growing tendency to use the machinery of contract to enforce social and economic policies. This became imperative in view of the new developments such as a dramatic rise in the commercial and consumer transactions, the increasing standardization of contracts, and the emergence of huge business entities. Numerous legislations are now in place to address the problem of inequality in the bargaining power. The earlier law paid little attention to the problem of inequality because it assumed that the parties to a contract were in position of equality. This was indeed an objectionable proposition but its impacts were not so visible. A significant increase in the statutorily implied contract terms imposing social duties; statutory and administrative restrictions on unfair trade practices; various measures aimed to regulate industry and market, protect human rights, and to promote social justice are examples of some of the most important responses of the law to the conditions of modern life. As noted in Paton's *A Textbook of Jurisprudence*:

> ...the law has interfered seriously with the parties' freedom "sometimes in the interests of the economically weaker party, sometimes in the hope of regulating an industry in order to protect it from foreign competition."[24]

As a result, we now see a remarkable change in the nature of a contract. The classical idea of a contract as based on an agreement between the parties has now considerably weakened.[25] Atiyah says, the law of contract is no longer seen as a negative instrument. "The tendency nowadays is to look on the law as a positive instrument for the achievement of justice."[26] A similar observation is made by Friedmann in his famous discussion on the changing nature of contract.[27] For him, the contract is becoming increasingly institutionalized and has to a large extent become the way by which social and economic policies find expression. He thus rightly finds that contract law has been vitally affected and modified by the pubic law. The state's growing involvement in the domain of private law in the interests of social justice is one of the most important contemporary developments of the post-classical period requiring a careful study of the impacts of public law on private law. As it is alleged, we now witness a return to ideas which prevailed before advent of individualism and the theory of freedom of contract.[28]

---

[23]On UNIDROIT Principles, see infra, Sect. 4.7 and Chap. 8.

[24]Paton & Derham (eds.) (1972), p. 452.

[25]Friedman (1972), p. 142.

[26]Atiyah (1961), p. 10.

[27]Friedman (1972), pp. 129–160.

[28]Pretorius (2004b), p. 100.

4.2 Theories of Contract

4.2.1 Will Theory

Considerable controversy surrounds the question—what is the source or basis of the contractual obligations? Many theories such as the will theory, objective and injurious reliance theories may be referred to in this regard which seek to explain the binding nature of contract, although none of these theories has been able to provide a satisfactory account of the development of the law of contract.

For a quite long time, the view indeed prevailed that contractual obligation was based on "inherent justice." As already noted, it is only in the nineteenth century the courts held for the first time that the source of the obligation of contract is the convergence of the wills of the parties to a contract. Throughout the nineteenth century during which much of the present-day law took shape the will theory was indeed the leading theory of contract but with the passage of time its significance has considerably declined. In view of the modern developments it has been largely replaced by the objective approach and reliance theories.[29]

According to the will or classical theory, a contract is binding because it is the outcome of the agreement between the parties or *consensus ad idem*. The theory is inspired by the ideologies of laisez faire and freedom of contract which were at their height in the nineteenth century. Since the will theory is based on the central idea that a party is bound because he has agreed to be bound, this logically follows that unless the parties' (real) will is *ad idem*, no contract shall be binding.[30]

But there are serious problems in accepting the view that a contract only results from the wills of the parties. A few points may be noted in this regard. First, in determining whether or not an agreement is reached, the law adopts an objective approach, as opposed to a subjective intention, and it is immaterial what was really intended by the parties.[31] An agreement or promise is understood as the manifestations of intention.[32] The objective approach demands some evidence of the agreement. The conduct of the parties should be such as that would lead a reasonable person to believe that an agreement was reached.[33] In other words, what the parties really intend or really agreed to is not important. What is important, rather, is the fact of agreement which must be established beyond doubt or unequivocally on the basis of some evidence as objectively indicating the parties' intention.[34] Here contracts under seal may be cited as an example. Contrary to simple agreements, they derive their binding force not from any agreement but from their "form" (see infra, Sect. 4.3.2).

---

[29]Id., p. 97; Horwitz (1974) p. 917.

[30]Paton & Derham (1972), p. 96.

[31]Atiyah (1961), p. 4; Pretorius (2004a), p. 232.

[32]Restatement (Second) of Contracts defines an agreement as "a manifestation of mutual assent on the part of two or more persons" (Section 3). See further Pretorius (2004a), pp. 231–33.

[33]Pretorius (2004a), ibid.

[34]Poole (2004), p. 32.

Secondly, the law prefers certainty over the subjective intentions of the parties. As noted in the Paton's *A Textbook on Jurisprudence*, it is for the convenience that the law provides for definite rules in regard to formation of contract.[35] The rules relating to the formation of contract under the English and Indian law of contract generally prefer certainty over the actual will of the parties.

Finally, the far-reaching and significant developments in the field of contract law which are attributable to the modern conditions have largely undermined the significance of the will theory.[36] Put differently, the rise of the large business entities, the growing standardization of contracts, impact of public law over the law of contract, as discussed above (Sect. 4.1) have led to the undermining of the will theory.[37]

4.2.2 Injurious Reliance Theory

While the will theory puts emphasis on the wills of the parties, the reliance theory attaches importance to the expectations reasonably created by the conduct of each party to a contract. According to this theory, the source of contractual obligation is not the promise as such but the fact of reliance on it.[38] In many cases, in order to be enforceable a promise needs to be relied on. For example, implied terms as to sale by description and fitness for purpose will not bind a seller unless it is shown that the buyer, in the case of sale by description, has actually relied on the descriptive words used by the seller; in the case of fitness for purpose, has relied on the seller's skill or judgment.[39]

However, the reliance theory is often criticized on the ground that although, in a number of cases, the reliance on the promise is necessary, there is no general requirement that a promise is actionable only upon reliance.[40] In fact, law does not treat mere reliance on the promise as enough.[41] As will be seen below, in most legal systems, intention to create legal relations is necessary to make a binding contract and in common law countries, in addition, consideration is necessary to support a promise. It has been rightly observed that the injurious reliance theory cannot serve as a basis for explaining "the whole law of contract".[42]

---

[35] Paton & Derham (eds.) (1972), p. 96.

[36] See Atiyah (1995), p. 13.

[37] Pretorius (2004a), p. 229.

[38] Poole (2004), p. 14.

[39] See infra, Chap. 6, Sect. 6.1.4.

[40] See Guest (ed.) (2006), p. 540.

[41] Paton & Derham (eds.), p. 447.

[42] Ibid.

4.3 Common Law Conception of Contract

4.3.1 Contracts as Agreement

As already stated, under the influence of the freedom of contract theory, for about a couple of century it has been the established principle that the basis of a contract is the agreement reached between the parties.[43] However, as already indicated, the principle is not absolute as in many cases contracts are not the result of agreements.[44] One prime example is contracts by deed which indisputably are not based on any agreement between the parties but derive their binding force from a set form.

Turning to the meaning of an agreement, it may be stated that in the legal sense, an agreement is not simply the subjective intention of the parties. Rather, it is an outward expression of a common intention as to the assurance contained in the promise.[45] Thus, unless a common intention to be bound by the promise is expressed or communicated by each to the other party no contract can be formed. In other words, although a meeting of minds is necessary for the formation of contract, it is also required that each party to a contract must express his intention to be bound by the promise to the other. The promise may be communicated expressly or it may be assumed from the conduct of the promise.[46] Differently put, the question—whether or not an agreement is reached—is to be determined objectively and not subjectively. Thus, what matters is not whether the parties actually agreed but whether their conduct is such as to lead a person acting reasonably to assume that they agreed.[47]

Contracts are normally defined by reference to agreements or promises. Indian Contract Act defines a contract in terms of an agreement. S. 2(h) provides: "An agreement enforceable by law is a contract."[48] And an agreement is defined by S. 2(e) as [e]very promise and every set of promises, forming the consideration for each other, is an agreement. The definition is somewhat reflective of a traditional approach as it defines a contract in terms of an agreement.[49] Defining a contract in this way is

---

[43] Atiyah (1961), p. 4; Pretorius (2004a), p. 102.

[44] Atiyah, ibid.

[45] Beatson et al. (2010), p. 30; Paton and Derham (eds.) (1972), p. 433; Austin (1954), pp. 330–31. Although modern contract law differs from the classical law in many vital respects, there are strikingly similar in respect of basic concepts.

[46] S. 3 of the Indian Contract Act 1872 ("the communication of proposals, the acceptance of proposals, and the revocation of proposals and acceptances, respectively, are deemed to be made by any act or omission of the [relevant] party, by which he intends to communicate such proposal, acceptance or revocation such proposal, acceptance or revocation…."); Austin, id., p. 330.

[47] Atiyah (1961), p. 4.

[48] This proposition is often criticized on the ground that the law generally does not "compel the performance of a contract." The normal remedy under the English law of contract is damages for the breach. See ibid., p. 20. Conditions of enforceability are dealt with by s. 10, which provides: "All agreements are contracts if they are made by the free consent of parties competent to contract, for a lawful consideration and with a lawful object, and are not …declared to be void."

[49] See Paton & Derham (eds.) (1972), p. 434.

problematical as contracts in many cases are not the outcome of agreements. Here, a reference may be made to the definition of a contract as given by the Restatement (Second) of the Law of Contracts. The definition reads:

> A contract is a promise or a set of promises for the breach of which the law gives a remedy or the performance of which the law in some way recognizes as a duty.[50]

The Restatement defines a contract in terms of a promise and is an improvement over the definition provided by the Contract Act. However, the "UNIDROIT Principles" adopts the traditional approach in defining a contract. Article 2.1.1 reads:

> A contract may be concluded either by the acceptance of an offer or by conduct of the parties that is sufficient to show agreement.

An agreement consists of (1) a promise or (2) mutual (or reciprocal) promises proffered and accepted.[51] In case (1), only one of the parties offers a promise and when accepted by the other, a unilateral contract (convention) comes into existence. For example, where A makes a public offer to pay INR 1000 to anyone who does a stipulated act, the contract in question is unilateral. Take yet another example, A promises B to render some service and if B accepts the promise, the contract in question is unilateral in nature.[52] On the other hand, in case (2), each party proffers a promise and performance of either of the promises depends on the performance of the other party. In other words, both parties are under obligation to make good their promises. This is called a bilateral contract.[53] For example, where A promises B to render a service and B promises A to render a service in return. In other words, in case (1) only one party is under obligation to make good the promise whereas in case (2), both parties are under obligation to perform the stipulated act in future, hence a bilateral contract. This is made explicit by the Indian Contract Act when it provides: [e]very promise and every set of promises… is an agreement (s. 2(e)). This is a traditional analysis of an agreement or actionable promise under both—Indian and English law which holds good in most cases.

It is indeed true that, in a traditional sense, an account of the offer–acceptance process given above is found as the most suitable method in identifying a contract as it applies in "the vast majority of cases."[54] But it is equally true that in many situations a contract may result from means other than "offer–acceptance." In *G. Percy Trentham Ltd v Archital Luxfer Ltd*,[55] it was accepted that although a contract in most cases comes into existence by the normal method of offer and acceptance, it can also come into existence as a result of performance. Steyn LJ noted:

> I am in any event satisfied that in this fully executed transaction a contract came into existence during performance even if it cannot be precisely analysed in terms of offer and acceptance.

---

[50] The final clause of the sentence aims to cover a situation where for the breach of a contract no remedy is provided. See Atiyah (1961), p. 21.

[51] Austin (1954), p. 329; Paton & Derham (eds.) (1972), p. 437.

[52] Ibid.

[53] Ibid. See also Beatson et al. (2010), p. 30.

[54] See *Gibson v Manchester City Council* [1979] 1 WLR 294.

[55] [1993] 1 Lloyd's Rep 25.

Thus, it is not necessary to find offer–acceptance in every case.[56] Notably, the "UNIDROIT Principles" clearly recognize that a contract may result from the conduct of the parties (Article 2.1.1) and a tendency is growing to determine the existence of a contract on the basis of the circumstances as a whole.[57]

4.3.2 Intention to Create Contract

Only those agreements are treated by law as enforceable which are intended to be legally binding.[58] For example, a mere statement of intention made in the course of negotiations, mere puffs, social and family arrangements do not normally result into a contract. Family and social arrangements are presumed to have no legal consequences, hence are not contracts.[59] But in certain circumstances where facts of a case clearly indicate a willingness on the part of the parties to enter into contractual relations, statements which are normally taken as mere puffs, as well as social and family arrangements may give rise to contractual liability.

One often-cited case where even an exaggerated statement was found as creating legal relations is *Carlil v Carbolic Smoke Ball Co.*[60] The defendants who were manufacturers of "carbolic smoke balls" advertised that these balls were miraculous cures for influenza. The advertisement stated that 100 pounds would be paid to anyone who contracted influenza after having used the ball as prescribed. It was also stated that 1000 pounds was deposited with a bank. The plaintiff, who used one of these balls but contracted influenza, sued for the reward as promised. It was held that normally such advertisements are treated mere puffs and are not intended to create binding contract, but taking into account the circumstances of the case including the reference to the deposit at the bank, the advertisement in question was more than a puff. According to the Court, from the circumstances of the case, it could be reasonably inferred that the parties contemplated a legally binding contract. Thus, statements, like mere puffs, which are normally taken as not intended to create legal relations may, in certain circumstances, turn out to be the statements giving rise to contractual liability.

Further, the test of determining an intention is an objective one. It may happen that the parties have not intended to enter into a binding contract, nevertheless, an intention to affect legal relations could reasonably be inferred taking into account the circumstances as a whole.

---

[56] See *Butler machine Tool Co. Ltd. v Ex-Cell-O-corporation (England) Ltd* [1979] 1 WLR 401; *New Zealand Shipping Co. v Satterthwaite* (1975) AC 154; *Gibson v Manchester City Council* [1978] 1 WLR 520 (the House of Lords in *Gibson v Manchester* disagreed with the view of the Lord Denning in Court of Appeal).

[57] See *Butler Machine Tool Co. Ltd. v Ex-Cell-O-corporation (England) Ltd* [1979] 1 WLR 401; *Gibson v Manchester City Council* supra note 54. For more fully discussion, see Poole (2004), pp. 37–38.

[58] See Beatson et al. (2010), pp. 70–71; Poole (2004), p. 162.

[59] See *Balfour v Balfour* [1919] 2 KB 571; *Gould v Gould* [1970] 1QB 275.

[60] [1893] 1 QB 256.

4.3.3 Necessity of Consideration

Under common law, as a general rule, in addition to the requirement of an intention to create legal relations, a promise in order to be enforceable needs to be supported by consideration in the sense of an exchange of promises. However, in certain small number of cases, where contracts are required to be made in a special form requirement of consideration is not insisted upon by the law (see Sect. 4.3.4). Notably, under civil law systems, on the other hand, a contract may be concluded without consideration. Under CISG and UNIDROIT Principles also, consideration is not a prerequisite for making a contract (see Chap. 8, Sect. 8.2.6.2).

Under English (common) law, consideration was traditionally understood as consisting of some act or promise which involves "some right, interest, profit or benefit accruing to the one party, or some forbearance, detriment, loss or responsibility, given, suffered, or undertaken by the other." However, the traditional notion that consideration involves some benefit to one party and some detriment to the other has fallen into disfavor. The modern authorities, instead, prefer the definition of consideration given by Sir Frederick Pollock which views consideration as the price for which the promise of the other is bought.[61] It is this idea of consideration as an exchange of promises which serves as basis to most commercial transactions. The definition of consideration contained in Indian Contract also regards consideration as the price for the promise. S. 2(d) of the Contract Act reads:

> When, at the desire of the promisor, the promisee or any other person has done or abstained from doing or does or abstains from doing, or promises to do or to abstain from doing, something, such act or abstinence or promise is called a consideration for the promise.

4.3.4 No General Requirement About Form

Traditionally, under the common law, contracts or covenants were required to be made in a fixed form. In fact, as Simpson tells and as has been noted above, the medieval common law of contract was a "formulary system" which put considerably heavy emphasis on form. All formal contracts were enforceable just because they conform to the requirement of a form. They derived their validity from the form and the form alone. Simple or informal contracts, on the other hand, were generally not regarded as enforceable unless there was something more than mere agreement between the parties.

However, as we move from the medieval to modern law, we notice a considerable decline in the significance of formal requirements. In other words, with the emergence of the doctrine of consideration the requirement of form has considerably reduced.

---

[61] de Cruz (2007), p. 304.

Section 10 of the Contract Act which defines a contract does not refer to the formal requirements at all. It reads:

> All agreements are contracts if they are made by the free consent of the parties competent to contract, for a lawful consideration and with a lawful object, and are not …expressly declared to be void.

Thus, there is in general no requirement of form. An oral agreement is as valid as a written one. It is only in respect of a small category of contracts that the law insists on the requirement of a form. The category includes: contracts by deed and such (simple) contracts which because of their special significance to the parties are required to be made in a particular form, for example, transactions related to transfer of an interest in an immoveable property[62] and a few number of other transactions mainly to protect a party such as, consumers, tenants, and so on.

Although the role of formal requirements has considerably diminished, the law in both India and England still recognizes "contracts by deed" which are valid because of their form. Section 25 of Contract Act provides that in certain cases, an agreement is contract even if it is without consideration. It reads as follows:

> An agreement made without consideration is void, unless—
>
> (1) it is expressed in writing and registered under the law for the time being in force for the registration of documents and is made on account of natural love and affection between parties standing in a near relation to each other; or unless
> (2) it is a promise to compensate, wholly or in part, a person who has already voluntarily done something for the promisor, or something which the promisor was legally compellable to do; or unless
> (3) it is a promise, made in writing and signed by the person to be charged therewith, or by his agent generally or specially authorized in that behalf, to pay wholly or in part a debt of which the creditor might have enforced payment but for the law for the limitation of suits.

Earlier, under English law, in order to be a deed a contract was required to be "signed, sealed and delivered." But the Law of Property (Miscellaneous Provisions) Act 1989 now does away the requirement of sealing and retains only the requirements of signature, attestation, and delivery.[63]

---

[62]For example, under Transfer of Property Act, 1882, transactions involving immoveable property such as sale, exchange, mortgage, lease and gift are in general required to fulfill certain formalities. Also, in cases of gift of moveable property and assignment of actionable claims certain legal formalities are required. However, in the case of the former, the formalities are optional. See Srivastava (2017), p. 42.

[63]For a more fully account of contracts by deed, see Beatson et al. (2010), pp. 76–78.

4.4 Civil Law Approaches

The common law conception of contracts, discussed above, is not quite different from the idea of contract in civil law countries. However, in a few respects, they differ significantly. First, while in common law countries the requirement of consideration, in the sense of *quid pro quo* for the promise,[64] is strictly, if not universally, adhered to, in civil law countries there is no rule that requires that an agreement must be supported by consideration. However, in civil law, the traditional requirement of *causa civils*, understood as a civil, legal reason for a contract may be regarded as similar to consideration.[65]

Secondly, under civil law system, the remedy of specific performance is a usual remedy whereas in common law countries, except India where in virtue of a recent amendment in the Specific Relief Act, 1967 the remedy of specific performance is made as a general remedy,[66] and this remedy is provided only exceptionally where the remedy of damages is found inadequate.[67] On the other hand, damage for breach of contract, a normal remedy in common law, is usually not awarded in civil law. In other words, it is only where specific relief is inadequate that the civil law system awards damages.[68]

Thirdly, while under common law systems, the significance of the requirement of a particular form for making a contract has in general been declined, and in civil law countries, a contract is generally required to be in a set form.

A further distinction between the two systems relates to the concept of good faith and fair dealing. While common law generally do not recognize good faith as an essential element of contract formation, in certain civil law countries such as Germany and Italy the requirement of good faith features prominently.[69] Further, the "good faith and fair dealing" is also incorporated into the UNIDROIT Principles as a fundamental concept and serve as basis of a number of Principles.[70]

4.5 Codification of English Contract Law

This Chapter is primarily concerned with the English and Indian law of contract. As will be seen below, both—Indian and English laws have a common background as

[64] Paton & Derham (eds.) (1972), p. 440.

[65] See de Cruz (2007), pp. 304–5; Paton & Derham (eds.) (1972), p. 441.

[66] See Specific Relief Act (Amendment) Act, 2018 introducing necessary changes in ss. 10, 20, and 21 in this regard. For further discussion, see Srivastava and Pathak (2018), pp. 346–53.

[67] See infra, Chap. 6, Sect. 6.3.2.2.

[68] de Cruz (2007) pp. 304–05; Paton & Derham (eds.) (1972) p. 441.

[69] See Furmston (2017), pp. 33–35.

[70] UNIDROIT Principles, Article 1.7 ((1) "Each party must act in accordance with good faith and fair dealing in international trade. (2) The parties may not exclude or limit." See in particular, comment to UNIDROIT Principles, Article 1.7).

based on common law and in many respects are strikingly similar, although there are notable differences.[71] Thus, in the following discussion, unless the context otherwise requires, a reference to the English law as it applies to England, Wales, and Northern Ireland includes a reference to the Indian law and vice versa.

It would be interesting to note that English law of contract is mainly based on case law.[72] In recent decades, however, a number of legislations were introduced in the area of the general law of contract.[73] Some of the most important statutes include: the Misrepresentation Act 1967, the Minors Contracts Acts 1987, and the Contract (Rights of Third Parties) Act 1999.

While much of the English law remains un-codified, this is not true of Indian law which has its own statute, namely the Indian Contract Act 1872. The Act, for the most part, codified the then existing English law.[74] However, since passing of the Contract Act, the legislative interventions have been scanty. This is despite the fact that there is a pressing need to reform the contract law to meet the modern conditions. It may also be noted that a great mass of case law interpreting the Act has been developed which also constitutes an authoritative source of the law. In fact, the case law which pre-dates the Contract Act may also be referred to and, as a matter of fact, it is routinely referred to by the courts in India.[75]

4.6 Standardized Contracts

Standard-form contracts, sometimes called, "contracts of adhesion", are commonplace in the present-day law of contract.[76] UNIDROIT Principles define standard terms of contracts as those terms of contract "which are prepared in advance for general and repeated use by one party and which are actually used without negotiation with the other party." Thus, they are not the result of negotiations between the parties but are actually imposed or dictated by a stronger party. This raises the issue of protecting a weaker party, such as a consumer or an employee. In view of this, in recent decades a number of statutes were enacted for the purpose. Here, mention may be made of the (English) Unfair Contract terms Act, 1977,[77] Consumer Rights Act,

---

[71]The common law is the basis of the law in other countries also, namely Australia, New Zealand, Canada, United States and certain countries of Africa. See Applebey (2001), p. 9.

[72]Diamond (1968), p. 361.

[73]Beatson et al. (2010), p. 18; ibid.

[74]See Diamond (1968), p. 362. The draft of the Indian Contract Act, was prepared in England between 1863 and 1806. It was then revised in India by James Fitzjames Stephen and was passed in 1872. Ibid.

[75]On the method of interpreting a codified statute, see Chap. 5, Sect. 5.1.4.

[76]See Beatson et al. (2010), pp. 5–6; Furmston (2017), pp. 26–29; Atiyah (1995) pp. 16–18.

[77]The Act of 1977 applies to terms that restrict or exclude liability i.e. "exemption clauses.' However, its provisions on consumer rights are now repealed and are incorporated in the Consumer Rights Act 2015 which gathers at one place all the statutory provisions about the rights of consumers.

2015[78] and the Consumer Protection Act, 2019 replacing the Consumer Protection Act, 1986. The Act of 2019 was enacted mainly to enhance the rights of consumers in the face of the emergence of e-commerce as an important mode of conducting business.

However, standard form contracts referred to above need to be distinguished from a kind of standard form contracts which contain terms on the basis of which most commercial transactions take place. Examples include: bills of lading, charterparties, and marine insurance contracts. "The standard clauses in these contracts have been settled over the years by negotiation by representatives of the commercial interests involved and have been widely adopted because…they facilitate the conduct of trade."[79]

4.7 Global Contract Law?

In recent decades, we have witnessed increasing interests in internationalization or even globalization of contract law (see Chap. 2). In 1971, the UNIDROIT decided to place on its agenda the elaboration of "Principles of International Commercial Contracts" and in 1980, it sets up a special Working Group for the purpose. As will be seen in Chap. 8, "Harmonization through International Restatements" the above initiative led to the publication in 1994, of the first edition of the UNIDROIT Principles of International Commercial Contracts (UNIDROIT Principles) to be followed by the publication of further editions in 2004, 2010, and 2016.[80] The UNIDROIT Principles are of the nature of soft-law and are aimed to achieving harmonization of the principles of contract laws through persuasion.

A similar initiative undertook by the UNCITRAL in 1967 led to the adoption of the 1980 United Nations Convention on Contracts for International Sale of Goods (CISG). Unlike the UNIDROIT Principles, CISG is a binding convention which provides for uniform rules on international sale of goods. It entered into force on January 1, 1988 and to date has been ratified by 90 states. It means that in these countries, the CISG is part of the domestic law on international sale of goods (see Chap. 7, Sect. 7.5).

4.8 Toward European Contract Law

Motivated by the desire of facilitating international trade and to establishing a common market, in recent decades we have witnessed several initiatives toward

---

[78] See Furmston (2017), pp. 259–62.

[79] Per Lord Diplock in *Schroeder Music Publishing Co. Ltd. v Macaulay* [1974] 3 All ER 616 at p. 524 (cited in Furmston (2017), pp. 26–27.

[80] UNIDROIT Principles can be accessed from: www.uniddroit.org.

standardization of contract laws at regional level. A brief account of such efforts is provided in Chap. 2 dealing with the international harmonization of trade laws. Here, we will only focus on the efforts directed at creation of the European contract law. Two such initiatives are particularly notable. The first is the creation of the Principles of European Contract Law ("PECL") by the Commission of European Contract Law (CECL) for the member countries of the European Union (EU).[81] The "PECL," published in 2003, is aimed at harmonizing general contract law within the EU and offers "an authoritative point of reference for the interpretation and development of the national legal systems in Europe."[82] Created as a restatement of law much like the UNIDROIT Principles it is a set of (model) rules intended to be used by the parties as the applicable law; by courts and arbitrators; and by legislatures in preparing the rules of contract.[83] In fact both—the PECL and UNIDROIT Principles have many common features. They are similar in terms of content; were created at approximately the same time; and have influenced one another.[84]

The second initiative relates to the project of the Draft Common Frame of Reference (DCFR) launched by Commission of the European Union as part of an Action Plan for promoting the development of general contract terms for the member countries of the EU, known as the Common Frame of Reference (CFR).[85] The Interim Outline Edition of DCFR was published in 2008 followed by the publication of the Outline Edition and the Full Edition respectively in February 2009 and October 2009. The Final Edition (model rules, comments, and comparative notes) consists of six volumes comprising about 6,100 pages.[86]

4.9 Formation of Contract

4.9.1 Offer (or Proposal)

4.9.1.1 Proposal Must Be Unequivocal

A proposal or offer is an expression or manifestation of willingness to enter into a binding contract. It is a final declaration of a readiness on the part of the offeror to

---

[81]The first edition (Part I) of PECL appeared in 1995 followed by the subsequent editions (Part II & Part III) in 1999 and 2003, respectively. See Whittaker (2009), p. 617.

[82]Eidenmüller et al. (2008), p. 661.

[83]Poole (2004), pp. 20–21; McKendrick (2000), p. 9.

[84]See Jansen and Zimmermann (2011) p. 628.

[85]See Beatson et al. (2010), p. 20; Whittaker (2009), p. 618; Jansen and Zimmermann (2011), pp. 625–62; Eidenmüller et al. (2008) pp. 659–708; Jansen and Zimmermann (2010), pp. 98–112. In 2005, CECL for the purpose formed two study groups: "Study Group on a European Civil Code" and" Research Group on Existing EC Private Law (or "Acquis Group"). See Whittaker, Simon, id, p. 618.

[86]Jansen and Zimmermann (2010), p. 98.

be bound. Here it is instructive to note the definition of proposal in Contract Act (s. 2 (a)):

> When one person signifies to another his willingness to do or to abstain from doing anything, with a view to obtaining the assent of that other to such act or abstinence, he is said to make a proposal.

Anson's Law of Contract provides a similar definition. It defines an offer as "intimation, by words or conduct, of a willingness to enter into contractual relations," and terms of which clearly indicate that it will become binding on the offeror as soon as it is accepted.

Although an offer need not be made expressly and may be inferred by conduct, in order to be valid, it must be sufficiently definite and unequivocal. Here reference may be made to CISG, Article 14(1), relevant part of which reads: A proposal…constitutes an offer if it is sufficiently definite and indicates the intention of the offeror to be bound in case of acceptance.[87]

4.9.1.2 Invitation to Treat and Offer Distinguished

An offer is distinguishable from "an invitation to treat." The former denotes a definite promise to enter into contractual relationship. It must be borne in mind that every statements or expressions of intention made in the course of negotiations do not constitute an offer. To be an offer, the expression of offer it must not leave any room for further negotiation.[88] Therefore, statements made merely to seek or supply information is not an offer. To bring home the point, a few examples may be given. In *Harvey v Facey*,[89] the plaintiffs asked the defendants, "Will you sell us Bumper Hall Pen?" and "Telegraph lowest cash price." Defendants replied that lowest price for Bumper Hall Pen was 900 pounds. The plaintiffs then telegraphed that they were ready to buy Bumper Hall Pen for 900 pounds. The Privy Council held that no contract was made as in starting the price the defendants were merely supplying the information which did not amount to an offer. Similarly, in another often-cited case, *Hyde v Wrench*,[90] the defendant offered to sell a piece of land to B for 1000 pounds. In reply, the plaintiff made a counter-offer to purchase the property for 950 pounds. The defendant rejected counter-offer of the plaintiff. It was held that no contract was concluded as the plaintiff's counter-offer amounted to the rejection of original offer made by the defendant.

An invitation to treat, on the other hand, is merely "an offer to negotiate" or "offers to receive offers" For example, a price list, a catalogue, advertisements in a newspaper and television, websites, and inviting tenders are not generally considered an offer but an invitation to offer.[91] The result is that a seller by merely advertising

---

[87]UNIDROIT Principles, Article 2.1.2 define a valid offer in a similar manner.

[88]Poole (2004), p. 38; Atiyah (1961), p. 31.

[89][1893] AC 552.

[90](1840) 3 Beav 334.

[91]See Beatson et al. (2010), pp. 34–37; McKendrick (2000), pp. 32–41; Poole (2004), pp. 40–47.

goods is not bound to supply the goods in question as soon as an order is placed. "If it were so, the merchant might find himself involved in any number of contractual obligations to supply wine of a particular description which he would be quite unable to carry out...."[92] Similarly, in *Partridge v Crittenden*,[93] it was found that the advertisement for sale of goods was an invitation to offer and not an offer. In that case, an advertisement was published showing the willingness to sell wild birds. Since it was a crime to offer wild birds for sale, the appellant was convicted. On appeal, the appellant was acquitted on the ground that the advertisement in question was not an offer but only an invitation to treat.[94] However, in certain situations a different view is possible, in particular, where the terms of the advertisement indicate a definite intention to be bound. In *Carlill v Carbolic Smoke Ball Co.* (already cited), it was held that the advertisement in question was an offer because the terms of the advertisement showed a definite promise to be bound.[95]

A similar view may be taken about display of goods for sale in a shop.[96] However, in a situation where it was clear that the goods could be sold to any one paying the displayed price, a different view is indeed possible.[97]

4.9.1.3 Communication of Proposal

The rule is well settled that an offer is not effective unless it is communicated to the offeree.[98] The requirement of communication ensures that there is the opportunity for acceptance and rejection of an offer. Since communication of an offer is necessary, it follows that there can be no valid acceptance if it is made in ignorance of an offer.[99] It also follows that cross-offers, when made in ignorance of each other, do not result into the acceptance of an offer. For example, where A and B make identical offers to each other in respect of the sale and purchase of a piece of land, it is clear that these (cross) offers cannot result into contract. "The two offers are isolated, independent acts, and are not given one in return for the other."[100] However, where one offer is made with reference to another it appears that a valid contract is concluded.[101]

---

[92] *Grainger & Son v Gough* [1896] AC 35 (per Lord Herschell).

[93] [1968] 1 WLR 1204.

[94] See also *Grainger & Son v Gough*, supra note 91; *Gibson v Manchester City Council* supra note 56.

[95] See Poole (2004), pp. 40–44.

[96] See *Pharmaceutical Society of GB v Boots Cash Chemists* [1953] 1 QB 401 (display of goods in a self-service store was not an offer); *Fisher v Bell* [1961] 1 QB 394 (display of flick-knife with a price tag was not an offer).

[97] For example, *Chapelton v Barry Urban District Council* [1940] 1 KB 532 (display of goods in a self-service store could be treated as an offer to sell).

[98] See Beatson et al. (2010), p. 39; Poole (2004), pp. 47–48.

[99] Ibid. See also *Lalman v Gauri Dutt* (1913) 11 All LJ 489.

[100] Atiyah (1961), pp. 35–36.

[101] See Beatson et al. (2010), p. 39.

Further, an offer in addition to statement can also be made by conduct such as the rendering of services.

Further, there is no requirement that an offer should be made to an ascertained or specific person and a general offer is as much valid as an offer made to a specific person. However, no contract can exist unless it is accepted by an ascertained person (Beatson et al. 2010, p. 37).

4.9.1.4 Termination and Revocation of Offer

An offer which has not been accepted may be terminated in any of the following ways.[102] First, an offer may be terminated by rejection or counter-offer. It is always open to the offeree to either accept the proposal, seek further information, or to reject it at all. Secondly, an offer is terminated upon withdrawal or revocation of an offer by the offeror. An offeror may revoke his offer at any time before its acceptance is complete. However, as Atiyah tells where an offeror promises to keep an offer open for a specified period of time and the promise is made by deed or for consideration the offer is not revocable during the specified period.[103] Thirdly, an offer is revocable by the lapse of time. This is self-evident. An offer cannot last for an indefinite period. Where a period is specified for acceptance of an offer, the offer will lapse if it is not accepted within the period. And where no time is specified, the offer will lapse after a reasonable time. Fourthly, an offer which is conditional can come to an end upon non-fulfillment of the condition.[104] Finally, an offer can come to an end upon death of the offeror or offeree. However, it seems that where a proposal is accepted before the notice of death of the offeror reaches the offeree, the offer may be treated as accepted.[105]

4.9.2 Acceptance

4.9.2.1 Offer and Acceptance Must Correspond: "Mirror Image" Rule

Acceptance may be defined as an expression or indication of assent to the offer which may be by words or conduct and must be made in the manner prescribed by the offeror.[106] Contract Act, 1872 provides: "when the person to whom the proposal is made signifies his assent thereto, the proposal is said to be accepted." A similar approach is adopted by CISG and UNIDROIT Principles. The former provides: "A statement made by or other conduct of the offeree indicating assent to an offer is an

---

[102] See Atiyah (1961), pp. 39–41.

[103] Id., p. 40.

[104] Furmston (2017), pp. 82–83; *Financing Ltd. v Stimson* [196] 3 All ER 386.

[105] For more fully discussion, see Furmston (2017), ibid.

[106] See Beatson et al. (2010), p. 40.

acceptance. Silence or inactivity does not in itself amount to acceptance" (Article 18).[107] Clearly, a mental assent is not sufficient to constitute an acceptance and the assent must be indicated to the offeror. There must be something more than that[108]; there must be "an external manifestation of assent."[109]

While an offer may be conditional, an acceptance must be absolute; must be made with reference to the offer and must correspond, that is to say, must exactly match with the offer.[110] The rule is sometimes expressed as the "mirror image" rule. Where an offeree makes a counter-offer or varies the terms of original offer while accepting it, acceptance will not be treated as valid. Therefore, "a conditional acceptance is no real acceptance at all."[111]

4.9.2.2 "Battle of Forms"

The problem of battle of form arises where the parties to a contract use their own standard terms in buying or selling the goods. In modern times the problem often arises as business people prefer to enter into contracts using a form that contains their own terms of business. If one prefers traditional approach of looking at the issue at hand, it is clear that as a result of the mirror image rule no contract will be made. However, in many cases, business people may find that the result is not appropriate.

Here reference may be made to UNIDROIT Principles, Article 2.1.2 which provides a solution to the problem based on the "Knock-out" doctrine. According to the Principles, "where the parties reach an agreement except on their standard terms, a contract is concluded on the basis of the agreed terms and of any standard terms which are common in substance." The solution suggested here is opposed to what may be called a "first shot" rule according to which an offeree by accepting the offer is considered to have waived its own standard terms.[112]

4.9.2.3 Communication of Acceptance

As a general rule, acceptance becomes effective only when it is communicated to the offeror ("receipt" rule).[113] However, this rule is not absolute and, as discussed

[107]UNIDROIT Principles, Article 2.1.6 defines an acceptance in identical terms.

[108]Beatson et al. (2010), p. 43; *Brogden v Metropolitan Railway Co.* (1877) 2 AC 666.

[109]Furmston (2017), p. 65.

[110]Atiyah (1961), p. 36; Poole (2004), p. 49.

[111]Atiyah (1961), ibid.

[112]See Beatson et al. (2010) p. 41 (citing *Chas Davis (Metal Brokers) Ltd v Gilyott & Scott Ltd* [1975] 2 Lloyd's Rep 422).

[113]Atiyah (1961), p. 37; *Carlill v Carbolic Smoke Ball Co.* [1893] 1 QB 256 (…as a general proposition, when an offer is made, it is necessary in order to make a binding contract, not only that it should be accepted, but that acceptance should be notified.) Id., p. 262. One important exception to this rule is that when an acceptance is sent through post, contract is formed at the very moment when the acceptance is dispatched (see the discussion below).

below, is subject to certain important exceptions. The rule will not apply when the requirement of the notification of acceptance is expressly or impliedly waived by the offeror himself. For example, in unilateral contracts performance of the condition in itself constitutes acceptance. In other words, performance of the condition clearly signifies the assent to the offer. (See *Carlill v Carbolic Smoke Ball Co.*, cited above.) Furthermore, when acceptance is sent through post, contract is taken as formed at the very moment when the acceptance is dispatched or posted ("dispatch" rule).

It may be noted that in applying the receipt rule a distinction is drawn between the oral and other means of communications or between the instantaneous and non-instantaneous means of communications. In *Entores Ltd v Miles Far East Corpn*[114] it was made clear that the rule that acceptance to an offer is not effective unless it reaches the offeror was confined to cases of instantaneous communication such as where the parties are in each other's presence or communicating over phone or similar devices. The Court of Appeal held that where the parties are in each other's presence or, though, separated in space, communication between them is in effect instantaneous, it is the general rule that communication of acceptance must be received by the offeror will apply.[115]

Where the parties are negotiating in the presence of each other or communicating to each other on telephone or by telex,[116] the rule that acceptance must reach the offeror or must be heard by him does not present any difficulty. In this case, the offeree knows that his communication has not reached the offeror. However, where the parties are communicating to each other through post or telegram the law treats the issue of communication differently and presumes that the communication of acceptance has reached the offeror the moment the letter of acceptance is posted. Basis of this rule can be traced to the decision of *Adams v Lindsell* decided in 1818 by the King's Bench.[117] Since that case, the rule has come to be settled that where acceptance is communicated by post or other means of non-instantaneous communication and the offeror has not designated any particular mode of acceptance or where postal acceptance does not seem unreasonable, the contract is concluded as soon as the letter of acceptance is posted or put in the course of transmission.[118] It follows then if the offeror wishes to revoke his offer he must do so before that time.

---

[114] [1955] 2 All ER 493.

[115] See also *Brinkibon Ltd. v Stahag Stahl und Stahlwarenhandels GmbH* [1983] 2 AC 34 approving the decision in *Entores*. The same (general) rule also applies to telex messages. Supreme Court of India has also adopted a similar approach. It was made clear in *Bhagwandas Goverdhandas Kedia v Girdharilal Parshottamdas & Co.* (AIR 1966 SC 543) that the rule that acceptance is not effective unless it reaches the offeror is confined to acceptance by instantaneous methods or where the parties are in each other's presence.

[116] Communication by telex is normally treated as instantaneous method of communication. However, the rule is not universal one. See D'Arcy (ed.) (2000), p. 56 (citing *Brinkibon Ltd. v Stahag Stahl und Stahlwarenhandels GmbH* (cited above).

[117] (1818) 1 B & Ald 681. See also *Household Fire and Carriage Accident Insurance Co. Ltd. v Grant* (1879) 4 Ex D 216; *Byrne v Van Tienhoven* (1880) 5 CPD 344.

[118] *Byrne v Van Tienhoven* ibid. (cited in Furmston (2017), p. 72). See also Poole (2004), p. 56.

However, the postal rule of acceptance which puts an offeror in a disadvantageous position gives rise to difficulty in situations where the letter of acceptance is lost or delayed. Here, the case of *Household Fire and Carriage Accident Insurance Co. Ltd. v Grant*[119] may be cited as illustrative of the problem. In that case, the plaintiff company posted a letter accepting the offer of the defendant for purchase of shares. The letter was lost in the post and never reached the offeror. But the claim by the liquidator of the plaintiff company against the defendant in respect of the value of the shares was upheld by the Court of Appeal. According to the Court, although the acceptance did not reach the offeror, the contract in question was valid and the defendant-buyer was liable to pay.

The postal rule as discussed above will not apply when it was unreasonable to send acceptance through post[120] or where delay or loss of acceptance was attributable to the fault on the part of the offeree. The reason for placing the risk of loss on the offeror is that he is better placed to bear the risk and it is he who has chosen the postal or other non-instantaneous means of communication.[121]

4.9.2.4 Indian Position

As already noted, Indian law on the subject broadly conforms to the position under English law as the rule in *Entores* applies to India. But there is one important difference for s. 4 of the Contract Act provides:

> The communication of an acceptance is complete—as against the proposer, when it is put in a course of transmission so as to be out of the power of the acceptor; as against the acceptor, when it comes to the knowledge of the proposer.

The provision incorporates the elements of both—the receipt and the dispatch rule. As against the offeror, it applies the dispatch rule as it says that the communication of an acceptance is complete as against the proposer, when it is put in a course of transmission. However, as against the offeree, it applies the receipt rule as it says that the offeree is bound only when acceptance "comes to the knowledge of the proposer."

It is accepted position that the rule contained in s. 4 of the Contract Act is confined to cases of acceptance through the post or other non-instantaneous means of communication. In a leading case on the subject, *Bhagwandas Goverdhandas Kedia v Girdharilal Parshottamdas & Co.*,[122] it was made clear by the Supreme Court that the provision of s. 4 applies only to the communication of acceptance by post. It follows then that acceptance through instantaneous means of communication is subject to the *Entores* rule.

---

[119](1879) 4 Ex D 216.

[120]See *Henthorn v Fraser* [1892] 2 Ch 27; Beatson et al. (2010), p. 47.

[121]See Comment to Article 2.1.6 UNIDROIT Principles. For differing views on the issue, see in particular Poole (2004), pp. 57–58.

[122]AIR 1966 SC 543.

4.9.2.5 Acceptance Through E-mail

Where acceptance of an offer is made by the use of electronic communications, that is, by means of data messages, a question arises as to the time when the contract is concluded.[123] Opinion on the issue is divided. It is sometimes suggested that acceptance of a proposal through e-mail should be treated as similar to non-instantaneous means of communication as there is considerable similarity between communication through e-mail and postal communication. The most convincing argument that may be offered in support of this view is that unlike the parties who are communicating in the presence of each other or speaking over telephone, the originator of the e-mail is not sure about the receipt of acceptance by the addressee or offeror. Therefore, it is the dispatch rule that should govern the issue of formation of contract by e-mail.[124] In other words, the moment an e-mail is dispatched[125] a contract should be taken as concluded. But the most preferred approach seems to be that acceptance through e-mail is similar to instantaneous means and the contract is concluded where e-mail is received.[126] Since opinion is divided on the issue and also that there is scanty of the authorities not only in regard to an acceptance by e-mail but also respecting other methods of communication like couriers, this area of law needs attention.[127]

Prescribed Mode of Acceptance

Where a particular mode of communicating acceptance is prescribed by the offeror, acceptance, as a general rule, must be made observing that method of communication.[128] However, the issue of the method of communication should be decided on the basis of the circumstances of a case. Where an offer is made by post, its acceptance by telegram would suffice.[129] But, where offer is made by telegram as the offeror is expecting a prompt reply, acceptance by post will not be sufficient.[130]

Where no particular method is prescribed, the acceptance may be sent by a mode which does not seem unreasonable in the circumstances of the case.

---

[123] Here a distinction may be made between e-mail messages and acceptance of an offer at the website. Poole (2004), p. 60.

[124] Poole (2004), ibid.; Padia (ed.), pp. 178–79.

[125] On the meaning of dispatch in the context, see s. 13(1), Information Technology Act (IT Act), 2000 ("Save as otherwise agreed to between the originator and the addressee, the dispatch of an electronic record occurs when it enters a computer resource outside the control of the originator"). Section 13 of the IT Act, 2000 lays down specific rules with regard to the time and place of dispatch and receipt of an electronic record.

[126] See Furmston (2017), p. 70; Collins (ed.) (2006), p. 377; *Bank of Baroda v Vysya Bank Ltd* [1994] 2 Lloyd's Rep 87.

[127] Beatson et al. (2010), pp. 48–49.

[128] *Manchester Diocesan Council for Education v Commercial & General Investments Ltd* [1970] 1 WLR 241.

[129] See Guest (ed.) (1977), p. 73.

[130] Furmston (2017), p. 68.

4.9.3 Consideration

4.9.3.1 Consideration Need Not Be Adequate but It Must Be Real and of Some Value

The meaning of consideration has already been discussed under Sect. 4.3.3 above. Now attention will be directed to the issues of the adequacy of consideration; the relationship between consideration and doctrine of privity of contract; promissory estoppel which in certain situations operate as an alternative to the doctrine of consideration.

The legal position on the issue of the adequacy of consideration is well settled. Once it is shown that consideration has some value in the eye of law, the court will not look into the question of the adequacy of consideration.[131] The underlying idea is that it is not for the courts to make bargain for the parties, it is the parties who make their bargain. Explanation 2, s. 25 of the Contract provides that "an agreement to which the consent of the promisor is freely given is not void merely because the consideration is inadequate." Illustration (f) attached to s. 25 runs as follows: A agrees to sell a horse worth Rs. 1000 for Rs. 10. A's consent to the agreement was freely given. The agreement is a contract notwithstanding the inadequacy of the consideration. However, in certain cases, in particular, in immoveable property transactions the courts may enquire into the issue of adequacy of consideration for deciding whether or not a contract is unconscionable.

4.9.3.2 Theory of "Privity of Contract"

At common law, since the middle of the nineteenth century the rule came to be established that only the parties can acquire rights and duties under the contract, and therefore, only they can enforce it. The rule is often expressed as the rule of "privity of contract." This is based on the premise that since a contract is a bargain a person who has not given consideration does not take part in a contract.

Tweddle v Atkinson[132] decision in 1861 is often cited as one of the early cases from which the doctrine originated. In that case an action for enforcing the contract by the beneficiary failed as he was found stranger to the contract. Wightman J said: "…it is now well established that no stranger to the consideration can take advantage of a contract, although made for his benefit." Later, in the early twentieth century the doctrine was affirmed in another important case on the subject, *Dunlop Pneumatic Tyre Co. Ltd. v Selfridge & Co. Ltd.*[133] It was held:

---

[131] See Furmston, id., p. 113; Beatson et al. (2010), p. 99; *De La Bere v Pearson Ltd* [1908] 1 KB 280. In *Commissioner of Income Tax, Bombay City I v Tulsidas* AIR 1961 SC 1023 Supreme Court made it clear that the phrase, "adequate consideration" excludes mere natural love and affection.

[132] (1861) 1 B & S 393 (per Wightman J). See also *Price v Easton* (1833) 4 B & Ad 433.

[133] [1915] AC 847.

> ...in the law of England certain principles are fundamental. One is that only a person who is a party to a contract can sue on it. Our law knows nothing of *jus quaesitum tertio* arising by way of contract. Such a right may be conferred by way of property, as for example, under a trust, but it cannot be conferred on a stranger to a contract...A second principle is that if a person with whom a contract not under seal has been made is to be able to enforce it consideration must have been given by him to the promisor or to some other person at the promisor's request.

In India also the doctrine is generally recognized. In *Jamna Das v Pandit Ram Autar Pande*,[134] the Privy Council took the view that a contract could not be enforced by a third party. The view of the Privy Council was later affirmed by the Supreme Court of India in *MC Chacko v State Bank of Travancore.*[135] It was held:

> It must be taken as well settled that except in the case of a beneficiary under a trust or in the case of a family arrangement, no right may be enforced by a person who is not a party to contract.[136]

4.9.3.3 Exceptions

Interestingly, there are a number of exceptions to the common law rule that a contract is not enforceable by a third party. Some of such exceptions that are particularly notable in the context of international trade include the contracts of carriage and the letters of credit.[137] Here reference may be made to the (English) Carriage of Goods by Sea Act 1992 under which a lawful holder of a bill of lading or a sea waybill or a delivery order has the right to sue the carrier for loss or damage to the goods, although none of these is a party to the contract of shipment between the carrier and shipper/consignor. Section 2(1) provides:

> Subject to the following provisions of this section a person who becomes:
>
> [a] the lawful holder of a bill of lading;
>
> [b] the person who (without being an original party to the contract of carriage) is the person to whom delivery of the goods to which a sea waybill relates is to be made...
>
> [c] the person to whom delivery of the goods to which a ship's delivery order relates is to be made...have transferred to and vested in him all rights of suit under the contract of carriage as if he had been a party to the contract.

Similarly, the letters of credit also constitute an exception to the privity doctrine.[138] A letter of credit is issued by a banker of the buyer on the instructions of the latter

---

[134] (1911–12) 39 IA 7.

[135] AIR 1970 SC 504.

[136] Courts in India, however, have created a number of exceptions to the doctrine of privity of contract for which a standard work on Indian contract law may be referred to.

[137] The devise of trust also constitutes an exception to the privity of contract doctrine. Under a trust, a beneficiary who is not a party to the contract is nevertheless able to enforce the terms of the trust. See Poole (2004), p. 490. Courts in India, however, have created a number of exceptions to the doctrine of privity of contract.

[138] A letter of credit is defined by the UCP 600 as an arrangement whereby the issuing bank, acting on the instructions of a customer undertakes to "make a payment to or t the order of a third party

for paying the seller upon tender of the specified documents, and it thus constitutes a contract between the buyer and the banker. However, under it the banker undertakes an obligation to make the payment to the seller, a third party against specified documents.[139]

4.9.3.4 Reform of the Law: Contracts (Rights of Third Parties) Act, 1999

The Contracts (Rights of Third Parties) Act, 1999[140] substantially alters the law of privity of contract as it confers upon a third party a limited right of action.[141] Section 1(1) of the Act provides that a person who is not a party to the contract may enforce the terms of the contract in his own right if the test of enforceability is satisfied. The third party may enforce the right of action under the contract even if it has not furnished consideration. And s. 1 (5) provides that the third party will have any remedy that would have been available to him in an action for breach of contract if he had been a party to the contract. The test of enforceability under s. 1(1) of the Act is satisfied where (1) the contract expressly confers upon a third party the right of action provided that the third party "must be expressly identified in the contract by name, as a member of a class or as answering a particular description"; and (2) the third party is expressly identified in the contract and the term purports to confer a benefit on the third party. However, the second situation will not apply if on a proper construction of the contract it appears that the parties did not intend the term to be enforceable by the third party.

However, the Act, though "carves out a general and wide-ranging exception" to the rule of privity, yet it leaves the rule unaltered for cases not covered by the statute.

4.9.3.5 Consideration and Promissory Estoppel

In certain cases, such as the discharge of existing duties, the equitable principle of promissory estoppel may be invoked as an alternative to consideration. But the real question is: to what extent promissory estoppel may operate as an alternative to consideration? Since the doctrine of consideration is not merely a rule of evidence nor merely a requirement of form but a necessary requirement for the formation of contract, it is clear that promissory estoppel can operate as an alternative to consideration only in a limited way.

---

or is to accept and pay bills of exchange drawn by the beneficiary" against stipulated document(s), provided that the terms and conditions of the Credit are complied with. See infra, Chap. 14.

[139]Beatson et al. (2010), p. 116.

[140]The Act does not apply to contracts entered into before May 11, 2000, i.e., the date on which the Act came into effect.

[141]See Poole (2004), pp. 485–87; McKendrick (2000), pp. 140–47.

Under the law of contract, the rule of promissory estoppel is generally understood to have evolved from the decision of the House of Lords in *Hughes v Metropolitan Railway Co.*[142] In that case, Lord Cairns observed that where the parties by their own act enter upon a course of negotiation which has led one of the parties to believe that the strict rights arising under the contract will not be enforced, the person who otherwise might have enforced those rights will not be allowed to enforce them where it would be inequitable having regard to the dealings which have thus taken place between the parties.

However, as already indicated, the doctrine of promissory estoppel can operate only in a limited manner. The doctrine is subject to the following conditions: First, the promisee must have relied upon the promise; secondly, he has changed his position to detriment; thirdly, it is inequitable for the promisor to go back upon his promise; and finally the promise only becomes final if the promisee cannot resume his position.[143] Additionally, the doctrine of promissory estoppels is generally suspensory as it does not extinguish the claim of the promisor.[144]

References

Applebey, G. (2001). *Contract law*. London: Sweet & Maxwell.

Atiyah, P. S. (1961). *An introduction to the law of contract*. Oxford: Clarendon Press.

Atiyah, P. S. (1995). *An introduction to the law of contract*. Oxford: Clarendon Press.

Austin, J. (1954). *Province of the jurisprudence determined* (p. 329). Delhi: Universal Book Publishing Co.

Barton, J. L. (1969). The early history of consideration. *Law Quarterly Review, 85*(371–92), 376.

Beatson, S. J., Burrows, A., & Cartwright, J. (2010). *Anson's law of contract*. Oxford: Oxford University Press.

Collins, S. L. (Ed.). (2006). *Dicey, Morris & Collins: The conflict of laws*. London: Sweet & Maxwell.

de Cruz, P. (2007). *Comparative law in a changing world*. Oxon: Routledge-Cavendish.

D' Arcy, L., Murray, C., & Cleave, B. (Eds.). (2000). *Schmitthoff's export trade: The Law and practice of international trade*. London: Stevens.

Diamond, A. L. (1968). Codification of the law of contract. *Modern Law Review, 31*(4), 361–389.

Eidenmüller, H., Faust, F., Christoph, H. C., Grigoleit, J., Nils, W. G., & Zimmermann, R. (2008). The common frame of reference for European Private Law: Policy choices and codification problems. *Oxford Journal of Legal Studies, 28*(4), 659–708.

Friedman, W. (1972). *Law in a changing society*. Delhi: Universal Book Co., Sweet & Maxwell.

Furmston, M. (Ed.). (2017). *Chesire, Fifoot, & Furmston's law of contract*. Oxford: Oxford University Press.

Guest, A. G. (Ed.). (1977). *Chitty on contracts* (Vol. I). London: Sweet & Maxwell.

---

[142](1877) 2 AC 439. A similar observation was made by Denning J. in *Central London Property Trust Ltd v High Trees House Ltd* [1947] KB 130. It was found that the promise to accept reduced rent on account of the war operated as (promissory) estoppel against the promisor even if there was no consideration.

[143]See *Emmanuel Ayodeji Ajayi v RT Briscoe (Nigeria) Ltd*, [1964] 3 All ER 556; McKendrick (2000), pp. 113–14. Beatson et al (2010), pp. 119-26.

[144]See Mckendrick, ibid.; Furmston (2017), p. 138. Poole (2004), pp. 139-40.

Guest, A. G. (Ed.). (2006). *Benjamin's sale of goods*. London: Sweet & Maxwell.

Horwitz, M. J. (1974). The historical foundations of modern contract law. *Harvard Law Review, 87*(918), 917–956.

James, P. S. (1979). *Introduction to English law* (pp. 272–273). London: Butterworths.

Jansen, N., & Zimmermann, R. (2010). "A European Civil Code in all but name": Discussing the nature and purposes of the Draft Common Frame of Reference. *Cambridge Law Journal, 69*(1), 98–112.

Jansen, N., & Zimmermann, R. (2011). Contract formation and mistake in European Contract Law: A genetic comparison of transnational model rules. *Oxford Journal of Legal Studies, 31*(4), 625–662.

McKendrick, E. (2000). *Law of contract*. Hampshire, London: Macmillan Press Ltd.

Padia, R. G. (Ed.). *Polluck & Mulla Indian Contract & Specific Relief Act*, (Vol. I, 13th ed.). LexisNexis.

Paton, G. W., & Derham, D. P. (Eds.). (1972). *A textbook of jurisprudence* (p. 437). Oxford: Oxford University Press.

Poole, J. (2004). *Textbook on contract law* (p. 14). Oxford: Oxford University Press.

Pretorius, C.-J. (2004a). The basis of contractual liability in America. *Comparative and International Law Journal of Southern Africa, 37*(2), 226–252.

Pretorius, C.-J. (2004b). The basis of contractual liability in English law and its influence on the South African law of contract. *Comparative and International Law Journal of Southern Africa, 37*(1), 96–128.

Simpson, A. W. B. (1975). *A history of the common law of contract: The rise of the action of assumpsit*. Oxford: Clarendon Press.

Srivastava, A. (2017). *Introduction to transfer of property act*. Jaipur: University Book House Pvt. Ltd.

Srivastava, R. C., & Pathak, A. (2018). *The principles of law of contract* (pp. 346–353). New Delhi: Bloomsbury Publishing India Pvt. Ltd.

Whittaker, S. (2009). A framework of principle for European contract law? *Law Quarterly Review, 125*, 616–647.

Online Resource

UNIDROIT: www.uniddroit.org.

Chapter 5
International Sale in Indian and English Law I: General Aspects

5.1 Statutes Governing Contract of Sale

5.1.1 General

It may be pointed out that in both countries—India and England—the law of sale of goods is to be found in distinct statutes. In other words, in India, England as well as other common law countries, a contract of sale, in general, is governed by the special rules of the law of sales developed as a distinct branch of law.[1] But this specialized branch of law cannot be totally separated from the general law of contract and in both countries the statutes on the sale of goods are supplemented by the general law of contract.[2] As will be seen below, the general law of contract continues to apply to a sale of goods contract to the extent that the former is not inconsistent with the express provisions of the statutes on sale of goods (see infra, Sect. 5.1.2).

Originally, the sale of goods law was part of the medieval era law merchant or the *lex mercatoria* which mainly consisted of mercantile customs. However, in the closing years of the nineteenth century as part of a drive toward unification of sales law, there came into existence, especially in the common law countries, specific statutes embodying principles of the law of sales.[3] The Sale of Goods Act, 1893 marked the first comprehensively codification of the English law of sale of goods as it then existed. Sir Chalmers who drafted the Act intended it to be the codification of the "existing law." Originally conceived to apply only to the common law jurisdictions, the Act of 1893 was later applied to Scotland.[4] It was subsequently adopted in many common law countries including India, Canada, and the USA. The Sale of Goods

[1]Poole (2006). p. 18; Bridge (1997), p. 1; Atiyah et al. (2010) p. 1.

[2]For a discussion on the relationship between the (English) Sale of Goods Act, 1979 and the general law of contract, see Bridge, id., pp. 4–5; Guest (ed.) (2006), p. 10.

[3]McCurdy (1927), p. 15.

[4]Guest (ed.) (2006), pp. 3–4.

A. Srivastava, *Modern Law of International Trade*, International Law and the Global South, https://doi.org/10.1007/978-981-15-5475-9_5

Act, 1930 (SoGA 1930) which applies to India; the Uniform Sales Act, 1906 of the USA (now replaced by the Uniform Commercial Code); and the Canadian legislation on the subject are based and modeled on the Act of 1893.

5.1.2 Sale of Goods Act, 1930

In India, the law relating to a contract of sale of goods, in general, is contained in SoGA 1930.[5] But a point which should constantly be kept in mind is that the specialized rules of the Act are supplemented by the general law of contract which is codified in the Indian Contract Act, 1872. The Contract Act applies to all contracts so also to a contract of sale of goods. In fact, up to July 1930, transactions involving the sale of goods were governed by the Contract Act, 1872 (Chap. 7, Ss. 76–123). But keeping in view of the development of trade and commerce on an unprecedented scale in the first quarter of the last century, a new legislation in the form of the present Act was passed which repealed and replaced Ss. 76–123 of the Contract Act.[6]

It may be noted that the provisions of the Indian Contract Act, 1872 continue to govern the sale of goods, even after the passage of the Act. But they apply only "insofar they are not inconsistent with the express provisions of this Act." This is expressly provided by s. 3 of the SoGA 1930:

> The unrepealed provisions of the Indian Contract Act, 1872, save insofar as they are inconsistent with the express provisions of this Act, shall continue to apply to contracts for the sale of goods.[7]

Further, s. 66 (e) also saves "any rule of law not inconsistent with [the Sale of Goods Act, 1930]."

5.1.3 Sale of Goods Act, 1979

The (English) Sale of Goods Act, 1979 (SoGA 1979), which has replaced the Sale of Goods Act, 1893, is the most important enactment governing the sale of goods transactions in the UK.[8] In contrast to the 1893 Act which had codified the nineteenth century law merchant, the 1979 Act simply consolidates the Act of 1893 and

[5] Act 3 of 1930, entered into force: July 1, 1930.

[6] See *Eighth Report of the Law Commission of India,* available at: http://lawcommissionofindia.nic.in.

[7] A similar provision is contained in the 1979 Act (s. 62 (2)) which shows that the law of sales, though a distinct body of law, cannot be totally separated from the general law of contract. See also Guest (ed.) (2006), p. 10; Bridge (1997), p. 1; Poole (2006), p. 18.

[8] SoGA 1979, which is a consolidating legislation bringing together the earlier Sale of Goods Act, 1893 and its amendments, applies to whole of the UK. See Guest (2006), p. 3.

incorporates subsequent legislative developments.[9] In addition to the 1979 Act, the Factors Act, 1889, the Unfair Contract Terms Act 1977, and the rules of common law also apply to sales transactions. In this way, SoGA 1979 cannot be regarded as a code of all particular rules governing the sale of goods.[10] The Act was amended by the Sale and Supply of Goods Act, 1994, the Sale of Goods (Amendment) Act, 1995, and the Sale of Goods (Amendment) Act, 1995 in addition to other amendment Acts of minor importance.[11]

As already stated, SoGA 1979 is declared to consolidate the 1839 Act.[12] In that way, it makes no attempt to create new rules or even revise the old 1893 Act. Rather, it intends to bring clarity to the law and make only necessary changes to the existing law. However, to the extent it modifies the existing law, SoGA 1979 may be taken to have the effect of codifying certain parts of the law relating to the sale of goods.[13] The 1979 Act expressly states that "[t]he rules of the common law, including the law merchant, except in so far as they are inconsistent with the express provisions of this Act… apply to contracts for the sale of goods."[14] It is thus "less than a code" and a "reworking" or redrafting of the old Act.[15] However, the earlier statute on the subject, namely the Sale of Goods Act, 1893, was stated to be a codifying statute.[16] Being a codifying statute, it was not simply a "restatement" or redrafting of the law. As will be seen below, the purpose of a codifying legislation is different from that of a consolidating statute. In construing a codifying statute, it is generally understood that a court is "not at liberty to go outside the code…." But in the case of a consolidating statute, the generally accepted view is that a court can freely refer to the case law that existed prior to the statute in construing its provisions provided that they are not unambiguous.

It also seems necessary to say a few words on the relationship between the laws of sale of goods and the consumer protection law. Both the statutes—SoGA 1930 and SoGA 1979, being based on the Act of 1893, are mainly concerned with the commercial sales. The 1893 Act attempted to state the effect of the case law of the nineteenth century which with a few exceptions overwhelmingly related to the commercial disputes.[17] However, since the twentieth century the contract law has increasingly come to tackle the issues related to the consumer protection and in recent years, as a response to a strong consumer movement, a new body of law on the protection of consumer has grown which, though distinct from the law of sale of goods, in many respects supplements it.[18] The consumer protection law addresses

[9]Bridge (1997), p. 2; Guest (2006), p. 4.

[10]Guest (2006), id, pp. 8–9.

[11]Id, p. 4; Atiyah et al. (2010), p. 3.

[12]Preamble to SoGA 1979; Furmston (2017), p. 191.

[13]de Cruz (2007), p. 419.

[14]SoGA 1979, s. 62(2).

[15]Bridge (1997), p. 6; de Cruz (2007), p. 419.

[16]See Atiyah et al. (2010), p. 3; Guest (ed.) (2006), id, pp. 8–9.

[17]Bridge (1997), p. 1.

[18]See Guest (ed.) (2006), pp. 753–754.

the problems of exemption clauses and unequal bargaining power of the parties and thus has the effect of modifying the law of sale of goods in some important respects. Some significant statutes on the consumer protection include the (English) Consumer Rights Act, 2015 and the Consumer Protection Act, 2019. However, the international trade law concerns solely with the commercial transactions, and a discussion of the consumer protection law will be out of place here.

5.1.4 Rules of Construction

As already stated, the Sale of Goods Act, 1893 was a codifying statute and it, therefore, stated the pre-1893 Common law on the subject in an orderly manner.[19] A codifying legislation is understood to make a fresh start and is not simply the restatement of law.[20] Therefore, the pre-1893 cases are not relevant to ascertain the law on any point specifically dealt with by the Act of 1893 unless the provision in question is ambiguous or it was intended to continue the established law.[21] As famously stated by Lord Herschell LC in *Bank of England v Vagliano Brothers,*[22] the proper course of interpreting a codifying statute is:

In the first instance to examine the language of the statute and to ask what is its natural meaning, uninfluenced by any considerations derived from the previous state of the law, and not to start with inquiring how the law previously stood, and then, assuming that it was probably intended to leave it unaltered, to see if the words of the enactment will bear an interpretation in conformity with this view.[23]

However, there is another approach which seeks to discover the true meaning of a term on a careful examination of the cases decided before the 1893 Act even where the term in question is not ambiguous.[24] As noted in *Benjamin's Sale of Goods*, as a matter of practice, recourse is often had to be the pre-1893 law by the courts in deciding a case under the Act of 1893 even where the statute is unambiguous.[25]

SoGA, 1930 is expressed to be "[a]n act to define and amend the law relating to the sale of goods" which largely reproduces the Act of 1893 with necessary modifications. The courts in India have taken the position that the English cases may

---

[19]Bharuka (2007), p. 2. See also Furmston (2017), p. 188.

[20]See Guest (ed.) (2006), pp. 5–6.

[21]Ibid; Atiyah et al. (2010), pp. 3–4; Furmston (2000), pp. 1–2; Mark (1967), p. 1; *Wallis v Pratt & Haynes* [1911] AC 394 at p. 398.

[22][1891] AC 107.

[23]Id., at pp. 144–45.

[24]See Bridge (1997), p. 5; Furmston (2000), p. 2.

[25]Guest (ed.) (2006), p. 6. See also Atiyah et al. (2010), p. 4.

be useful in interpreting the Act despite its being a codifying legislation and have not hesitated in borrowing from the English decisions in interpreting the Act.[26]

As stated earlier, in contrast to the 1893 Act, SoGA 1979 is a consolidating legislation which is to be construed differently from a legislation which is expressly stated to be a codifying statute. Since a consolidating statute does not attempt to alter or amend the existing law, recourse to the previous case law is treated as legitimate in order to ascertain true meaning of a term.

5.2 Nature of "Contract of Sale"

5.2.1 General

A clear understanding of the term, "contract of sale" is critical for the study of the law of sale of goods as contained in both—SoGA 1930 and SoGA 1979. Both enactments commonly use the expression, "contract of sale" to denote two entirely different things—a "sale," where property in the goods is transferred from the seller to the buyer; and an "agreement to sell" whereby a seller merely agrees to transfer the property in goods at a future time. In the latter case, only a contractual relationship is created between the parties. The use of the term, "contract of sale" to refer both—a present sale as well as an agreement to sell—may be for the reason that under laws of England and India, a contract is understood to include both a mere contract which creates only a contractual relationship between the parties; and a contract which results in transfer of property. Since "sale" and "agreement to sell" denote different ideas and the rules which apply to them are also not the same, the use of the expression "contract of sale" which may sometimes refer to sale and sometimes agreement to sell is a source of confusion. As has been pointed out, "contract of sale" is originally a term of the Roman law and was used for the reason that under that law, the transfer of property in the goods could not take place by a mere contract.[27] But use of the same expression in the English and Indian law to denote both—a contract as well as a conveyance—seems somewhat strange and even "confusing".[28]

Here it also needs emphasis that the basic concepts of the laws of sales of both countries—India and England cannot be understood without the help of the general contract law. Some basic terms, such as property, owner used in the Act of 1930 and also in the 1979 Act have been left undefined. This gap in the law is to be filled by the concepts of the contract law.

---

[26]See *Consolidated Coffee Ltd v Coffee Board, Bangalore* AIR 1980 SC 1468, at p. 1490; *Ranjit Udeshi v State of Maharashtra* AIR 1965 SC 881. In interpreting Indian legislations, the courts in India have made 'sobered' use of the foreign decisions. See Patnaik (2016), pp. 386–87.

[27]McCurdy (1927), p. 17. In the Roman law, both terms, "contract of sale" or "contract to sell" used to denote the same thing. Ibid.

[28]Ibid.

5.2.2 *Contract of Sale as (Present) "Sale" and "Agreement to Sell"*

Section 4 of the Act of 1930 [which corresponds to S. 2 of the 1979 Act] defines the expression "contract of sale" as "...a contract whereby the seller transfers or agrees to transfer the property in goods to the buyer for a price." It further provides that "[w]here under a contract of sale the property in the goods is transferred from the seller to the buyer, the contract is called a sale, but where the transfer of the property in the goods is to take place at a future time or subject to some condition thereafter to be fulfilled, the contract is called an agreement to sell."

A few points need consideration. First, the Act of 1930, closely following the English statute, namely the Sale of Goods Act, 1893 (now replaced by SoGA 1979) uses the term, "contract of sale" to include both sale and agreement to sell as it states that a contract of sale is a contract whereby the seller "*transfers or agrees to transfer* the property in goods...." According to the definition, the term "contract of sale," thus, includes both present sale and agreement to sell.[29] While in the case of the former, also referred to as an executed contract,[30] property in the goods passes from the seller to the buyer, in the case of the latter, treated as an executory contract, the property in the goods does not pass. In other words, a contract of sale as defined by s. 4 operates both as a conveyance (or transfer) and as a contract.[31] But there is a good deal of difference between the two. Whereas a sale of goods is a conveyance or actual transfer which may involve the element of contract or not, agreement to sell is *mere* contract whereby the seller only *agrees to transfer* the property in goods. In the case of sale, property in the goods, that is to say, ownership passes from seller to buyer. But in the case of "agreement to sell," to use the terminology of the Act, property in the goods does not pass from the seller to buyer. In the latter case, it passes at "a future time or subject to some condition thereafter to be fulfilled." Further, since an agreement to sell is *merely* an agreement or contract it creates only personal rights that is to say, proprietary rights in *personam* or contractual rights as opposed to proprietary rights in *rem* and does not give rise to the right in respect of the subject-matter of the sale.[32] For example, if an agreement to sell is breached by a seller, the buyer can only claim damages and cannot sue in respect of the goods.

However, under the Acts of 1930 and 1979, though it seems somewhat strange because in some cases sale is purely a conveyance, a sale operates both as a conveyance and as a contract or to use the phrase used in Chalmers' Sale of Goods Act, 1893, "a contract plus conveyance."[33] S. 4 of the 1930 Act states, "[w]here under a contract of sale the property in the goods is transferred from the seller to the buyer, the contract is called a sale." The result is that a sale takes place under a

---

[29] *Ashington Piggeries Ltd v Christopher Hill Ltd* [1972] AC 441.

[30] See Mark (1967), p. 13.

[31] Ibid ("An agreement to sell...is a contract pure and simple; whereas a sale...is a contract plus a conveyance.").

[32] See Guest (ed.) (2006), p. 27.

[33] Sieghart (1963), p. 12.

contract in two ways.[34] First, where a contract itself operates as transfer of property from a seller to a buyer[35]; and secondly, when an agreement to sell is performed. The latter also operates as a transfer of property in the goods to the buyer.[36]

Secondly, a contract of sale of goods is described as a contract whereby the seller transfers "the property in goods" to the buyer. However, the term "the property in goods" is not defined. S. 2 (11) [corresponding to s. 61 (1) of the 1979 Act] simply says that "property" means the general property in goods, and not merely special property. In the absence of a complete definition of the term property in goods the only inference that can be drawn is that since sale is understood as a transfer of absolute or the best possible interest possessed by the transferor, the sale of goods means transfer of ownership or equivalent interest in the subject-matter of the transaction.

Finally, a contract of sale as defined by s. 4 of the Act, first of all, is a contract. In other words, contract of sale is a consensual or voluntary transaction under which one party agrees to sell and the other party agrees to buy. In other words, in a sale of goods transaction, one party promises to sell and other promises to buy "goods" for money consideration. Being an agreement, it has to satisfy the requirements of a valid contract. Hence the questions relating to the capacity of the parties, consideration, formation of the contract, and illegality unquestionably arise. Further, a contract of sale, like any other contract, can be avoided if it is vitiated by fraud, misrepresentation, mistake, or undue influence. It may further be noted, since a sale transaction is a transfer of property in goods from one party to another, it is a transaction between two different persons. A person cannot be both—the seller and the buyer, although one co-owner may sell to another. It may also be noted that a contract of sale dealt with under the Act applies to sale of goods and goods only, rather all kinds of goods. Thus, where the subject-matter of the transaction is not goods, the Act will obviously not govern the transaction. Definition of goods will be discussed below, suffices it to state here that the term "goods" embraces all kinds of moveable property except money and actionable claims with this difference between the indian and English law that shares are included under the Indian law. Finally, under a contract of sale, one party (seller) promises to sell and the other party (buyer) promises to buy goods for money consideration. It follows, then, if consideration is not in the form of money the contract in question will not be a contract of sale.

5.2.3 Agreement to Sell Is Mere a Contract

As stated above, a sale is both a contract and a conveyance while an agreement to sell is *mere* a contract. While a sale transaction results in the transfer of property in

[34]Ibid.

[35]SoGA 1930, s. 20 provides that in the case of "an unconditional contract for the sale of specific goods in a deliverable state, the property in the goods passes to the buyer when the contract is made...".

[36]Guest (ed.) (2006), p. 27.

the goods from seller to buyer, an agreement to sell has no such effect and gives rise only to personal remedy. S. 4 (3) of the 1930 Act provides that "where under the contract of sale the property in the goods is transferred from the seller to the buyer, the contract is called a sale, but where the transfer of the property in the goods is to take place at a future time or subject to some condition thereafter to be fulfilled, the contract is called an agreement to sell." And S. 4 (4) provides that an agreement to sell becomes sale when the time elapses or the conditions are fulfilled subject to which the property in the goods is to be transferred.

The distinction between "sale" and "agreement to sell" is important because in the case of the former the buyer acquires rights in respect of the goods and the seller has the right to sue for the price while in the case of the latter a party normally has only the right to sue for damages if the other party breaches his obligations under the contract. To put it another way, in the case of the former, the parties to a sale transaction has proprietary rights in *rem* while in the case of the latter, the parties to contract have only personal remedy. Further, in the case of agreement to sell, since the seller remains to be the owner it is he who has to bear the risks of loss or damage to the goods but once the agreement is executed, that is to say, if the sale is complete, it is the buyer who bears the risks of loss or damage to the goods. S. 26 of the Act provides: "Unless otherwise agreed, the goods remain at the seller's risk until the property therein is transferred to the buyer, but when the property therein is transferred to the buyer, the goods are at the buyer's risk whether delivery has been made or not."

5.3 Sale of Goods Distinguished from Other Related Transactions

5.3.1 General

A contract of sale of goods whereby the "seller transfers or agrees to transfer the (general) property in goods to the buyer for a price"[37] is distinguishable from other transactions relating to goods, such as exchange of goods, bailment, pledge, and hire purchase agreement; as well as transactions concerning services and work contract. Here a brief account of the distinction between a sale of goods transaction and other related transactions is provided highlighting the new developments and similarities in Indian and English law on the subject as a detailed discussion will be outside the scope of this book.

[37] SoGA 1930, s. 4.

5.3.2 Bailment and Pledge

A contract of carriage of goods is an example of a bailment contract and a carrier is subject to the duties of a bailee. A transaction of bailment, thus, deserves special mention in the present work which is devoted to the rules of the international trade transactions. In bailment, possession of goods is delivered by the bailor to the bailee for a limited purpose on the condition that the goods shall be redelivered to the bailor upon fulfillment of the purpose.[38] For example, where goods are deposited with a person for the purpose of safe custody or carriage, the transaction in question is treated as bailment. S. 148 of the Contract Act, 1872 defines a bailment in similar terms. It provides that a bailment contract is the "delivery of goods by one person to another for some purpose, upon a contract that they shall, when the purpose is accomplished, be returned or otherwise disposed of according to the directions of the person delivering them." In bailment, after the fulfillment of the purpose for which goods are delivered, the bailee is, thus, under obligation to redeliver the goods to the bailor or any other person at the bailor's direction.[39] Further, the goods may be hired, or lent, or given by way of security for a loan, and the transaction in question will be a bailment transaction. Where goods are delivered for hire, the bailment in question, as opposed to a sale of goods transaction, involves transfer of special property in the goods to the bailee.

Significantly, the relationship created by bailment is not always contractual. In other words, it is a transaction which is *sui generis*.[40] Since bailment is not always a result of contract, the consideration is not an essential element of it.[41] As Supreme Court of India emphasized in *State of Gujarat v Memon Mahomed HaziHasam*,[42] the bailment is governed by the Contract Act only to the extent it is based on a contract "but it is not correct to say that there cannot be a bailment without an enforceable contract."

Where possession of goods is delivered by way of security for payment of a debt, the transaction in question is a pledge. In other words, pledge is a bailment of goods

---

[38]See Furmston (2017), p. 118; Guest (ed.) (2006) p. 51; Bridge (1997), p. 51; Padia (2006), pp. 2028–30.

[39]See Guest (ed.) (2006), pp. 51–52; Bridge (1997), p. 51. Duties of the bailor and the bailee are dealt with in ss. 149–172 of the Contract Act. Bailee's duties include but are not limited to: duty to take reasonable care (ss. 151–52); not to act inconsistent with the conditions of the bailment (s. 153); not to make unauthorized use of the goods (s. 154); not to mix the bailor's goods with his own (ss. 155–57); to restore and return the goods (159–61); and to return profits to the bailor (s. 163). Bailor's duties include: duty to disclose faults in the goods bailed (s. 150); duty to repay necessary expenses (s. 158) and duty to make good the loss sustained by the bailee (s. 164). See further Padia (2006), ibid.

[40]See *State of Gujrat v Memon Mahomed HaziHasam* AIR 1967 SC 1885; *Trustees of the Port of Bombay v Premier automobiles Ltd.* AIR 1981 SC 1992; *Building and Civil Engineering Holidays Scheme Management Ltd. v Post Office* [1965] 1 All ER 163.

[41]See Furmston (2017), pp. 118–19 and the authorities cited therein including *Chesworth v Farran* [1966] 2 All ER 107; *Building and Civil Engineering Holidays Scheme Management Ltd. v Post Office* [1965] 1 All ER 163. See also Padia (2006), p. 2032.

[42]AIR 1967 SC 1885, at p. 1888; ibid.

by one party (the pledgor) to another (the pledgee) in order to secure a debt owed to the pledgee by the pledgor.[43] Ss. 172–76 of the Contract Act deal with pledge while in England it is generally governed by the Consumer Credit Act, 1974. But there is little difference between the law of two countries.[44]

It may further be stated that where the pledgor makes default in repaying the debt owed by him the pledgee will have the right to sell the goods after giving notice to the pledgor.[45] A pawnee's other rights include the right to retain the goods for payment of the debt or the performance of the promise[46] and the right to extraordinary expenses incurred for the preservation of the goods.[47]

5.3.3 *Mortgage*

A mortgage of goods is the transfer of property in "goods" from one party, called the mortgagor, to the other party, called the mortgagee, in order to secure a debt.[48] Thus, what distinguishes a mortgage from a sale is that while in the latter ownership in the goods is transferred from seller to buyer with the result that the seller ceases to have any interest in the goods sold, in a mortgage of the goods, the property in goods is transferred to secure a debt which is owed to the transferee (mortgagee) by the transferor (the mortgagor) and the mortgagor retains the right to redeem the mortgaged property. However, although in the mortgage of goods, general property in the goods passes, it does not pass absolutely.[49] Further, in determining whether a transaction amounts to a sale of goods transaction or a mortgage of goods, it is the substance of transaction and not the form which should be taken into consideration, for the Act of 1979 would not apply to a transaction if it appears to be sale transaction but is intended to operate as a mortgage.[50] In India, mortgage of immoveable property is dealt with by the Transfer of Property Act, 1882 but there is no statutory law on the mortgage of goods or moveable property.

A pledge resembles mortgage of goods but there are some important differences between the two. First, in a mortgage of goods, the mortgagor transfers general property, in contrast to special property, in the goods while in a pledge, the pledgor retains general property in the goods and transfers only special property in the goods. A second point of distinction is that the possession of the goods may not always be

[43] A pledge is defined by the Contract Act (s. 172) as "the bailment of goods as security for payment of a debt or performance of a promise." On pledge of goods see Padia (2006), pp. 2030–38.

[44] *Lallan Prasad v Rahmat* AIR 1967 SC 1322, at 1325.

[45] Contract Act, s. 176.

[46] Id, s. 173.

[47] Id, s. 175.

[48] On mortgage, see Guest (ed.) (2006), pp. 57–58; Guest (ed.) (1977), p. 4413.

[49] Guest (2006), ibid.

[50] See Act of 1979, s. 62 (4). See also Guest (2006), ibid.

with the mortgagor but in the case of pledge, a pledgor is bound to transfer possession of goods to the pledgee.[51]

5.3.4 *Exchange or Barter*

An exchange or barter of goods transaction has a close resemblance with a sale of goods transaction. In both cases, ownership in a thing or "goods" is transferred for some valuable consideration. Hence, a distinction between the two must carefully be drawn. There is one important difference between a sale and an exchange. As stated above (Chap. 1, Sect.1.3.1, in a sale transaction, consideration for transfer of property in goods must be in the form of money, that is to say, price. It is this feature of a sale which clearly distinguishes it from an exchange of goods. In a sale of goods, consideration is in the form of money which may be paid or promised, while in an exchange ownership of one thing is exchanged for another. In other words, where ownership of one thing or goods is exchanged for money, the transaction is a sale of goods but where one thing or goods is exchanged for another, the transaction is called "exchange."[52] For example, where a ten-rupee note is exchanged for coins or one book is exchanged or another the transaction will amount to an exchange.

In India, an exchange of things is governed by the provisions of the Transfer of Property Act, 1882.[53] Since the term, things, refers to both types of property, moveable and immoveable property, the provisions of the Transfer of Property Act apply to an exchange of goods as well as immoveable property such as land and things attached to the land. Section 118 which defines an exchange reads as follows:

> **118. Exchange defined**—When two persons mutually transfer the ownership of one thing for the ownership of another, neither thing or both things being money only, the transaction is called an exchange.
>
> A transfer of property in completion of an exchange can be made only in manner provided for the transfer of such property by sale.

A reading of the above said provision shows that an exchange is a *mutual* transfer of ownership of one thing for the ownership of another. Where both things that are exchanged are money only, for example where one currency note is exchanged for another or one type of coin is exchanged for another the transaction is an exchange; or where one thing (not being money) is exchanged for another thing the transaction is exchange, for example one piece of land is supplied in return for another piece of land or a car or some other valuable thing is exchanged for furniture.

However, difficulties arise in a case of a part exchange where the goods are exchanged or bartered in return for the goods and money. For example, where a

---

[51] On distinction between a pledge and mortgage of moveable property, see Padia (2006), p. 2043.

[52] See *Ram Kristo v Dhankisto* AIR 1969 204; *Commr. of Income Tax v Motor &General Stores (P) Ltd* AIR 1968 SC 200. See also Canton (1976), pp. 589–92; Bridge (1997), pp. 50–51; Atiyah et al. (2010), pp. 10–11; Guest (2006), pp. 33–35.

[53] See Ss. 118–121 of Transfer of Property Act, 1882.

buffalo, on the one hand, is exchanged for a cow as well as some money, on the other hand, the question arises whether the transaction in question is a sale or an exchange. So far as Indian law is concerned there is little doubt that the transaction will amount to an exchange in virtue of s. 118 of the Transfer of Property Act.[54]

Under English law the position is different. In deciding whether a contract of such a type is barter or a sale, "intention of the parties" is to be looked into by the courts. Where the parties to a contract treat it as a sale and "use a terminology more appropriate to sale, the contract would be held *such* (a sale of goods) even if the substantial consideration is supplied in goods rather than money."[55] The view has been expressed that since the price is central to the idea of a sale transaction unless there is evidence to buy the goods for an agreed price, the transaction in question will be treated as a barter and not as a sale transaction.[56] In the Irish case of *Flynn v Mackin and Mahon*[57] where a new car was to be bartered in return for an old car and some money, it was held that in the absence of any agreement as to the price, the transaction was a barter or exchange and not a sale.[58]

Since an exchange transaction is quite different from a sale of goods, the rules governing the latter will not directly apply to the former. The view has been expressed that in an exchange transaction an action for the price of the goods will not lie.[59] In India, the position is, however, different. S. 118 of the Transfer of Property Act, 1882 explicitly state that a transaction involving an exchange of goods or immoveable property is to be treated like a sale transaction and shall be made like the latter. Further, S. 120 of the Transfer of Property Act states that the rights and duties of the parties to an exchange shall exactly be the same as in the case of a sale. Thus, in an exchange, every party is both a seller and a buyer. A party will be treated a seller in respect of the things he is giving and a buyer in respect of the things he is receiving. Under Indian law, the distinction between a sale and exchange, thus, is of academic importance only.

Here, it also seems necessary to say a few words on counter trade arrangements. A counter trade is an important trade transaction in international trade in which goods are counter traded between two countries. The essential feature of a counter trade is that it is a method by which two export sales are linked—one which originates from the exporter's country and the other which originates from that of the importer.[60] Although it may take place in various ways, but it commonly occurs in the form of a barter or counter (or reciprocal) sale arrangements between two countries. In the

[54]See Nair and Paul (2015), p. 982. See also *Ismail Shah v Saleh Muhammad* AIR 1925 Lahore 326; *Ram Badanlal v Kunwar Singh* AIR 1938 All 229.

[55]Atiyah et al. (2010), p. 10. See also Furmston (2000), pp. 10–11.

[56]Canton (1976), p. 591.

[57][1974] IR 101.

[58]Canton (1976), p. 589. A similar view was expressed in *Aldridge v Johnson*, (1875) 7 E&B 885, *Dawson (Clapham) Ltd. V Dutfield,* [1936] 2 All ER 232; *Chappell & Co. Ltd. v Nestle Co. Ltd.* [1960] AC 87: cited in Canton, ibid.

[59]Guest (ed.) (2006), pp. 33; Bridge (1997), p. 51.

[60]D'Arcy et al. (2000), p. 11; Chuah (2009), p. 21.

latter case, a seller enters into a separate contract with the importer-buyer and agrees to purchases some specific goods of the country of import, in lieu of the price of the goods supplied by him. Thus, there are two distinct contracts of sale—export sale contract and reciprocal sale contract. In contrast, in a barter trade, there is only single agreement. Here, the kind of transaction involved may be described as the counter trade or reciprocal sale.[61]

5.3.5 Contract for Supply of Services

A distinction needs to be drawn between a contract of service and a contract of sale of goods for the main reason that the rules governing the latter, in general, are not applicable to the former.[62] The Acts of 1930 and 1979 generally exclude supply of services. Further, the implied duties of a seller of goods and a supplier of services are different. Under the Supply of Goods and Services Act 1982, a supplier of services is subject only to duties of due or reasonable care and skill while a seller's duties are generally strict.[63]

As has already been noted in Chap. 1, services, unlike goods, defy a clear definition. Services are made up of a different types of economic activities that are intangibles; cannot be counted and in many cases cannot be stored.[64] Activities included in services are as diverse as the carriage of goods, insurance, banking, telecommunications, engineering, tourism, management and consulting, architecture, medical treatment, and construction.[65] On the basis of a number of distinctive characteristics services exhibit, they are clearly distinguishable from goods and in some cases, for example, the deposit and carriage of goods, it is clear enough that the contract in question is a contract of service. But in many cases, it is not easy to draw a distinction between a contract of sale and a contract of service for contracts of sale, very often, involve the element of service also.

In distinguishing between a contract of service and a contract of sale of goods, the courts in India and England have adopted the "substance of the contract" test. They have consistently taken the view that it is only where a contract is predominantly a

---

[61]See UNCITRAL *Legal Guide on International Countertrade Transactions* (New York: United Nations, 1993), A/CN.9/SER.B/3.

[62]There are also other reasons for making such a distinction. See Atiyah et al. (2010), p. 22.

[63]Act of 1982, ss. 12–16. Part (a) of the Act governs those contracts which transfer goods but not the ownership in goods, such as a bailment contract. In these cases, implied terms about quality or fitness similar to those of the 1979 Act apply. Provisions of Part (b) govern contracts for supply of services and require that services are carried out with reasonable skill and care (s. 13); and in a reasonable time (s. 14). See also Atiyah et al. (2010), id, p. 23; Guest (2006), p. 29. Before the Supply of Goods and Services Act, 1982, the supplier of services, under the existing common law regime, was also strictly liable as regards goods and liable for lack of due care as regards services. But there were many exceptions to this rule. See Atiyah et al. (2010) ibid.

[64]Footer (1994), pp. 661–63.

[65]Ibid; Grunfeld (1961), p. 68.

contract for supply of skill and labor (or work), it will be termed as a contract for service. In other words, where the preponderant part of the transaction consists of the obligations to supply services the transaction in question will be the contract for the supply of services. But, where transfer of "goods" element is predominant and the goods supplied are not merely collateral or incidental for the purpose of a particular contract, the contract in question will be a contract of sale.[66] In *Robinson v Graves*,[67] Greer LJ in laying down the "substance of the contract" test observed:

> [Where]…skill and labour have to be exercised for the production of the article and…it is only ancillary to that that there will pass from the artist to his client or customer some materials in addition to the skill involved in the production of the portrait, that does not make any difference to the result, because the substance of the contract is the skill and experience of the artist in producing the picture.[68]

In *Robinson v Graves*, it was found that the contract to paint a portrait was one for skill and labor and not the contract for the sale of goods. It was so because "the substance of the contract" was the skill and experience of the artist.

A similar approach has been adopted by the courts in India.[69] For example, in *State of Andhra Pradesh v Kone Elevators (India) Ltd*,[70] the Supreme Court relying on the substance of the contract test held that in determining the nature of the transaction what is important is the substance and not the form of the contract. It was found that since the skill and labor employed for converting the main components into the end product were only incidentally used and, therefore, the delivery of the end product by the assessee to the customer amounted to a sale and not a works contract. The following observations of the Court, which also apply to a contract for skill and labor, are instructive:

> If the intention is to transfer for a price a chattel in which the transferee had no previous property, then the contract is contract for sal… In a "contract of sale," the main object is the transfer of property and delivery of possession of the property, whereas the main object in a contract for work is not the transfer of the property but it is one for work and labour… Therefore, in judging whether the contract is for a sale or for work and labour, the essence of the contract or the reality of the transaction as a whole has to be taken into consideration. The pre-dominant object of the contract, the circumstances of the case and the custom of the trade provides a guide in deciding whether transaction is a "sale" or a "works contract."[71]

Considerable difficulty, however, arises in classifying a contract under which services are to be provided as contained onto some physical medium, for example, a contract for the supply of computer software incorporated onto hardware or a film. Such a contract, in general, is treated as a contract for the supply of goods or "tangible

---

[66]See *Cammell Laird & Co. v Manganese Bronze & Brass Co.* [1934] AC 402.

[67][1935] 1 KB 579.

[68]Id., p. 587.

[69]See *State of Rajasthan v Man industrial Corporation Ltd* AIR 1969 SC 1245; *Vanguard Rolling Shulter & Steel Works v Commr of Sales Tax* AIR 1977 SC 1505.

[70](2005) 3 SCC 389.

[71]See also *Hindustan Aeronautics Ltd v State of Karnataka* AIR 1984 SC 744.

service" and not a contract for the provision of services.[72] In *St. Albans City & District Council v International Computer Ltd*,[73] Sir Iain Glidewell considered the issue at some length and observed, obiter, that although a program, of itself, is not a good, a disk carrying the program was clearly a good and where "the disk is sold or hired... but the programme is defective ... there would prima facie be a breach of the term as to quality and fitness for purpose implied by the 1979 Act or the 1982 Act."[74]

St. Albans concerns the claim for damages due to an error in the software supplied by the defendant company. Under the contract entered into by the plaintiff with the defendant company, the plaintiff was licensed to use the programme while the property in the programme, that is, intangible instructions remained with the defendant company. Although the issue whether software is goods or not has not squarely arisen, Sir Glidewell went on to consider the question whether a contract for the transfer into a computer of a programme, in the absence of any express term as to quality or fitness for purpose, is subject to an implied term that the programme will be reasonably fit for the purpose. He made a distinction between a case where the programme is transferred directly by a licensor to a user's a computer without making use of a disk or any tangible thing and a case where the programme is transferred as contained onto a disk and concluded that while in the former case there is no transfer of goods, the latter case involved the supply of goods.

Sir Glidewell's approach in treating a contract for supplying software contained onto a physical medium as a contract for the supply of goods is not without difficulty.[75] It ignores the point that the dominant purpose of a contract, under which goods are supplied *simply* as a means by which services or intangible things are used, is to make use of services and not the tangible things. As Bridge observes that contrary to the worlds of cars and video recorders where intangible things are supplied for the better use of tangible things, in the world of computers tangible things are supplied for the purpose of making use of intangible things and the tangible things accompanying services are simply the "integument" for covering the programme.[76] "It is not a case of the disk being unusable without a program: the disk is merely the integument of the program," he adds. Bridge, thus, concludes that supply of software should appropriately be treated as the provision of service, "even if it comes with a disk."[77]

---

[72]Footer (1994), pp. 661–62; *Advent Systems Ltd. v Unisys Corp.* (1991) 925 F2d 670 (software is a "good"); *Toby Constructions Products Pvt. Ltd. v Computer Bar (Sales) Pty Ltd.* [1993] 2 NSWLR 48 ("...the sale of a whole computer system, including both hardware and software, was a sale of goods with the new South Wales legislation..." For the purposes of the levy of sales tax, the sale of a software programme on a CD/floppy disc, is held to be the "goods" by the Supreme Court of India (*Tata Consultancy Services v. State of AP* (2005) 1 SCC 308).

[73][1996] 4 All ER 481 (Court of Appeal).

[74]Id., p. 493.

[75]For a criticism of the approach of Sir Glidewell, see Bridge (1997), pp. v–vi.

[76]Id., p. vi.

[77]Ibid.

5.3.6 Work and Materials Contract

Since the statutes on the sale of goods transactions do not apply to a work and materials contract a distinction should also be drawn between a sale of goods contract and a contract of work and materials.[78] It may be noted that the latter was traditionally treated as a sub-group of the contract for the provision of services.[79] However, in England and Wales and Northern Ireland, the Sale and Supply of Goods Act 1982 in respect of a contract for "the transfer of goods" now provides for implied duties as to quality and fitness for purpose akin to those to be found under the Act of 1979. This has led the distinction between two classes of contracts "irrelevant"[80] or to borrow the words used in *Benjamin's Sale of Goods* as "much less important."[81] Also, in recent years a tendency has grown to apply the sale of goods law to cases where a contract has elements of both—goods and services. But the distinction between the two classes of contracts to some extent is still important.[82]

A work and materials contract is a contract for the supply of services as well as the goods which are most usually the case where goods supplied are to be fitted in a construction.[83] Examples include shipbuilding contracts[84]; and contracts for installation of kitchen appliances.[85] In that way, a contract of work and materials is a separate species of contract which is distinct from a contract for services and goods

[78]Before the Supply of Goods and Services Act, 1982, the common law principles identical or similar to those to be found in SoGA 1979 in respect of a seller's implied duties were applied to work and materials contract, barter and hire-purchase agreements.

[79]Atiyah et al. (2010), p. 21.

[80]A contract for "the transfer of goods" is defined by the 1982 Act as "a contract under which one person transfers or agrees to transfer to another the property in goods, other than an excepted contract." It is intended to cover those transactions which result in the transfer of *goods* (but not the ownership in goods) from one person to another. See Act of 1982, s. 1. It includes a variety of contracts such as a contract for the sale of goods; a hire-purchase agreement, and contracts intended to operate by way of mortgage, pledge, charge, or other security. Ibid. It is also explained by s.1 of the 1982 Act that a contract for the transfer of goods shall remain so "whether or not services are also provided or to be provided under the contract..." See *Samuels v Davis* [1943] 2 All ER 3; *Young& Marten Ltd. v McManus Childs Ltd.* [1969] 1 AC 454. See also Atiyah et al. (2010), p. 23.

[81]Guest (ed.) (2006), p. 37.

[82]Bridge (1997), p. 347. For a discussion of different reasons why it is still important to make a distinction between a contract of sale of goods and a contract of service, see Atiyah, id, pp. 21–22; Guest, ibid; Bridge, p. 46. Since under the Supply of Goods and Services Act, 1982 implied terms as to quality and fitness are similar to those implied under the Act of 1979 in respect of a contract of sale of goods the difference between the contract of sale and a contact of work and materials has now become less important.

[83]Atiyah et al. (2010), p. 21; Bridge (1997), p. 347.

[84]*StoczinaGdanska SA v Latvian Shipping Co.* [1996] 2 Lloyd's Reports, p. 132.

[85]*Jones v Gallagher* [2005] 1 Lloyd's Reports, p. 377.

as well[86] and has to be treated separately.[87] In other words, a work and materials contract is distinguishable from the contracts of services since in the former, goods supplied are integral and not merely collateral to the purpose of the contract.[88] In that way, a work and materials contract is a composite and indivisible contract but at the same time is divisible into one for sale of goods and other for supply of labor and services.[89] The part of the transaction related to the goods is to be governed by the sale of goods law and the remainder by a different law.[90] In India, support for this position is to be found in some important decisions of the Supreme Court, whereas in England, the case law on the point has not sufficiently grown.[91]

However, in India, the initial approach was to treat the works contract as "inseparable and indivisible." In an old case, the *State of Madras v. Gannon Dunkerley & Co. (Madras) Ltd*,[92] decided in 1958, it was held by the Supreme Court that a building contract was not a contract of sale of goods for it was one and a composite contract which is inseparable and indivisible, and which consists of several elements which include not only a transfer of property in goods but labor and service elements as well. However, on the recommendation of the Law Commission of India, which in its 61st Report had recommended to amend Article 366 of the Constitution of India so as to widen the scope of the definition of "sale or purchase of goods" to include within its ambit a "works contract," the Constitution (46th Amendment) Act was passed in 1983. The 46th Amendment inserted a new sub-clause (29A) to Article 366[93] which provided for levying of tax on the sale or purchase of goods involved in the execution of works contract.[94] Thus a legal fiction was introduced by the 46th Amendment whereby the works contract can be altered into a contract which is divisible into one for sale of goods and other for supply of labor and services.[95] Thus the goods element involved in the execution of the works contract came to be taxed by the State Legislatures. Later, the Finance Act, 1994 introduced a new category service tax to be levied on the labor and service element of such contracts. The result was that the works contracts could be taxed by the Parliament as well

[86] Bridge, however, thinks that the distinction between a contract of work and materials and a contract of sale of goods is a matter of degree only for labor is inherent in the manufacture of goods. Bridge (1997), p. 46.

[87] *State of Madras v Gannon Dunkerley & Co. (Madras) Ltd* (the first *Gannon Dunkerley* case) 1959 SCR 379.

[88] Bridge (1997), p. 46.

[89] See *State of Madras v Gannon Dunkerley & Co. (Madras) Ltd* (1993) 1 SCC 364 (the second *Gannon Dunkerley* case); *Commissioner, Central Excise and Customs, Kerala and others v Larsen and Toubro Limited and others* AIR 2015 SC 3600.

[90] See also Bridge (1997), p. 47 and pp. 347–48.

[91] Ibid.

[92] 1959 SCR 379.

[93] The Constitution (Forty-sixth Amendment) Act, 1982, S. 4.

[94] The Constitution of India, Article 366 (29-A) provides that "tax on the sale or purchase of goods," inter alia, includes "a tax on the transfer of property in goods (whether as goods or in some other form) involved in the execution of a works contract.".

[95] *Second Gannon Dunkerley case*, (1993) 1 SCC 364.

as the State Legislatures. The Parliament could only tax service element contained in such contracts and states could only tax the "goods" element. And in a further development, the 2007 amendment introduced a new category, "works contract" as being a separate and distinct subject matter of taxation and expressly made works contracts liable to service tax.[96]

5.3.7 *Hire-Purchase Agreement*

In India, a hire-purchase agreement is governed by the Hire-Purchase Act, 1972 (Act No. 26 of 1972) and in England it is now governed by the Hire-Purchase Act, 1964, the Supply of Goods (Implied Terms) Act, 1973, and the Consumer Credits Act, 1974.[97] It is essentially a bailment of the goods together with an option to purchase them and is not a contract of sale of goods.[98] If the option to purchase is exercised, the hire-purchase agreement converts into a sale of goods. But until the option is exercised, the hirer is not the owner of the goods. What distinguishes it from a sale of the goods is the fact that a bailee of the goods with an option to purchase (but not under any obligation to purchase) is certainly not a purchaser, that is, a person who agreed to buy goods.[99] In *Helby v Mathews*,[100] the plaintiff, a dealer agreed to hire a piano to A at monthly rent. If A continued to pay the monthly rent for 36 months the ownership would pass to A. But A was entitled to terminate the agreement whenever he pleased. After paying four installments A pledged the piano to the defendant. It was held by the House of Lords that since A was not under any obligation to buy the piano but had only an option to purchase, the transaction in question was a hire-purchase agreement and no title passed to the defendant. Under a hire-purchase agreement the hirer or the bailee agrees to hire the goods for a period and has the option to buy the goods at the end of the period. The bailee does not become the owner of goods until all the payments are made.

The real problem in making a distinction between a sale and hire-purchase arises in cases where buyer takes the possession of the goods under a contract of sale and agrees to make the payment in installments. Though this transaction has a close resemblance with a hire-purchase contract, it is a pure contract of sale which is normally termed as a credit sale and should not be confused with a hire-purchase

---

[96] *Commissioner, Central Excise and Customs, Kerala and others v Larsen and Toubro Limited and others (Larsen and Toubro Case)*, AIR 2015 SC 3600. In *Larsen and Toubro*, the Supreme Court while dealing with the issue whether service tax can be levied on indivisible works contracts prior to the introduction of the Finance Act, 2007 which expressly makes such contracts liable to service tax has emphasized that the two components of the works contract should be completely segregated "for if some element of transfer of property in goods remains when a service tax is levied, the said levy would be found to be constitutionally infirm.".

[97] See Guest (ed.) (2006), p. 20.

[98] Atiyah et al. (2010), p. 13; Guest (2006) ibid.

[99] See *Helby v Matthews* [1895] AC 471.

[100] Ibid.

agreement. In a credit-sale agreement, the property passes to the buyer at once who can pass a good title in favor of a third party, although full payment is not made. But where the passing of property is made conditional on payment of the installments, the transaction is a hire-purchase contract and not a sale of the goods.

5.4 Subject-Matter of Contract of Sale

5.4.1 Meaning of Goods

Since quite different principles of law govern the sale of immoveable and moveable property, a discussion of the meaning of the "goods" under the Acts of 1930 and 1979 is crucial.[101] Both the Acts define the term, "goods" by reference to moveable property and exclude things in action and money from the definition of goods. Since sale is a transaction in which goods are exchanged or agreed to be exchanged for money the reason for excluding money is obvious. The reason for excluding things in action or actionable claims from the scope of the two Acts is that the assignment or transfer of actionable claims is governed by the separate rules of law.[102] The transfer of actionable claims is required to be evidenced by writing but there is no such requirement in the case of a sale of goods. Under the Acts of 1930 and 1979, a sale of goods may be in writing or may take place orally, that is to say, informally.

S. 2 (7) of the 1930 Act which defines the term, "goods," provides:

> Goods means every kind of moveable property other than actionable claims and money; and includes stock and shares, growing crops, grass, and things attached to or forming part of the land which are agreed to be severed before sale or under the contract of sale.

S. 61 (1) of the Act of 1979 defines goods in a similar manner:

> Goods includes all personal chattels other than things in action and money, and in Scotland all corporeal moveables except money; and in particular "emblements, industrial growing crops, and things attached to or forming part of the land which are agreed to be severed before sale or under the contract of sale.

Both statutes, that is, Act of 1979 and the Act of 1930 have adopted a definition of goods which is similar in many respects. They expressly exclude actionable claims[103] with this difference that under the Indian law stock and shares would be goods while under the English law shares are generally not considered as included in the definition

---

[101]Under both—Indian and English law—a transfer of immoveable property or an interest therein generally requires certain legal formalities. See Law of Property (Miscellaneous Provisions) Act, 1989, s. 2 and Transfer of Property Act, s. 9 which require that such a transfer must fulfill certain formal requirements. Apart from this, in many other important respects the rules governing transfer of land and goods differ considerably, for example, the rules affecting the interests of third party.

[102]In India, transfer of actionable claims is governed by the Transfer of Property Act, 1982 (Ss. 120–137).

[103]On the definition of actionable claims, see s. 3 of the Transfer of Property Act, 1882.

of goods.[104] A further similarity between the Indian and English law is that under both laws, personal chattels, as opposed to chattels attached to land, are goods. Also, under both enactments, "growing crops, grass, and things attached to or forming part of the land which are agreed to be severed before sale or under the contract of sale" are covered while "fixtures" are excluded. The effect of the use of the phrase, "industrial growing crops grass, and things attached to or forming part of the land which are agreed to be severed before sale or under the contract of sale," is intended to do away certain distinctions drawn in the nineteenth century case law between *fructus naturals* (such as grass and timber regarded at common law as things attached to land) and *fructus industrials* (things considered independent of land and grown by the labor of the year such as growing crops or fruits).[105]

Difficulties in interpreting the term, goods, however, continue to arise because, as Bridge points out, the definition of "goods" under the both Acts is not based on a carefully drawn distinction between the goods and land or between goods and the immoveable property but is based on the decisions of the courts which are often inconsistent.[106] Contrary to the Act of 1930, the definition of goods in the 1979 Act is not intended to be exhaustive and in the absence of an exhaustive definition of land the problem of overlap between the meanings of land and goods is bound to arise. The Law of Property (Miscellaneous Provisions) Act, 1989 does not contain any definition of land, and the definition of land contained in the Law of Property Act of 1925 is unhelpful as not being capable of making a clear demarcation between land and goods.[107] Under Indian law also, there does not exist any clear and exhaustive statutory definition of immoveable property or land. However, in India, the cumulative effect of the Transfer of Property Act, the General Clauses Act, and the case law based on these statutes is to establish the meaning of land with sufficient clarity and precision.

The issue whether computer software falls within the definition of "goods" has given rise to a good deal of controversy. As already noted, in *St. Albans City and District Council v International Computers Ltd*,[108] in the Court of Appeal, Sir Iain Glidewell, took the view that the disk carrying a software program fell within the definition of goods, but the program, of itself, was not. According to him, if a program was directly transferred by the licensor to the user's system without making use of any tangible thing, it would fall outside the Act of 1979 as well as the Supply of Goods and Services Act, 1982 attracting only fault-based liability under the common law.

In altogether different regulatory context, the Supreme Court of India in *Tata Consultancy Services v State of AP*[109] clearly took the view that the sale of a software

---

[104]Bridge (1997), p. 29.

[105]Guest (ed.) (2006), p. 82; Bridge (1997), p. 24; *English Hop Growers Ltd v Dering* [1928] 1 KB 174, 178–79. On the case law characterizing things either as land or chattels, see Bridge, id., pp. 23–24; Guest (2006), id., pp. 80–81.

[106]See Bridge, ibid.

[107]Id., p. 80.

[108][1996] 4 All ER 481 (Court of Appeal).

[109](2005) 1 SCC 308. See also: *Commr of Sales Tax v MP Electricity Board* (1969) 1 SCC 200.

program contained on a disk was a sale of goods transaction and "as such was assessable to sales tax." The case concerned the issue of the levy of sales tax on the sale of computer software and it is for that purpose, the Court was to interpret the term "goods" as used in Article 266 of the Constitution of India. It was held that "in India, the test to determine whether a property is "goods", for the purposes of sales tax, is not whether the property is tangible or intangible or incorporeal. Rather, the test is whether the item concerned is capable of abstraction, consumption and use and whether it can be transmitted, transferred, delivered, stored, possessed, etc. Admittedly, in the case of software, both canned and uncanned, all of these are possible."[110] While referring to its earlier decisions, such as *Associated Cement Companies Ltd v Commr of Customs*[111] *State of AP v National Thermal Power Corpn. Ltd*[112]; and *CCE v. Acer India Ltd*[113]; the Supreme Court went on to observe:

In our view, the term goods, as used in Article 366 (12) of the Constitution and as defined under the said Act [the Andhra Pradesh General Sales Act, 1957] is very wide and includes all types of moveable properties, whether those properties be tangible or intangible.... The copyright in that program may remain with the originator of the program. But the moment, copies are made and marketed, it becomes goods, which are susceptible to sales tax. Even intellectual property, once it is put on to a media, whether it be in the form of books, or canvas (in case of painting) or computer discs or cassettes, and marketed would become "goods." We see no difference between a sale of a software program on a CD/Floppy disc from a sale of music on a cassette/CD or a sale of a film on a video cassette/CD.[114]

5.4.2 Existing or Future Goods

A clear understanding of the different types of goods is important because passing of property in the goods, that is to say, transfer of general property in goods, depends on the kind of goods involved and the intention of the parties.[115] The Acts of 1930 and 1979 recognize various subdivisions of goods. There may be existing or future goods. Further, goods can also be subdivided into specific goods, ascertained, or unascertained goods. Here mention may be made of s. 6 of the 1930 Act which provides that the subject-matter of sale may be existing or future goods. It reads as follows:

---

[110](2005) 1 SCC 308, at p. 323.

[111](2001) 4 SCC 593.

[112](2002) 5 SCC 203.

[113](2004) 8 SCC 173.

[114]Id., p. 329.

[115]S. 19 (1) of SoGA 1930 provides that "where there is a contract for the sale of specific or ascertained goods the property in them is transferred to the buyer at the such time as the parties to the contract intend to be transferred.".

(1) The goods which form the subject of a contract of sale may be either existing goods, owned or possessed by the seller, or future goods.
(2) There may be a contract for the sale of goods the acquisition of which by the seller depends upon a contingency which may or may not happen.
(3) Where by a contract of sale the seller purports to effect a present sale of future goods, the contract operates as an agreement to sell the goods.

Under the scheme of the two Acts, all goods are either existing or future goods.[116] Since no property can pass in future goods classifying goods as either existing or future goods seems necessary. Further, existing goods are goods which are already in the ownership or possession of the seller while future goods are goods which are not yet in existence or not yet acquired by the seller. "There may be a contract for the sale of goods *the acquisition of which by the seller depends upon a contingency which may or may not happen.*" S. 2 (6) defines future goods as "good to be manufactured or produced or acquired by the seller after the making of the contract of sale." It may also be pointed out that although property cannot pass in future goods an agreement in regard to future goods is perfectly valid for s. 6 (3) of the 1930 Act [s. 5(3) of the 1979 Act] provides that where the seller purports to effect a present sale of future goods, the contract is an agreement to sell.

5.4.3 Specific, Unascertained, and Ascertained Goods

A further division of goods into specific and unascertained goods is made under both the Acts—SoGA 1930 and SoGA 1979.[117] "Specific goods" are goods identified and agreed on at the time a contract of sale is made.[118] In other words, they are capable of being identified at the time when a contract of sale is made. The definition of "specific goods" under the 1979 Act is now amended to include "an undivided share, specified as a fraction or percentage, of goods identified and agreed on as aforesaid."[119] It may also be noted that according to s. 20 of the 1930 Act, "where there is an unconditional contract for the sale of specific goods in a deliverable state, the property in the goods passes to the buyer when the contract is made." Further, at the time of contract goods are either specific or unascertained.[120] Unascertained goods can be later ascertained but they, as noted above, cannot become specific goods since specific goods are those goods which are capable of being identified at the time of contact of sale.[121]

[116]See Bridge (1997), p. 39.

[117]Id, p. 41.

[118]Act, 1930, s. 6 (14) [Act of 1979, s. 61 (1); *Kursell v Timber Operators and Contractors Ltd* [1927] 1 KB 298.

[119]Sale of Goods (Amendment) Act, 1995, s. 2 (d). See also Bridge (1997) p. 42; Guest (2006) p. 82.

[120]Schnitzer (2006), p. 8; Bridge, id, p. 42.

[121]Schnitzer, ibid.

The expressions, "ascertained goods" or "unascertained goods" remained undefined by the Act of 1930 and the Act of 1979. But it may be stated that certain quantities of sugar or grain which are not seperated fom the bulk are the examples of unascertained goods. Thus, generic goods, such as 100 tons of sugar and future goods are unascertained goods.[122] But when identified or sufficiently appropriated, unascertained goods can become ascertained, although, as stated above, they cannot become specific.[123] In fact, the absence of the definition of the term "ascertained goods" in the statute book is a glaring omission as under the old (English) law drawing a distinction between ascertained and unascertained goods was important. According to the original version of s. 16 of the 1979 Act, property in the unascertained goods could not pass until they had been ascertained.[124] *Kursell v Timber Operators and Contractors Ltd*[125] is illustrative of the problem. In *Kursell*, a contract was concluded for the sale of all the timber in a forest which conformed to certain specified measurements and a delivery date was also fixed. But soon after the contract of sale was concluded the seller's rights in the forest were revoked. This led to a dispute between the parties about the passing of property in the goods in question. The Court held that since the goods in question, that is, trees were neither identified nor agreed at the time of contract no property in them could pass from the seller to the buyer.

The rule that no property in unascertained goods could pass from the seller to the buyer unless goods had been ascertained proved troublesome in modern conditions which led to the insertion of s. 20 A to the 1979 Act by the Amendment Act of 1995 referred to the above.[126] As a result, now property in an undivided share of a bulk can pass even before ascertainment as soon as the buyer has paid the price. The following part of s. 20 A is relevant to quote here:

20 A (1) This section applies to a contract for the sale of a specified quantity of unascertained goods if the following conditions are met—

(a) The goods or some of them form part of a bulk which is identified either in the contract or by subsequent agreement between the parties; and
(b) The buyer has paid the price for some or all of the goods which are the subject of the contract and which form part of the bulk.

(2) Where this section applies then (unless the parties agree otherwise), as soon as the conditions specified in paragraphs (a) and (b) of subsection above are met or at such later time as the parties may agree—

(a) property in an undivided share in the bulk is transferred to the buyer, and

---

[122]Guest (ed.) (2006), p. 97.

[123]Per Atkin LJ in *Re Wait* 1 Ch 606, at 630 (ascertained goods mean goods identified in accordance with the agreement after the time a contract of sale is made).

[124]1979 Act, s. 16 [corresponding to s. 18 of the 1930 Act] in its original form provided that in the case of the contract of sale of unascertained goods, no property in the goods passes unless and until the goods are ascertained. For further discussion on the rules relating to passing of property in goods, see Chap. 7.

[125][1927] 1 KB 298.

[126]See Atiyah et al. (2010), p. 332.

(b) the buyer becomes owner in common of the bulk.

Thus, unless the parties otherwise agree, property in a specified quantity of unascertained goods forming part of an identified bulk passes if the buyer has paid the price for some or all of the goods (see further Chap. 6, Sect. 6.2.2).

References

Atiyah, P. S., Adams, J. N., & Macqueen, H. (eds.) (2010). *Atiyah's sale of goods*. New Delhi: Dorling Kindersley.

Bharuka, G. C. (ed.) (2007). *Pollock & mulla: The sale of goods act*. New Delhi: LexisNexis.

Bridge, M. (1997). *The sale of goods*. Oxford: Oxford University Press.

Canton, E. M. C., & Clare, F. M. (1976). Sale of goods and barter. *Modern Law Review, 39*, 589–592.

Chuah, J. C. T. (2009). *Law of international trade: Cross-Border commercial transactions*. Sweet & Maxwell, (2009), South Asian Edition, 2011, p. 21.

De Cruz, P. (2007). *Comparative law in a changing world London*. New York: Routledge-Cavendish.

D'Arcy, (2000). *Schmitthoff's export trade: The law and practice of international trade*. London: Stevens.

Footer, M. E. (1994). Global and regional approaches to the regulation of trade in services. *International and Comparative Law Quarterly 43*, 61–678.

Furmston, M. P. (Ed.). (2017). *Chesire, Fifoot & Furmston's law of contract*. Oxford: Oxford University Press.

Furmston, M. (2000). *Sale & supply of goods*. London, Sydney: Cavendish Publishing Ltd.

Grunfeld, C. (1961). Reform in the law of contract. *Modern Law Review, 24*, 68.

Guest, A. G. (Ed.). (1977). *Chitty on contracts* (Vol. 2). London: Sweat & Maxwell.

Guest, A. G. (Ed.). (2006). *Benjamin's sale of goods*. London: Sweet & Maxwell.

Mark, M. (ed.). (1967). *Chalmers" Sale of Goods Act*. 1893 Including the Factors Acts 1889 &1890 London: Butterworths.

McCurdy, W. E. (1927). Some differences between the English and the American law of sale of goods. *Journal of Comparative Legislation and International Law, 9*, 15–39.

Nair, H., & Paul, B. (Eds.). (2015). *Mulla The Transfer of Property Act* (12th ed.). New Delhi: LexisNexis.

Padia, R. G. (Ed.). (2006). *Mulla Indian contract and specific relief acts* (13th ed., Vol. 2). New Delhi: LexisNexis Butterworths.

Patnaik, A. K. (Ed.). (2016). *Principles of statutory interpretation by GP Singh*. LexisNexis: New Delhi.

Poole, J. (2006). *Textbook on contract law*. Oxford, New York: Oxford University Press.

Schnitzer, S. (2006). *Understanding international trade law*. Law Matters Publishing.

Sieghart, P.(ed.) (1963). *Chalmers" sale of goods act, 1893*. London: Butterworths.

UNCITRAL (1993). *Legal guide on international countertrade transactions*. A/CN.9/SER.B/3. New York: United Nations.

Reports and Online Resource

Eighth Report of the Law Commission of India, available at: http://lawcommissionofindia.nic.in.

Chapter 6
International Sale in Indian and English Law II: Rights and Duties, Passing of Risks and Remedies

6.1 Rights and Duties of Seller and Buyer

6.1.1 Nature of Contract Terms

The rights and duties of the parties usually depend on the "terms" incorporated into their contract.[1] Therefore, for a full grasp of the subject-matter under discussion, it is necessary to begin with a note on the true nature of the contractual terms. Notably, neither the Sale of Goods Act, 1930 (SoGA 1930) nor the (English) Sale of Goods Act, 1979 (SoGA 1979) define a "term" as such. Rather they define, "condition" and "warranty" which are different categories of a term. *Black's Law Dictionary* defines a "term" as "a contractual stipulation" as distinguished from a "misrepresentation" which is an untrue statement made at the time of the contract. The latter becomes a term only if it is incorporated into the contract.[2] A similar definition is to be found in the *New International Webster's Dictionary* which reads as follows: "the condition or stipulation according to which something is to be done."[3] While these dictionary definitions make the underlying idea of the terms sufficiently clear, it is still needed to examine the issue in some detail and for that purpose it may be helpful to consider first different kinds of the pre-contractual statements.

It is worth appreciating here that not all statements or promises made in the course of negotiations leading to a contract do become the terms of a contract. As we have already noted, vague or extravagant statements made by a party to a contract, called mere puffs or opinions, are not generally regarded actionable (see Chap. 4,

[1]For a discussion on the contract terms, see Beatson et al. (2010), pp. 133–39; Furmston (2017), pp. 177–213; McKendrick (2000), pp. 175–219; Atiyah et al. (2010), pp. 86–87; Poole (2004), pp. 180–89.

[2]Garner (ed.), *Black's Law Dictionary* (2009), p. 1608.

[3]*New International Webster's Comprehensive Dictionary of the English Language* (2004), p. 1294.

A. Srivastava, *Modern Law of International Trade*, International Law and the Global South, https://doi.org/10.1007/978-981-15-5475-9_6

Sect. 4.3.2). It is then unlikely that they are treated as the terms of a contract.[4] Similarly, a mere representation or misrepresentation about a fact needs to be distinguished from a term of a contract for the simple reason that the latter is not of the nature of an enforceable promise. A misrepresentation is rather a false statement about an existing fact which induces a party to enter into the contract.[5] If made fraudulently or negligently, a misrepresentation is indeed actionable and the innocent party is entitled to set aside the contract and claim damages under the (English) Misrepresentation Act, 1967[6]; it, nevertheless, cannot of itself serve as the basis for contractual liability.

Although a mere representation as such is generally not treated as the contractual term, it nevertheless may become the term of the contract provided that an intention to be bound is shown to be present. It may be noted that the intention is a question of fact and therefore each case has to be decided in the light of its peculiar circumstances.[7] In practice, making a precise distinction between a mere representation and a statement incorporated as a term is, however, quite complicated and sometimes the line dividing the two gets blurred. Notably, in ascertaining the intention of the parties, modern cases place considerable emphasis on the objective criteria such as the conduct of the parties, possession of special information, the means to obtain the necessary information, the degree of reliance placed on the description of goods, and the notion of reasonableness.[8] As noted in *Atiyah's Sale of Goods*, when they (courts) think it is appropriate to impose liability on the maker of the statement, the courts are more willing to treat a statement about the goods as the terms of the contract.[9]

---

[4]However, no clear-cut line can be drawn between puffs and contractual terms and in many cases, the dividing line gets blurred. The statements about goods that might be treated as puffs in the early twentieth century are likely to be held by courts these days as terms of the contract. See, in particular, infra, Chap. 4; Guest (2006), p. 507.

[5]A misrepresentation is not necessarily fraudulent. A negligent or even innocently made statement may amount to misrepresentation. See further, McKendrick (2000), pp. 268–79.

[6]Apart from the Misrepresentation Act, 1967, a negligent or fraudulent representation was actionable as a tort under common law as a result of the decision of the House of Lords in *Hedley Byrne & Co. v Heller & Partners Ltd* [1964] AC 465. See Poole (2004), pp. 162—63; Beatson et al. (2010), p. 136. For a discussion of the difference between the liability under the common law and that under the Act of 1967, see, in particular, McKendrick (2000), pp. 276–79.

[7]See further Poole (2004), pp 163–67; Beatson et al. (2010), pp. 143–35.

[8]See *Couchman v Hill* [1947] All ER 103 ("The printed condition that the vendor will take no responsibility for errors of description of things or animal specifically offered for sale on inspection is reasonable for visible defects, but for qualities or attributes which are invisible it is not reasonable"); *Inntrepreneur Pub Co. v East Crown Ltd* [2000] 2 Lloyd's Rep. 611; *Harling v Eddy* [1951] 2 All ER 212; *Dick Bentley Productions Ltd v Harold Smith (Motors) Ltd* [1965] 1 WLR 623; *Beale v Tayor* [1967] 1 WLR 1193. For a more fully discussion of various criteria to ascertain an intention to be bound, see Furmston, (2017), pp. 178–83; Guest (ed.) (2006), pp. 517–20; Atiyah et al. (2010), pp. 93–94.

[9]Atiyah et al., id, p. 94; Guest (2006), id, pp. 517–19.

6.1.2 *Classification of Terms*

6.1.2.1 General

Since all the terms of a contract are not of equal importance, in order to specify the precise obligations they impose on the parties, they are to be divided into different categories: conditions, warranties, and innominate (or intermediate) terms. Traditionally, the contractual terms were understood to fall into two broad categories: conditions and warranties. Where a term is so important for the parties that it "goes to the root of the contract" it is a condition. The breach of a condition gives rise to the right to treat the contract as repudiated or discharged and also the right to claim damages.[10] In other words, in the case of the breach of a condition, the innocent party has the option to terminate the contract and claim damages for loss suffered by him or her.[11] A warranty, in contrast, is a term of lesser significance. The breach of a warranty does not discharge the innocent party from further performance of the contract. It only gives rise to the right to claim damages.[12]

As will be noted below, in addition to these two categories of the terms of a contract, there has evolved a new category of the contractual terms, namely the intermediate terms which because of their peculiar character cannot neatly be described as conditions or warranties. The legal consequences of the breach of such terms depend on the degree of the gravity of the breach and not the ab initio classification of the terms as either conditions or warranties. As explained below, if the breach of intermediate terms is considered serious, the innocent party is entitled to treat the contract as repudiated and claim damages; if the breach is so slight that it would be unreasonable to treat the contract as repudiated, it is treated as a warranty and the innocent party can only claim damages.

6.1.2.2 Condition

As stated above, a "condition" is a term of major importance to the contract. It is *so* essential or important to the contract in question that its non-fulfillment entitles the other party to treat the contract as rescinded. S. 12 of the SoGA 1930 reads: "A condition is a stipulation essential to the main purpose of the contract the breach of which gives rise to a right to treat the contract repudiated." To put it another way, a condition is such an important stipulation in the contract that its performance by one party is a condition of the liability of the other party.[13] Describing a condition,

---

[10] SoGA 1979, s. 11 (3); *Photo Production Ltd. v Securicor Transport Ltd* [1980] AC 826. 21 In the case of the breach of a condition the innocent party is entitled to terminate the contract even if he has not suffered any damage. See: *Re Moore & Co.* [1921] 2 K.B. 519; McKendrick (2000), p. 207.

[11] He or she, however, can waive his or her right to terminate the contract and claim only damages.

[12] *Photo Production Ltd. v Securicor Transport Ltd* [1980] AC 826.21.

[13] Guest (ed.) (2006), p. 523. The term condition as it is used here is imported into the law of contract from the law of conveyancing. Id., p. 54.

Diplock LJ in *Photo Production Ltd v Securicor Transport Ltd*[14] stated that "any failure by one party to perform a particular obligation, irrespective of the gravity of event that has in fact resulted from the breach, shall entitle the other party to elect to put an end to all primary obligations of both parties remaining unperformed."[15] One example of a condition as contained in s. 14 (a) of the 1930 Act is that in a contract of sale of goods, there is an implied condition that the seller has a right to sell the goods "unless the circumstances of the contract are such as to show a different intention."[16] A further example is furnished by s. 15 of the Act, which provides that in a contract for the sale of goods by description there is an implied condition that the goods shall correspond with the description. Moreover, since a condition is a term which goes to the root of the contract its breach entitles the innocent party to treat the contract repudiated and claim damages for the loss suffered by him or her. He or she may, in alternative, waive his right to treat the contract discharged and claim only damages.[17]

Here a few points may be added. First, in deciding whether a particular contractual term is a condition or warranty, it is not the label but the "construction of the contract" which is crucial. S. 12 (4) of the SoGA, 1930 provides that whether a stipulation in a contract of sale is a condition or a warranty depends in each case on the construction of the contract. A stipulation may be a condition, though called a warranty in the contract. Similarly, s. 11 (3) of the SoGA 1979 provides:

Whether a stipulation in a contract of sale is a condition, the breach of which may give rise to a right to treat the contract as repudiated, or a warranty, the breach of which may give rise to a claim for damages but not to a right to reject the goods and treat the contract as repudiated, depends in each case on the construction of the contract….

It is worth noting that under contract law the terms, condition, and warranty carry specific meanings and as a matter of fact they are terms of art. However, in practice it is not unlikely that they are used in a variety of senses. Therefore, it is only logical that emphasis should be placed on the intention of the parties and not the form. Secondly, a condition with which we are concerned here is a promissory condition as opposed to a contingent condition. The latter refers to some event which is uncertain and upon the happening or non-happening of which the performance of the contract is based. A contingent condition is of two types—condition precedent and condition subsequent. A condition precedent refers to a specified but uncertain event upon the occurrence of which a contract comes into effect. On the other hand, a condition subsequent is a condition on the happening of which a previously made contract comes to an end.

[14][1980] AC 827.

[15]Id., p. 849.

[16]The corresponding provision is contained in s. 12 (1) of SoGA 1979.

[17]Beatson et al. (2010), p. 149.

6.1.2.3 Warranty

A warranty is a subsidiary or less important term of a contract.[18] Its breach does not give rise to the right to treat the contract as discharged by breach but only the right to claim damages. S. 12(3) of SoGA 1930 provides: "A warranty is a stipulation collateral to the main purpose of the contract, the breach of which gives rise to a claim for damages but not to a right to reject the gods and treat the contract as repudiated." For example, in a contract of sale, there is an implied warranty on the part of the seller that the buyer "shall have and enjoy quiet possession of goods."[19] As explained in *Benjamin's Sale of Goods*, when in the nineteenth century a usage grew which treated the word condition as meaning a promise breach of which would entitle the innocent party to treat the contract as discharged by breach, the word, "warranty" came to be understood as a promise which was "less important terms of a contract." Its breach did not give rise to right to treat the contract repudiated.[20] It is this meaning attributed to a warranty in the nineteenth century in England which was adopted in the Sale of Goods Act 1893 (now reenacted as the SoGA 1979). Notably, the Act of 1930 adopted the same meaning attributed to a warranty under the English law which remains unaltered.

6.1.2.4 Innominate or Intermediate Terms

The traditional approach of categorizing all contractual terms as either conditions or warranties came to be questioned in the latter half of the twentieth century. A particularly instructive case on this point is: *Cehave NV v Bremer Handelsgesellschaft mbH* (*The Hansa Nord*)[21] which expressly rejected the argument that the SoGA 1979 exhaustively divided all terms as either conditions or warranties. The Court of Appeal, relying on its previous decision in *Hongkong Fir Shipping Co. Ltd. v Kawasaki Kisen Kaisha Ltd*,[22] held that there also existed a third category of terms, namely intermediate terms which fell midway between conditions and warranties. According to the Court, the term, "shipped in a good condition" was similar to a stipulation as to quality, such as "fair average quality" and if a small portion of the goods sold was a little below that standard, the buyer would have no right to reject the whole goods in question. Lord Denning MR observed:

> In my opinion, therefore, the term "shipped in good condition" was not a condition strictly so called: nor was it a warranty strictly so called. It was one of those intermediate stipulations which gives no right to reject unless the breach goes to the root of the contract.

---

[18] See McKendrick (2000), p. 218; Beatson et al. (2010), p. 143; Guest (2006), p. 521.

[19] S. 14 (b) of SoGA 1930.

[20] Guest (2006), p. 521.

[21] [1976] QB 44.

[22] [1962] 2 QB 2.

In contrast to the traditional approach of classifying all terms at the time of the contract itself as either conditions or warranties on the basis of their relative importance, in the case of innominate terms, emphasis is on the seriousness of the breach of terms. According to the new approach if the breach is not serious enough to justify repudiation of the contract, the innocent party will not be entitled to treat the contract as discharged.

Another important case dealing with the issue is *Hong Kong Fir Shipping* case (cited above) which had already shown that in addition to conditions and warranties there were many stipulations of complex character of which the legal effect depended on the seriousness of the breach. In that case, the Court of Appeal emphasized the need to pay attention to actual consequences of the breach, rather ab initio classification of the contractual terms as either conditions or warranties. According to the Court, certain terms could not be classified, at the time of the contract, either as a condition or warranty. To quote:

> The question to be answered is, does the breach of the stipulation go so much to the root of the contract that it makes further performance of the contract impossible, or in other words, is the whole contract frustrated? If yea, the innocent party may treat the contract as at an end. If nay, his claim sounds in damages only.

In *Hong Kong Fir Shipping* case, a question arose whether the obligation to deliver a seaworthy vessel was a condition to the charterer's liability under the charterparty contract, a breach of which entitled the charterer to treat the contract repudiated and to declare him as relived from the obligations under the contract in question? It was argued that unseaworthiness of the vessel was as important as departure from the voyage and was a condition that any breach of which entitled the charterer to treat it as going to the root of the contract and to declare himself no longer bound by it. Both the courts—the Queen's Bench Division and the Court of Appeal found that there was no breach of a condition which entitled the charterers to treat the contract as repudiated.[23]

According to Upjohn LJ, the stipulation as to the seaworthiness is not a condition in the strict sense and since the only unseaworthiness alleged, serious though it was, was the insufficiency and incompetence of the crew, "that surely cannot be treated as going to the root of the contract for the parties must have contemplated that in such an event the crew could be changed and augmented."[24] Referring to the familiar categorization of stipulations in a contract as either conditions or warranties, Upjohn LJ expressed the opinion that that classification reflected the old position and "when considering the remedies to which one party may be entitled today for breach of a stipulation by the other the decision whether the stipulation is a condition or warranty may not provide a complete answer."[25] According to him:

> Where, however, upon the true construction of the contract, the parties have not made a particular stipulation a condition, it would in my judgment be unsound and misleading to conclude that, being a warranty, damages is necessarily a sufficient remedy.

---

[23]Ibid.

[24]Id., p. 64.

[25]Id., p. 63.

Delving into the issue of the distinction between condition and warranty as stipulations of a contract, Diplok LJ expressed similar opinion. He went on to suggest:

There are, however, many contractual undertakings of a more complex character which cannot be categorized as being "conditions" or "warranties,"... Of such undertakings all that can be predicated is that some breaches will and others will not give rise to an event which will deprive the party not in default of substantially the whole benefit which it was intended that he should obtain from the contract; and the legal consequences of a breach of such an undertaking, unless provided for expressly in the contract, depend upon the nature of the event to which the breach gives rise and do not follow automatically from a prior classification of the undertaking as a "condition" or a "warranty."[26]

6.1.3 Reform of the Statute Law

SoGA 1930 as well as SoGA 1979 rely on the traditional common law approach in classifying terms. Thus, all the terms under these enactments are either conditions or warranties.[27] In other words, the statutes assume that the distinction between conditions and warranties is exhaustive; that all terms are to fall within one group or another as there is no scope for any other category of terms. Thus, both the statutes in classifying terms place emphasis on the relative importance of different terms but ignore consequences of the breach. An advantage of the traditional approach, however, is its emphasis on certainty and simplicity which is undeniably of considerable importance in commercial transactions.[28]

Here it may be of some interest to note that SoGA 1979 has, to a certain extent, accommodated the new approach in regard to the classification of the contractual terms. In accommodating the intermediate terms, s. 15 A of the SoGA 1979, as amended by the Sale and Supply of Goods Act, 1994, provides that in non-consumer transactions, unless a contrary intension appears or is to be implied from the contract, the buyer has no right to reject the goods if the breach of a term as to quality or fitness for purpose is so slight that it would not be reasonable for the buyer to reject the goods.[29] The relevant part of s. 15A reads:

(1) Where in the case of a contract of sale—
 (a) The buyer would, apart from this subsection, have the right to reject goods by reason of a breach on the part of the seller of a term implied by sections 13, 4 or 15 above, but,

---

[26] Id., p. 70.

[27] See Beatson et al. (2010), p. 144; McKendrick (2000), p. 212; Atiyah et al. (2010), pp. 86–87; Furmston (2017), p. 207.

[28] For further discussion on the significance of certainty in (international) commercial transactions, see Beatson et al. (2010), p. 147; Furmston (2017) ibid.

[29] For further discussion, see Guest (ed.) (2006), pp. 608-09.

(b) The breach is so slight that it would be unreasonable for him to reject them, then, if the buyer does not deal as consumer, the breach is not to be treated as a breach of condition but may be treated as a breach of warranty.

(2) This section applies unless a contrary intention appears in, or is to be implied from, the contract.

6.1.4 Seller's Duties: Implied Terms as to Title, Description, and Quality

While the contracting parties are free to agree upon by express words, the terms they wish to insert into their contract, in many cases, law use the device of implied terms to fill the gaps in the express terms. Thus, apart from express contractual terms, there are also implied terms which have their source in custom, legislations, and decisions of the court.[30] These terms are implied in many branches of commercial law, including marine insurance, negotiable instruments, hire-purchase, and sale of goods. But here we will draw our attention to the statutory implied terms defining a seller's obligations under a contract of sale.

The statutory implied terms defining a seller's duties in respect of title, correspondence with description, quality, and fitness for purpose are contained in SoGA 1930 (ss. 14–17) and SoGA 1979 (ss. 12–15). Originally recognized by the mercantile custom and usages of the nineteenth century, these terms were subsequently codified by the Sale of Goods Act, 1893 and reproduced in SoGA 1930 and SoGA 1979.[31] As will be seen below, while significant changes have been made in the English law as originally contained in the Act of 1893 and SoGA 1979, Indian law remains unaltered. Notably, the English law (the law as it applies to England, Wales, and the Northern Ireland) has undergone significant changes since 1973 mainly as a result of the legislative intervention. It may also be noted that the statutory implied terms, just referred to above, are classified as conditions and warranties and can be excluded or varied by an express agreement.[32]

6.1.4.1 Implied Terms as to Title

Since a seller need not be the owner of the goods sold, it is necessary to imply a term in a contract of sale to the effect that the seller has the right to pass a good title to protect a buyer from the claims of a third party. The meaning is that if after the completion of sale it turns out that the seller has no right to pass a good title, the buyer

[30] It may be noted that only in limited situations terms will be implied by courts or custom. For a discussion of the terms implied by custom and courts, see Furmston (2017), pp. 184–87 & 192–206; Beatson et al. (2010), pp. 152–59.

[31] See Farwell LJ in *Bristol Tramways v Fiat Motors,* [1910] 2 KB 831, at p. 838.

[32] However, under the SoGA 1979 (s. 55), in consumer transactions implied terms cannot be excluded or varied by the contracting parties.

will have the right to repudiate the contract and/or to claim damages. The relevant part of s. 14 of SoGA 1930 [s. 12 of SoGA 1979] which deals with the implied term as to title states:

14. Implied undertaking as to title, etc.—In a contract of sale, unless the circumstances of the contract are such as to show a different intention, there is—

(a) an implied condition on the part of the seller that, in the case of a sale, he has a right to sell the goods and that, in the case of an agreement to sell, he will have a right to sell the goods at the time when the property is to pass.
(b) xxx.
(c) xxx.

In *Niblett Ltd v Confectioners' Materials Co. Ltd.*,[33] certain quantity of condensed milk bearing the name "Nissley Brand" was sold. Since selling of the goods under the "Nissley Brand" was an infringement of the registered trademark of a well-known manufacturer of condensed milk, the buyers were stopped from reselling it and were compelled to sell the goods unlabeled at the best price obtainable. It was held by the Court of Appeal that the sellers were in breach of the implied condition as to title for "if a vendor can be stopped by process of law from selling he has no right to sell."[34]

Section 14 further provides that unless the circumstances of the contract are such as to show a different intention, there is—

(a) xxx;
(b) an implied warranty that the buyer shall have and enjoy quiet possession of the goods;
(c) an implied warranty that the goods shall be free from any charge or encumbrance in favour of any third party not declared or known to the buyer before or at the time when the contract is made.

The implied terms relating to a seller's duties in respects of quiet possession of the goods and freedom from encumbrance are expressed as warranties. It means that a breach of these duties will not entitle a buyer to claim the remedy of termination of the contract. He can only bring a suit for damages.

It has been suggested that except in a few cases the implied warranty as to quiet enjoyment of the goods does not confer upon a buyer any "additional rights".[35] The view has also been expressed that when a buyer is already protected by the implied condition about title of the goods the warranty of quiet possession of the goods seems to be superfluous as regards the cases where a buyer's possession of the goods is disturbed by a third person.[36] As has already been noted, a breach of the duty to pass a good title under s. 14 entitles a buyer to treat the condition as warranty and bring an action for damages. In *Atiyah's Sale of Goods*,[37] Singleton LJ is quoted as

---

[33] [1921] 3 KB 387.

[34] Id., p. 398 (Per Scrutton LJ).

[35] See Atiyah et al. (2010), p. 115; Bridge (1997), p. 405.

[36] Bharuka (2007), pp. 155–56.

[37] Atiyah et al. (2010), p. 115.

stating: "In any event if there was a breach of the implied condition the plaintiff was entitled to treat that as a breach of warranty."[38]

According to S. 14 (c) there is an implied warranty on the part of the seller that the buyer's title to the goods shall be free from any charge or encumbrance in favor of any third party. Thus, where a buyer is forced to discharge any such encumbrance, he is entitled to recover the amount from the seller. S. 69 of the Indian Contract Act confers upon a buyer the right to recover any amount he is compelled to pay on behalf of the seller.

6.1.4.2 Rule of *Caveat Emptor*

Before we proceed to discuss implied terms as to description, and quality, it seems appropriate to say a few words about the rule of *caveat emptor*. The rule was traditionally understood as stating that a buyer receives the goods as "they are."[39] But as will be seen below, ss. 15–17 of SoGA 1930 [ss. 13–15, SoGA 1979] now impose upon a seller a number of duties as to the description and quality of goods. It is thus fairly clear that the maxim that a buyer buys goods as they are is of little significance in modern law of sales as the rule does not apply in a vast majority of cases. The doctrine of *caveat emptor* will only apply to cases not covered by the description, quality, and sample-related provisions of the Act. The preamble to s. 16 of the SoGA 1930 which incorporates the rule makes it explicit: "subject to the provisions of the Act and of any other law for the time being in force, there is *no implied warranty or condition as to the quality or fitness for any particular purpose of goods* supplied under a contract of sale...."[40]

However, the description requirement of s. 15, as will be seen below, applies to practically all sales except when a buyer, in buying specific goods, is relying on his own judgment. Similarly, where the merchantability and fitness for purpose requirements provided for by s. 16 will apply the rule of *caveat emptor* has no application. However, since s. 16 applies only to professional sales, it may be stated that the rule of *caveat emptor* has a fair scope in cases of private sales. The rule has its origin in the sales of goods of medieval times when all sales took place in market overt.[41] But since the sales of nowadays are quite different from those of early times and that the implied terms now take account of a buyer's need, albeit partially, the relevance of the rule of caveat emptor has considerably diminished.[42]

---

[38] *Mason v Burningham* [1949] 2 KB 545.

[39] See Guest (2006), p. 551; Bridge (1997), p. 272.

[40] Under the SoGA 1979, after the remodeling of s. 14, the rule of *caveat emptor* appears as a subsection and not as the preamble.

[41] Bridge (1997), p. 272.

[42] See Bridge (1997), p. 272.

6.1.4.3 Sale by Description

Section 15 of the SoGA 1930 provides:

> Where there is a contract for the sale of goods by description, there is an implied condition that the goods shall correspond with the description; and,
>
> If the sale is by sample as well as by description, it is not sufficient that the bulk of the goods corresponds with the sample if the goods do not also correspond with the description.

Section 15 reproduces the law as originally found in the Act of 1893. Its English law counterpart s. 13 which is also based on the Act of 1893 was, however, amended in 1973 by the Supply of Goods (Implied Terms) Act which inserted subsection (3):

A sale of goods is not prevented from being a sale by description by reason only that, being exposed for sale or hire, they are selected by the buyer.

S. 13 (3) of SoGA 1979 does not introduce a new principle. It only affirms the position that the "sale by description" is not restricted to the unascertained and future goods but is extended to the sale of specific goods as well "so long as it is sold not merely as the specific thing, but as a thing corresponding to a description."[43] In other words, where specific goods are bought not as specific goods as such or as "they are" but in reliance upon the description the sale in question will be a sale by description.[44] In fact, before the insertion of s. 13 (3), it had been well settled that even where the buyer had inspected the goods the sale in question was sale by description provided that buyer had relied on the description.[45] In *Varley v Whipp*,[46] a purchaser who agreed to purchase a second-hand reaping machine described as "new the previous year and only used to cut 50 acres" was allowed to reject the goods when he came to know that it was an old machine. *Varley v Whipp* was not a case of the sale of specific goods as such but the sale of specific goods by description. A similar view is taken in many cases. These cases show that even where the buyer has seen the goods or even where goods are selected by the buyer himself, for example, in the self-service shop or store, the sale in question will amount to sale by description provided that the buyer has relied on the description.[47] To quote Lord Wright in *Grant v Australian Knitting Mills Ltd*[48]:

There is a sale by description even though the buyer is buying something displayed before him on the counter: a thing is sold by description, though it is specific, so

[43] See, in particular, Guest (2006), pp. 538–39; Atiyah et al. (2010), pp. 15--51.

[44] Even if the buyer has examined the goods the sale is a sale by description provided that the buyer has relied on description. See *Wallis, Son & Wells v Pratt & Haynes* [1911] AC 394; *Beale v Taylor* [1967] 1 WLR 1193; Guest AG (ed.) (2004), p. 541.

[45] See in particular *Beale v Taylor*, ibid; *Varley v Whipp* [1900] 1 QB 513; Guest (2006), pp. 538–39; Atiyah et al. (2010), pp. 150–51.

[46] [1900] 1 QB 513.

[47] See, in particular, *Thornett and Fehr v Beers & Son* [1919] 1 KB 486; *Grant v Australian Knitting Mills Ltd* [1936] AC 85; *Morelli v Fitch and Gibbons,* [1928] 2 K.B. 636; *Ashington Piggeries Ltd v Christopher Hill Ltd*, [1972] AC 441; *Godley v Perry* [1960] 1 WLR 9; *Beale v Taylor* [1967] 1 WLR 1193; Atiyah et al. (2010), p. 150; Guest (2006), pp. 540–41; Beatson et al. (2010), p. 160.

[48] *Grant v Australian Knitting Mills Ltd*, ibid.

long as it is sold not merely as the specific thing but as a thing corresponding to a description, e.g. woolen undergarments, hot- water bottle, a second- hand reaping machine, to select a few obvious illustrations."[49]

Thus, the scope of the sale by description is very wide. Except where specific goods are bought by a buyer relying on his own judgment a sale is sale by description.[50] It may also be noted that the phrase, "sale by description" covers not just professional but also private sales.[51]

6.1.4.4 Implied Terms as to Quality

S. 16 of the SoGA, 1930 provides for the implied conditions about quality and fitness for the particular purpose. It reads as follows:

16. Implied conditions as to quality or fitness.—Subject to the provisions of this Act and of any other law for the time being in force, there is no implied warranty or condition as to the quality or fitness for any particular purpose of goods supplied under a contract of sale, except as follows:—

(1) Where the buyer, expressly or by implication, makes known to the seller the particular purpose for which the goods are required, so as to show that the buyer relies on the seller's skill or judgment, and the goods are of a description which it is in the course of the seller's business to supply (whether he is the manufacturer or producer or not), there is an implied condition that the goods shall be reasonably fit for such purpose: Provided that, in the case of a contract for the sale of a specified article under its patent or other trade name, there is no implied condition as to its fitness for any particular purpose.
(2) Where goods are bought by description from a seller who deals in goods of that description (whether he is the manufacturer or producer or not), there is an implied condition that the goods shall be of merchantable quality: Provided that, if the buyer has examined the goods, there shall be no implied condition as regards defects which such examination ought to have revealed.
(3) An implied warranty or condition as to quality or fitness for a particular purpose may be annexed by the usage of trade.
(4) An express warranty or condition does not negative a warranty or condition implied by this Act unless inconsistent therewith.

As will be noticed below, while s. 16, just quoted above, remains unaltered, its English law counterpart, s. 14 of SoGA 1979 has undergone substantial modifications since 1973 and, in its present form, is worded differently from its original version found in the 1893 Act. Therefore, for a full appreciation of the implied duties of the

---

[49] Id., p. 100.

[50] Atiyah et al. (2010), p. 151; Guest (ed.) (2006), pp. 541–42. Where it was clear that the buyer bought the goods relying on his own judgment, the sale was not a sale by description. See *Harlingdon and Leinster Enterprises Ltd. v Christopher Hull Fine Art Ltd* [1991] 1 QB 564.

[51] On professional sales, see supra, Sect. 6.1.4.3.

seller about quality under English and Indian law, it seems imperative to compare new s. 14 with its original version.

Of all the major changes introduced in s. 14, the most important one was brought about by the Sale and Supply of Goods Act, 1994 which, with respect to a seller's duty who sells in the course of business, substituted the requirement of the merchantable quality by that of the satisfactory quality. Although the Supply of Goods (Implied Terms) Act, 1973 had provided the definition of the term, "merchantable quality" which was retained in the SoGA 1979 the statutory definition met with strong criticism and was ultimately abandoned.[52] The concept of merchantable quality shall be dealt with below, suffices to state here that this concept which appeared to be sufficiently precise in the context of commercial sales found inadequate when applied to consumer sales.[53]

The current version of s. 14 (2) which contains the seller's implied obligation as to quality provides that thère is an implied term (condition) that, where the goods are sold in the course of a business, the goods supplied shall be of satisfactory quality. The relevant part of the current version of s. 14 reads:

(2) Where the seller sells goods in the course of a business, there is an implied term that the goods supplied under the contract are of satisfactory quality.

(2A) For the purposes of this Act, goods are of satisfactory quality if they meet the standard that a reasonable person would regard as satisfactory, taking account of any description of the goods, the price (if relevant) and all the other relevant circumstances."

(2B) For the purposes of this Act, the quality of goods includes their state and condition and the following (among others) are in appropriate cases aspects of the quality of goods—

(a) fitness for all the purposes for which goods of the kind in question are commonly supplied,
(b) Appearance and finish,
(c) Freedom from minor defects,
(d) Safety, and
(e) durability

(2C) The term implied by subsection (2) above does not extend to any matter making the quality of goods unsatisfactory—

(a) which is specifically drawn to the buyer's attention before the contract is made,
(b) where the buyer examines the goods before the contract is made, which that examination ought to reveal, or
(c) in the case of a contract for sale by sample, which would have been apparent on a reasonable examination of the sample.

---

[52]For more discussion on this aspect, see Atiyah et al. (2010), pp. 157–58.

[53]Atiyah, id, p. 157; Guest (ed.) (2006), p. 558.

The reader will notice that s. 14 (2) does more than simply laying down the requirement of supplying the goods of satisfactory quality. It defines the term, "satisfactory quality" by reference to the (general) standard of a reasonable man and specifies "description of the goods," and "the price" as the matters to be taken into account for the purpose (s. 2A). The definition is also supplemented with specific aspects of quality which seek to provide guidance in this respect. These, as stated above, include: fitness for all the purposes for which goods are commonly supplied; appearance and finish; freedom from minor defects; safety; and durability (s. 2B). However, the definition of "satisfactory quality" has not escaped criticism. The view has been expressed that since the general "satisfactory quality" requirement will remain the overriding consideration in determining whether or not the goods are of satisfactory quality, the change in practical terms comes to almost nothing.[54]

A second major change is aimed to making the (implied) term of merchantable (now satisfactory) quality free from the shackles of the description requirement.[55] In the original version, the two requirements—the merchantable quality and sale by description—were interconnected, that is, the merchantability quality provision of s. 14 applied only in cases of sale by description. In order to get the benefit of the merchantable quality condition, it was necessary to show that the goods were "bought by description from a seller who deals in goods of that description." However, the Supply of Goods (Implied Terms) Act, 1973 replaced the requirement of sale by description found in original s. 14(2) by one that the seller sells "in the course of a business."[56]

A third major change is the substitution of the original s. 14 (1) by new s. 14 (3) which deals with the implied condition about fitness for particular purpose. A differently worded s. 14 (3) provides that where a buyer, expressly or by implication, makes known to a seller (who sells the goods in the course of business) "any particular purpose for which the goods are being bought, there is an implied condition that the goods supplied under the contract are reasonably fit for the purpose, whether or not that is a purpose for which such goods are commonly supplied except where the circumstances show that the buyer does not rely, or that it is unreasonable for him to rely, on the skill or judgment of the seller or credit-broker." Insertion of new s. 14 (3) involves two important implications. First, s. 14 (3), like s. 14(2), also replaces sale by description requirement for one that the seller sells goods in the course of business. Secondly, under new s. 14 (3), where a buyer makes known to a seller any particular purpose for which the goods are being bought it will be presumed that the buyer has relied on the seller as there is *no* need of showing reliance. Rather, burden of proof is on the seller to prove that there was no reliance or that reliance was unreasonable. However, under the original arrangement, the burden of proof was on the buyer. He had to show that he relied on the seller's skill or judgment, although in most cases it could be inferred from the circumstances.[57]

---

[54]Atiyah et al. (2010), p. 177.

[55]Bridge (1997), p. 290; Guest (ed.) (2006), pp. 551–52.

[56]Guest (2006), id, p. 552.

[57]Bridge (1997), p. 334.

Having noted the changes made in the English law on the subject, we now turn to a brief discussion of the fitness for purpose and merchantable quality requirements respectively contained in ss. 16 (1) and 16 (2) of the SoGA 1930.[58] As already noted, s. 16 is modeled on the original Act of 1893 which for well over a century remains unchanged. Thus, discussion on s. 16 undertaken here corresponds to the pre-1973 position under English law.

Turning now to s 16 [s. 14 of SoGA 1979], the first issue to be examined is its scope of application. Here it is of some interest to note that the scope of s. 16 is narrower than that of s. 15 dealing with sale by description [s. 13 of SoGA 1979].[59] As already noted, s. 15 covers not just private sales but also a sale that occurs in the course of business. In other words, s. 15 applies even if the goods are sold not by a person who deals in goods of that description. S. 16 (1), on the other hand, applies only where "the goods are of a description which it is in the course of the seller's business to supply (whether he is the manufacturer or producer or not)" and s. 16 (2) applies only "where goods are bought by description from a seller who deals in goods of that description (whether he is the manufacturer or producer or not)." Thus, s. 16 excludes from its purview all private sales and only applies when goods are bought from a seller who deals in goods of that description.[60]

The next issue to be considered in this context is the relationship between subsections (1) and (2) of s. 16 dealing with the requirements of fitness for particular purpose and merchantability, respectively. It may be noted that while s 16 (1) speaks of the buyer's special needs and purpose, s 16 (2) speaks of the merchantable quality of the goods. But it may happen that goods are of merchantable quality and yet do not fulfill the condition of fitness for the particular purpose for which the goods are bought[61] or do not fit the buyer's special needs.[62] Similarly, it is also likely that the goods are fit for the particular purpose for which they are bought but they are not of the merchantable quality. The question of relationship between subsections (1) and (2) of s. 16 assumes significance because of their drafting style which gives the

[58]Notably, under s. 14 the two requirements are given in reverse order. Under the new arrangement, the provision on fitness for purpose is placed in subsection (3) while the merchantable quality requirement remains as subsection (2).

[59]For further discussion, see Atiyah et al. (2010), pp. 152–53.

[60]Id, p. 197.

[61]For example, as will be noted below, in *Henry Kendall v Lillico* (cited below), the goods in question were not found fit for the particular purpose for which they were bought, nevertheless, were found "merchantable" under original s. 14 (2) of SoGA 1979 (corresponding to s. 16 (2) of SoGA 1930. Similarly, in *Bristol Tramways v Fiat Motors* [1910] 2 K.B. 831, the goods in question, omnibuses, were not fit for the purpose for which they were required, but were found "merchantable." See below.

[62]*Jones v Just* (1868) 3 Q.B. 197. See also *Jones v. Padgett* (1890) 24 QB 650 (The plaintiff bought a certain quantity of indigo blue cloth. But cloth in question proved to be not fit for the purpose for which it was bought. He sued for breach of an implied term of merchantability. But the plaintiff failed. The cloth was found to be of merchantable quality as it was suitable for other purposes for which cloth of that description was ordinarily used and as he had not told the defendant the particular purpose for which he wanted it).

impression that two subsections dealing with fitness for purpose and merchantable quality tests are distinct and unrelated.[63]

Fitness for a Particular Purpose

In order to invoke s. 16 (1), the buyer must have told the seller *the particular purpose* for which he is buying the goods so that he can show that he is relying on the seller's skill or judgment; and the goods must be of a description "which it is in the course of the seller's business to supply."[64]

Obviously, the most usual application of s. 16 (1) involves the sale of a multipurpose goods. In the purchase of this kind of goods, the buyer in order to obtain the protection of s. 16 (1) must expressly or by implication make it known to the seller *the particular purpose* for which the goods are required. For example, where goods sold could be used for a number of different purposes the seller has complied with the implied terms as to quality and fitness if the goods in question are fit for the ordinary uses. But if the buyer makes it known to the seller that the goods required are not for the ordinary use but for "the particular purpose," the seller will be in breach of his obligations as to quality or fitness if the goods in question are not fit for that particular purpose. However, the purpose must be "stated with sufficient particularity to enable the seller to exercise his skill or judgment in making or selecting appropriate goods."[65]

"A particular purpose means a given purpose, known or communicated. It is not necessarily a narrow or closely particularised purpose."[66] In *Henry Kendall & Sons v William Lillico & Sons Ltd* (cited above) it was stated that the term "particular" was used in the sense of "specified" rather than as opposed to the term "general."[67] Further, a purpose may be stated in wide terms, for example, "a car to drive on the road"[68] or it may be specified, for example, "an omnibus for heavy traffic in a hilly district."[69] To quote Lord Pearce in *Henry Kendall & Sons v William Lillico & Sons Ltd* (cited above):

> The less circumscribed the purpose, the less circumscribed will be, as a rule, the range of goods which are reasonably fit for such purpose. The purpose of a car to drive on the road will be satisfied by almost any car so long as it will function reasonably; but the narrower purpose of an omnibus suitable to the crowded streets of a city can only be achieved by a narrower range of vehicles.

---

[63]The drafting style of s. 16 [old version of s. 14 of SoGA 1979] has been criticized as it gives the impression that two subsections dealing with fitness for purpose and merchantable quality tests are distinct and unrelated. Considerable doubt persists as to the precise scope of subsections (1) and (2). Do they deal with the obligations that are totally distinct and unrelated? Or they are envisaged as containing interrelated obligations? See generally Davies (1969), pp. 74–91.

[64]*Henry Kendall & Sons v William Lillico & Sons Ltd* [1969] 2 A.C. 31, at p. 79.

[65]Id., p. 80. For more fully discussion, see Atiyah et al. (2010), pp. 195–97.

[66]Per Lord Pearce in *Henry Kendall & Sons v William Lillico & Sons Ltd* [1969] 2 A.C. 31, p. 114.

[67]Id., p. 123.

[68]*Bartlett v. Sydney Marcus Ltd* [1965] 1 W.L.R. 1013; *Baldry v. Marshall* [1925] 1 K.B. 260 ["a comfortable car suitable for touring purposes"].

[69]*Bristol Tramways v Fiat Motors Ltd* [1910] 2 K.B 831.

In the case of *Priest v Last*[70] which concerns the sale of the multipurpose goods, it was held that the seller was in breach of his obligations about fitness of the goods where a hot water bottle was not found fit for a particular purpose for which it was required, though it ordinarily had only one purpose.

In *Bristol Tramways v Fiat Motors* (cited above), the plaintiffs bought from the defendants the Fiat omnibus and "six Fiat omnibus chassis." Although the contract contained no mention of the particular purpose for which they were required, it was made known to the defendants that the omnibus and six chassis were required for heavy traffic in a hilly district. But the goods in question were not fit for heavy traffic. In an action for breach of terms, the Court found that since the plaintiffs relied upon the defendants' skill or judgment, there was an implied condition that the omnibuses should be reasonably fit for the declared purpose.

The proviso to s. 16 (1) of SoGA 1930 states that "in the case of a contract for the sale of a specified article under its patent or other trade name, there is no implied condition as to its fitness for any particular purpose." But the proviso will have application only in those cases where a buyer orders goods under their trade name so as to show that he does not base his decision on the seller's skill or judgment.[71]

Merchantable Quality

S. 16 (2) of SoGA 1930 provides that "where goods are *bought by description* from a seller who deals in goods of that description (whether he is the manufacturer or producer or not), there is an implied condition that the goods shall be of merchantable quality." However, if the buyer has examined the goods, there shall be no implied condition as regards defects which such examination ought to have revealed.

The obligation of the seller about merchantable quality of the goods, in the first place, like the obligation in respect of fitness for purpose, applies only to a seller who deals in goods of that description. Secondly, the requirement of the merchantable quality only applies to the sale by description dealt with under s. 15 of the SoGA 1930. Thirdly, unlike the parallel obligation in respect of fitness for the particular purpose, the obligation in respect of merchantable quality is not dependent on reliance by the buyer on the seller's skill or judgment.

Explaining the phrase, "merchantable quality" as used in the original version of s. 14 (2) of the Sale of Goods Act, 1893 which corresponds to s. 16 (2) of SoGA 1930[72], the House of Lords in *Henry Kendall & Sons v William Lillico & Sons Ltd* (cited

---

[70] [1903] 2 K.B 148.

[71] See *Baldry v Marshall* [1925] 1 KB 260.

[72] As already stated, the merchantable quality requirement was retained in the 1979 Act until it was replaced in 1994 by the term "satisfactory quality." The relevant parts of S. 14 (2) of the Sale of Goods Act, 1979 reads as follows:

(1) …there is no implied condition or warranty about the quality or fitness for any particular purpose of goods supplied under a contract of sale.
(2) Where the seller sells goods in the course of a business, there is an implied term that the goods supplied under the contract are of satisfactory quality.

above) took the view that merchantable quality means "commercially saleable." Lord Reid stated:

> ...Merchantable can only mean commercially saleable. If the description is a familiar one it may be that in practice only one quality of goods answers that description—then that quality and only that quality is merchantable quality. Or it may be that various qualities of goods are commonly sold under that description—then it is not disputed that the lowest quality commonly so sold is what is meant by merchantable quality: it is commercially saleable under that description. I need not consider here what expansion or adaptation of the statutory words is required where there is a sale of a particular article or a sale under a novel description.

It is important to note that "merchantable" does not mean "good, or fair, or average quality."[73] Goods may be even of the inferior quality yet they may be found merchantable. Merchantable does not mean that the goods in question, "if only meant for one particular use in ordinary course, is fit for that use;"[74] does not mean "that the thing is saleable in the market simply because it looks all right."[75] In fact, the issue of merchantability is related to the description under which the goods are sold. The following passage from the judgment of Mellor J in *Jones v Just*,[76] quoted by Lord Reid in *Henry Kendall & Sons v William Lillico*, succinctly makes the point:

> It appears to us that, in every contract to supply goods of a specified description which the buyer has no opportunity to inspect, the goods must not only in fact answer the specific description, *but must also be saleable or merchantable under that description.*[77]

In *Henry Kendall & Sons*, Lord Reid stated in so many words that the goods would be "unmerchantable" only when they "would not have been used by a reasonable man for any purpose." Lord Reid went on to say:

> If the description in the contract was so limited that goods sold under it would normally be used for only one purpose, then the goods would be unmerchantable under that description if they were of no use for that purpose. But if the description was so general that goods sold under it are normally used for several purposes, then goods are merchantable under that description if they are fit for any one of these purposes: if the buyer wanted the goods for one of those several purposes for which the goods delivered did not happen to be suitable, though they were suitable for other purposes for which goods bought under that description are normally bought, then he cannot complain.

In *Henry Kendall & Sons*, the House of Lords held that the goods in question, that is, the ground nut meal, were not fit for the purpose for which they were required, therefore, the plaintiff must succeed under s. 14 (1) of the old SoGA 1979. However, the Court also found that since the goods in question were still merchantable, the plaintiff must fail under subsection (2) of s. 14 of SoGA 1979.

---

[73] *Taylor v Combined Buyers* [1924] NZLR 627, at p. 645.

[74] *Grant v. Australian Knitting Mills Ltd.* [1936] A.C. 85, p. 99.

[75] Ibid.

[76] (1868) L.R. 3 Q.B. 197.

[77] [Emphasis supplied].

In *Shine v General Guarantee Corp.*,[78] a 1981 Fiat X1-9 sports car was sold second hand in 1982. The car was stated to be in good condition. But it was subsequently found that for about 24 hours the car had been wholly submerged in water and had been "written off" by the insurance company. In an action for damages, it was held that the car was not of merchantable quality unless it was sold with "a substantially reduced price to reflect the risk they are taking." Hence, there was a breach of the implied condition of merchantable quality under the law.

6.1.4.5 Sale by Sample

Sale by sample is regulated by s. 17 of SoGA 1930 [s. 15 of SoGA 1979]. Subsection (1) of s. 17 which is almost identical to its counterpart in English law, describes a sale by sample in these words:

A contract of sale is a contract for sale by sample where there is a term in the contract, express or implied, to that effect.

A reading of s. 17 (1) suggests that merely because a sample is provided to the buyer, a sale is not the sale by sample. It is only where there is an express or implied term to that effect a sale will be described as a sale by sample.

In an old case on the subject, *James Drummond & Sons v Van Ingen*,[79] Lord Macnaghten famously stated that the purpose of the office of a sample "is to present the real meaning and intention of the parties with regard to the subject matter of the contract which, owing to the imperfection of language, it may be difficult or impossible to express in words." Thus the sale by sample has the effect of largely replacing the description by words of the goods.[80]

Such as there is the requirement in the case of sale by description that the goods must correspond with contract description so also in the case of sale by sample, there is the requirement that the bulk must correspond with the sample. S. 17 (2) provides that a contract of sale by sample implies the conditions: (a) that the bulk shall correspond with the sample in quality; (b) that the buyer shall have a reasonable opportunity of comparing the bulk with the sample; and (c) that the goods shall be free from any defect, rendering them un-merchantable, which would not be apparent on reasonable examination of the sample.[81] Here mention should also be made of s. 41 which provides that "where goods are delivered to the buyer which he has not previously examined, he is not deemed to have accepted them unless and until he has had a reasonable opportunity of examining them for the purpose the purpose of ascertaining whether they are in conformity with the contract."

---

[78] [1988] 1 All ER 911.

[79] [1887] 12 AC 284.

[80] Furmston (2000), p. 128.

[81] S. 17 (2) of the Act of 1930.

6.1.5 *Exclusion of Implied Terms*

The terms set out in Ss. 14–17 can be contracted out by the parties. S. 62 of SoGA 1930 [s. 55 of SoGA 1979] enables a seller or a buyer to negative or vary by express agreement, the terms implied under the Act.

62. Exclusion of implied terms and conditions.—Where any right, duty or liability would arise under a contract of sale by implication of law, it may be negatived or varied by express agreement or by the course of dealing between the parties, or by usage, if the usage is such as to bind both parties to the contract.

The provision contained in s. 62 is based on s. 55 of the Sale of Goods Act, 1893 which has now been replaced by s. 55 (1) of the new Sale of Goods Act, 1979. The new provision has considerably restricted the power of a seller to negative his obligations as implied by the 1979 Act as it is now subject to the Unfair Contract Terms Act, 1977 (now Consumer Rights Act, 2015).[82] But Indian law remains unaltered which is unsatisfactory from the perspective of protecting a buyer from the unreasonable application of the provision.

6.1.6 *Buyer's Duties*

6.1.6.1 Duty to Accept the Goods and Pay for Them

Where the seller is willing and ready to deliver the goods, the buyer is under obligation to accept the goods and to pay for them. It is a buyer's duty to pay the price of the goods which he has either purchased or agreed to purchase in accordance with a contract of sale. The non-payment of price may entitle the (unpaid) seller to claim lien over the goods if he has not parted with the possession of the goods and if other conditions provided for in s. 47 are fulfilled. In certain circumstance, the unpaid seller, under s. 50 of the Act, has also the right of "stopping the goods in transit" if the buyer becomes insolvent. This aspect of the matter will be discussed in some detail below under "Remedies of Seller and Buyer."

S. 31 of the Act imposes upon a buyer the duty to accept the goods and pay for them. The text of s. 31, which is identical to s. 27 of SoGA 1979 reads as follows:

It is the duty of the seller to deliver the goods and of the buyer to accept and pay for them, in accordance with the terms of the contract of sale.

---

[82]See Atiyah et al. (2010), p. 216. S. 55 (1) of the Sale of Goods Act, 1979 reads as under: "Where any right, duty or liability would arise under a contract of sale by implication of law, it may (subject to the Unfair Contract Terms Act, 1977) be negatived or varied by express agreement or by the course of dealing between the parties, or by usage, if the usage is such as to bind both parties to the contract.".

6.1.6.2 Delivery of the Goods and Payment of the Price as Concurrent Conditions

Although a buyer is under duty to pay the price of the goods which he either purchased or agreed to purchase, it, in itself, does not entitle a seller to bring an action for the price. As will be seen below, a seller is entitled to sue for the price only when "the property in the goods has passed to the buyer and the buyer wrongfully neglects or refuses to pay for the goods according to the terms of the contract."[83]

It is also relevant to refer to s. 32 of SoGA 1930 which is identical to s. 28 of SoGA 1979:

> Unless otherwise agreed, delivery of the goods and payment of the price are concurrent conditions, that is to say, the seller shall be ready and willing to give possession of the goods to the buyer in exchange for the price, and the buyer shall be ready and willing to pay the price in exchange for possession of the goods.

Thus, within the terms of s. 32 of SoGA 1930, unless otherwise agreed, delivery of the goods and payment of the price are concurrent conditions, that is to say, they should take place simultaneously. S. 32 is based on the principle of law contained in s. 51 of the Indian Contract Act, 1872 dealing with delivery and payment-related obligations of the parties in a contract based on reciprocal promises. The result is that the seller is not bound to deliver, if the buyer is not ready and willing to pay the price on delivery. Similarly, the buyer is not bound to pay the price, and is not liable to an action for failure to accept the goods, if the seller was not ready and willing to let the buyer have the goods on demand.[84]

But where the seller and buyer agreed that the payment will precede delivery of the goods or vice versa, s. 32 will not apply. Therefore, it is perfectly valid for the parties to agree that the buyer will pay in advance and as a matter of fact this often happens in international sales where the buyer agrees to pay through the letter of credit.[85] Conversely, it may also be agreed upon that the buyer is to take delivery of the goods before paying the price.

6.2 Passing of Property and Risks

6.2.1 General

The event of passing of property, that is, the transfer of ownership in the goods, is of critical significance in a sale transaction for certain important legal consequences

[83]However, it may happen that property in the goods passes to the buyer before delivery of the goods and before the buyer accepts them. See Guest AG (ed.) (2006), p. 970.

[84]S. 51 of the Indian Contract Act provides that "when a contract consists of reciprocal promises to be simultaneously performed, no promisor need perform his promise unless the promisee is ready and willing to perform his reciprocal promise."

[85]Furmston (2000), p. 32.

flow from it. When property in the goods passes from the seller to the buyer the risks of loss or damage to the goods, as a general rule, also pass from the former to the latter unless otherwise agreed.[86] Further, the passing of property has a bearing on the issue of payment of the price and is also important in the event of insolvency either of the seller or the buyer.

Indian and English laws on the subject, based on the common law, are contained respectively in ss. 18–26 of the SoGA 1930 and ss. 16–20 of SoGA 1979 Act. It may be noted that until 1995, when English law on the passing of property was reformed, both Indian and English laws on the subject were remarkably similar; even after the change, both laws remain broadly similar since the change of the law primarily affects the rules governing the passing of property in respects of a specified quantity of goods forming an undifferentiated part of the bulk. In both laws, the transfer of ownership in the goods is not linked either to the delivery of possession of the goods or payment of the price rather is based on the factors like, intention of the parties, nature of the goods, and special agreements between the parties. This peculiarity makes the rules of the passing of property in the goods a bit complicated.

In discussing the rules on passing of property and risks we will first discuss Indian law which may be taken as reflecting the pre-1995 position of English law to be followed by a note on the changes made under the English law.

6.2.2 Passing of Property

Under the SoGA 1930, ss. 18–26 determines the question when property in the goods is to pass from the seller to the buyer. In this regard, ss. 18 and 19 provide certain basic rules, according to which, the passing of property, in the first place, depends on the intention of the parties and the nature of goods in question.

S. 18 Goods must be ascertained—Where there is a contract for the sale of unascertained goods, no property in the goods is transferred to the buyer unless and until the goods are ascertained.

S. 19 Property passes when intended to pass—(1) Where there is a contract for the sale of specific or ascertained goods the property in them is transferred to the buyer at such time as the parties to the contract intend it to be transferred.

(2) For the purpose of ascertaining the intention of the parties regard shall be had to the terms of the contract, the conduct of the parties and the circumstances of the case.

(3) Unless a different intention appears, the rules contained in Sections 20–24 are rules for ascertain the intention of the parties as to the time at which the property in the goods is to pass to the buyer.

From the above said provisions the following rules are discernible:

---

[86]See s. 26 of SoGA 1930.

1. Property cannot pass until and unless the goods are ascertained.[87] In *Laurie & Morewood v Dudin & Sons*,[88] there were 200 quarters of maize, as part of 618 quarters of maize, but which had never been separated. It was held by the Court of Appeal that the plaintiffs had no claim as owners, because at the time of contract, the goods were not ascertained.
2. If the goods in question are specific or ascertained, the property passes when intended to pass. In *Usha Beltron v State of Punjab*,[89] the contract of sale provided that property in the goods would not pass till after delivery and after successful testing and issuance of take-over certificate. The Supreme Court, on the basis of s. 19 of the SoGA 1930, found that in these circumstances of the case, the property in the goods had not passed at the relevant time since the take-over certificate was not issued. It needs to be noted that in international trade it is commonly intended that the property does not pass until payment is made or assurance is given.[90]
3. The parties are free to decide on the basis of the agreements between them when property in the goods is to pass (s. 19, SoGA 1930). For example, in an international contract of sale, the parties may decide that property will pass on shipment of the goods; or delivery of the shipping documents; or cash against documents.
4. Where parties to a contract of sale have formed no intention as to the time when property is to pass, which is normally the case with the consumer sales, their intention is to be ascertained on the basis of the provisions of ss. 20–24, SoGA 1930.

Section 19 (3) provides that in the absence of an agreement as to the relevant intention, the passing of property will take place on the basis of the rules set out in ss. 20–25. These sections lay down specific rules about the passing of property which may be summarized as follows:

1. Where there is an unconditional contract for the sale of specific goods in a deliverable state property in the goods passes when the contract is made (s. 20). The phrase "deliverable state" means "in such a state that the buyer would under the contract be bound to take delivery of [goods]."[91]
2. Even if there is a contract for the sale of specific goods if the seller is bound to do something for putting the goods into deliverable state, the property in the goods shall not pass "until such thing is done and the buyer has notice thereof" (s. 21).

---

[87] SoGA 1930, s. 18.

[88] [1926] 1 KB 223.

[89] (2005) 7 SCC 58.

[90] See Guest (2006), p. 1393.

[91] *Underwood Ltd v Burgh Castle Brick and Cement Syndicate* [1922] 1 KB 243. In *Underwood* case, the contract was for the sale of a specific type of engine which had to be delivered in London. The engine was damaged during transit. It was held by the Court of Appeal that the engine was not in a deliverable state because the plaintiffs were bound to do something, which they had not done, for the purpose of putting the engine into a deliverable state. Therefore, property could not pass from the seller to the buyer.

In *Jute and Gunny Brokers v Union of India*,[92] the goods were not ascertained when the *pucca* delivery orders were issued. It was held by the Supreme Court that "till appropriation takes place and goods are actually delivered, they are not ascertained. The contract therefore represented by the *pucca* delivery orders is a contract for the sale of unascertained goods and no property in the goods is transferred to the buyer in view of s. 18 of the Indian Sale of Goods Act till the goods are ascertained by appropriation, which in this case takes place at the time only of actual delivery."

3. Where anything remains to be done in relation to the goods for the purpose of ascertaining the price of the goods, "the property does not pass until such act or thing is done and the buyer has notice thereof" (s. 22).
4. The property in the unascertained goods passes to the buyer when the goods are unconditionally appropriated to the contract if there is assent from the both parties. Meaning is that either party to the contract may appropriate the goods to the contract if other party assents.
5. The goods will normally be deemed to have been unconditionally appropriated when they are delivered to the buyer or the carrier and the seller does not reserve the right of disposal (s. 23 (2)).
6. In the cases (1) where there is a contract for the sale of specific goods or (2) where goods are subsequently appropriated to the contract, the seller may reserve the right of disposal of the goods until certain conditions are fulfilled (s. 25).

Reform of the English Law

Under the law[93] as it stood before 1995, a contract for the sale of the specified quantity of goods forming part of an identified bulk, for example, 100 tons of wheat out of 1000 tons in a bulk, was treated as a sale of unascertained goods.[94] Consequently, no property in the goods could pass from the seller to buyer. This happened even if the buyer had paid the price. Thus the buyer was at a considerable risk if the seller became insolvent before ascertainment of goods. This is particularly problematic in the context of international trade where the goods involved often remain undifferentiated or unascertained at the time of contract of sale. Therefore, in an attempt to provide adequate statutory protection to the buyer of the undifferentiated part of a bulk, the Sale of Goods (Amendment) Act, 1995 was passed amending SoGA 1979. Here certain relevant changes may be noted. First, by the Act of 1995 a new Section 20 A was inserted which provided that the property in an undivided share of a bulk can pass even before ascertainment as soon as the buyer has paid the price. Secondly, s. 16 was made subject to s. 20 A. Thirdly, it was made clear that an undivided share, specified as a fraction or percentage, of goods identified and agreed on at the time the contract is made is included in the definition of "specific goods." Fourthly, the principle of "ascertainment by exhaustion" was recognized amending s. 18 of SoGA 1979. A differently worded s. 18, inter alia, provides that where there is a contract for

[92]AIR 1961 SC 1214.

[93]See, in particular, Burns (1996), pp. 260–71.

[94]SoGA 1979, s. 16 [SoGA 1930, s. 19]. See also *Re Wait* [1927] 1 Ch. 606.

the sale of a specified quantity of unascertained goods in a deliverable state forming part of a bulk which is identified … and the bulk is reduced to (or less than) that quantity, then, if the buyer under the contract is the only buyer to whom goods are then due out of the bulk—(a) the remaining goods shall be taken as appropriated to that contract at the time when the bulk is so reduced; and (b) the property in those goods then passes to that buyer.

The following part of s. 20 A is relevant to quote here:

> 20 A (1) This section applies to a contract for the sale of a specified quantity of unascertained goods if the following conditions are met—
>
> (a) The goods or some of them form part of a bulk which is identified either in the contract or by subsequent agreement between the parties; and
> (b) The buyer has paid the price for some or all of the goods which are the subject of the contract and which form part of the bulk.
>
> (2) Where this section applies then (unless the parties agree otherwise), as soon as the conditions specified in paragraphs (a) and (b) of subsection above are met or at such later time as the parties may agree—
>
> (a) property in an undivided share in the bulk is transferred to the buyer, and
> (b) the buyer becomes owner in common of the bulk.

6.2.3 Passing of Risks

The basic rule is contained in s. 26 of SoGA 1930 [s. 20 of SoGA 1979], according to which risks and property, unless otherwise agreed, pass simultaneously.[95]

S. 26. Risk *prima facie* passes with property—Where otherwise agreed, the goods remain at the seller's risk until the property therein is transferred to the buyer, but when the property therein is transferred to the buyer, the goods are at the buyer's risk whether delivery has been made or not:

Provided that where delivery has been delayed through the fault of either buyer or seller, the goods are at the risks of the party in fault as regards any loss which might not have occurred but for such fault:

Provided also that nothing in this section shall affect the duties or liabilities of either seller or buyer as a bailee of the goods of the other party.

It may be noted that the rule that the property and risks pass together may be modified in practice.[96] This is particularly true in international sales contract. For example, in an FOB ("free on board") sale, property and risks pass on shipment of the goods, that is to say, when the goods are placed on board the ship.[97] But in a CIF ("cost, insurance, freight") sale, although risks of loss or damage of the goods

[95] See also the discussion on the passing of property and risks in Chap. 3.

[96] D'Arcy et al. (2000), p. 76; Furmston (2000), p. 90.

[97] *Pyrene and Co. v Scindia Navigation Co. Ltd.*, [1954] 2 QB 402; *Colonial Insurance Co. of New Zeeland v Adelaide Marine Insurance Co.* (1886) 1 AC 128; *Contship Container Lines Limited v*

pass on shipment, property passes only when shipping documents are tendered to the buyer.

Wimble, Sons & Co. Ltd. v Rosenberg & Sons is a good illustrative case on the transfer of risks in an FOB contract. In *Wimble*, by a contract of June 27, 1912, Messrs. Rosenberg & Sons, the defendants, bought 200 bags of rice FOB Antwerp. Defendants-buyers sent the plaintiffs instructions to ship the rice to Odessa and to pay freight. The instructions to ship the rice were given in writing omitting the customary request according to which the vendor was to inform the buyer about the name of the ship and the date of the proposed shipment. The rice was actually shipped on board a steamer called the *Egyptian* on August 24, 1912. The defendants knew nothing about it until the 29th, when an invoice and bill of lading reached them, and they were requested to pay against documents. They immediately on receipt of the bill of lading attempted to insure the bags of rice, but they failed. The buyers refused to pay for the rice.

In an action for the price, it was argued by the defendants that the plaintiffs, under s. 32 (3) of the Sale of Goods Act, 1893,[98] were under duty to give notice to the buyers enabling them to insure the goods and since the same was not done the voyage was at the risk of the sellers. While taking the position that s. 32 (3) applied to an FOB contract, the Court ruled that in the present case, the buyers had sufficient knowledge to enable them to insure the goods; and that, therefore, "there was no obligation upon the plaintiffs, under S. 32 (3), to give notice to the defendants of the shipment on a particular ship."

As stated by the Supreme Court in *Contship Container Lines Limited v D. K. Lall and Others*[99]: "[I]n the case of FOB contracts, ...once the seller has placed the goods safely on board at his cost and thereby handed over the possession of the goods to the ship in terms of the Bill of Lading or other documents, the responsibility of the seller ceases and the delivery of the goods to the buyer is complete. The goods are from that stage onwards at the risk of the buyer."[100]

D. K. Lall and Others AIR 2010 SC 1704; *Wimble, Sons & Co. Ltd. v Rosenberg & Sons* [1913] 3 KB 743.

[98]The corresponding provision is contained in s. 39 (3) of the Sale of Goods Act, 1930. S. 39 (3) reads as follows: "Unless otherwise agreed, where goods are sent by the seller to the buyer by a route involving sea transit, in circumstances in which it is usual to insure, the seller shall give such notice to the buyer as may enable him to ensure them during their sea transit, and if the seller fails so to do, the goods shall be deemed to be at his risk during such sea transit."

[99]AIR 2010 SC 1704.

[100]On the FOB contract, see supra, Chap. 3.

6.3 Remedies of Seller and Buyer

6.3.1 Remedies Under General Law of Contract

Under the general law of contract,[101] a breach of the terms of a contract usually gives rise to the right to (1) terminate or avoid a contract for breach or non-performance; (2) damages; and (3) specific performance. Apart from these, an innocent person can also claim the remedy of restitution (or restitutionary remedies). The remedy of restitution seeks to compel the defendant to restore the benefit received by him to the right person. The object is the prevention of gain by the defaulting promisor at the expense of the promisee, that is, the prevention of unjust enrichment. But this remedy, strictly speaking, more properly falls under the law restitution;[102] therefore, is beyond the scope of this book.

Turning now to the position under the law of sale of goods, it may be stated that the remedy of damages is the most important remedy and is commonly available to the seller and the buyer. The remedy of specific performance can be claimed only as an exceptional remedy. Only a buyer can avail this remedy which is confined to a case where the buyer cannot be compensated in terms of money (however, see infra, Sect. 6.3.2.2). As far as the remedy of termination or recession of contract of sale for breach is concerned, it has already been noted that where the breach is so serious so that it amounts to fundamental breach, the innocent party is entitled to treat the contract as discharged.[103] The meaning is that the innocent party is not only entitled to refuse to accept further performance he is also excused from further performance of the contract.[104]

6.3.1.1 Termination for Breach

The non-performance or performance of an obligation in a manner which is inconsistent with the requirements of the contract results in the discharge of contract by breach giving rise to the right to terminate or rescind the contract.[105] However, a breach does not automatically result in the termination or discharge of a contract.

[101]On remedies available to a seller or a buyer, see Atiyah et al. (2010), pp. 447–559; Guest (2006), pp. 871–1116; Furmston (2000), pp. 155–178; Bharuka GC (ed.), pp. 359–499.

[102]For a discussion of the restitutionary remedy, see Poole (2004), pp. 471–75. Remedy of restitution is recognized by s. 65 of Indian Contract Act. S. 65 reads as follows: "When an agreement is discovered to be void, or when a contract becomes void, any person who has received any advantage under such agreement or contract is bound to restore it, or to make compensation for it to the person from whom he received it."

[103]Discharge by breach is different from discharge by agreement and by operation of law. On discharge by breach, see Beatson et al. (2010), pp. 507–23.

[104]See Guest (ed.) (2006), p. 603.

[105]Various terms are used to denote the situation of discharge by breach—termination, rescission or avoidance. As will be seen at the appropriate place, while the 1980 Convention on Contracts for

It only enables an innocent party to treat the contract as discharged. The innocent party may treat the contract as subsisting in which case he is said to have affirmed the contract by accepting the breach.[106] In other words, a breach of contract provides the innocent party an option to put an end to the contract; and regard himself as absolved from further performance of the contract. In this sense, the option of termination of a contract for non-performance can be used as a defense by the innocent party as he can resist the claim for damages by the repudiating party. It may also be noted that the termination of contract frees both—the innocent as well as the repudiating party from further performance of the contract.[107]

Obviously, it is not the every breach of a contract which entitles a party to treat the contract as discharged. Here classifying the terms into conditions, warranties, and innominate terms assumes significance. As has already been noted that conditions are those terms of a contract which go to the root of a contract and their breach may justify the termination of a contract. On the other hand, a breach of warranties does not entitle the innocent party to terminate the contract. It only gives rise to the right to claim damages for loss.[108]

6.3.1.2 Anticipatory Breach of Contract

Further, the innocent party may terminate a contract not only for present breaches but also for anticipatory breaches of contract. This leads us to a discussion of the rule of anticipatory breaches which is now in order.

The anticipatory breach occurs where one of the parties repudiates the contract, that is to say, commits a fundamental breach of contract before the performance of contract becomes due.[109] Like the present breaches, the anticipatory breach does not automatically result in the termination of contract. It rather entitles the innocent party to terminate or avid the contract.[110]

---

the International Sale of Goods (CISG) uses the term, avoidance, the UNIDROIT Principles uses the term, termination of contract. On rescission of the contract, see Atiyah (1961), pp. 210–14.

[106]Beatson et al. (2010), pp. 507–09. See also *Photo Productions Ltd v Securicor Transport Ltd* [1980] AC 827.

[107]See CISG, Article 81 ("Avoidance of contract releases both parties from their obligations under it, subject to any damages which may be due").

[108]Under CISG, a contract may be terminated or avoided for a fundamental breach of contract which is defined in Article 25 as a kind of breach which "results in such detriment to the other party as substantially to deprive him of what he is entitled to expect under the contract..." However, the terminology of the "fundamental breach of contract" is not usually employed under the English common law to describe a kind of breach which is so serious so as to entitle a party to terminate a contract for breach. See Bridge (2010), p. 916; Atiyah et al. (2010), pp. 224–25; Poole (2006) pp. 206–08.

[109]See Article 72 of the CISG, infra, Chap. 7, Sect. 7.8. It may also be noted that the anticipatory breach doctrine is has its origins in the common law and in civil law countries this doctrine is generally not recognized. See Strub (1989), p. 484.

[110]Beatson et al. (2010), p. 514.

While the rule of anticipatory breach remains un-codified under the English law,[111] Indian Contract Act, s. 39 and SOGA 1930 s. 60 expressly recognize this rule.

39. Effect of refusal of party to promise wholly—When a party to a contract has refused to perform, or disabled himself from performing, his promise in its entirety, the promisee may put an end to the contract, unless he has signified, by words or conduct, his acquiescence in its continuance.

One of the illustrations attached to s. 39 reads as follows:

A, a singer, enters into a contract with B, the manager of a theatre, to sing at his theatre two nights in every week during next two months, and B engages to pay her 100 rupees for each night's performance. On the sixth night A willfully absents herself from the theatre. B is at liberty to put an end to the contract.

Similarly, s. 60 of SoGA provides:

Where either party to a contract of sale, repudiates the contract before the date of delivery, the other party may either treat the contract as subsisting and wait till the date of delivery, or he may treat the contract as rescinded and sue for damages for the breach.

6.3.1.3 Damages

Damages are Compensatory

As already stated, damages are the most important remedy under the common law of contract.[112] Under Indian and English law, as a general rule, all breaches of contractual terms give rise to this remedy.[113] They are available for failure of performance; as well as insufficient and defective performance of the contract. Notably, damages are intended to compensate for the loss or damage suffered by the innocent party.[114] Hence, they are compensatory in nature;[115] are not punitive; cannot be awarded to punish the party who has breached the contract.[116] In fact, the law of contract does not recognize any role for punishment of the party who has breached the contractual obligation as its sole purpose is to enforce the contractual obligations.[117] Although it is rare in practice, damages may well be awarded where the loss suffered by the plaintiff is negligible or the plaintiff has suffered no loss at all. The reason is self-evident. The innocent party is entitled to the remedy of damages as a matter of right. But in such a case, the plaintiff is entitled to only nominal damages.[118]

---

[111] Strub (1989)???, p. 481.

[112] See *Photo Production Ltd v Securicor Transport Ltd* [1980] AC 827.

[113] Guest (ed.) (2006), p. 603.

[114] Fuller and Perdue (1936), p. 52.

[115] See Atiyah (1961), p. 223; Beatson et al. (2010), p. 534.

[116] *Addis v Gramophone Co. Ltd.* [1909] AC 488; *Cooperative Insurance Society Ltd Argyll Strres (Holding) Ltd* [1998] 1 AC 1; *Malik v Bank of Credit & Commerce International SA* [1998] 1 Ac 20.

[117] See Poole (2004), pp. 405; Atiyah et al. (2010), p. 223.

[118] Atiyah, id, p. 223.

A further point to note is that in order to succeed in an action for damages, the claimant needs to prove that the other party has breached the contract and the loss sustained by him is the result or consequence of the breach. In other words, before the remedy of damages is awarded, the test of causation needs to be satisfied.[119] Here, a couple of questions further arise. Whether the defendant is liable for all those losses which the innocent party may have suffered or is liable in respect of only those losses which are not too remote? This question relates to the remoteness of damage to be discussed below. Another question relates to the measure or assessment of damages, that is to say, quantifying the sum payable by the party breaching the contract. This needs to be borne in mind that the questions related to the assessment of damages and the remoteness of damage, though related, are considered as distinct and independent questions. In the case of the former, we are primarily concerned with the rules that are helpful in arriving at the amount payable by the party breaching the contract whereas in the case of the latter we are concerned with the question—what kind of loss is actually recoverable?[120] Or what losses should be taken into account in assessing damages?

Assessment of damages

Under the law of contract, the purpose of awarding damages is to place the aggrieved party in the position he would have been had the contract been performed.[121] It follows then the aggrieved party is entitled to be compensated for loss of expected gains or profits[122] which extend to loss of the particular benefit the innocent party is expected to receive.[123] Here, the law seeks to compel the defendant to pay the value of the (lost) performance. The object is to put the plaintiff in as good a position as he would have occupied had the defendant performed his promise. The interest protected in this case is sometimes, called the expectation interest.[124] Loss of expected profit is measured on the basis of the "market price rule" discussed below (Sect. 6.3.4.3).

Where the aggrieved party has in reliance on the promise of the defendant incurred expenses toward preparation of the performance of the contract, the law seeks to compensate him for loss which his reliance on the promise has caused him. The purpose is "to put the innocent person in as good a position as he was before the promise was made."[125] The interest protected here may be called the reliance interest.

---

[119] See *C & P Haulage v Middleton* [1983] 1 WLR 1461. On causation, see Beatson et al. (2010), p. 543; Poole (2006), pp. 429–31.

[120] Fawcett and Carruthers (2008), pp. 95–96.

[121] See the judgment of the Court of Exchequer in *Robinson v Harman* [1848] 1 Exch 850. The judgment is widely regarded as laying the foundations for the law for contractual damages. See also *Surrey Country Council v Bredero Homes Ltd* [1993] 1 WLR 1361; Fuller and Perdue (1936), pp. 52–53; Merrett (2009), p. 469. In tort, by contrast, damages are awarded to put the plaintiff back in the position he would have been had the tort not been committed. See Louise (2009) ibid.

[122] See Beatson et al. (2010), p. 539; Poole (2004), p. 410.

[123] Beatson et al. (2010), p. 540.

[124] Fuller and Perdue (1936), p. 53.

[125] Id, p. 54.

Remoteness of Damage

Traditional Test: Rule in *Hadley v Baxendale*

According to the conventional law of remoteness as derived from the judgment of Alderson B in the Court of Exchequer in *Hadley v Baxendale*,[126] given as back as 1854, damages are recoverable only for such losses which are not "too remote." A loss is not too remote if it arises either (1) naturally, that is, in the usual course of things as a consequence of the breach, that is, or (2) as a consequence of special circumstances but may reasonably be supposed to have been in the contemplation of both parties as the defendant was given necessary information. The difference between the two heads of the rule is that in case (1), damage is obviously not too remote as it occurs in normal course of things. But the kind of loss covered in case (2), is, in the ordinary sense, abnormal as it does not arise naturally; is nonetheless recoverable as is reasonably supposed to be in the contemplation of the parties because the defendant has been given sufficient notice of the special circumstances to enable him to appreciate that this kind of loss would occur.[127] It was later clarified that knowledge necessary to charge the defendant with responsibility under the second head of the rule may be both—actual as well as imputed.[128] Further, under both cases, in order to be recoverable, loss in question must be reasonably contemplated as a "not unlikely" consequence of the breach.[129]

To quote from the judgment of Alderson B in *Hadley v Baxendale*:

> Where two parties have made a contract which one of them has broken, the damages which the other party ought to receive in respect of such breach of contract should be such as may fairly and reasonably be considered either arising naturally, i.e., according to the usual course of things, from such breach, of contract itself, or such as may reasonably be supposed to have been in the contemplation of both parties, at the time they made the contract, as the probable result of the breach of it.

In *Hadley v Baxendale*, production in the plaintiff's mill was suspended due to the breakage of a crankshaft. It was necessary to send the crankshaft to the makers "as a pattern for a new one." The defendants-carriers promised to deliver the shaft to the makers. But the only information given to them was that the article inquestion was the broken shaft of a mill. Owing to the neglect on the part of the defendants, the delivery of the shaft was delayed resulting in the loss of profit to the mill-owners. The plaintiff sued for the recovery of lost profits. It was held that in the circumstances of the case the defendants were not responsible. According to the Court, since the

---

[126][1854] 9 Ex 341.

[127]See *The Pegase* [1981] 1 Lloyd's Rep 175; *Seven Seas Properties Ltd v Al-Essa (No. 2)* [1993] 3 All ER 577.

[128]*Victoria Laundry (Windsor) Ltd v Newman Industries Ltd* [1949] 1 All ER 997 (affirmed in *Koufos v Czarnikow Ltd* (*The Heron II*).

[129]*The Henron II* [1969] 1 AC 350. This, however, is now relevant only as the standard or default rule as based on the traditional test of remoteness. Under the new test, foreseeability of the loss as a likely consequence of the breach is not necessary for deciding that the loss is not too remote. See: *Transfield Shipping Inc of Panama v Mercator Shipping Inc of Monrovia* [2009] 1 AC 61, at p. 9; Kramer (2009), p. 408.

special circumstances were not brought to the notice of the defendants, it could not reasonably be supposed that a delay in the delivery of the crankshaft to the maker would result in loss of profits to the mill owner. As Alderson B categorically stated: "[I]f the special circumstances were wholly unknown to the party breaking the contract, he, at the most, could only be supposed to have had in his contemplation the amount of injury which would arise generally..."

The judgment of Alderson B is often interpreted as laying down two distinct rules of remoteness, one for normal loss and another for abnormal one. Under the so-called, first rule, damages are recoverable for those losses which arise in the normal course of things; under the so-called second rule, damages are recoverable for a loss which is greater than the normal arising as a result of the special circumstances of the case, although, in order to charge the defendant with responsibility, it must be shown that he had knowledge, whether actual or imputed, about the special circumstances at the time the contract was made. However, as it was clarified in a number of cases, including *Victoria Laundry* and *Koufos v Czarnikow Ltd* (*The Heron II*), the rule in *Hadley v Baxendale* cannot be viewed as consisting of two separate tests and the two heads of the rule in *Hadley v Baxendale* are actually part of one general principle.[130]

Here a couple of illustrations attached to s. 73 of Contract Act incorporating the *Hadley v Baxendale* rule may be referred to:

(1) A contracts to sell and deliver 50 maunds of saltpeter to B, at a certain price be paid on delivery. A breaks his promise. B is entitled to receive from A, by way of compensation, the sum, if any, by which the contract price falls short of the price for which B might have obtained 50 maunds of saltpeter of like quality at the time when the saltpeter ought to have been delivered.
(2) A, a builder, contracts to erect and finish a house by the first of January, in order that B may give possession of it at the time to C, to whom B has contracted to let it. A is informed of the contract between B and c. A builds the house so badly that, before the first of January, it falls down and has to be re-built by B, who, in consequence, loses the rent which he was to have received from C, and is obliged to make compensations to C for the breach of his contract. A must make compensation to B for the cost of rebuilding of the house, for the rent lost, and for the compensation made to C.

[130] *The Pegase*, [1981] 1 Lloyd's Rep 175; *Khophraror v Woolwich Building Society*, [1996] 4 All ER 119 (Per Evans LJ, "...it may often be the case that the first and second parts of the rule overlap, or at least that it is unnecessary to draw a clear line of demarcation between them"); Furmston (2017), p. 756.

The judgment of Alderson B has been the subject of considerable discussions and has had profound impact on the later decisions.[131] A particularly instructive case is *Victoria Laundry (Windsor) Ltd v Newman Industries Ltd.*[132] In that case, the plaintiff, a launderer, and a dyer entered into an agreement with the defendant to purchase a new boiler. But the supply of the boiler was considerably delayed. This resulted in the loss of profits as well as certain lucrative dying contracts. The plaintiff sought to recover damages for both—(ordinary) loss of profit resulting from the delay in supply of the boiler as well as additional losses. The Court of Appeal held that the plaintiff was entitled to damages for loss of profit attributable to the delay in the supply of boiler as it must be presumed that the defendant had anticipated some loss for the reason of delay. But addition losses were not recoverable as the defendants had no knowledge of an "especially profitable contract."

The rule in *Hadley v Baxendale* as originally formulated by Alderson B and refined in the Court of Appeal in *Victoria Laundry* was reexamined and rewritten in the House of Lords in a leading case of *Koufos v Czarnikow Ltd* (*The Heron II*) (cited above). Contrary to the approach of Asquith LJ in *Victoria Laundry* case that in order to be recoverable, loss should have been foreseen as "liable to result" from the breach, in *The Henron II*, the House of Lords relied on a different basis of remoteness. It was clarified that the real question, unlike torts, was not whether the loss was reasonably foreseeable or not. Rather the real question was whether the probability of the occurrence of the loss was within the reasonable contemplation of the parties as a "not unlikely" consequence of the breach at the time of contract. This was a remarkable departure from the position taken in *Victoria Laundry*. It was clarified that the test of remoteness in contract is stricter (or narrower) than the test in tort. In contract, for it to be recoverable, a loss must not *merely* be foreseeable but must be within reasonable contemplation of the parties at the time of the contract.[133]

---

[131] The judgment has been applied in a number of cases. For example, *Victoria Laundry (Windsor) Ltd v Newman Industries Ltd* [1949] 1 All ER 997; *The Pegase*, ibid; *Khophraror v Woolwich Building Society*, ibid wherein a claim to damages for exceptional losses under the second branch to the of *Hadley v Baxendale* rule was rejected because necessary facts could not be brought to the knowledge of the defendants. See also *Parsons (H.) (Livestock) Ltd v Uttley Ingham & Co. Ltd.* [1978] QB 791; *Brown v KMR Services Ltd*, [1995] 4 All AR 119; *Islamic Republic of Iran Shipping Lines v Ierax Shipping Co. of Panama, The Forum Craftsman* [1991] 1 Lloyd's Rep 81 & *Koufos v Czarnikow Ltd* (*The Heron II*), [1969] 1 AC 350. The cases, however, while broadly agreeing to the approach of Alderson B have made departures in some respects. See Beatson et al. (2010), pp. 546–47; Guest (2006), pp. 988–89; Poole (2004) pp. 436–37.

[132] [1949] 1 All ER 997.

[133] McKendrick (2000), p. 418; Poole (2004), p. 436; Furmston (2017), p. 753.

New Approach: "Extent of Liability" Principle

As already noted, in order to be recoverable, the loss must be within the reasonable contemplation of the parties as not unlikely consequence of a breach. But problem with this theory is that it does not provide any guidance as to the degree of likelihood necessary to make the loss recoverable.[134] This has led the House of Lords to give an alternative test of remoteness in *Transfield Shipping Inc v Mercator Shipping Inc, The Achilleas.*[135] According to the new test, the loss must be treated as too remote unless the defendant has accepted the liability for such loss under the contract.[136] The new approach looks at the issue of remoteness from the standpoint of the scope of the contractual duty of the defendant.[137]

In *The Achilleas*, under a time charterparty, the charterers undertook to redeliver the ship (*The Achilleas*) to the plaintiff-owners by May 2, 2004. But they did not redeliver the ship until 11 May. Meanwhile, the ship-owners had entered into a follow-on fixture under which they were bound to deliver the ship to the new charterers by 8 May. When it became clear that the ship would not be redelivered before 8 May, the owners renegotiated the follow-on fixture. Since rates had fallen, they had to reduce the freight from $39,500 to $31,500 daily. The owners claimed damages for the whole period of the follow-on fixture, that is, 191 days and 11 h. The defendants admitted that they were liable for the breach but said that their liability was restricted to the difference between the market price and the charter rate for the overrun period between 2 and 11 May. The Court of Appeal, relying on the traditional test of remoteness, held that the owners were entitled to damages for the whole period and not only for the overrun period.

In the House of Lords the decision was reversed. While Lord Rodger and Lady Hale found that the loss was too remote as it could not have been reasonably foreseen as a likely consequence, Lord Hoffmann and Lord Hope, adopting a new approach, held that since the defendants did not assume responsibility for a lost fixture, they were not liable for the loss to the plaintiff.[138] The position adopted by Lord Hoffmann and Lord Hope is grounded in the belief that responsibility for damages under a contract is based on "the intention of the parties" as objectively ascertained because "all contractual liability is voluntarily undertaken."[139] However, this new approach toward remoteness has been criticized on the ground that it runs contrary to the approach of the House of Lords in *The Heron II*.

---

[134]Kramer (2009). pp. 408–15 LQR vol. 125.

[135][2009] 1 AC 61. See also, *South Australia Asset Management Corp v York Montague Ltd* [1997] 1 AC 191 (*SAAMCO*).

[136]See in particular observations of Lord Hoffmann and Lord Hope in *Transfield Shipping Inc v Mercator Shipping Inc, The Achilleas* (cited above). For a critique, see Peel (2009), pp. 6–12.

[137]See Kramer (2009), pp. 408–15; Beatson et al. (2010), pp. 547–49.

[138]See also *South Australia Asset Management Corp v York Montague Ltd* [1997] AC 191, wherein Lord Hoffman took the similar position when he stressed that the real question in such type of cases relates to the scope of the duty undertaken by the defendant.

[139]Peel, id p. 9.

The new approach to remoteness as adopted by the majority in House of Lords in *The Achilleas* was recently adopted by the Court of Appeal in the case of *Supershield Ltd v Siemens Building Technologies FE Ltd*.[140]

Statute Law: Indian Position

The rule in *Hadley v Baxendale* is recognized by s. 73 of the Indian Contract Act.[141] It reads as follows:

Compensation for loss or damage caused by breach of contract—When a contract has been broken, the party who suffers by such breach is entitled to receive, from the party who has broken the contract, compensation for any loss or damage caused to him thereby, which naturally arose in the usual course of things from such breach, or which the parties knew, when they made the contract, to be likely to result from the breach of it.

Such compensation is not to be given for any remote and indirect loss or damage sustained by reason of the breach.

XXX

Here, it may be useful to reproduce a few illustrations attached to s. 73:

1. A hires B's ship to go to Bombay, and there takes on board, on the first of January, a cargo, which A is to provide, and to bring it to Calcutta, the freight to be paid when earned. B's ship does not go to Bombay, but A has opportunities of procuring suitable conveyance for the cargo upon terms as advantageous as those on which he had chartered the ship. A avails himself of those opportunities, but is put to trouble and expense in doing so. A is entitled to receive compensation from B in respect of such trouble and expense.
2. A contracts to buy of B, at a stated price, 50 maunds of rice, no time being fixed for delivery. A afterwards informs B that he will not accept the rice if tendered to him. B is entitled to receive from A, by way of compensation, the amount, if any, by which the contract price exceeds that which B can obtain for the rice at the time when A informs B that he will not accept it.

"Mitigation" Rule

The principle is well settled that a claimant is under a duty to take all reasonable steps for avoiding or minimizing his loss arising from the breach.[142] In other words, the claimant cannot recover damages where he could have avoided the loss by taking reasonable steps to minimize the loss.[143] He cannot claim compensation for a loss

[140] [2010] 1 Lloyd's Rep 349. For further discussion, see Beatson et al. (2010), pp. 548–49.

[141] See *AKAS Jamal v Molla Dawood Sons & Co.* (1916) 1 AC 175; *Pannalal Janakidas v Mohanlal* AIR 1951 SC 144.

[142] This is an oversimplification. The true position is that the claimant is really under no duty to mitigate his loss. The law only requires that the claimant will not be compensated for a loss which could have been avoided by taking reasonable steps. See Beatson et al. (2010), p. 955; Guest (2006), p. 997.

[143] *British Westinghouse Electric and Manufacturing Co. Ltd. v Underground Electric Railways Co. of London Ltd.* [1912] AC 673; Guest (2006), p. 997; Poole (2004), p. 438.

which is really attributable not to the breach by other party but to his own failure to act reasonably after the breach.[144] The compensating advantage obtained by the claimant by mitigating the loss will be deducted from the damages.[145] Explanation attached to s. 73 of Indian Contract Act which incorporates the mitigation rule provides:

In estimating the loss or damage arising from a breach of contract, the means which existed of remedying the inconvenience caused by the non-performance of the contract must be taken into account.

For example, where A promises to sell to B 1000 kg rice for INR 50,000 but fails to deliver the rice at the time fixed for delivery. Here, B should mitigate his loss by purchasing the rice at the market for he may not recover those losses which could be avoided by him.

However, the claimant is only required to take such steps toward the minimization of loss which are reasonable in the ordinary course of business. In other words, he is not required to do more than taking reasonable steps.[146]

6.3.2 Remedies Under Law of Sale of Goods

6.3.2.1 Seller's Remedies Against the Goods

A seller, in addition to personal remedies (discussed below, Sect. 6.3.4.3), has certain remedies against the goods themselves, called real remedies.[147] Real rights or remedies refer to those rights which can be exercised against the goods as in certain cases recourse to personal remedies, is not satisfactory. A seller, therefore, can use the goods in his possession as a security for the limited purpose of recovering the price of the goods sold.[148]

The relevant rules are contained in ss. 45–54 of SoGA 1930 [ss. 38–47 of SoGA 1979]. The wording of these rules is almost identical to their English law counterparts. This is not surprising as both statutes are based on the old 1893 Act and derive their language from it.

S. 46 of SoGA 1930 [s. 39 of SoGA 1979] gives an unpaid seller[149] the following rights against the goods:

1. A lien on the goods for the price while he is in possession of them;
2. In case of the insolvency of the buyer, a right of stopping the goods in transit after he has parted with the possession of them; and

---

[144] Beatson et al. (2010), p. 555.

[145] Ibid.

[146] What is reasonable will mainly depend on the circumstances of the case. See McKendrick (2000), p. 414; Poole (2006), pp. 439–40.

[147] On real remedies, see Guest (ed.) (2006), pp. 871–956; Atiyah et al. (2010), pp. 445–46.

[148] Guest (2006) id, p. 872.

[149] An unpaid seller is defined in s. 45 of SoGA 1930 [s. 38 of SoGA 1979].

3. A limited right of resale

S. 46 of SoGA 1930 provides that subject to this Act (Act of 1930) and of any law for the time being in force and "notwithstanding that the property in the goods may have passed to the buyer," the above said rights accrues to a seller by implication of law. It further provides that if the property in goods has not passed to the buyer, the unpaid seller has the right of "withholding delivery similar to and co-extensive with his rights of lien and stoppage in transit where the property has passed to the buyer."

Right of Lien

The right of lien given to an unpaid seller[150] is a right to retain possession of the goods for the purpose of securing the payment. It is of the nature of a security by virtue of which the unpaid seller can enforce his rights to be paid.[151] Spelling out the meaning of the right of lien, s. 47 (1) of SoGA 1930 [s. 40 of SoGA 1979] states that, subject to the provisions of the Act, the unpaid seller "who is in possession of them is entitled to retain possession of them until payment or tender of the price in a case: where the goods have been sold without any stipulation as to credit."

However, the right of lien gives the seller only limited protection which lasts until the payment is made and the exercise of this right is indeed restricted in many ways. First, this right can be exercised by an unpaid seller only when he has the actual possession of the goods sold. Once the goods are handed over to a carrier for the purpose of transmission to the buyer or to an agent of the buyer, or where the buyer obtains possession of the goods with the consent of the seller, a seller's lien comes to an end.[152] Secondly, the right of lien is only a statutory right and does not exist independently of the Act. Thirdly, this right is merely the right to retain the possession of the goods sold and does not confer upon the seller any proprietary right over the goods in question nor it confers upon him the right of sale. The right of resale given to the unpaid seller is independent from the right of lien. Lastly, the seller generally has no right of lien when he sells the goods on credit. However, there are two exceptions to this rule and the right of lien can be exercised even if the goods

[150] The unpaid seller is defined by S. 45 (1) according to which a seller is 'deemed' to be an unpaid seller: "(a) when the whole of the price has not been paid or tendered; (b) when a bill of exchange or other negotiable instrument has been received as conditional payment, and the condition on which it was received has not been fulfilled by reason of the dishonour of the instrument or otherwise."

[151] *Kemp v Falk* (1882) 7 AC 573.

[152] See Atiyah et al. (2010), pp. 454–55. Termination of the right of lien is dealt with in S. 49 of the Act. It reads as follows:

(1) The unpaid seller of goods loses his lien thereon—
(a) when he delivers the goods to a carrier or other bailee for the purpose of transmission to the buyer without reserving the right of disposal of the goods;
(b) when the buyer or his agent lawfully obtains possession of the goods;
(c) by waiver thereof.
(2) The unpaid seller of goods, having a lien thereon, does not lose his lien by reason only that he has obtained a decree for the price of the goods.

are sold on credit in the following two situations: (a) where the term of credit has expired; and (b) where the buyer becomes insolvent.[153]

Right of Stoppage in Transit

The right to stop the goods in transit which accrues to an unpaid seller by virtue of S. 46 of SoGA 1930 [s.39 of SoGA 1979] is available to the seller only when the buyer has become insolvent and so long the goods are in transit. If the buyer obtains possession of the goods, the transit of the goods comes to an end. S. 50 of SoGA 1930 [s. 44 of SoGA 1979] which deals with the conditions for the exercise of the right of stoppage in transit provides that "[s]ubject to the provisions of this Act, when the buyer becomes insolvent, the unpaid seller who has parted with the possession of the goods has the right of stopping them in transit, that is to say, he may resume possession of the goods as long as they are in the course of transit, and may retain them until payment or tender of the price."

The right of stoppage in transit raises an important issue about the meaning of the course of transit which is addressed by s. 51 of SoGA 1930 which is identical to its English law counterpart, s. 45 of SoGA 1979. The term "course of transit" is defined as follows:

51. Duration of transit—

(1) Goods are deemed to be in course of transit from the time when they are delivered to a carrier or other bailee for the purpose of transmission to the buyer, until the buyer or his agent in that behalf takes delivery of them from such carrier or other bailee.

(2) If the buyer or his agent in that behalf obtains delivery of the goods before their arrival at the appointed destination, the transit is at an end.

(3) If, after the arrival of the goods at the appointed destination, the carrier or other bailee acknowledges to the buyer or his agent that he holds the goods on his behalf and continues in possession of them as bailee for the buyer or his agent, the transit is at an end and it is immaterial that a further destination for the goods may have been indicated by the buyer.

(4) If the goods are rejected by the buyer and the carrier or other bailee continues in possession of them, the transit is not deemed to be at an end, even if the seller has refused to receive them back.

(5) When goods are delivered to a ship chartered by the buyer, it is a question depending on the circumstances of the particular case, whether they are in the possession of the master as a carrier or as agent of the buyer.

(6) Where the carrier or other bailee wrongfully refuses to deliver the goods to the buyer or his agent in that behalf, the transit is deemed to be at an end.

(7) Where part delivery of the goods has been made to the buyer or his agent in that behalf, the remainder of the goods may be stopped in transit, unless such part delivery has been given in such circumstances as to show an agreement to give up possession of the whole of the goods.

---

[153]Section 47 of SoGA 1930 [41(1) of SoGA 1979]. See further, Atiyah et al. (2010), pp. 451–52.

An important point to note is that the right to stop the goods in transit is not linked to the transfer of the property in the goods. Thus, when the bill of lading is tendered to the buyer and consequently property in the goods has passed to him, the unpaid seller does not lose his right of stoppage.[154]

Right of Resale

S. 54 of SoGA 1930 [s. 48 of SoGA 1979] gives an unpaid seller the right of sale of a limited nature to enforce his right to receive the price of the goods. This right can be exercised:

(a) Where the goods are of a perishable nature, or

(b) where the unpaid seller who has exercised his right of lien or stoppage in transit gives notice to the buyer of his intention to re-sell, the unpaid seller may, if the buyer does not within a reasonable time pay or tender the price, re-sell the goods within a reasonable time and recover from the original buyer damages for any loss occasioned by his breach of contract, but the buyer shall not be entitled to any profit which may occur on the re-sale. If such notice is not given, the unpaid seller shall not be entitled to recover such damages and the buyer shall be entitled to the profit, if any, on the re-sale.

It may be noted that s. 54 deals with the unpaid seller's right of resale who exercised his right of lien, or the right of stoppage and regained possession of the goods. It is intended to apply to a case where property has passed to the original buyer. Here passing of property to the original buyer does not affect the right of the second buyer. It is important to note that in the case of resale of the goods under s. 54 the (second) buyer acquires a good title as against the original buyer even if the property in the goods has already passed to the original buyer. This result follows from s. 54 (3) which states

> Where an unpaid seller who has exercised his right of lien or stoppage in transit re-sells the goods, the buyer acquires a good title thereto as against the original buyer, notwithstanding that no notice of the re-sale has been given to the original buyer.

The principle is that where the unpaid seller who has exercised his right of lien or stoppage in transit gives notice to the buyer of his intention to re-sell, and if the buyer does not within a reasonable time pay or tender the price, the property in the goods reverts to the seller who can, in exercise of the right of resale, transfer it to the second buyer and in that case the second buyer acquires a good title thereto as against the original buyer.[155] This was made clear by the Court of Appeal in *Ward (RV) v Bignall.*[156] In that case, the defendant agreed to buy two used cars—a Ford Zodiac and a Vanguard estate car—from the plaintiffs for 850 Pound. The defendants paid 25 Pound towards the price and left the home of the plaintiff for arranging the rest of the amount. Subsequently, he repudiated the contract and declined to make payment and take delivery of the cars. His offer to buy the Zodiac car alone for 500

[154]Chuah (2009), p. 128; Atiyah et al. id., pp. 460–61.

[155]D'Arcy et al. (2000), p. 103.

[156][1967] 1 Q.B. 534.

Pound was rejected by the plaintiffs who requested the defendant to make payment and take delivery of both cars. No express right of resale had been reserved by the plaintiffs in case of the defendant's default. The defendant failed to make payment and take delivery, and the plaintiffs subsequently resold the Vanguard elsewhere for 350 Pound. They brought an action against the defendant claiming damages being the balance of the purchase price of both cars. The judgment was given for the plaintiffs. However, the Court of Appeal held that the plaintiffs-sellers were not entitled to the price of the Zodiac car since the resale of the Vanguard car had rescinded the original contract.

The Court of Appeal clarified the scope of application of s. 48 (3) of the Sale of the Goods Act, 1979 (which is identical to s. 54 (2) of the Act of 1930). According to the Court, s. 48 (3) is "limited to cases where the property in the goods at the time of resale had already passed to the original buyer." The Court further held since a stipulation as to time of payment is not of the essence of a contract of sale unless a different intention appears from the terms of the contract failure by the buyer to pay on the stipulated date does not in itself entitle the unpaid seller to treat the contract as repudiated. "He remains liable to deliver the goods to the buyer upon tender of the contract price."[157] But, according to the Court, the purpose of s. 46 (3) of the English Sale of Goods Act [which is identical to s. 54 (2) of the Indian Act of 1930] is:

to make time of payment of the essence of the contract whenever the goods are of a perishable nature, and to enable an unpaid seller, whatever the nature of the goods, to make payment within a reasonable time after notice of the essence of the contract.[158]

6.3.2.2 Seller's Personal Remedies

Where a buyer makes default in payment of the price or refuses to accept the goods, the law gives a seller certain personal remedies in the form of actions for the price and damages. The normal rule may be stated like this. Where property in the goods has passed to the buyer, the seller may bring an action for the price S. 55, SoGA 1930 [s. 49, SoGA 1979]. But where property in the goods has not passed, the seller's remedy is to sue for damages S. 56, SoGA 1930 [s. 50, SoGA 1979]. However, as will be seen below, in certain exceptional situations, a different rule may apply.[159]

Action for Price
55. Suit for price—

(1) Where under a contract of sale the property in the goods has passed to the buyer and the buyer wrongfully neglects or refuses to pay for the goods according to the terms of the contract, the seller may sue him for the price of the goods.

---

[157] Id., pp. 549–50 (Per Diplok LJ).

[158] Id., p. 550 (Per Diplok LJ), [emphasis supplied].

[159] See s. 55 (2), SoGA 1930 [s. 49 (2) SoGA 1979].

(2) Where under a contract of sale the price is payable on a day certain irrespective of delivery and the buyer wrongfully neglects or refuses to pay such price, the seller may sue him for the price although the property in the goods has not passed and the goods have not been appropriated to the contract.

Under s. 55(1) of SoGA 1930 [s. 49 (1) of SoGA 1979], the passing of property in the goods to the buyer is a pre-condition for bringing an action for the price. But in a situation covered under s. 55 (2), that is to say, where the contract specifically provides that the price is to be paid on a fixed date irrespective of passing of property in the goods, the action for price will lie even if property in the goods has not passed. In both situations, the question of delivery is not important.[160] Applying the principle of s. 55 to international sales contracts, it may be stated that in a FOB contract, where property passes upon shipment, the seller cannot sue for the price before shipment of the goods and since in a CIF contract passing of property is linked to the delivery of shipping documents and not shipment of goods, seller cannot sue for the price until delivery of such documents.

Damages for Non-acceptance of Goods

Section 56 [s. 50 (1) of SoGA 1979] gives a seller the right to bring an action for damages for non-acceptance of the goods:

56. Damages for non-acceptance—Where the buyer wrongfully neglects or refuses to accept and pay for the goods, the seller may sue him for damages for non-acceptance.

The section makes wrongful neglect or refusal to pay the price on the part of the buyer a pre-condition for claim for damages on the part of the seller. It is intended to apply to both cases—where property in the goods has not passed to the buyer; and where property in the goods has passed to the buyer but he wrongfully neglects or refuses to accept and pay for the goods. In the former case, the claim for damages is a normal remedy whereas in the latter case, damages may be claimed as an alternative remedy to the remedy of bringing an action for the price under s. 55.[161]

Assessment of Damages: Market Price Rule

Here a brief discussion on the issue of the measure of damages may also be made. The discussion that follows here has the relevance for both—a seller and a buyer.

In this respect, ss. 50 and 54 SoGA 1979 lays down the following rules[162]:

(1) the measure of damages is the estimated loss directly and naturally resulting, in the ordinary course of events, from the buyer's breach of contract (s. 50(2));
(2) where there is an available market for the goods in question the measure of damages is prima facie to be ascertained by the difference between the contract price and the market or current price at the time or times when the goods ought to have been accepted or (if no time was fixed for acceptance) at the time of the refusal to accept (s. 50(3));

---

[160] See *Bungu Steel Furniture Pvt Ltd v Union of India* AIR 1967 SC 378; Guest (2006), p. 970.
[161] See Atiyah et al. (2010) p. 485; Guest (ed.) ibid.
[162] See, Beatson et al. (2010), p. 557; Atiyah et al, id., pp. 488–94.

(3) Nothing in this Act affects the right of the buyer or the seller to recover interest or special damages in any case where by law interest or special damages may be recoverable, or to recover money paid where the consideration for the payment of it has failed (s. 54 [s. 61 of SoGA 1930].

The above-said rule (1) incorporates the first branch of the rule in *Hadley v Baxendale*. This is intended to apply to a situation where application of the market price rule incorporated in s. 50 (3) (rule (2) above) is likely to lead to incorrect assessment or there is no available market for the purpose of applying the market price rule. The above said rule (2) or s. 50 (3) SoGA 1979 or the market price rule, as it is called, merely lays down a method of the assessment of damages based on the difference between the contract price and the market or current price. Further, this, as will be seen below, is only a prima facie rule and may well be avoided where it is likely to result in incorrect assessment of damages.[163] The above-said rule (3) applies to a situation where the seller or the buyer, as the case may be, claims special damages under the second limb of the *Hadley v Baxendale* rule.[164]

Market Price Rule and Modern Conditions

Ss. 50 (3) and 51 (3) of SoGA 1979[165] incorporate the "market price" rule of common law settled well before the enactment of the Act of 1893.[166] The rule requires that a buyer or seller's claim for damages should be assessed on the basis of the difference between the contract price, that is, selling or buying price, as the case may be, and the market or current price of the goods at the breach date.

The rule raises a few incidental but difficult questions. The first such question relates to the meaning of an "available market" for the purpose of applying the market price rule. Various approaches are possible depending on the context to which they relate to.[167] But for the present purpose, it is quite helpful to refer to the view adopted by Jenkins LJ according to which the most relevant factor in identifying a market is the situation where prices are determined by the supply and demand.[168]

Another question relates to the significance of the market price rule, especially in in situations when prices are already fixed. Put differently, the question that needs to be considered is: whether a seller can claim damages for the loss of profits where as a result of a fixed retail price of the goods in question there is little or no difference between the contract price and the market price? The question was raised in two cases involving similar facts—*Thompson (WL) Ltd v Robinson (Gunmakers) Ltd*

[163] Guest (2006), p. 1005; Atiyah et al. (2010), pp. 492–93.

[164] Guest, AG (ed.) id, p. 991.

[165] S. 51 (3) relates to a buyer's claim for damages for non-delivery of goods by a seller.

[166] Guest (ed.) (2006) p. 1006; Atiyah et al. (2010) p. 485.

[167] It is simply not possible to give a universally agreed definition of "market" as the concept varies from context to context. It may refer to "a particular level of trade" (*Heskell v Continental Express Ltd* [1950] 1 All ER 1033); a situation where there is a sufficient demand for the goods (*Thompson (WL) Ltd. v Robinson (Gunmakers) Ltd* [1955] Ch 177). For a more fully discussion, see Guest (ed.) (2006), pp. 1006–12; Atiyah et al. (2010), pp. 486–88.

[168] See *Charter v Sullivan* [1957] 2 QB 117.

(cited above) and *Charter v Sullivan* (cited above). In both cases, the seller claimed damages for non-acceptance of the goods by the buyer. The buyer's reply, in both cases, was that since there was no difference between the contract price and the market price of the goods in question, the seller could claim only nominal damages. But two cases differed in one important respect which led to two different outcomes. While in *Thompson (WL) Ltd* case supply of the goods exceeded demand, in *Charter v Sullivan* case it was opposite that was true. In *Thompson (WL) Ltd* case, the court, therefore, found that although there was no difference between the contract price and market price, the plaintiff-seller could still recover loss of expectations because there was loss of one sale. Since the market price rule of s. 50 (3) of SoGA 1979 was likely to lead an unsatisfactory solution, it was ignored by the Court. But in *Charter v Sullivan* involving a situation where demand exceeded supply, a different view was taken by the court. The Court of Appeal found that in view of the excess of demand over supply, the plaintiff-seller was able to sell all the goods he had; therefore, he was only entitled to nominal damages.

6.3.2.3 Buyer's Remedies

A buyer's remedy, in the first place, is to reject the goods if they do not conform to the contract description or of not the right quality. He can also in certain situations repudiate the contract; can bring an action for damages for non-delivery of the goods or for the breach of warranty. In addition to these, he has also the remedy of specific performance of the contract of sale. These remedies are dealt with in Ss. 57–60 of SoGA 1930 and 51–53 of SoGA 1979. S. 57 is about the right of damages for non-delivery of the goods and s. 59 deals with the claim for damages for breach of warranty. The remedy of specific performance is provided in s. 58 of the Act.

Right to Reject the Goods

The right to reject the goods accrues to a buyer in a good number of cases. Obviously, in all cases where a seller breaches a condition the buyer is entitled to terminate the contract of sale and as part of this has the right to reject the goods.[169] For example, where the seller fails to deliver the goods of contract description or fails to deliver the goods of right quality, the buyer will have the right to reject the goods and/or to claim damages. In other words, a breach of a condition or an innominate term where the consequences of the breach goes to the root of the contract entitles the buyer to reject the goods. See infra, Sect. 6.1.4.

However, under SoGA 1979, s. 30 (2A), a buyer who is not a consumer may not reject the goods for slight breaches in respect of delivery of wrong quantity of goods. The provision similar to the original s. 30 is contained in s. 37 of SoGA 1930.

---

[169] See Guest (ed.) (2006), p. 610; *Kwei Tek Chao v British Traders & Shippers Ltd* [1954] 2 QB 459.

Loss of the Right to Reject

A buyer's right to reject the goods is lost by acceptance of the goods. S. 35 (1) of SoGA 1979 provides:

35. (1) The buyer is deemed to have accepted the goods[subject to subsection (2) below—

(a) When he intimates to the seller that he has accepted them, or
(b) When the goods have been delivered to him and he does any act in relation to them which is inconsistent with the ownership of the seller.

However, loss of the right of rejection by acceptance is linked to the buyer's opportunity to examine the goods. Subsection (2) of s. 35 provides:

35. (2) Where goods are delivered to the buyer, and he has not previously examined them, he is not deemed to have accepted them under subsection (1) above until he has had a reasonable opportunity of examining them for the purpose—

(a) of ascertaining whether they are in conformity with the contract, and
(b) in the case of a contract for sale by sample, of comparing the bulk with the sample.

It is further provided by s. 35 that although a buyer is deemed to have accepted the goods when after the lapse of a reasonable time he retains the goods without intimating to the seller that he has rejected them, he is not deemed to have accepted the goods merely because—(a) he asks for, or agrees to, their repair by or under an arrangements with the seller, or (b) the goods are delivered to another under a sub-sale or their disposition (subsections (4) and (6) of s. 35).

A further point to note is that the right of rejection may also be lost by waiver. Where a buyer does not use the option of rejecting the goods and is content with the claim for damages only, he is said to have waived his right of rejection by affirming the contract of sale.[170]

Claim for Damages

Section 57 which deals with the buyer's claim for damages for non-delivery of the goods reads as follows:

57. Damages for non-delivery—Where the seller wrongfully neglects or refuses to deliver the goods to the buyer, the buyer may sue the seller for damages for non-delivery.

This section will apply irrespective of the fact whether the property in the goods has passed to the buyer or not. Furthermore, s. 59 provides:

59. Remedy for breach of warranty—

(1) Where there is a breach of warranty by the seller, or where the buyer elects or is compelled to treat any breach of a condition on the part of the seller as a breach of warranty, the buyer is not by reason only of such breach of warranty entitled to reject the goods; but he may—

[170]Guest AG (ed.) id, p. 614.

(a) set up against the seller the breach of warranty in diminution or extinction of the price; or

(b) sue the seller for damages for breach of warranty.

(2) The fact that a buyer has set up a breach of warranty in diminution or extinction of the price does not prevent him from suing for the same breach of warranty if he has suffered further damage.

Thus, a buyer has claim for damages in two situations: (a) where the seller wrongfully neglects or refuses to deliver the goods to the buyer (S. 57); and (b) where there is a breach of warranty by the seller, or where the buyer elects any breach of a condition as a breach of warranty.

Specific Performance of Contract

S. 58 of SoGA 1930 which is similar to s. 52 of SOGA 1979 gives a buyer the remedy of specific performance of contract by virtue of which he can get the terms of the contract performed. An order of specific performance requires the party in breach of a contract to perform his primary obligations arising under the contract.[171] But this is not a usual remedy in a contract of sale of goods and the court will order the specific performance only when the buyer cannot be compensated in terms of money. Under common-law-based systems, the rule is that the remedy of specific performance shall not be granted where damages provide adequate relief. Thus, recourse to specific performance is of no avail where the goods sold are not in some sense unique.[172]

In India, under the general law of contract the remedy of specific performance is regulated by the provisions of the Specific Relief Act 1963[173] and in the specific context of the sale of goods it is governed by s 58 of SOGA. The latter is expressly stated to be subject to the former. The underlying principle of these provisions is that the specific performance will not be ordered where damages are the adequate remedy. Since the goods can ordinarily be obtained in the market, in the case of sale of goods, the remedy of specific performance has a restrictive scope. However, as already noted in Chap. 4 (Sect. 4.4), things have radically changed with the coming into effect of a recent amendment to the Specific Relief Act; as a result, the remedy of specific performance is no longer an exceptional one and can be claimed by both buyer and seller. However, s. 58 of SoGA 1930 envisages only a limited role for the specific performance remedy.

58. Specific performance—Subject to the provisions of Chap. 2 of the Specific Relief Act, 1877[174] (1 of 1877), in any suit for breach of contract to deliver specific or ascertained goods, the Court may, if it thinks fit, on the application of the plaintiff, by its decree direct that the contract shall be performed specifically, without giving the defendant the option of retaining the goods on payment of damages. The decree may be unconditional, or upon such terms and conditions as to damages, payment

[171] McKendrick (2000), p. 441.

[172] Beatson et al. (2010), p. 576.

[173] Under English law this remedy remains un-codified.

[174] Specific Relief Act, 1963.

of the price, or otherwise, as the Court may deem just, and the application of the plaintiff may be made at any time before the decree.

A reading of s. 58 shows first that the remedy of specific performance is given only to a buyer and not to a seller.[175] Secondly, it is a discretionary remedy and the courts will not be willing to order specific performance when replacement of the goods is available in the market. Since the goods can ordinarily be obtained in the market and the buyer can adequately be compensated in terms of money, there is little scope for the applicability of s. 58 in normal conditions.[176] Further, s. 58 applies to the sale of specific or ascertained goods. However, in recent years, a tendency has grown to grant specific performance in the sale of unascertained goods also.[177]

References

Atiyah, P. S., Adams, J. N., & Macqueen, H. (2010). *Atiyah's sale of goods*. New Delhi: Dorling Kindersley.

Atiyah, P. S. (1961). *An introduction to the law of contract*. Oxford: Clarendon Press.

Beatson, J., Burrows, A., & Cartwright, J. (2010). *Anson's law of contract*. Oxford: Oxford University Press.

Bharuka, G. C. (ed.) (2007). *Pollock & Mulla: The sale of goods act*. New Delhi: LexisNexis.

Bridge, (2010). Avoidance for fundamental breach of contract under the UN Convention on the International Sale of Goods. *International and Comparative Law Quarterly, 59*(4), 911–940.

Bridge, M. (1997). *The sale of goods*. Oxford: Oxford University Press.

Burns, T. (1996). Better late than never: The reform of the law on the sale of goods forming part of a bulk. *Modern Law Review, 59*(2), 260–271.

Chuah, J. C. T. (2009). *Law of international trade: Cross-Border commercial transactions*. London: Sweet & Maxwell, First South Asian Edition 2011.

D'Arcy, L., Murray, C., & Cleave, B. (eds.) (1990). *Schmitthoff's export trade: The law and practice of international trade*. London: Stevens.

Davies, C. (1969). Merchantability and fitness for purpose: Implied conditions of the sale of goods Act 1893. *Law Quarterly Review, 85,* 74–91.

Fawcett, J. J., & Carruthers, J. M. (2008). *Chesire, North and Fawcett: Private international law*. Oxford: Oxford University Press.

Fuller, L. L. & Perdue, W. R. (1936). *The reliance interest in contract damages: 1 Yale Law Journal, 46* (1) 52–96,

Furmston, M. (2000). *Sale & supply of goods*. London, Sydney: Cavendish Publishing Ltd.

Furmston, M. P. (2017). *Chesire, Fifoot, & Furmston's law of contract*. Oxford: Oxford University Press.

Garner, B. A. (Ed.). (2009). *Black's law dictionary*. Thomson Reuters: West.

Guest, A. G. (ed.) (2006). *Benjamin's sale of goods*. London: Sweet & Maxwell.

Kramer, A. (2009). The new test of remoteness in contract Law. *Quarterly Review, 125*(408–15), 408.

McKendrick, E. (2000). *Law of contract*. Hampshire, London: Macmillan Press Ltd.

[175] It may be noted that s. 58 uses the terms, plaintiffs and defendants and not buyers and sellers.

[176] See *Societe des Industries v Bronx Engineering Co. Ltd.* [1975] 1 Lloyd's Rep 465.

[177] See Atiyah et al. (2010), p. 559 citing *Sky Petroleum v VIP Petroleum* [1974] 1 All ER 954 wherein the English Court granted the remedy of specific performance in the case of sale of unascertained goods in the extraordinary circumstances of the case.

Merrett, L. (2009). Costs as damages. *Law Quarterly Review, 125,* 468–490.
New International Webster's Comprehensive Dictionary of the English Language (2004). Trident Press International, p. 1294.
Peel, E. (2009). Remoteness revisited. *Law Quarterly Review, 125,* 6–12.
Poole, J. (2004). *Contract law*. Oxford: Oxford University Press.
Strub, M. G. (1989). The convention on the international sale of goods: Anticipatory repudiation provisions and developing countries. *International and Comparative Law Quarterly, 38*(3), 475–501.

Chapter 7
UN Convention on Contracts for the International Sale of Goods

7.1 Toward Uniform Regulation of International Sales Contracts

As noted in Chap. 2, efforts toward unification of domestic laws governing international sales transactions gathered momentum with the establishment of International Institute for the Unification of Private Law (UNIDROIT) in 1926. UNIDROIT's great efforts led to the adoption in 1964 of the first international conventions on the subject containing in their annexes, the "Uniform Law for International Sale of Goods" (ULIS)[1] and the "Uniform Law on the Formation of Contracts for International Sale of Goods" (ULF),[2] also referred to as the "Uniform Laws." However, they failed in gaining the trust of the international community and were mainly criticized for showing a strong preference for the laws and practices which favored the Western, developed world grounded in civil law traditions.[3] Though, Uniform Laws proved inadequate, it would be a mistake to suggest that they were of no significance. Their failure exposed the gaps and weaknesses in the then scheme of the things which needed to be addressed for erecting an internationally acceptable convention. Above all, it did not diminish the hopes of reaching an agreement on a subject as complex as the uniform law on international sales. The main contribution of the Uniform Laws lies in preparing the ground for further negotiations which eventually led to the adoption of the UN Convention on Contracts for International Sale of Goods (CISG).[4]

[1]For the text, see 13 AJCL 453–56 (1964).

[2]For the text, see 13 AJCL 470–74 (1964).

[3]See Viejobueno (1995), p. 200; Suy (1981), p. 141; MGilbey (1989), pp. 475–501; Bergsten (2015), pp. 7–9.

[4]Adopted on April 11, 1980; entered into force on January 1, 1988; currently, 85 states are parties. India is not a party. For the text, see 19 ILM 668-69 (1980), the text together with explanatory note can also be accessed from: http://www.uncitral.org/pdf/english/texts/sales/cisg/V1056997-CISG-e-book.pdf. All judicial decisions concerning the CISG are available at: http://www.cisg.law.pace. On CISG, see Bridge (2010), pp. 911–40; Moens and Gillies (2006), pp. 1–46; Carr (2014), pp. 57–92;

A. Srivastava, *Modern Law of International Trade*, International Law and the Global South, https://doi.org/10.1007/978-981-15-5475-9_7

Therefore, when UNCITRAL undertook efforts toward unification of sales laws in 1967, it did not have to start a fresh. It rightly confined itself to a less ambitious project, that is, to "review and revise" the "existing texts" of Uniform Laws to make them widely acceptable. It then wasted no time in establishing a working group with a clear mandate of suggesting such modifications in the existing texts which were needed for this purpose. The working group identified a number of areas of concern where international cooperation was most needed. These relentless efforts bore fruit when in 1977 a draft Convention on the subject as based on the text submitted by the working group was adopted by UNCITRAL. It was this draft that finally took the form of a convention, known as CISG. The Convention was adopted at a Diplomatic Conference held in Vienna. Significantly, the Vienna Conference was attended by delegates from 62 countries representing all major legal traditions, though most of them belonged to the developed world.[5]

As Preamble to the CISG stresses, CISG, being an instrument containing uniform rules on international sale of goods, can contribute greatly toward the removal of legal barriers in international trade and promote the development of international trade which "is an important element in promoting friendly relations among States."[6]

7.2 Reconciling Divergent Approaches

A notable feature of CISG is that it successfully incorporates the elements of both major systems—common and civil law—and also tries to address the concerns of developing countries.[7] While ULF and ULIS had a clear preference for concepts and principles grounded in the civil law tradition, CISG endeavors to forge a common ground on many contentious issues such as those related to the requirement of consideration, formation of contracts, and remedies for breach. Here a brief reference to some of most important compromises made in the text of the Convention may be made.

The first important compromise relates to the requirement of consideration. Since the concept is not familiar to the civil law countries, the text omits any reference to considerationas an element of the contract. Secondly, with respect to the formation of contract, CISG adopts a solution that suits to countries from both—civil and common law traditions. While broadly conforming to the position under common

Chuah (2009) pp. 149–68; Explanatory Note by the UNCITRAL Secretariat on the United Nations Convention on Contracts for the International Sale of Goods (2010), pp. 33–42; Strub (1989), pp. 475-501; Eorsi (1983), p. 333; Honnold (1979), pp. 223–230; Lookofsky (1991), pp. 403–16; Ndulo (1989), pp. 1–25; Bridge (2007), pp. 505–98.

[5]Bonell (2008) pp. 1–28.

[6]Notably, the international trading system of the World Trade Organization aimed at regulating international trade, also stresses promoting free trade among nations in the interests of friendly relations among states.

[7]The earlier conventions—ULIF and ULIS were frequently criticized as adopting a drafting style which favoured the countries of civil law tradition.

law, it tries to address the gap between the civil and common law rules on the acceptance and revocation of offer. Here, two important departures from common law may be noted. One, according to CISG, an acceptance is complete only when it reaches the offeror. Two, while under the common law an offer is revocable at the will of the offeror unless it is accepted, under CIS an offeror cannot revoke an offer when there is: either a promise on the part of the offeror that the offer will not be revoked; or offeree acts in reliance of the offer.[8] A third important area of compromise relates to remedies for breach of contract. Here attention may be drawn to two most important provisions. First, under CISG, as it is the case with civil-law-based systems, the remedy of specific performance is a normal remedy as not based on inadequacy of the remedy of damages. Secondly, the Convention expressly incorporates the common law principle of the anticipatory breach of contract (articles 71 and 72), although serious difference surfaced between developing and developed countries on this aspect.[9] As developing countries feared that the anticipatory breach provisions might be abused by the parties from the developed countries, necessary compromises were made to reduce their apprehensions.[10]

7.3 Interpretation of the Convention

Notably, CISG, unlike ULIS and ULF, do incorporate provisions which are helpful in interpreting the text of the Convention itself and the terms of the contract to which the Convention applies. Article 7(1) which deals with the interpretation and "filling of gaps" issues provide that in interpreting the Convention "regard is to be had to its international character and to the need to promote uniformity in its application and the observance of good faith in international trade." Since the provisions of the Convention are to be applied and interpreted by the national courts, importance of such a provision cannot be overstated. Given the ample scope of different and unique interpretations of the Convention's provisions, it seems crucial to provide some guidance in regard to interpretations of the Convention.[11] Since the CISG lays down uniform rules intended to be applied uniformly, the domestic courts should not allow their views to be colored by the domestic principles of the law of contract. Instead, they should promote uniformity in applying the Convention to an international contract of sale of goods.

Regarding the filling of gaps in the coverage of the Convention, Article 7 (2) provides that "questions concerning matters governed by this Convention which are not expressly settled in it are to be settled in conformity with the general principles on which it is based or, in the absence of such principles, in conformity with the law applicable by virtue of the rules of private international law." Gaps exist if

---

[8]See Sect. 7.6 below. See also Viejobueno (1995), p. 206.

[9]See in particular, MGilbey (1989), pp. 457–501.

[10]Ibid.

[11]See Moens and Gillies (2006), p. 11.

certain matters are not expressly settled by a convention and are left to be governed by implication. An example of such a matter which is not expressly settled by the Convention is the right of interest provided for by Article 78 of the Convention.[12] According to Article 78 a right to interest arises "if a party fails to pay the price or any other sum that is in arrears." However, Article 78 does not provide any indication regarding the rate of interest and whether it is simple or compound.[13]

Further, Article 7(2) of the Convention uses also the concept of "good faith" as a tool of interpretation. The Convention is to be interpreted in the light of the principle of good faith. But the term "good faith" is not defined and its precise meaning is not clear.[14] Since the concept is susceptible to various interpretations, it is possible that "some national courts will interpret this provision more broadly than others."[15] However, recourse to the principle of good faith may be useful in many ways. It can give the courts sufficient flexibility in applying the provisions of the Convention; can prevent a domestic court acting too hastily.[16] The CISG also contains a provision on the interpretation of the statements made by and other conduct of a party. Article 8 (1) provides that for the purposes of the Vienna Convention "statements made by and other conduct of a party are to be interpreted according to his intent where the other party knew or could not have been unaware what the intent was."

7.4 Scheme of Convention

CISG is divided into four parts. The first part, comprising Chaps. 1 (articles 1–6) and II (articles 7–13) deal, respectively, with "sphere of application" and "general provisions." General provisions include but are not limited to such aspects as the interpretation of the Convention, applicability of the mercantile usage, and the requirement of form. The second part (articles 14–24) contains the rules regarding formation of the contract, that is to say, rules about what constitutes a valid offer and acceptance, requirements of communication of offer and acceptance, revocation, and the conclusion of contract. The third and which is also the largest part, titled "sale of goods" (articles 25–88) deals with general provisions (articles 25–29), obligations of the seller (articles 30–44), remedies for breach of obligations by the seller (articles 45–52), obligations of the buyer (articles 54–60), remedies for breach of contract by the buyer (articles 61–65), and passing of risks (articles 66–70); and also contains provisions which commonly apply to the seller and the buyer such as those related to anticipatory breach (articles 71–72), instalment sale (Article 73), measure of damages (Articles 74–77), mitigation of damage (Article 77), and entitlement to

[12]See Bridge (2007), p. 536.

[13]Ibid.

[14]Muna Ndulo, p. 9.

[15]Bridge (2007), p. 534.

[16]Muna Ndulo p. 9.

interest (Article 78). The fourth part contains final provisions like implementation, ratification, accession, and reservations to the Convention.

7.5 Scope of Application

7.5.1 Automatic Application of the Convention

As already noted in Chap. 2 (Sect. 2.2.1), a notable feature of CISG is that, unless the parties show a preference for a different law, it is directly applicable to a contract of sale between the parties of the ratifying states displacing the domestic law. In other words, once the conditions of the applicability of CISG are met, it can supersede the concerned domestic law—the substantive as well as conflict of laws rules provided that the parties have not excluded its application. Article 1 (1) provides

(1) This Convention applies to contract of sale of goods between parties whose places of business are in different States:
   (a) When the States are Contracting States; or
   (b) When the rules of private international law lead to the application of the law of a Contracting State.
(2) "The fact that the parties have their places of business in different States is to be disregarded whenever this fact does not appear either from the contract or from any dealings between, or from information disclosed by, the parties at any time before or at the conclusion of the contract."
(3) Neither the nationality of the parties nor the civil or commercial character of the parties or of the contract is to be taken into consideration in determining the application of this Convention.

Article 1 (1) speaks of two situations in which CISG may apply. First, as provided under Article 1 (1) (a), CISG applies to a situation where the parties have their places of business in different contracting states provided that this fact appears "either from the contract itself, or in any dealings between the parties or from information disclosed by the parties at any time before or at the conclusion of the contract."[17] The reader will notice that in a situation covered by Article 1(1) (a), the Convention applies directly, without recourse to private international law rules. In other words, under Article 1 (1) (a), CISG applies as part of the domestic law of a state party.[18]

Conflict of Law Rules

Another situation in which CISG applies is given in Article 1(1) (b), according to which, the Convention applies when the parties have their places of business in

[17]CISG, Article 1 (2): "The fact that the parties have their places of business in different States is to be disregarded whenever this fact does not appear either from the contract or from any dealings between, or from information disclosed by, the parties at any time before or at the conclusion of the contract."

[18]Bridge (2007) p. 513.

different states and the rules of private international law lead to the application of the law of a contracting state.[19] In this second situation, the parties' location in different states (not their location in different contracting states) is required. In other words, under Article 1 (1) (b) the application of convention is dependent on the application of the private international law rules of the forum. Thus, CISG, unlike the Uniform Laws which applied without recourse to conflict of laws rules, does not altogether dispense with the applicability of the conflict of law rules. Unlike a situation covered by Article 1 (1) (a), where the Convention applies directly, under Article 1 (1) (b) it applies when the private international law rules of the forum directs so.

7.5.2 Notion of Internationality

As noted in Chap. 1 (Sect. 1.3.3), CISG in identifying an international trade transaction relies on the location of the parties' places of business in different contracting states. All other requirements such as the shipment of goods from one country to another or the nationality of the parties are not relevant in determining the applicability of the Convention. The result is that where a seller and a buyer have their places of business in a common contracting state "A" but under the contract between them the goods in question are to move from state "A" to state "B" or from state "B" to state "A," CISG will not apply for the obvious reason that the both parties have their places of business in state "A." To put it differently, under the CISG it is only the location of the parties' place of business in two different contracting states which is important in determining the international character of the transaction.

Here it may be recalled that this is in contrast to the criteria of internationality adopted by the Uniform Laws. Under Uniform Laws (Article I), in addition to the parties' location in two different countries, it is necessary that the cross-border movement element is present. [20]

7.5.3 Coverage of the Convention

CISG applies to contracts of sale of goods only. Although the expression "sale of goods" is not defined by the Convention, it may be stated that for the purpose of the Convention the expression covers a sale of manufactured or produced goods. This meaning is borne out from the provision of Article 3 (1). The relevant phrase is: "...contracts for the supply of *goods to be manufactured or produced* are to be considered sales." Since Articles 2 and 3 exclude certain kinds of goods and transactions from the scope of the Convention, they are indeed helpful in specifying

---

[19]Id, Article 1(1) (b). But according to Article 95, a contracting state may declare at the time of ratifying the Convention that it will not be bound by this criterion of applicability.

[20]Ndulo (1989), pp. 7–8. See also Chap. 2, Sect. 2.4.1

with sufficient precision the kinds of goods covered under the Convention. Article 2 provides that the Convention does not apply to sale of goods bought for personal, family or household use, unless the seller, at any time before or at the conclusion of the contract, neither knew nor ought to have known that the goods were bought for any such use. It further provides that sale of goods by auction; securities; negotiable instruments, and money; electricity; ships and aircraft are also excluded. It also states that sales on execution or otherwise by authority of law are also excluded. However, in the absence of any express provision it is not clear whether exchange of goods is covered or not. As has been noted in the previous chapter, the sale of goods is clearly distinguishable from "exchange" for in the case of latter one kind of goods is exchanged for another kind of goods.

It may also be noted that CISG excludes a contract of service from its scope of application. According to Article 3 (2), the Convention "does not apply to contracts in which the preponderant part of the obligations of the party who furnishes the goods consists in the supply of labour or other services." Thus, where in a contract of supply of goods the preponderant part of the suppliers' obligations consists of the supply of labor or skill, such contracts are excluded from the purview of the CISG. As has already been noted in Chap. 5, a contract of service is distinguishable from a contract of sale of goods in that the former is essentially a contract for supply of labor or skill. It is the accepted position that where the substance of the contract is the supply of service for production of goods, the resulting transaction is a contract of service. Here the provision contained in paragraph 1 of Article 3 is relevant, which states that contracts for the supply of goods…"are to be considered sales" unless the party ordering the goods undertakes to supply "a substantial part" of the necessary materials.

Matters Excluded

The Convention further restricts its scope of application by providing in Article 4 that it deals only with the issues concerning the formation of a contract and the contractual rights and obligations of the parties *inter se*. Like the Uniform Laws, CISG only sets forth rights and obligations of the parties *inter se* thus leaving the conflict of rights situations unaddressed.[21] Article 4 expressly provides that the Vienna Convention is not concerned with the issues of validity and the rights of third parties. A reading of Article 4 makes clear that the Convention addresses only contractual rights arising out of a contract of sale of goods and not the proprietary rights:

> This Convention governs only the formation of the contract of sale and the rights and obligations of the seller and the buyer arising from such a contract. In particular, except as otherwise expressly provided in this Convention, it is not concerned with:
>
> (a) The validity of the contract or of any of its obligations or of any usage;

---

[21] In a "conflict of rights" situation, a dispute is not between a buyer and seller as such but between persons claiming rights over the same property or "goods" in the same capacity. For example, where a dispute is between a buyer, on the one hand, and a person who also claims to be interested in the property, the issue is concerning the "conflict of rights."

(b) The effect which the contract may have on the property in the goods sold.

It may be recalled that CISG, like the Uniform Laws, contains only substantive law on international sales and following the approach of the Uniform Laws it primarily lays down general principles on the subject giving the parties free hand in deciding which special terms should govern their contract.

7.6 Formation of Contract of Sale

Offer–Acceptance Model

Notably, the Convention is based on an offer and acceptance model of contract and an accepted offer within the terms of the Convention is prerequisite for formation of the contract of sale. The rules laid down by the CISG in this regard (articles 14–24) are broadly similar to the domestic laws of India and England on the subject although in certain respects the Convention makes departure from them which will be pointed out in due course.

As already noted, a contract of sale is formed only upon acceptance by the promisee of a proposal or offer. An offer is an intimation of a willingness on the part of the offeror to enter into a contract. It indicates that it is to become legally binding on the promisor or offeror upon its acceptance. An offer needs to be distinguished from an "invitation to treat." The latter is merely a statement of intention which is not intended to be binding (see Chap. 4, Sect. 4.10).

No Requirements About a Particular Form

Under CISG, a contract is not subject to any requirements about a form and an oral contract is as much valid as the one in written form.[22] Article 11 explicitly states that a "contract of sale need not be in or evidenced by writing." However, Article 96 of the Convention allows the contracting states to make reservation in this regard. To quote the text of Article 12 in full:

> Any provision of Article 11, Article 29 or Part II of this Convention that allows a contract of sale or its modification or termination by agreement or any offer, acceptance or other indication of intention to be made in any form other than in writing does not apply where any party has his place of business in a Contracting State which has made a declaration under Article 96 of this Convention. The parties may not derogate from or vary the effect of this article.

Offer

While there is in general no requirement that an offer must be addressed to a specific person, under the CISG in order to be a valid proposal, an offer must be addressed to a specific person. According to Article 14 (1), an offer to be valid must be addressed

[22] See Duca and Duca (1998), pp. 48–49; Bridge (2007), pp. 558–59.

to a specific person; must be sufficiently definite; and must indicate the intention to be bound if accepted. An offer is sufficiently definite if it indicates the goods and explicitly or implicitly "fixes or makes provision for determining the quantity and the price." Further, Article 14 (2) provides that "[a] proposal other than one addressed to one or more specific persons is to be considered merely as an invitation to make offers, unless the contrary is clearly indicated by the person making the proposal."

An offer may be revoked at any time before it is accepted. Recognizing this common law rule of the revocability of an offer, Article 16 (1) provides that "[u]ntil a contract is concluded, an offer may be revoked if the revocation reaches the offeree before he has dispatched an acceptance." However, paragraph (2) of Article 16 incorporating the civil law rule on revocation of offer provides that an offer is not subject to revocation where a time is fixed for making the acceptance. It states that an offer cannot be revoked if it (a) indicates, whether by stating a fixed time for acceptance or otherwise, that it is irrevocable; or (b) was reasonable for the offeree to reply on the offer as being irrevocable and the offeree has acted in reliance on the offer. In this way, the Convention takes a middle position between the common law rule of the revocability of the offer before acceptance and the civil law rule of the general revocability for the offer for a fixed time limit.[23] Here it is important to note that the rule laid down by Article 16 (2) to the effect that an offer is not subject to revocation where a time is fixed for the acceptance makes a departure from the common law rule relating to revocation of an offer.[24]

Acceptance

Article 18 of CISG lays down the rules regarding the acceptance of an offer. Since acceptance is more than a mental assent, in order to constitute a contractually important acceptance it must be communicated to the offeror. Article 18 (1) states that acceptance of an offer may be made by means of a statement or other conduct of the offeree. Since communication of an acceptance is necessary, "silence or inactivity does not in itself amount to acceptance." Further, Article 18 (2) provides that an acceptance becomes effective only after the indication of assent reaches the offeree. It also provides:

> An acceptance is not effective if the indication of assent does not reach the offeror within the time he has fixed or if no time is fixed within a reasonable time, due account being taken of the circumstances of the transaction, including the rapidity of the means of communication employed by the offeror. An oral offer must be accepted immediately unless the circumstances indicate otherwise.

However, it may be noted that in some cases performance of an act, such as dispatch of goods or payment of the price, amounts to valid acceptance.[25] Here it is also important to note that a reading of Article 24 which defines the meaning of "reaches" in relation to the communication of offer, acceptance and revocation

---

[23]See further Carr (2014), p. 75.

[24]See Chap. 4 (Sect. 4.9.1.4); Beatson et al. (2010), p. 57.

[25]CISG, Article 18 (3). See also *Explanatory note,* supra note 4.

suggest that CISG does not recognize the postal acceptance rule of the common law and no distinction is drawn between acceptance by instantaneous and non-instantaneous means of communication.[26] As already noted, in the case of the acceptance by post, the common rule is that the communication of acceptance is complete as soon as the letter of acceptance is posted.

"Mirror Image" Rule

International trade, more often than not, raises the issue of establishing the exact terms on which the contract of sale is concluded. Where a reply to an offer is on a standard form which contains additions, limitations, or other modifications not to be found in the original offer, a question naturally arises whether the terms of the contract will be treated as modified or the original offer will be treated as rejected? Common law rule on this point is simple, which states that if offer and acceptance do not match the offer will be treated as rejected and the additional terms of the acceptance will constitute counter-offer. This rule is known as the "mirror image" rule according to which offer and acceptance must match (see supra, Chap. 4, Sect. 4.9.2). Article 19 of CISG while stating in paragraph (1) that "a reply to an offer which purports to be an acceptance but contains additions, limitations, or other modifications is a rejection of the offer and constitutes a counter-offer," in paragraph (2) makes a departure from this rule and provides that however, if the additional or different terms contained in the acceptance do not materially alter the terms of the offer, the acceptance amounts to a valid acceptance, unless the offeror without undue delay objects to those terms. But if the offeror does not object, the terms of the contract are the terms of the offer with the modifications contained in the acceptance.

7.7 Performance Obligations

7.7.1 Obligations of Seller

Part III of the CISG deals with a number of issues that are relevant in the context of the performance of the contract of sale of goods, that is to say, the obligations of the seller and the buyer. As already noted, this Part also deals with the remedies available to a seller and buyer for breach of the obligations by the other party, and passing of risk. It consists of four chapters—Chap. 1 (general provisions), Chap. 2 (obligations of the seller and remedies for their breach), Chap. 3 (obligations of the buyer and remedies for their breach), and Chap. 4 (passing of risk). However, in this section we shall only focus on the performance obligations, and the issues pertaining to remedies will be discussed in a separate section.

[26]**Article 24**: For the purposes of this part of the Convention, an offer, declaration of acceptance or any other indication of intention "reaches" the addressee when it is made orally to him or delivered by any other means to him personally, to his place of business or mailing address or, if he does not have a place of business or mailing address, to his habitual residence.

Article 30 of the Convention lists three general obligations of a seller: obligations to deliver the goods; obligation to deliver any documents relating to the goods; obligation to transfer the property in the goods. Articles 31–34 provide detailed rules regarding delivery and handing over of goods. In addition, articles 35–40 lay down rules as to a seller's duty to deliver goods of the right quality and description; articles 41–43 deal with the obligation to deliver goods free from any claim of the third party. However, the Convention does not lay down the rules regarding the transfer of property in goods from the seller to the buyer which are left to be decided on the basis of the applicable law.

7.7.1.1 Duty to Deliver Goods of Right Quality and Quantity

Obligation to deliver goods is dealt with by Article 31 which applies to a situation where there is no agreement between the seller and the buyer regarding the delivery of the goods to "any other particular place." According to Article 31, if a contract of sale involves carriage of goods, the seller's obligation consists of handing the goods over to the first carrier for transmission to the buyer or where; or if the contract of sale does not involve carriage of goods and the contract relates to specific goods, or unidentified goods to be drawn from a specific stock or to be manufactured or produced, and the parties knew that the goods were at a particular place or to be manufactured or produced at a particular place, the seller's obligation consists of in placing the goods at the buyer's disposal at that place; and in all other cases, the seller's obligation consists of in placing the goods at the buyer's disposal at the place where the seller had his place of business at the time of the conclusion of the contract.

Further, a seller must deliver the goods of the required quality, quantity, and description (Article 35 (1)). The conformity requirements are laid down in Article 35 (2) according to which except where the parties have otherwise agreed, the goods do not conform with the contract unless they: "(a) are fit for the purposes for which goods of the same description would ordinarily be used; (b) are fit for any particular purpose expressly or impliedly made known to the seller at the time of the conclusion of the contract, except where the circumstances show that the buyer did not rely, or that it was unreasonable for him to rely, on the seller's skill and judgment; (c) possess the qualities of goods which the seller has held out to the buyer as a sample or model; (d) are contained or packaged in the manner usual for such goods or, where there is no such manner, in a manner adequate to preserve and protect the goods." Article 35 (3) provides that the buyer may not complain of a lack of conformity where at the time of contract "the buyer knew or could not have been unaware of such lack of conformity. It may also be noted that the buyer is required to examine the goods, upon their arrival, as soon as practicable" (Article 38). He will lose the right to rely on a lack of conformity if notice to the seller specifying the nature of the lack of conformity is not given within a reasonable time (Article 39) (see Sect. 7.7.2).

Defective (*peius*) and Different (*aliud*) Goods

In this context, it may be noted that CISG does not draw a distinction between defective or inferior goods (*peius*) and different goods (*aliud*). Whatever merit there may be in making such a distinction, it does not have much practical relevance in the scheme of things adopted under CISG. For example, under Article 46 (2) a buyer's right to require substitute goods following a fundamental breach is not dependent upon a distinction between the inferior and different goods. Bridge points out that CISG neither recognizes nor rejects expressly the distinction between defective and different goods and the delivery of goods different from those contracted for should be treated as a case of non-delivery of goods.[27]

7.7.1.2 Duty to Deliver Goods Free from Right of a Third Party

Additionally, a seller must deliver goods which are free from any right or claim of a third party unless the buyer has consented (Article 41); deliver goods free from a claim based on "industrial property or other intellectual property" (Article 42). However, "the buyer loses the right to rely on the provisions of Article 41 or Article 42 if he does not give notice to the seller specifying the nature of the right or claim of the third party within a reasonable time after he has become aware or ought to have become aware of the right or claim" (Article 43(1)). However, the requirement of notice will not apply where he knew of the right or claim of the third party and the nature of it (Article 43(2)).

7.7.2 Obligations of Buyer

7.7.2.1 Obligation to Accept the Goods and to Pay

A buyer has two main obligations under the Vienna Convention: to take delivery of the goods and to pay for them. Article 53 provides: "The buyer must pay the price for the goods and take delivery of them as required by the contract and this Convention." In regard to the duty to pay the price, Article 54 provides that "the buyer's obligation to pay the price includes taking such steps and complying with such formalities" as required under the contract or any other relevant laws. And Article 59 provides that the buyer must pay the price on the date fixed by the contract and the Convention without the need for any request by the seller. Regarding a buyer's duty to take delivery, Article 60 provides that such an obligation consists of "(a) in doing all the

---

[27]See Bridge (2010), p. 927.

acts which could reasonably be expected of him in order to enable the seller to make delivery; and (b) in taking over the goods."

7.7.2.2 Obligation to Inspect the Goods

As already noted, a buyer is required to inspect the goods upon their arrival to enable him to give notice of any lack of conformity within a reasonable time. Article 38 provides:

> (1) The buyer must examine the goods, or cause them to be examined, within as short a period as is practicable in the circumstances.
> (2) If the contract involves carriage of the goods, examination may be deferred until after the goods have arrived at their destination.
> (3) If the goods are redirected in transit or redispatched by the buyer without a reasonable opportunity for examination by him and at the time of the conclusion of the contract the seller knew or ought to have known of the possibility of such redirection or redispatch, examination may be deferred until after the goods have arrived at the new destination.

Further, according to Article 39, the buyer will lose the right to rely on a lack of conformity of the goods if he does not give notice to the seller of the lack of conformity within a reasonable time after he has discovered it or ought to have discovered it. In any event, the buyer must give the seller notice of non-conformity of the goods "at the latest within a period of two years from the date on which the goods were actually handed over to the buyer, unless this time limit is inconsistent with a contractual period of guarantee."

7.7.2.3 Determination of Price of Goods

Notably, under CISG a contract can be validly made on "open price" term.[28] According to this rule, a contract is formed even if the parties have not fixed the price. Article 55 provides, where a contract, which though has been validly made, "does not expressly or implicitly fix or make provision for determining the price, the parties are considered, in the absence of any indication to the contrary, to have impliedly made reference to the price generally charged at the time of the conclusion of the contract for such goods sold under comparable circumstances in the trade concerned."

[28] See Duca and Duca (1998) pp. 51–52.

7.8 Remedies

7.8.1 Remedies in General

It may be noted that the rights and obligations of the seller and the buyer are reciprocal to each other, that is, a seller's claim for damages is linked to the buyer's obligations and a buyer's claim for remedies is linked to the obligations of a buyer. It is for this reason under CISG a buyer's remedies are provided in Part III, Chap. 2 in conjunction with the obligations of the seller while remedies of a seller are provided in Chap. 3 (Part III) in conjunction with the obligations of the buyer.

Remedies which are available to both—the seller and the buyer—include: (a) specific performance of the contract (articles 46 (for buyer) and 62 (for seller)); (b) damages (articles 74–77); and (c) termination (or avoidance) of the contract for fundamental breach (articles 47 and 49 (for buyer) and 64); avoidance for anticipatory (fundamental) breach (Article 72); fixing additional time for performance (Articles 47 and 49 (for buyer) and Articles 63 (1) and 64 (for seller)); and suspension (Article 71). In addition, CISG provides for the remedy of reduction of price (Article 50) and right of cure (Articles 37 and 48) to be claimed by the buyer and the seller, respectively.

The reader will notice that in making provisions for remedies, CISG makes significant departures from Indian and English law on the subject. Certain remedies like fixing additional time for performance (Articles 47 and 63) and suspension (Article 71) are not familiar in common-law-based systems. Furthermore, while under the common law, the remedy of damages, which is aimed at to compensate the aggrieved party for any loss or damage, is the primary remedy and the remedy of specific performance is only supplementary to the remedy of damages. Under the Vienna Convention the remedy of specific performance is provided as a general rule for it is not limited to those cases where damages are not the adequate remedy.

7.8.2 Specific Performance

In the case of specific performance, a court directs the defendant to perform his obligations in accordance with the terms of the contract. As already noted, in civil law systems, the remedy of specific performance is a primary remedy and the role of damages is only supplementary in remedying the innocent party. In conformity with the position in the civil law systems, CISG provides for the remedy of specific performance as a general rule.[29] However, Article 28 limits the scope of the remedy of specific performance by providing that a "court is not bound to enter a judgment for specific performance unless the court would do so under its own law in respect of similar contracts of sale not governed by this convention." It may also be noted

[29] Id, p. 63.

that, as it is the case with the remedy of avoidance, simply by claiming the remedy of specific performance the claimant—whether buyer or seller—does not lose the right to claim damages.[30]

Article 46 (1) states that the buyer may require performance by the seller of his obligations unless the buyer has resorted to a remedy which is inconsistent with this requirement. While under Article 46 (1), a buyer has the right to require performance by the seller of his obligations, according to paragraph (2) of Article 46, where the goods do not conform and the non-conformity amounts to a fundamental breach within the meaning of Article 25, the buyer may request for substitute goods provided the request for substitute goods is made along with the notice of non-conformity or within a reasonable time after notice. Moreover, the buyer also has the right to require the seller to remedy any lack of conformity by repair unless it would be unreasonable in the circumstances provided the request is made in conjunction with the notice of non-conformity or within a reasonable time after notice.

The seller's remedy of specific performance is provided under Article 62 according to which, in the exercise of his right to specific performance, a seller may require the buyer to pay the price, take delivery, or perform his other obligations, unless the seller has resorted to a remedy which is inconsistent with this requirement. It has been already noted that a buyer has two main obligations: to pay the price; and to take delivery of the goods and it is the breach of these obligations that entitles a seller to seek the remedy of specific performance.

7.8.3 Avoidance for Fundamental Breach of Contract

In some extreme cases, CISG allows the parties—the seller (Article 64) and the buyer (Article 49)—to avoid or terminate the contract for non-performance or what may be called a breach of the contract by the other party. The effect of avoidance, according to Article 81 of the Vienna Convention, is that it releases both parties from their contractual obligations.

It may be noted that in order to claim the remedy of avoidance—whether to be claimed by a seller or a buyer—the claimant must show that there has been a fundamental breach of obligation in the sense of Article 25. Article 64 which gives a seller the right to avoid a contract of sale reads as follows:

> (1) The seller may declare the contract avoided: (a) if the failure by the buyer to perform any of his obligations under the contract or this Convention amounts to a fundamental breach of contract;
>
> Or (*b*) if the buyer does not, within the additional period of time fixed by the seller in accordance with paragraph (1) of article 63, perform his obligation to pay the price or take delivery of the goods, or if he declares that he will not do so within the period so fixed.

---

[30]See Article 46 (3) and 61 (2).

(2) However, in cases where the buyer has paid the price, the seller loses the right to declare the contract avoided unless he does so: (a) in respect of late performance by the buyer, before the seller has become aware that performance has been rendered; or (b) in respect of any breach other than late performance by the buyer, within a reasonable time: (i) after the seller knew or ought to have known of the breach; or (ii) after the expiration of any additional period of time fixed by the seller in accordance with paragraph (1) of article 63, or after the buyer has declared that he will not perform his obligations within such an additional period.

Further, According to Article 25, a breach is fundamental "if it results in such detriment to the other party as substantially to deprive him of what he is entitled to expect under the contract, unless the party in breach did not foresee and a reasonable person of the same kind would not have foreseen such a result."

Under the CISG, there are two alternative routes to the avoidance of a contract for non-performance.[31] The first such situation arises where it is shown the other party has committed a fundamental breach of contract. The second situation where the contract can be avoided is: if the other party to fails to perform the contract during an additional time of reasonable length fixed by the aggrieved party.

7.8.4 Fixing Additional Time

As already stated, a party to a contract may avoid the contract even if the breach is not fundamental one within the meaning of Article 25. This right accrues to a seller or buyer, as the case may be, if a party fixes an additional period of time of reasonable length to enable the other party to perform its obligations but the other party fails to perform within that period. The right or option to fix an additional period of time for performance of the contract by the other party is recognized by Articles 47 (1) and 49 (1) for buyer and articles 63 (1) and 64 (1) for the seller. This option is available to both, the buyer as well as the seller.

In respect of a buyer, Article 47 (1) provides that "the buyer may fix an additional period of time of reasonable length for performance by the seller of his obligations." But if the buyer has received notice from the seller that he will not perform within the period so fixed, the buyer may not, during that period, resort to any remedy for breach of contract. A corresponding provision is contained in Article 63 which allows a seller to fix an additional period of time.

The provision recognizing the right of a party to fix an additional period of time for performance by the other party, known as the concept or procedure of *Nachfrist*, is based on German law.[32]

---

[31] See Bridge (2010), p. 912.

[32] Duca and Duca (1998), pp. 75–76.

7.8.5 Anticipatory Breach of Contract

Article 72 which incorporates the principle of anticipatory breach of contract provides:

> If prior to the date for performance of the contract it is clear that one of the parties will commit a fundamental breach of contract, the other party may declare the contract avoided. (2) If time allows, the party intending to declare the contract avoided must give reasonable notice to the other party in order to permit him to provide adequate assurance of his performance. (3) The requirements of the preceding paragraph do not apply if the other party has declared that he will not perform his obligations.

And Article 71 provides:

> A party may suspend the performance of his obligations if, after the conclusion of the contract, it becomes apparent that the other party will not perform a substantial part of his obligations as a result of: (a) a serious deficiency in his ability to perform or in his creditworthi-ness; or (b) his conduct in preparing to perform or in performing the contract. (3) A party suspending performance, whether before or after dispatch of the goods, must immediately give notice of the suspension to the other party and must continue with performance if the other party provides adequate assurance of his performance.

The doctrine of anticipatory breach of contract is a well-established principle of common law.[33] It has long been established that an aggrieved party can immediately avoid the contract in question for anticipatory repudiation of a contract and need not wait till the date for performance of the contract once it becomes clear that one of the parties will commit a fundamental breach of contract.

7.8.6 Damages

As stated above, both the seller and the buyer are entitled to claim damages from the party in breach of the contract. Articles 74–77 of the Vienna Convention lay down the rules on the remedy of damages. Article 74 which contains the main provision provides that "…damages for breach of contract by one party consist of a sum equal to the loss, including loss of profit, suffered by the other party." It further provides that such damages, however, "may not exceed the loss which the party in breach foresaw or ought to have foreseen at the time of the conclusion of the contract in the light of the facts and matters of which he then knew or ought to have known as a possible consequence of the breach of contract." Thus, Article 74 besides defining damages also incorporates the rule of remoteness of damage. It includes both direct and the consequential loss.[34] Further, Article 74 allows counterclaims. But the right to make counterclaims is limited to claims arising under the Convention.

Mention may also be made of Article 77 according to which, an aggrieved party's claim for damages is subject to the condition that he or she must take such measures

---

[33] See generally MGilbey (1989), pp. 475–501.

[34] Bridge (2007), p. 590.

as are reasonable in the circumstances to mitigate the loss, including loss or profit. "If he fails to take such measures, the party in breach may claim a reduction in the damages in the amount by which the loss should have been mitigated."

7.8.7 Reduction of Price

Where the goods do not conform to the contract, a buyer is given a "novel" remedy of reduction of price.[35] According to Article 50, "[i]f the goods do not conform with the contract and whether or not the price has already been paid, the buyer may reduce the price in the same proportion as the value that the goods actually delivered had at the time of the delivery bears to the value that the goods actually delivered had at the time of the delivery bears to the value that conforming goods would have had at that time...."

The provision on the remedy of reduction of price in the Vienna Convention is significant in that it has its origin in the civil law tradition. Although the remedy is similar to the remedy of damages in that it grants relief to the buyer measured in the form of money.[36] However, it is not as such a right to damages. Rather, reduction of price is a kind of "self-help" which entitles a buyer to modify the price provision in a contract of sale.[37] It should be kept in mind that this remedy, being separate from the remedy of damages, should not be confused with the right to set off.

7.8.8 Seller's Right of Cure

Where a seller has delivered the goods before the date for delivery, any defective delivery up to that date may be cured by him subject to the condition that the exercise of this right does not cause the buyer "unreasonable inconvenience" or "unreasonable expense." Article 37 provides:

> If the seller has delivered gods before the date for delivery, he may up to that date, deliver any missing part or make up any deficiency in the quantity of the goods delivered, or deliver goods in replacement of any non-conforming goods delivered or remedy any lack of conformity in the goods delivered provided that the exercise of this right does not cause the buyer unreasonable inconvenience or unreasonable expense.

However, the buyer retains any right to claim damages as provided for in this Convention.

---

[35] Duca and Duca (1998), pp. 82–83.

[36] Bergsten and Miller (1979), p. 255.

[37] Bridge (2007), p. 588.

References

Beatson, S. J., Burrows, A., & Cartwright, J. (2010). *Anson's law of contract*. Oxford: Oxford University Press.
Bergsten & Miller. (1979). The remedy of reduction of price. *American Journal of Comparative Law, 27*(2/3), 255–277.
Bergsten, E. E. (2015). Thirty-five years of the United Nations Convention on Contracts for the International Sale of Goods: Expectations and deliveries. In *Thirty-five years of uniform sales law: Trends and perspectives, (7–12), Proceedings of the High Level Panel held during the Forty-eighth Session of the United Nations Commission on International Trade Law*. New York: United Nations.
Bonell, M. J. (2008). The CISG, European contract law and the development of a world contract law. *American Journal of Comparative Law, 56*(1), 1–28.
Bridge, M. (2007). *The international sale of goods: Law and practice*. Oxford: Oxford University Press.
Bridge, M. (2010). Avoidance for fundamental breach of on tract under the UN Convention on the International Sale of Goods. *International & Comparative Law Quarterly, 59,* 911–940.
Carr, I. (2014). *International trade law*. London, New York: Routledge-Cavendish.
Chuah. (2009). *Law of International Trade: Cross-Border commercial transactions*. Sweet& Maxwell, Thomson Reuters, South Asian Edition 2011.
Duca, L. D., & Duca, P. D. (1998). Internationalization of sales law—Practice under the Convention on international Sale of Goods—A primer for attorneys and international traders. In S. Ziegel Jacob (Ed.), *New developments in International commercial and consumer law* (pp. 37–85). Oxford: Hart Publishing.
Eorsi. (1983). A propos the 1980 Vienna convention on contraction on contracts for the international sale of goods. *American Journal Comparative Law* 333.
Explanatory Note by the UNCITRAL Secretariat on the United Nations Convention on Contracts for the International Sale of Goods. (2010). In *United Nations Convention on Contract for International Sale of Goods* (pp. 33–42). New York: United Nations.
Honnold, J. (1979). The draft convention on contracts for the International sale of goods: An overview. *American Journal of Comparative Law, 27*(2/3), 223–230.
Lookofsky, J. M. (1991). Loose ends and contorts in international sales: Problems in the harmonization of private law rules. *American Journal of Comparative Law, 39*(2), 403–416.
MGilbey, S. (1989). The convention on the international sale of goods: Anticipatory repudiation provisions and developing countries *International & Comparative Law Quarterly, 38*(3), 475–501.
Moens & Gillies. (2006). *International trade & business: Law, policy and ethics*, pp. 1–46. Oxon, New York: Routledge-Cavendish.
Ndulo, M. (1989). The Vienna sales convention 1980 and the hague uniform laws on International sale of goods 1964: A comparative analysis. *International and Comparative Law Quarterly, 38*(1), 1–25.
Suy, E. (1981). Achievements of the United Nations Commission on International Trade Law. *International Lawyer, 15* (1), 141, 139–147.
Viejobueno, S. (1995). Progress through compromise: The 1980 United Nations convention on contracts for the international sale of goods. *Comparative & International Law Journal of South Africa, 28*(2), 200–207.

Chapter 8
Harmonization Through International Restatements

8.1 Non-state Law

As already noted (Chap. 2, Sect. 2.4.3), it is one of the most important characteristics of the modern movement toward harmonization that it does not just rely on the binding instruments such as treaties, statutes, judicial decisions, and customs but also places considerable reliance on the "non-state norms" or to be found in the soft-law, non-binding instruments such as the codes of practices, and doctrinal writings or "normative" principles like the UNIDROIT Principles of International Commercial Contracts (UNIDROIT Principles) and the Hague Principles on the Choice of law in International Commercial Contracts (the Hague principles).[1] At the cost of repetition it may be stressed that in situations, where a high degree of harmonization is not considered desirable or where it cannot be achieved, harmonization through codification of trade practices and restatements of laws or what sometimes is called, "rules of law" to refer to non-state law, has commonly been resorted to by the international community. Furthermore, the non-binding nature of these instruments provides the business community and states a greater scope for cooperating in the process of internationalization of the law of contract and is also helpful in achieving the maximum uniformity possible in the field of international trade law.[2] Here, we will direct our attention to a couple of the most important soft-law instruments aimed at harmonizing trade laws, namely the UNIDROIT Principles and the Hague Principles.

[1]See Bonell (1992), pp. 617–33; Kozolchyk (1998), pp. 151–79.

[2]See Kozolchyk, id, p. 153.

A. Srivastava, *Modern Law of International Trade*, International Law and the Global South, https://doi.org/10.1007/978-981-15-5475-9_8

8.2 UNIDROIT Principles

8.2.1 UNIDROIT Principles as a Restatement of General Contract Law

As already noted in Chap. 2, the efforts of the International Institute for Unification of Trade Law (UNIDROIT) were initially confined to international conventions or model laws, but for several decades it has directed its efforts toward formulation of non-binding, soft-law instruments. In 1971, the Governing Council of the UNIDROIT decided to include the elaboration of "Principles of International Commercial Contracts" in the Work Programme of the Institute and in 1980, it set up a special Working Group for preparing the various draft chapters of these Principles. Finally, in 1994, the first edition of the UNIDROIT Principles was published, followed by the publication of further editions in 2004, 2010, and 2016.[3] It may also be noted that the successive editions of UNIDROIT Principles are not intended to be a revision of the previous editions.[4]

The UNIDROIT Principles, prepared by a group of experts representing all major legal systems of the world, "represent a non-binding codification or "restatement" of the general part of international contract law."[5] As the Preamble states, these Principles set forth "general rules for international commercial contracts." Their objective is to provide a balanced set of rules covering virtually all the most important topics of general contract law, such as formation, interpretation, validity including illegality, performance, non-performance and remedies, assignment, set-off, plurality of obligors and of obligees, as well as the authority of agents and limitation periods. Further, the UNIDROIT Principles are designed for use throughout the world irrespective of the differences in the legal traditions and the economic and political conditions of various countries. Significantly, they do not intend to unify the existing domestic laws. Rather they "enunciate common principles and rules to the existing legal systems and to select the solutions that are best adapted to the special requirements of international commercial contracts."[6]

Preamble to the UNIDROIT Principles further provides that the Principles shall apply where the parties to an international contract have agreed that their contract is to be governed by them. They may also apply where the parties have agreed that "their contract be governed by general principles of law, the lex mercatoria or the like"; or "when the parties have not chosen any law to govern their contract." Thus, they provide a useful alternative to the choice of the domestic laws. In fact,

[3]UNIDROIT Principles can be accessed from: www.uniddroit.org.

[4]UNIDROIT Principles 2016, "Introduction," ibid.

[5]Model Clauses for the Use of the UNIDROIT Principles of International Commercial Contracts, UNIDROIT Principles Model Clause No. 1. 29 (a), International Institute for the Unification of Private Law (UNIDROIT), Rome (2013) [hereinafter referred to as the Model Clauses]. The text can be accessed from: www.uniddroit.org.

[6]Bonell (1992), p. 622.

the Principles are especially useful for a situation where a dispute is submitted to arbitration. Arbitrators can very well apply the UNIDROIT principles even in the absence of a choice of law clause or where they are authorized to decide the dispute simply according to the general principles of law, the *lex mercatoria* or the like.[7] Furthermore, Preamble to the UNIDROIT Principles also states that the Principles may be used "to interpret or supplement international uniform law instruments; to interpret or supplement domestic law; and may also serve as a model for national and international legislators." Finally, the Principles may also serve as a guide for drafting of international commercial contracts.[8]

8.2.2 Non-Mandatory Nature of "Principles"

As it is stated in the Preamble, UNIDROIT Principles are a non-binding codification or "restatement" of the general part of international contract law prepared by an independent group of experts. Therefore, being soft-law instruments these Principles cannot bind the parties to an international contract unless they have agreed that their contract is to be governed by these Principles. According to the Comment to the Principles, the parties to a contract "may in each individual case either simply exclude their application in whole or in part or modify their content so as to adapt them to the specific needs of the kind of transaction involved. Being not binding principles they are particularly useful in resolution of transnational commercial disputes through arbitration."[9]

8.2.3 Interpretation of "Principles"

As it is the case with the 1980 UN Convention on Contracts for the International Sale of Goods (CISG), UNIDROIT Principles incorporate provisions in regard to their interpretation. These provisions are similar to those contained in the CISG. The first rule of the interpretation contained in Article 1.6.1 provides that in interpreting these Principles, regard is to be had to their international character and their purposes, including the need to promote uniformity in their application. The message of this provision is clear. These Principles should be viewed "autonomously," and in interpreting their texts the adjudicator should not be guided by the law of a particular country.[10]

The second rule of the interpretation contained in Article 1.6.2 provides that the issues which fall within the scope of UNIDROIT Principles "but not expressly settled

[7]See Bonell (2006), p. 45.

[8]Id., p. 628.

[9]UNIDROIT Principles 2016, supra note 3.

[10]Bonell (2006), p. 79.

by them are as for as possible to be settled in accordance with their underlying general principles."

8.2.4 Scheme of the "Principles"

The current edition of UNIDROIT Principles is organized into 11 chapters dealing with a wide variety of aspects concerning international contracts, namely pre-contractual negotiations requirements, formation of contract, illegality, interpretation, performance, termination, and remedies. "Principles," in particular, contain provisions on scope of application (Preamble); general provisions (Chap. 1); formation of contract, and authority of agents (Chap. 2); avoidance of obligations, and illegality (Chapter 3); interpretation (Chap. 4); content, third party's rights, and conditions (Chap. 5); performance and hardship (Chap. 6); non-performance including: non-performance in general, right to performance, termination, and damages (Chap. 7); set-off (Chap. 8); assignments of rights, transfer of obligations, and assignment of contracts (Chap. 9); periods of limitation (Chap. 10); and plurality of obligors and obliges (Chap. 11). Each article is accompanied by comments and illustrations which may be regarded as the integral part of the Principles.

8.2.5 Scope of Application

8.2.5.1 Notion of Internationality

As already noted in the introductory Chapter, international and domestic law instruments in defining an international contract use various criteria in determining the international character of a contract. However, UNIDROIT Principles, notably, adopt an altogether different approach to the issue. They do not lay down a specific criterion of internationality and are based on the premise that the Principles exclude only those situations where no international element at all is involved.[11] Thus, the principles adopt a quite liberal approach toward defining an international commercial contract.

It may also be noted that although UNIDROIT Principles are created to apply to international commercial contracts, the parties may agree to apply these to a domestic contract.

8.2.5.2 Commercial Contracts

UNIDROIT Principles are intended to apply only to "commercial contracts." Although the term, "commercial contracts" is not defined, it is understood that

[11] See Comment to UNIDROIT Principles, supra note 3.

the Principles do not cover consumer contracts. As it is suggested, the commercial contracts should be viewed in the broadest possible sense, so as to include most economic transactions within its ambit, such as transactions related to supply of services, exchange of goods, and professional contracts.[12] It may be noted that, unlike CISG, the scope of the UNIDROIT Principles is not limited to just sale of goods contract but includes also service transactions.[13]

8.2.6 Formation of Contract

8.2.6.1 Offer and Acceptance Model

UNIDROIT Principles, like CISG, rely on the offer–acceptance model in determining the existence of an agreement and a contract may be concluded simply by the acceptance of an offer. Principles also suggest that a contract may be taken as concluded by the conduct of the parties. In the context of international commercial transactions this has special significance. In view of the complex nature of cross-border transactions, it is only logical that a contract is taken as concluded also by conduct of the parties provided that conduct is sufficient to show the agreement. Article 2.1.1 which deals with manner of formation of contract clearly provides:

> A contract may be concluded either by the acceptance of an offer or by conduct of the parties that is sufficient to show agreement.

Under UNIDROIT Principles, in order to constitute a valid offer, the proposal must be "sufficiently definite and indicates the intention of the offeror to be bound in case of acceptance" Article 2.1.2. It hardly needs saying that domestic laws of India and England, and CISG (Article 14 (1)) adopt a similar approach.

The rules regarding the communication and revocation of offer are also similar to those of CISG. Article 2.1.3 provides:

> (1) An offer becomes effective when it reaches the offeree.
> (2) An offer, even if it is revocable, may be withdrawn if the withdrawal reaches the offeree before or at the same time as the offer.

Regarding revocation of offer, Article 2.1.4.1 provides that an offer is revocable before the offeree has dispatched an acceptance. However, an offer cannot be revoked if it indicates that it is irrevocable or where the offeree, acting reasonably finds the offer irrevocable and has acted in reliance on the offer.

In respect of the mode of acceptance, Article 2.1.6.1 provides that an offer may be accepted by a statement or other conduct of the offeree. Further, an acceptance becomes effective when it reaches the offeror. An acceptance may be withdrawn if

[12] Ibid, p. 44.

[13] It is for the reason that the scope of application of the UNIDROIT Principles is wider than CISG, the former adopts solutions different from those provided for in the latter. Bonell (1992), p. 622.

the withdrawal reaches the offeror before or at the same time as the acceptance would have become effective.

8.2.6.2 Is Consideration not Necessary?

Article 3.1.2 provides:

> A contract is concluded, modified or terminated by the mere agreement of the parties, without any further requirement.

The above provision clearly indicates that under UNIDROIT Principles a contract may be concluded without consideration. As already stated, the requirement of consideration is not universally recognized as in civil law systems a contract may be concluded without consideration. It may also be recalled here that CISG adopts a similar approach. Article 29 (1) of GISG provides: "A contract is concluded, modified or terminated by the mere agreement of the parties."

8.2.6.3 No Requirement as to a Particular Form

According to Article 1.2, a contract is not required to be in a prescribed form. An oral contract is as much valid as a contract in writing. It reads:

> Nothing in these Principles requires a contract, statement or any other act to be made in or evidenced by a particular form. It may be proved by any means, including witnesses.

As already noted, the modern law does not generally insist on the requirement of form for the conclusion of a contract. Only limited types of contracts are subject to the requirement of form (see Chap. 4, Sect. 2.3.4). The rule that a contract is not subject to any requirement about form is of particular relevance in international trade where various modern means of communication are used in making a contract. Further, the provision of Article 1.2 applies also to any statement or act, other than a contract.

8.2.7 Validity and Enforcement

8.2.7.1 Matters Not Covered

In contrast to the 1980 CISG, UNIDROIT Principles do contain provisions regarding the validity of contracts. However, "Principles" do not deal with all the grounds of invalidity of a contract to be found in the various national legal systems. As Article 3.1.1 makes clear the lack of capacity as a ground of invalidity of a contract is not covered by "Principles." According to the comment to Article 3.1.1, "the reason for its exclusion lies in both the inherent complexity of questions of status and the extremely diverse manner in which these questions are treated in domestic law."

8.2.7.2 Grounds of Invalidity

Notably, under UNIDROIT Principles, the initial impossibility of a contract is not a ground of invalidity. Article 3.1.3 clearly provides that the mere fact that at the time of the conclusion of the contract the performance of the obligation assumed was impossible does not affect the validity of the contract. This is in contrast to many legal systems in which a contract is considered void for initial impossibility. For example, s. 56 (1) of Indian Contract Act provides that an agreement to do an act impossible in itself is void. Furthermore, under the UNIDROIT Principles a contract is not void simply because at the time of making of the contract "a party was not entitled to dispose of the assets to which the contract relates does not affect the validity of the contract" (Article 3.1.3)). Thus, in contrast to the position in some countries, under Article 3.1.3.2, a contract of sale is not void simply because a party professing to transfer assets was not entitled to dispose of the assets.

Under UNIDROIT Principles, the grounds of invalidity are: serious mistake; fraud; threat; and gross disparity. Mistake is defined as an erroneous assumption related to both—facts or law. Further, a party may avoid a contract on the basis of mistake only if, the mistake is serious, that is to say, it is of "such importance that a reasonable person in the same situation as the party in error would only have concluded the contract on materially different terms or would not have concluded it at all if the true state of affairs had been known, and (a) the other party made the same mistake or caused the mistake, or knew or ought to have known of the mistake and it was contrary to reasonable commercial standards of fair dealing to leave the mistaken party in error; or (b) the other party had not at the time of avoidance acted in reliance on the contract"(Article 3.2.2).

Similarly, a party may avoid a contract for threat only if it is so imminent and serious that the person so threatened has no reasonable alternative but to conclude the contract on the terms proposed by the other party (Article 3.2.5).

8.2.8 Third Parties' Rights

As already noted, a contract normally does not confer rights upon the third parties.[14] But the Principles recognize the right of the parties to create rights in favor of a third party, the beneficiary. Article 5.2.1 provides:

> (1) The parties (the "promisor" and the "promisee") may confer by express or implied agreement a right on a third party (the "beneficiary").
>
> (2) The existence and content of the beneficiary's right against the promisor are determined by the agreement of the parties and are subject to any conditions or other limitations under the agreement.

[14]However, after the enactment of the Contracts (Rights of Third Parties) Act, 1999, the parties if they wish can create rights in favor of the third parties (supra, Chap. 4, Sect. 4.9.3.4).

However, the beneficiary must be clearly identifiable. Article 5.2.2 provides: "The beneficiary must be identifiable with adequate certainty by the contract but need not be in existence at the time the contract is made." Furthermore, the rights created by the contract on the beneficiary may be modified or revoked until the beneficiary has accepted them or reasonably acted in reliance on them.

8.2.9 Performance Obligations

8.2.9.1 "Order of Preference" Rule

The "order of performance" rule determines when does each party's performance under a bilateral contract become due? It applies only in a bilateral contract in which each party undertakes an obligation to perform.[15] In this context, Article 6.1.4 provides two rules which are intended to apply in a situation where the parties have not made any specific arrangements. First, the parties are bound to perform the contract simultaneously unless the circumstances indicate otherwise; secondly, where the performance of only one party's obligation requires a period of time, for example in construction and most service contracts, that party is bound to perform first.[16] Comment to the UNIDROIT Principles provides the following illustrations to bring home the point:

(a) A and B agree to barter a certain quantity of oil against a certain quantity of cotton. Unless circumstances indicate otherwise, the commodities should be exchanged simultaneously.

(b) A promises to write a legal opinion to assist B in an arbitration. If no arrangement is made as to when A should be paid for the services, A must prepare the opinion before asking to be paid.

Regarding the time of performance, Article 6.1.1 provides three rules: First, where the contract fixes the precise time for performance the contract must be performed by that time; secondly, where the contract does not fix a precise moment but a period of time for performing the contract, the contract must be performed at any time within that period unless circumstances indicate that the other party is to choose a time; finally, in any other case, the contract must be performed within a reasonable time.

With regard to the situations where a contract is silent on the question of the place of performance and from the circumstances it is not determinable where the contract is to be performed, Article 6.1.6 gives two rules. According to the first rule, a party is to perform its obligations at its own place of business. And the second rule which is specific to monetary obligations states that the contract is to be performed at the obligee's place of business.

---

[15] See Fontaine (1992), p. 653.

[16] See Comment to the UNIDROIT Principles 2016, supra note 3.

8.2.9.2 Exemption Clauses

Exemption clauses refer to those contract terms which limit or exclude one party's liability for non-performance or which permits one party to render performance substantially different from what the other party reasonably expected. Since exemption causes may have the effect of giving one party excessive advantages which appear unconscionable from the circumstances, Article 7.1.6 of UNIDROIT Principles provides that they may not be invoked if it would be grossly unfair to do so, having regard to the purpose of the contract.

It may also be noted that the exemption clauses are different from those which are limited to defining the obligations undertaken by the party in question. Comment to the "Principles" contains the following example to distinguish the former from the latter:

> A hotelkeeper exhibits a notice to the effect that the hotel is responsible for cars left in the garage but not for objects contained in the cars. This term is not an exemption clause for the purpose of this Article since its purpose is merely that of defining the scope of the hotelkeeper's obligation.

8.2.10 Remedies

8.2.10.1 Remedies in General

Under UNIDROIT Principles, a party to a contract is entitled to a number of remedies many of which are also provided by CISG. These remedies include: (a) the right to require performance of monetary and non-monetary obligations (articles 7.2.1 and 7.2.2); (b) damages (articles 7.4.1 through 7.4.13); and (c) termination (or avoidance) of the contract for fundamental breach (articles 7.3.1 through 7.3.2 and 7.3.5); termination for anticipatory (fundamental) termination or breach (Article 7.3.3); adequate assurance of due performance (Article 7.3.4); fixing additional time for performance (Article 7.1.5); restitution (Article 7.3.6); and the right of cure by the non-performing party (Article 7.1.4).

8.2.10.2 Specific Performance

UNIDROIT Principles recognize the right to demand performance of contract by a party, known as the right of specific performance. As already noted, while this right is generally recognized across all major system of law, in common law countries this right is generally restricted in the sense that it is available only to a buyer and only in exceptional circumstances. Under the Principles, however, each party has the right to demand performance of the contract by the other party.

Article 7.2.1 which deals with the case of the performance of monetary obligation states:

> Where a party who is obliged to pay money does not do so, the other party may require payment.

Further, Article 7.2.2 which sets out rules about performance of non-monetary obligation reads as follows:

> Where a party who owes an obligation other than one to pay money does not perform, the other party may require performance, unless
>
> (a) performance is impossible in law or in fact;
> (b) performance or, where relevant, enforcement is unreasonably burdensome or expensive;
> (c) the party entitled to performance may reasonably obtain performance from another source;
> (d) performance is of an exclusively personal character; or
> (e) the party entitled to performance does not require performance within a reasonable time after it has, or ought to have, become aware of the non-performance.

In setting out the rule of specific performance, UNIDROIT Principles follow a less restrictive approach and are similar to the approach of civil law. The remedy is not a discretionary one and is available to both parties, though, it is subject to certain limitations.

Repair and Replacement of Defective Performance

In the present context, it may further be noted that under UNIDROIT Principles the right to specific performance also includes the right of the party who has received a defective performance to require cure of the defect. Article 7.2.3 dealing with the right to repair and replacement of defective performance provides that "[t]he right to performance includes in appropriate cases the right to require repair, replacement, or other cure of defective performance."

8.2.10.3 Damages

Article 7.4.1 of UNIDROIT Principles recognizes a party's right to damages for loss sustained as a result of the non-performance of the contract. It reads as follows:

> Any non-performance gives the aggrieved party a right to damages either exclusively or in conjunction with any other remedies except where the non-performance is excused under these Principles.

Thus, except where the non-performance is excused, the aggrieved party is entitled to claim damages. The right "arises from the sole fact of non-performance." In other words, in order to be entitled to claim damages it is enough for the aggrieved party simply to prove the non-performance.[17]

Article 7.4.2 makes it clear that the right to damages means the right to "full compensation." The loss sustained by the aggrieved party includes "both any loss

[17] See Comment to UNIDROIT Principles, ibid.

which it suffered and any gain of which it was deprived, taking into account any gain to the aggrieved party resulting from its avoidance of cost or harm."

8.2.10.4 Termination for Non-performance

It is interesting to note that the UNIDROIT Principles provide for the remedy of termination for non-performance instead of breach and distinguishes between the excused non-performance and non-excused non-performance. As Furmston suggests, the reason for using the terminology of the non-performance is that for many purposes the same rules can be applied to both—excused as well as non-excused—non-performances.[18] A further point to note is that under "Principles" as far as the right to terminate a contract for non-performance is concerned, it arises only for a kind of non-performance which is a fundamental one and is dealt with separately by Article 7.3.1 (right to terminate the contract) and Article 7.3.3 (anticipatory non-performance). The right of termination for the non-performance arises in both cases—excused and non-excused non-performances.[19]

Non-performance is defined by Article 7.1.1, which reads as follows:

> Non-performance is failure by a party to perform any of its obligations under the contract, including defective performance or late performance.

Thus, under "Principles" the "non-performance" includes not only the complete failure of performance but also the defective performance.

8.2.10.5 Termination for Fundamental Non-Performance

Article 7.3.1 of UNIDROIT Principles, like CISG (Articles 64 and 49), entitles a party to terminate the contract for fundamental non-performance or breach.[20] Para (1) states:

> A party may terminate the contract where the failure of the other party to perform an obligation under the contract amounts to a fundamental non-performance.

Further, Para (2) provides that in determining whether or not a non-performance amount to a fundamental non-performance regard shall be had, in particular, to whether

> (a) the non-performance substantially deprives the aggrieved party of what it was entitled to expect under the contract unless the other party did not foresee and could not reasonably have foreseen such result;
>
> (b) strict compliance with the obligation which has not been performed is of essence under the contract;

[18] Furmston (1992), p. 672.

[19] Ibid.

[20] UNIDROIT Principles consistently uses the term, non-performance to refer to breach of contract.

(c) the non-performance is intentional or reckless;

(d) the non-performance gives the aggrieved party reason to believe that it cannot rely on the other party's future performance;

(e) the non-performing party will suffer disproportionate loss as a result of the preparation or performance if the contract is terminated.

Para (3) gives the aggrieved party the right to terminate the contract where the other party fails to perform within the additional time allowed under Article 7.1.5.

It may also be noted that a contract may also be terminated where "adequate assurance of due performance" is not provided upon demand (Article 7.3.4). The right to demand adequate assurance is given by Article 7.3.4 which states that a party who reasonably believes that there will be a fundamental non-performance by the other party may demand adequate assurance of due performance and may meanwhile withhold its own performance.

Effect of termination for non-performance is provided by Article 7.3.5. According to Para (1), termination of the contract releases both parties from their future obligation. Further, the exercise of the right of termination does not preclude a claim for damages for non-performance (Para (2)).

Requirement of Notice

According to Article 7.3.2, a party may not exercise the right of termination unless notice to the other party is given. Para (1) states:

> The right of a party to terminate the contract is exercised by notice to the other party.

Obviously, the requirement of notice is intended to avoid any loss due to uncertainty as to whether the aggrieved party will accept the performance.

8.2.10.6 Termination for Anticipatory Non-Performance

Article 7.3.3 recognizes the principle of anticipatory breach of contract. It states:

> Where prior to the date for performance by one of the parties it is clear that there will be a fundamental non-performance by that party, the other party may terminate the contract.

Article 7.3.3 is similar to Article 72 of CISG dealing the right of anticipatory breach. As Comment to UNIDROIT Principles states that this right can be exercised only when the aggrieved party is clear that there will be non-performance, and a suspicion, even a well-founded one, is not sufficient to give rise to the right anticipatory breach. Furthermore, the non-performance in question must be fundamental and the notice of termination must be given to the non-performing party.

8.2.10.7 Fixing Additional Time (*"Nachfrist"*)

UNIDROIT Principles, like CISG, recognize the principle of granting additional time for performance.[21] Article 7.1.5 reads as follows:

(1) In a case of non-performance the aggrieved party may by notice to the other party allow an additional period of time for performance.

(2) During the additional period the aggrieved party may withhold performance of its own reciprocal obligations and may claim damages but may not resort to any other remedy. If it receives notice from the other party that the latter will not perform within that period, or if upon expiry of that period due performance has not been made, the aggrieved party may resort to any of the remedies that may be available under this Chapter.

(3) Where in a case of delay in performance which is not fundamental the aggrieved party has given notice allowing an additional period of time of reasonable length, it may terminate the contract at the end of that period. If the additional period allowed is not of reasonable length it shall be extended to a reasonable length. The aggrieved party may in its notice provide that if the other party fails to perform within the period allowed by the notice the contract shall automatically terminate.

8.2.10.8 Curing the Non-Performance

Like CISG, UNIDROIT Principles recognize the right of cure the defective performance provided that certain conditions are met. Article 7.1.4 provides:

(1) a non-performing party may cure any non-performance provided that (a) without undue delay, it gives notice indicating the proposed manner and timing of the cure; (b) cure is appropriate in the circumstances; (c) the aggrieved party has no legitimate interest in refusing cure; and (d) cure is effected promptly.

(2) The right to cure is not precluded by notice of termination.

(3) Upon effective notice of cure, rights of the aggrieved party that are inconsistent with the non-performing party's performance are suspended until the time for cure has expired.

(4) The aggrieved party may withhold performance pending cure.

(5) Notwithstanding cure, the aggrieved party retains the right to claim damages for delay as well as for any harm caused or not prevented by the cure.

---

[21] Article 7.1.5 incorporates the principle of *Nachfrist* which has already been noted in the context of remedies under CISG.

8.3 Hague Principles on Choice of Law in International Commercial Contracts

8.3.1 Hague Principles as Restatement of General Principles Concerning Choice of Law

The 2015 Hague Principles[22] set forth "general principles concerning choice of law in international commercial contracts" (Preamble). Significantly, they are the first soft-law instrument developed by the Hague Conference on Private International Law (HCCH).[23] As already stated, the "Principles" are not part of true law as they are neither promulgated by legislatures nor are customs of merchants. In this way, they are not legally binding. Rather, they are of the nature of restatement of law (see Chap. 2, Sect. 2.4.3). Being a soft-law instrument, the Principles are useful in many ways. As stated in the Preamble, first, they may be used as a model for national, regional, supranational, or international instruments; secondly, they may be used to interpret, supplement, and develop rules of private international law; and finally, they may be applied by courts and arbitral tribunals. Further, as Commentary to the Principles on Choice of Law in International Commercial Contracts states, through promulgation of "Principles," HCCH encourages states to incorporate them into their domestic law "in a manner appropriate for the circumstances of each State."[24] They are aimed to harmonize the choice of law rules across the world and to promote the principle of party autonomy.

8.3.2 Applicability of "The Hague Principles"

Turning to the applicability of the principles, it may be stated that the Hague Principles only apply to the principle of choice of law in international commercial contracts. Article 1 (1) categorically states that "Principles" specifically do exclude consumer or employment contracts. Further, Para (2) states that they do not cover the following matters: (a) the capacity of natural persons; (b) arbitration agreements and agreements on choice of court; (c) companies or other collective bodies and trusts; (d) insolvency;

[22]The text with Commentary to the Principles on Choice of Law in International Commercial Contracts is available at the official website of HCCH: https://www.hcch.net.

[23]See Principles on Choice of Law in International Commercial Contracts, "Foreword." The Hague: The Hague Conference on Private international Law.

[24]Commentary to the Hague Principles, supra note 22.

(e) the proprietary effects of contracts; (f) the issue of whether an agent is able to bind a principal to a third party.

Commercial Contracts

"Principles" do not define the term, "commercial" contracts. Rather, Article 1 (1) simply indicates that they apply to those contracts in which each party "is acting in the exercise of its trade or profession." As Commentary to the Hague Principles states, this "affirmative" definition of commercial contracts is significant because "it introduces an autonomous concept for determining when the Principles apply." Further, as Commentary explains, "Principles" do not use the term "commercial contracts" because the term is not used uniformly in all the countries. In certain countries, a distinction is made between the civil and commercial transactions but the expression, "commercial contracts" as used under the Principles is nothing to do with this distinction. Also, in some other states contracts between businesses and consumers are considered to be "commercial but these Principles are not concerned with them."[25]. Notably, a similar approach is adopted by the UNIDROIT Principles and some uniform law instruments, such as CISG (supra, Chap. 7, Sect. 7.5.3) and 2005 Electronic Communications Convention (infra, Chap. 9, Sect. 9.3.2).

8.3.3 Criteria of Internationality

Principles are intended to apply to international commercial contracts, that is to say, contracts which are entered into by the parties from different countries or jurisdictions. As already noted in the introductory chapter, an international contract may be defined variously depending on the legal regime to which they are subject to.

According to Article 1, Para (2), for the purpose of Principles, "a contract is international unless each party has its establishment in the same State and the relationship of the parties and all other relevant elements, regardless of the chosen law, are connected only with that State."

The definition given above is a negative one, which is meant to apply to all those contracts which are not purely domestic ones.[26] Thus, like UNIDROIT Principles, Article 1 defines an international contract in a broadest possible manner and excludes only those contracts in which each party is located or has its establishment in one state and the relationship between the parties and all other relevant criteria, such as making of the contract, performance of the contract, regardless of the chosen law, is connected only with that state.[27] In other words, if any of these elements, for example, nationality of the parties, is not connected with the same state, the contract in question will be covered by these Principles.

[25]Ibid. See also Symeonides (2013), p. 881.

[26]Symeonides, Symeon C., id, p. 879.

[27]Where a party has more than one establishment, according to Article 12, "the relevant establishment is the one that has the closest relationship to the contract at the time of its conclusion.".

8.3.4 *Principle of Party Autonomy*

The basic objective of the Hague Principles is to "affirm" and promote the principle of party autonomy (Preamble).[28] According to the principle of party autonomy, the parties to an international contract can themselves determine the law to govern their contract. As will be noted at the appropriate place in this book, the law so chosen by the parties replaces the law that would otherwise have governed their contract (see further infra, Chap. 15). Defining the principle, Article 2 states:

Article 2 Freedom of choice

(1) A contract is governed by the law chosen by the parties.

(2) The parties may choose—

  (a) the law applicable to the whole contract or to only part of it; and

  (b) different laws for different parts of the contract.

(3) The choice may be made or modified at any time. A choice or modification made after the contract has been concluded shall not prejudice its formal validity or the rights of third parties.

(4) No connection is required between the law chosen and the parties or their transaction.

The principle of party autonomy is an old principle of private international law and is adhered to in most of the countries. The significance of "Principles" then lies in the fact that they are intended to promote the principle of party autonomy in countries where it has still not been fully established.[29]

Para 4 makes it clear that the law chosen by the parties may not have any connection with the parties. In other words, the parties are free to choose a law other than the law of their country and can rightly choose the law of a third country or embodied in an international agreement or the "rules of law" embodied in a restatement like the UNIDROIT Principles.

8.3.5 *Overriding Mandatory Principles and Public Order"*

As explained at the appropriate place in this book, the principle of party autonomy is not absolute and is subject to certain restrictions. Where the law chosen by the party is inconsistent with the mandatory rules of forum or public policy, the principle cannot be given effect to (see further Chap. 15). Article 11 states:

Article 11 Overriding mandatory rules and public policy (ordre public)

(1) These Principles shall not prevent a court from applying overriding mandatory provisions of the law of the forum which apply irrespective of the law chosen by the parties.

---

[28] See Symeonides (2013), p. 878.

[29] See id, p. 876.

(2) The law of the forum determines when a court may or must apply or take into account overriding mandatory provisions of another law.
(3) A court may exclude application of a provision of the law chosen by the parties only if and to the extent that the result of such application would be manifestly incompatible with fundamental notions of public policy (ordre public) of the forum.
(4) The law of the forum determines when a court may or must apply or take into account the public policy (ordre public) of a State the law of which would be applicable in the absence of a choice of law.
(5) These Principles shall not prevent an arbitral tribunal from applying or taking into account public policy (ordre public), or from applying or taking into account overriding mandatory provisions of a law other than the law chosen by the parties, if the arbitral tribunal is required or entitled to do so.

Article 11 thus places certain limits on the applicability of the principle of party autonomy. It sets out the circumstances in which the principle can be applied. It identifies two situations in which a forum may refuse to apply the principle of party autonomy. First, where law so chosen by the parties is in conflict with the forum's mandatory rules of law or what may be termed, "overriding mandatory provisions" of law. Second, the forum may refuse to apply the law chosen by the parties to the extent that the result would be "manifestly incompatible with fundamental notions of public policy (*ordre public*)."[30]

8.3.6 Choice of Law: Express and Implied Choice

A choice of law may be made by the parties expressly or tacitly. Article 4 states:

Article 4 Express and tacit choice

A choice of law, or any modification of a choice of law, must be made expressly or appear clearly from the provisions of the contract or the circumstances. An agreement between the parties to confer jurisdiction on a court or an arbitral tribunal to determine disputes under the contract is not in itself equivalent to a choice of law.

Express choice of law clauses frequently appears in the (main) contract. However, in the absence of such clauses, a tacit choice of law may clearly appear from the provisions of the contract or the circumstances. However, the contract or the circumstances of the case should conclusively indicate a tacit choice of law. Further, as Commentary states, in order to be an effective choice of law the concerned choice must be a real one "although not expressly stated in the contract;" and "a presumed intention imputed to the parties does not suffice."

[30]Commentary to the Hague Principles, supra note 22.

8.3.7 No Requirements as to Form: Validity of the Choice of Law Clauses

Under the Hague Principles, the choice of law contracts, whether made expressly or tacitly, need not to comply with any requirements of form. This is made clear by Article 5 which states that "[a] choice of law is not subject to any requirement as to form unless otherwise agreed by the parties." Thus, it does not need to be in writing, or registered or attested by witnesses. The same rule applies to a modification of a choice of law (see Art. 2(3)). The provision is based on the policy that the parties' intention should not be impeded by formalistic requirements.[31]

8.3.8 Scope of the Chosen Law

According to Article 9, the law chosen by the parties, as a general rule, governs all aspects of their contractual relationship. For that purpose, it includes a "non-exhaustive" and illustrative list of issues governed by such law. The text of Article 9 reads as follows:

> (1) The law chosen by the parties shall govern all aspects of the contract between the parties, including but not limited to—
> (a) interpretation;
> (b) rights and obligations arising from the contract;
> (c) performance and the consequences of non-performance, including the assessment of damages;
> (d) the various ways of extinguishing obligations, and prescription and limitation periods;
> (e) validity and the consequences of invalidity of the contract;
> (f) burden of proof and legal presumptions;
> (g) pre-contractual obligations.
>
> (2) Paragraph 1(e) does not preclude the application of any other governing law supporting the formal validity of the contract.

Article 9 is based on the principle that, unless the parties agree otherwise, the law chosen shall govern all aspects of the contract. The contract should be governed by the law chosen by the parties from its formation until its end. This approach ensures legal certainty, and uniformity of results and, in doing so, reduces the incentive for forum shopping.[32]

---

[31] Ibid.

[32] Ibid.

References

Bonell, M. J. (1992). Unification of law by non-legislative means: The UNIDROIT Draft Principles for International commercial contracts. *American Journal of Comparative Law, 40*(3), 617–633.
Bonell, M. J. (Ed.). (2006). *The UNIDROIT Principles in Practice.* New York: Transnational Publishers.
Fontaine, M. (1992). Content and performance. *American Journal of Comparative Law, 40*(3), 645–655.
Furmston, M. P. (1992). Breach of contract. *American Journal of Comparative Law, 40*(3), 671674.
Kozolchyk, B. (1998). The UNIDROIT Principles as a model for the unification of the best contractual practices in the Americas. *American Journal of Comparative Law, 46*(1), 151–179.
Symeonides, S. C. (2013). The Hague principles on choice of law for international contracts: Some preliminary comments. *American Journal of Comparative Law, 61*(4), 873–899.

Official Documents and Online Resources

Hague Principles on the Choice of law in International Commercial Contracts (the Hague Principles), Hague Conference on Private International Law (HCCH): www.hcch.net
Model Clauses for the Use of the UNIDROIT Principles of International Commercial Contracts, UNIDROIT Principles Model Clause No. 1. 29 (a), International Institute for the Unification of Private Law.
UNIDROIT Principles of International Commercial Contracts (UNIDROIT Principles), International Institute for Unification of Trade law (UNIDROIT): www.uniddroit.org.
(UNIDROIT), Rome (2013): www.uniddroit.org.

Part III
Electronic Commerce

Chapter 9
Harmonization of Laws Concerning Electronic Communications in International Contracts

9.1 UNCITRAL Model Law on Electronic Commerce

9.1.1 General

Electronic commerce (e-commerce), explained below, has numerous advantages over the traditional, paper-based transactions[1] resulting in the massive increase in the use of it in the field of international trade over the last few decades. The advent of internet technology in the early 1990s has provided further impetus to the growth of e-commerce raising the issue of harmonizing the laws governing the modern means of communications, including communications through electronic means. Thus, in the wake of the rise of electronic commerce and the massive increase in the use of internet for recording and communicating information in the field of international trade, the United Nations Commission on International Trade Law (UNCITRAL) has adopted a series of important legislative instruments directed toward harmonizing national laws for facilitating e-commerce. These instruments include: the 1996 Model Law on Electronic Commerce ("MLEC"),[2] the 2001 Model Law on Electronic Signatures ("MLES"),[3] and the 2005 United Nations Convention on the Use of Electronic Communications in International Contracts ("Electronic Communications Convention").[4]

---

[1] See generally, Lucking-Reiley and Spulber (2001), pp. 55–68.

[2] Adopted on June 12, 1996. The Model Law includes an additional article 5 *bis* as adopted by the UNCITRAL in June 1998. For the text, see *Model Law on Electronic Commerce with Guide to the Enactment*, New York: United Nations 1996. The text of the Model Law as well as the Guide to the Enactment is also available at the official website of UNCITRAL: https://uncitral.un.org/.

[3] Adopted on December 12, 2001. For the text, see *Model Law on Electronic Signatures with Guide to the Enactment*, New York: United Nations 2001. The text of the Model Law as well as the Guide to the Enactment is also available at the official website of UNCITRAL: https://uncitral.un.org/.

[4] Adopted on November 23, 2005, entered into force on March 1, 2013. For the text of the Convention together with the Explanatory note by the UNCITRAL secretariat, see United Nations Convention

A. Srivastava, *Modern Law of International Trade*, International Law and the Global South, https://doi.org/10.1007/978-981-15-5475-9_9

MLEC was adopted with a view to removing legal obstacles to the use of the modern techniques of communications and to creating "a more secure legal environment" for electronic commerce. The objectives of the Model Law include facilitating the use of electronic commerce and recognizing and providing equal treatment to both—the modern techniques of communications as well as the paper-based documentation. Although a model law, unlike an international convention, is not a legally binding instrument, it is, nevertheless, considered considerably useful in harmonizing national laws (see Chap. 2, Sect. 2.4.2). In this context, the EC Model Law offers national legislators a set of internationally acceptable (model) rules as to how a number of legal issues arising in the context may be addressed. As the Guide to the Enactment (the Guide) states, the model law was adopted because in many countries the existing legislations on communication and storage of information was "inadequate" or "outdated" as they did not contemplate the use of electronic commerce.[5] Further, the EC Model Law is at best a "framework" law as it is not conceived as setting out all the rules considered necessary for facilitating the use of the "modern techniques" for recording and communicating information in states that adopt the Model Law; not intended to include every aspect of electronic commerce.[6]

The Model Law is divided into two parts—Part I and Part II. Part I deals with "electronic commerce in general" and Part II deals with electronic commerce in specific areas. While the latter consists of a single chapter dealing with carriage of goods, the former consists of three chapters—Chap. 1 (articles 1–4) dealing with the general aspects; Chap. 2 (articles 5–10) dealing with the legal recognition and requirements in data messages; and Chap. 3 (articles 11–15) devoted to the issues concerning communication of data messages.

9.1.2 Electronic Commerce in General

9.1.2.1 Scope of Application

The text of Article 1, MLEC which defines the sphere of application reads as follows:

Model Law applies to any kind of information in the form of a data message used in the context of commercial activities.

It may be noted that while the Model Law is prepared to apply to commercial transactions there is nothing in the text to prevent its application to other fields. Although not specifically directed to the issues arising in the context of consumers, it can also be extended to consumer transactions.[7] A further point to note is that the

---

on the Use of Electronic Communications in International Contracts, New York: United Nations 2007. The text of the Convention as well as the Explanatory note by the UNCITRAL secretariat on the Convention is also available at the official website of UNCITRAL: https://uncitral.un.org/.

[5]The Guide, supra note 2, Para 3.

[6]See ibid.

[7]Ibid.

applicability of the Model Law is not restricted to international transactions and it may well be applied to a transaction which is purely domestic one.

9.1.2.2 Electronic Commerce: Meaning

"Electronic commerce" is commonly understood as agreements concluded through the exchange of email, purchases made at internet websites, payments made by electronic means, and other similar activities.[8] In other words, the phrase refers to those commercial transactions which are conducted by means of either electronic data interchange (EDI) or the internet.

The EC Model Law does not define e-commerce. However, the Guide to MLEC states that the notion includes various modes of transmission based on electronic techniques, such as "communication by means of electronic data interchange (EDI); transmission of electronic messages involving the use of either publicly available standards or proprietary standards; transmission of free-formatted text by electronic means, for example through the internet."[9]

A key term in the present context is EDI which may be defined as "point-to-point communications done over proprietary networks, rather than over the Internet."[10] The Model Law defines it as "the electronic transfer from computer to computer of information using an agreed standard to structure the information" (Article 2 (b)). In other words, EDI, unlike internet, is "the inter-community computer-to-computer communication of information using an agreed standard to structure the information. In EDI, unlike internet, communications take place within closed networks.[11] Internet commerce typically makes use of open standards and off-the-shelf technology on a global network, while EDI relies on customized hardware and software.[12]

Another key term in the context is "data message" which is defined by the Model Law as "information generated, sent, received or stored by electronic, optical or similar means including, but not limited to, electronic data interchange (EDI), electronic mail, telegram, telex or telecopy" (Article 2(a)). The definition covers all kinds of data messages that might be generated, stored, or communicated. It clearly states that a data message is any "information… by electronic, optical or similar means… As the Guide to MLEC suggests the use of the term, "similar means" indicates that the definition intends to include all means of communication and storage of information that might be used to perform functions parallel to the functions performed by the means listed in the definition…." Further, it is not limited to communication only but also encompasses computer-generated records that are not intended for communication.

---

[8] Maggs (Maggs 2002), p. 665.

[9] The Guide, supra note 1, Para 7.

[10] Lucking-Reiley and Spulber (2001), p. 56. In comparison to EDI, "Internet commerce offers considerable advantages in terms of cost and convenience."

[11] See Carr (2014), p. 103.

[12] Lucking-Reiley and Spulber (2001), p. 56.

9.1.2.3 "Functional Equivalence" Approach

Model Law is based on the premise that if certain conditions (provided for in articles 6–8) are fulfilled, both—data messages and paper documents—should be treated as performing similar functions. Thus, it adopts an approach of functional equivalence according to which, a contract formed on the basis of data messages cannot be denied legal effect and thus cannot be discriminated against paper documents. Article 5 states.

Article 5 Legal recognition of data messages
Information shall not be denied legal effect, validity or enforceability solely on the grounds that it is in the form of a data message.

Article 5 thus gives legal recognition to information communicated or stored by data messages and clearly says that "data messages should not be discriminated against i.e., that there should be no disparity of treatment between data messages and paper documents." The Guide states that by stating that "information shall not be denied legal effectiveness, validity or enforceability solely on the grounds that it is in the form of a data message," Article 5 merely indicates that the form in which "certain information is presented or retained cannot be used as the only reason for which that information would be denied legal effectiveness, validity or enforceability."

A related provision is contained in Article 9 which is intended to establish the admissibility of data messages as evidence. Article 9 (1) states:

> In any legal proceedings, nothing in the application of the rules of evidence shall apply so as to deny the admissibility of a data message in evidence:
>
> (a) on the sole ground that it is a data message; or,
> (b) if it is the best evidence that the person adducing it could reasonably be expected to obtain, on the grounds that it is not in its original form.

Further, Para (2) of Article 9 states that "information in the form of a data message shall be given due evidential weight."

9.1.2.4 Requirements as to Writing, Signature, and Original

As already stated, in order to enable a data message to be treated in a way similar to the paper documents, it needs to fulfill certain legal requirements set out in a set of provisions contained in articles 6 (writing), 7 (signature), and 9 (originals). Article 6 provides the basic standard to be met by a data message in order to be considered as equivalent to the requirement that "information to be in writing." Article 6 states: "Where the law requires information to be in writing, that requirement is met by a data message if the information contained therein is accessible so as to be usable for subsequent reference" (Para 1).

Similarly, Article 7 states that the requirement of signature is met in relation to a data message if:

(a) a method is used to identify that person and to indicate that person's approval of the information contained in the data message; and

(b) that method is as reliable as was appropriate for the purpose for which the data message was generated or communicated, in the light of all the circumstances, including any relevant agreement.

Article 8 is intended to address the requirement for presentation of originals in a paper-less environment. It states that where the law requires information to be presented or retained in its original form, that requirement is met by a data message if:

(a) there exists a reliable assurance as to the integrity of the information from the time when it was first generated in its final form, as a data message or otherwise; and

(b) where it is required that information be presented, that information is capable of being displayed to the person to whom it is to be presented.

9.1.2.5 Formation of Contract, Validity, and Enforcement

The issue of contract formation and the validity of a contract based on electronic communications is dealt with by Article 11 which states:

Article 11 Formation and validity of contracts

(1) In the context of contract formation, unless otherwise agreed by the parties, an offer and the acceptance of an offer may be expressed by means of data messages. Where a data message is used in the formation of a contract, that contract shall not be denied validity or enforceability on the sole ground that a data message was used for that purpose.

(2) xxx.

Article 11 makes it clear that an offer and an acceptance can be made by data messages. This obvious provision was made to make it clear that a contract can validly be made by electronic means.[13] As the Guide indicates, Para (1) covers not merely the cases in which both the offer and the acceptance are communicated by electronic means but also cases in which only the offer or only the acceptance is communicated electronically.

9.1.2.6 Time and Place of Dispatch and Receipt of Data Messages

Ascertaining the time and place of dispatch and receipt of communication is of key significance in the context of formation of contract through the use of modern communication techniques. Notably, Article 15 which addresses the issue adopts the criterion of the place of business of the parties rather than the location of the parties in ascertaining time and place of dispatch and receipt of communication. It would be relevant here to quote the text of Article 15 in full.

[13]The Guide to MLEC, Para 76.

Article 15. Time and place of dispatch and receipt of data messages

(1) Unless otherwise agreed between the originator and the addressee, the dispatch of a data message occurs when it enters an information system outside the control of the originator or of the person who sent the data message on behalf of the originator.

(2) Unless otherwise agreed between the originator and the addressee, the time of receipt of a data message is determined as follows:

(a) if the addressee has designated an information system for the purpose of receiving data messages, receipt occurs:

i. at the time when the data message enters the designated information system; or

ii. if the data message is sent to an information system of the addressee that is not the designated information system, at the time when the data message is retrieved by the addressee;

(a) if the addressee has not designated an information system, receipt occurs when the data message enters an information system of the addressee.

(3) Paragraph (2) applies notwithstanding that the place where the information system is located may be different from the place where the data message is deemed to be received under paragraph (4).

(4) Unless otherwise agreed between the originator and the addressee, a data message is deemed to be dispatched at the place where the originator has its place of business, and is deemed to be received at the place where the addressee has its place of business. For the purposes of this paragraph:

   (a) if the originator or the addressee has more than one place of business, the place of business is that which has the closest relationship to the underlying transaction or, where there is no underlying transaction, the principal place of business;

   (b) if the originator or the addressee does not have a place of business, reference is to be made to its habitual residence.

9.1.3 E-Commerce in Specific Areas

Part two of the Model Law contains rules to be applied to the specific areas, in particular, carriage of goods. During the preparation of the Model Law, it was noted that in the specific area of carriage of goods "a legal framework facilitating the use of such [electronic] communications was most urgently needed."[14] Articles 16 (dealing with the scope of Chap. 1 which specifically relates to carriage of goods) and 17 (dealing with transport documents) therefore contain provisions that apply any transport documents whether "negotiable," such as the transferable bill of lading or "non-negotiable."[15] The principles embodied in these articles are applicable not only to maritime transport but also to transport of goods by road, rail, and air.[16]

[14]Id, Para 108.

[15]On the meaning of the negotiable transport documents in the specific context of the carriage of goods, see Chap. 10.

[16]The Guide, Para 110.

As the Guide to the Model Law indicates, Article 16 is intended to cover a wide range of documents in relation to a contract of carriage dealt with in the Chap. 1 of Part two.[17] It states that the following actions in connection with a carriage of contract are included within the scope of Chap. 1:

(a) (i) furnishing the marks, number, quantity or weight of goods; (ii) stating or declaring the nature or value of goods; (iii) issuing a receipt for goods; (iv) confirming that goods have been loaded;
(b) (i) notifying a person of terms and conditions of the contract; (ii) giving instructions to a carrier;
(c) (i) claiming delivery of goods; (ii) authorizing release of goods; (iii) giving notice of loss of, or damage to, goods;
(d) giving any other notice or statement in connection with the performance of the contract;
(e) undertaking to deliver goods to a named person or a person authorized to claim delivery;
(f) granting, acquiring, renouncing, surrendering, transferring or negotiating rights in goods;
(g) acquiring or transferring rights and obligations under the contract.

The list of actions given above is not exhaustive and is only illustrative.

9.2 UNCITRAL Model Law on Electronic Signatures

9.2.1 General

MLES is based on Article 7 of MLEC which sets out the conditions to be fulfilled in regard to meeting the requirement of a signature in relation to a data message. It offers a set of internationally acceptable (model) rules to guide the national legislators in establishing a legal regime for electronic signatures. The objectives of the Model Law include the encouragement of facilitating the use of electronic signatures and providing equal treatment for all documents whether they are in electronic format or they are paper-based. The objectives of the Model Law include enabling or facilitating the use of electronic signatures and providing equal treatment to both—paper-based documents and data messages. According to the accompanying Guide to the Enactment, "[b]y incorporating the procedures prescribed in the Model Law (and also the provisions of the UNCITRAL Model Law on Electronic Commerce) in its national legislation… an enacting State would appropriately create a media-neutral environment."[18] As a supplement to MLEC, MLES sets forth essential principles for facilitating the use of electronic signatures. However, like MLEC, this new Model Law is also a "framework" law and thus is not meant to contain all the rules and

---

[17] Id, Para 111.

[18] Guide to Enactment of the Model Law on Electronic Signatures, Para. 5.

regulations that may be necessary (in addition to contractual arrangements between users) to implement the modern authentication techniques in an enacting state.[19]

As Guide to the Enactment of the MLES states, in drafting the new Model Law, every effort was made to ensure consistency with the MLEC. It is for this reason the former instrument reproduces the general provisions of the latter: Articles 1 (Sphere of application), 2 *(a), (c) and (d)* (Definitions of "data message," "originator," and "addressee"), 3 (Interpretation), 4 (Variation by agreement), and 7 (Signature).[20]

As already noted, a model law is recommendatory in nature which only encourages the states to enact their laws on the basis of the rules incorporated into its text. While adopting a model law, a state is free to make necessary modifications to suit its domestic conditions. This is also true about this new Model Law which gives sufficient flexibility in incorporating its text into national legislations.[21]

9.2.2 Scope of Application

The "sphere of application" is dealt with by Article 1 which states:

Law applies where electronic signatures are used in the context of commercial activities. It does not override any rule of law intended for the protection of consumers.

MLES prefers a technology-neutral approach and is intended to cover all factual situations where electronic signatures are used, irrespective of the specific method authentication. Here mention may also be made of Article 3 which states that this Model Law shall not be applied so as to exclude, restrict, or deprive legal effect of any method of creating an electronic signature that satisfies the requirements of Article 6, or otherwise meets the requirements of applicable law. A further point to note is that MLES, like MLEC, though prepared for commercial transactions may well be applied to all kinds of data messages to which a legally significant electronic signature is attached. In other words, the scope of the Model Law may be extended by an enacting state to cover electronic signatures outside the commercial sphere.[22]

9.2.3 Electronic Signature

Article 2(a) defines an "electronic signature" as

> data in electronic form in, affixed to or logically associated with, a data message, which may be used to identify the signatory in relation to the data message and to indicate the signatory's approval of the information contained in the data message.

[19] Id, Para 69.

[20] Id, Para 66.

[21] Id, Para 27.

[22] Id, Para 88.

The definition is intended to cover all traditional uses of a handwritten signature and is based on the functional equivalence principle. Further, in consistent with the technology-neutral approach, the above-said definition does not promote any specific technology.[23] It encompasses all those technologies that could be used for creating a "legally significant signature."[24] The definition stresses two purposes of electronic signatures: identifying a person and associating that person with the content of a document.

9.2.4 Reliability Requirements

It may also be noted that an electronic signature as defined above must meet the reliability requirements stated in Para 3 of Article 6. According to Para 3, an electronic signature is considered to be reliable if: *(a)* The signature creation data are …linked to the signatory and to no other person; *(b)* The signature creation data were, at the time of signing, under the control of the signatory and of no other person; *(c)* Any alteration to the electronic signature, made after the time of signing, is detectable; and *(d)* Where a purpose of the legal requirement for a signature is to provide assurance as to the integrity of the information to which it relates, any alteration made to that information after the time of signing is detectable.

9.2.5 Functional Equivalence Principle

Like MLEC, the new Model Law is based on the functional equivalence principle according to which various techniques that may be used to communicate or store information electronically and a paper document should be treated equally.

9.2.6 Obligations of the Parties

Articles 8–11 set out the rules regarding the obligations and liabilities of the various parties: the signatory (Article 8); any certification services provider (Articles 9 and 10); and the relying party (Article 11). Where any of these parties fails to satisfy the requirements of these articles shall bear the legal consequences in this regard.

According to Article 8, each signatory shall: *(a)* exercise reasonable care to avoid unauthorized use of its signature creation data; *(b)* utilize means made available by the certification service provider pursuant to Article 9 or otherwise use reasonable efforts

[23] See Carr (2014), p. 126.

[24] The emphasis on legally significant signature seems necessary because "electronic signatures" could be used for purposes other than legally significant purposes. See Para 93.

to notify any person likely to rely on electronic signatures if: (i) the signatory knows that the signature creation data have been compromised; or (ii) the circumstances known to the signatory give rise to a substantial risk that the signature creation data may have been compromised; *(c)* exercise reasonable care to ensure the accuracy and completeness of all material representations made by the signatory that are relevant to the certificate throughout its life cycle.

In the same way, Article 9 makes a certification service provider subject to the following duties: (1) to act in accordance with representations made by it with regard to its policies; (2) to ensure the accuracy and completeness of its all material representations that are relevant to the certificate throughout its life cycle; (3) to provide reasonably accessible means that enable a relying party to ascertain from the certificate: (a) the identity of the certification service provider; (b) that the signatory had control of the signature creation data; and (c) that signature creation data were valid at or before the time when the certificate was issued; (4) to make available certain additional information where they are relevant; (5) and to utilize "trustworthy systems, procedures and human resources" in performing its services.

Further, Article 10 lists a number of factors to be taken into account in interpreting the above-mentioned phrase, "trustworthy systems, procedures and human resources." According to the Guide to the Enactment the list is based on a flexible notion of trustworthiness, which could vary in content depending upon what is expected of the certificate in the context in which it is created.[25]

According to Article 11, a relying party is under duty to take reasonable steps to verify the reliability of an electronic signature; and where an electronic signature is supported by a certificate, "to take reasonable steps to verify the validity, suspension or revocation of the certificate" and "to observe any limitation with respect to the certificate."

9.3 2005 United Nations Convention on the Use of Electronic Communications in International Contracts

9.3.1 General

The 2005 Electronic Communications Convention is based on the model laws, discussed above. Accordingly, it is aimed at removing "obstacles to the use of electronic communications in international contracts, including obstacles that might result from the operation of existing international trade law instruments."[26] According to the Explanatory Note, the purpose of the Convention is "to offer practical solutions for issues related to the use of electronic means of communication in

[25] Para 147.

[26] See Preamble to the Convention, supra note 4. See also Faria and Angelo (2006), p. 689.

connection with international contracts."[27] Significantly, the Convention is primarily meant to establish uniform rules for the issues that are specifically related to the use of electronic communications in international contracts.[28] In fact, it provides an "interpretative framework" to adapt existing rules regarding paper documents to support contracts formed through electronic means without specifically addressing the substantive contractual issues.[29]

9.3.2 Scope of Application

The Convention applies to an exchange of electronic communications[30] related to the formation or performance of an international contract. For the purpose of the Convention, an international contract is defined as the contracts between parties located in two different states. Article 1 provides that the "Convention applies to the use of electronic communications in connection with the formation or performance of a contract between parties whose places of business are in different States" (Para 1). Thus, it is not necessary that states in question be contracting states. However, "[t]he fact that the parties have their places of business in different States is to be disregarded whenever this fact does not appear either from the contract or from any dealings between the parties or from information..." (Para 2). Notably, following the approach adopted by CISG, the Convention in specifying the international character of a contract does not take into account the criterion of the nationality of the parties (Para 3).

Secondly, as the accompanying Explanatory Note states, the word "contract" in the Convention is used in a broad sense and covers "any form of legally binding agreement" whether or not it is usually considered contracts. For example, an arbitration agreement is a contract within the meaning of the Convention although it is not normally treated a contract.[31]

A further point to note is that the Convention does not apply to certain categories of contracts or transactions listed in Article 2. These mainly include contracts related to personal, family, or household purposes; transactions related to certain financial service markets; negotiable instruments and similar documents.

---

[27] Explanatory Note, id, Para 3.

[28] Id, Para 3.

[29] Faria and Angelo (2006), p. 690.

[30] Electronic communication is defined to include any statement, declaration, demand, notice or request, including an offer and the acceptance of an offer, made by electronic, magnetic, optical or similar means in connection with the formation or performance of a contract. Article 4 (a).

[31] Explanatory Note, Para 57.

9.3.3 Functional Equivalence Principle

Article 8 of the Convention gives legal recognition to contracts resulting from the exchange of electronic communications and reiterates this fundamental principle that a contract should not be denied validity or enforceability solely because they result from the exchange of electronic communications. However, for applying this principle, the conditions set out in Article 9 (which are similar to those mentioned in MLEC, Articles 6, 7, and 8) must be fulfilled.

Further and as already stated, the Convention does not generally address the issues concerning contract formation and other related issues in order to avoid establishing a duality of legal regimes for electronic and paper documents.[32]

9.3.4 Dispatch and Receipt of Electronic Communications

The rules regarding time and place of dispatch and receipt of electronic communications are contained in Article 10 which are similar to those contained in Article 15 of MLEC (see above, Sect. 9.1.2.6). As already stated, domestic legal system adopts divergent approaches to the issue of the time and place of contract formation and UNCITRAL does not make any attempt to interfere with the domestic laws and to offer a different set of rules in this regard. Instead, the Convention offers "guidance" regarding the adaptation of the concepts and principles developed by the domestic laws in the context of paper-based transactions to an electronic environment.[33]

9.4 General Usage for International Digitally Ensured Commerce (GUIDEC)

Finally, mention may be made of a key initiative of International Chamber of Commerce (ICC) toward promoting e-commerce and in particular addressing the issue of "information security"—the General Usage for International Digitally Ensured Commerce (GUIDEC) adopted in 1997,[34] which was subsequently issued in 2001 as GUIDEC II.[35] GUIDEC seeks to establish "a general framework for the ensuring and certification of digital messages, based upon existing law and practice

[32]Faria and Angelo (2006), p. 691.

[33]Explanatory Note, Para 175.

[34]Adopted on November 6, 1997. For the GUIDEC text, see International Chamber of Commerce: General Usage for International Digitally Ensured Commerce, 37 *International Legal Materials* 714 (1998).

[35]Available at the official website of ICC: www.iccwbo.org.

in different legal systems and provides a detailed explanation of ensuring and certification principles, particularly as they relate to information system security issues and public key cryptographic techniques."[36]

GUIDEC is meant for international business community. Preface to the text states: "[it] assumes practices in which transacting parties are expert commercial actors, operating under the lex mercatoria."[37] According to the GUIDEC text, the document includes "the core concepts, best practices and certification issues in the context of international commercial law and practice." Another most important feature of GUIDEC relates to its emphasis on the open network communications systems, like Internet. It addresses issues pertaining to information security which are the most significant barriers to global electronic commerce over open networks.[38] Significantly, GUIDEC recognizes the pubic key cryptography, a digital signature technology, known in the GUIDEC as "ensuring a message."[39] GUIDEC text explains: "Because an ensured message is difficult to forge, its use binds the signatory, precluding a later repudiation of the message."[40]

References

Carr, I. (2014) p. 103.

Faria, José, & Angelo, Estrella. (2006). The united nations convention on the use of electronic communications in international contracts: an introductory note. *International and Comparative Law Quarterly, 55*(3), 689–693.

Fox, Jr. William F. (2001). The international chamber of commerce's guidec principles: private-sector rules for digital signatures. *International Lawyer, 35*(1), 71–78.

Lucking-Reiley, David, & Spulber, Daniel F. (2001). Business-to-business electronic commerce. *Journal of Economic Perspectives, 15*(1), 55–68.

Maggs, Gregory E. (2002). Regulating electronic commerce. *American Journal of Comparative Law, 50*(Supplement), 665–685.

Official Texts and Online Resources

Explanatory Note by the UNCITRAL Secretariat on United Nations Convention on the use of Electronic Communications in International Contracts (the *Explanatory Note*) (2007): New York: United Nations.

General Usage for International Digitally Ensured Commerce (GUIDEC II). www.iccwbo.org.

General Usage for International Digitally Ensured Commerce (GUIDEC I). 37 *International Legal Materials, 714* (1998).

---

[36]GUIDEC text, id., p. 716.

[37]Ibid.

[38]Id., p. 719.

[39]Use of the phrase, "ensuring a message" in place of digital signature by GUIDEC, is "the central contribution." See Fox, Jr. William F. (2001), p. 76.

[40]GUIDEC text, p. 721.

Guide to Enactment of the Model Law on Electronic Signatures, at: https://uncitral.un.org/.
International Chamber of Commerce (ICC). www.iccwbo.org.
Model Law on Electronic Commerce with Guide to the Enactment (the *Guide*). https://uncitral.un.org/.
United Nations Commission on International Trade Law (UNCITRAL): https://uncitral.un.org/.

Part IV
Contracts of Carriage of Goods

Chapter 10
Maritime Carriage

The chapter first explains certain key terms used in maritime carriage; secondly, it discusses the duties of a carrier under the traditional, common law rules and then goes on to discuss the key aspects of the liability schemes established by the international conventions on the subject.

10.1 Key Terms

Contract of Affreightment
A "contract of affreightment" or a contract for carriage of goods by sea, as distinguished from a contract for carriage of passengers, generally refers to a contract concluded between a ship-owner/carrier, on the one hand, and the cargo-owner/shipper, on the other, whereby the former, for the reward called, freight, agrees to carry goods from one place to another.[1] Such a contract may be either a charterparty or a contract of shipment contained in or evidenced by a bill of lading as explained below.

Charterparty
Where cargo is to be carried in bulk and is sufficient to occupy the entire space or a great part of a ship, it is normal for the parties—the ship-owner or carrier and the cargo-owner—to enter into a contract of carriage, termed, charterparty, under which the entire ship or a principal part of it is hired to carry the goods.[2] In other words, under a charterparty concluded between a ship-owner/carrier, on the one hand and a charterer (hirer of a ship)/shipper, on the other, the entire ship is hired for undertaking a voyage or series of voyages for a specified period of time. A charterparty contains the terms defining various responsibilities of the parties and is mainly governed by

[1]See 1978 United Nations Convention on the Carriage of Goods by Sea (the Hamburg Rules), Article 1(6); Chorley and Giles (1970), pp. 103–04.

[2]See Aikens et al. (2006), p. 18; Chorley and Giles, id., pp. 108–09; Carr (2014), pp. 154–55.

A. Srivastava, *Modern Law of International Trade*, International Law and the Global South, https://doi.org/10.1007/978-981-15-5475-9_10

common law. Further, although there is no requirement in the law that a charterparty must be in writing, it is usually to be found in the written form.[3]

Voyage Charterparty, Time Charterparty, and Demise Charterparty
A charterparty may take the three main forms—voyage charterparty, time charterparty, and demise charterparty. Where the ship is chartered for a specified voyage, for example, from Chennai to Singapore, the charterparty in question is the voyage charterparty. Under the time charterparty, on the other hand, the ship is chartered for a specified duration, for example, from January 15, 2019 to January 14, 2020.

Under the demise charterparty, the ship-owner transfers the possession or control of the ship to the charterer and it is the charterer who is responsible for equipping and manning the ship during the specified voyage(s) or duration, as the case may be. The position is similar to the lease of a piece of land wherein the leaseholder obtains possession of the land for certain duration. But this type of charterparty is now less common. From a legal point of view, the charterer by demise steps into the shoes of the ship-owner and it is he who can invoke the rules of the limitation of the ship-owner's liabilities.[4]

Bills of Lading
A charterparty is most commonly used when an entire ship or a great part of it is hired for carriage of goods. But where the shipper wishes to transport the small quantity of goods, it is the bill of lading contract which is most commonly used. A bill of lading,[5] as explained below, refers to a document issued by the carrier/master of the ship or some other person acting as agent for the ship-owner or carrier after the goods are loaded on board the ship.[6] It is the duty of the carrier/master of the ship to issue a bill of lading within a reasonable time and a failure to do so is likely to be treated a breach of contractual or statutory duty.

A bill of lading serves three important purposes: First, it serves as the receipt for the goods received by the carrier in which case its work is similar to that of a freight bill. Originally, a bill of lading only served as the receipt of goods. Its sole purpose was to acknowledge the shipment of the goods as described in it.[7] Secondly, it serves as a (written) evidence of the contract of carriage between the carrier and the shipper where holder of the bill is the shipper. However, as will be seen below, upon endorsement, it contains the terms of a contract of carriage between the carrier and the consignor where holder of the bill is the endorsee or consignee.[8] Thirdly, it serves as a ("negotiable") document of title of goods upon endorsement of which the

---

[3]Chorley and Giles, id., p. 110.

[4]See Carr (2014), p. 156; Chorley and Giles, id., p. 182.

[5]A bill of lading is to be distinguished from an electronic bill of lading (discussed below).

[6]Hague-Visby Rules (cited below), Article III rule 3: "After receiving the goods into his charge, the carrier, or the master or agent of the carrier shall, on demand of the shipper, issue to the shipper a bill of lading….".

[7]See Duncan (1917), p. 681; *The Maurice Desgagnes* [1977] 1 Lloyd's Rep. 290.

[8]A consignee is the person to whom the goods are delivered by the ship-owner/carrier. He is not generally a party to the contract of carriage.

rights and duties of the shipper under the contract of carriage stand transferred to a third party like, the endorsee.[9]

In view of various uses of the bill of lading, in a charterparty also, it is normally issued in favor of the charterer-shipper for he may wish to sell the goods during their transit. In that case, the bill of lading serves the purpose of a document of title through which property in the goods may be transferred during transit of the goods.

Bill of Lading as Receipt of Goods

After goods are loaded on board the ship, the shipmaster or any other person acting as agent of the ship-owner issues a bill of lading which acknowledges the shipment of the goods.[10] The bill of lading in the hands of the shipper serves as a receipt for the quantity and condition of the goods received and for leading marks[11] and is the prima facie evidence that the shipper has shipped the goods. Where the bill of lading indicates that the goods have been shipped in good order upon endorsement, the consignee can use it as an evidence of the fact that the goods were shipped in that good condition. A clean bill of lading operates as an estoppel against the carrier and he is stopped from claiming that the goods were damaged at the time of shipment unless he shows that damage could not be "apparent" on the reasonable inspection.[12]

Bill of Lading as Evidence of Contract of Carriage

As already stated, the bill of lading is not merely a receipt of goods. It also contains or evidences the terms of contract of carriage between the carrier and the shipper.[13] However, in the hands of a shipper the bill is not the contract, but only evidence of the contract and a shipper is not bound by such terms of the bill if he is not aware of them.[14] This is for the reason that a bill of lading is not treated as embodying all the terms agreed between the carrier and the shipper and it is not unlikely that the bill does not contain all terms of the original contract or modifies them. Thus, where the bill is endorsed or transferred to a third party it is a contract of carriage. The Court of Appeal in *Cho yang Shipping Co. Ltd. v Coral (UK) Ltd*[15] held:

---

[9]Section 2 of the Carriage of Goods by Sea Act, 1992 (COGSA 1992) provide as follows: "...Subject to the following provisions of this section, a person who becomes the lawful holder of a bill of lading;... shall (by virtue of becoming the holder of the bill...) have transferred to and vested in him all rights of suit under the contract of carriage as if he had been a party to that contract...." See also *The Maurice Desgagnes* [1977] 1 Lloyd's Rep. 290.

[10]Originally a bill of lading, like a mate's receipt, only served as the receipt of goods. Its sole purpose was to acknowledge the shipment of the goods as described in it. Chorley and Giles (1970), p. 160.

[11]See Hague-Visby Rules, Article III(3).

[12]See *Brandt v Liverpool, Brazil and River Plate Steam Navigation Co.* [1924] 1 KB 575; *Compania Naviera Vascongada v Churchill & Sim* [1906] 1 KB 237; Aikens et al. (2006), pp. 78–79.

[13]Aikens et al., id., p. 13.

[14]See *Crooks v Allan* [1879] 5 QBD 38 (A bill of lading is not the contract, but only evidence of the contract; and it does not follow that a person who accepts the bill of lading ....binds himself to abide by all its stipulations.); *The Ardennes* [1951] 1 KB 55.

[15][1997] 2 Lloyd's Rep 641.

> ...in English law, the bill of lading is not the contract between the original parties but is simply evidence of it ... Indeed, though contractual in form, it may in the hands of a person already in contractual relation with the carrier ... be no more than a receipt.... Therefore, as between shipper and carrier, it may be necessary to inquire what the actual contract between them was; merely to look at the bill of lading may not in all cases suffice.[16]

Earlier indeed the position was different but since the passing of the Bills of Lading Act 1855, a consignee or endorsee has the right to sue in respect of the goods "as if the contract contained in the bill of lading had been made with [consignee or endorsee] himself."[17] As explained by the Court in *Leduc v Ward,*[18] in a charterparty, as between the ship-owner and the charterer, the bill of lading merely serves the purpose of a receipt for the goods shipped for "all the other terms of the contract of carriage are contained in the charterparty; and the bill of lading is merely given...to enable the charterer to deal with the goods while in the course of transit"; but

> ...[w]here the bill of lading is indorsed over, as between the ship-owner and the endorsee, the bill of lading must be considered to contain the contract, because the former has given it for the purpose of enabling the charterer to pass it on as the contract of carriage for the goods.[19]

Bill of Lading as a Document of Title

Bill of lading is a document of title also.[20] As a result, the endorsement and delivery of the bill of lading operates as a symbolic delivery of the cargo. As Bowen LJ in *Sanders v Maclean*[21] said, "It is a key which in the hands of the rightful owner is intended to unlock the door of the warehouse, floating or fixed, in which the goods may chance to be." Since the bill of lading is a document of title, the shipper or charterer can transfer property in the goods while the goods are in the course of transit.

A further quality of a bill of lading is that it is "negotiable" in the sense of being transferable. However, it is not negotiable in true sense of the term.[22] The result is that a consignee and endorsee of the goods, though, obtains a good title to the goods referred to in the bill, they, in absence of a notice about the defect in title of the transferor, do not get a better title than the transferor himself has. Negotiability in the context only means that the endorsee or any other transferee takes in the shoes of the original party to the bill of lading. Thus, a bill of lading is not a true

---

[16]Id., p. 643.

[17]Bill of Lading Act 1855, s. 1.

[18][1888] 20 QBD 475.

[19]Id., at 479.

[20]A document of title refers to a document which represents goods and enables a holder of it to claim title to the goods to which it refers to.

[21][1883] 11 QBD 327.

[22]Aikens (2006), p. 14. The significance of true negotiable document of title is that its holder (transferee) receives the goods or money, as the case may be, free from the defects, if any, in the title of the transferor provided that he fits to the description of a *bonafide* transferee for value. See infra, Chap. 14.

negotiable instrument. Since the rights of its holder are subject to the title of the original party, the negotiation of the instrument of lading is practically the same as that of a non-negotiable, ordinary instrument.

The right of the holder of the bill of rights is recognized by the COGSA 1992. Section 2 of the Act provides that a lawful holder of a bill of lading by virtue of becoming the holder of the bill "have transferred to and vested in him all rights of suit under the contract of carriage as if he had been a party to the contract." Significantly, the new Act, unlike its predecessor—the Bills of Lading Act, 1855—enables the (lawful) holder of a bill of lading to sue the carrier in contract irrespective of the question irrespective of the fact whether property in the goods has passed or not. Under the Act of 1855, a consignee or endorsee of a bill of lading acquired the right to sue on the contract only where property has passed to the consignee or endorsee.

Electronic Bill of Lading

A modern development in the context relates to the growing interest in the use of an electronic bill of lading. Obviously, the expenses incurred by the shippers, consignees, and carriers due to the delays caused by the handling of paper documents will considerably be reduced if a paper-based bill of lading is replaced by the electronic bill of lading. Further, electronic documents are more secure than their paper-based counterparts. Significantly, recognizing the significance of the electronic bill of lading in the modern times, the Comité Maritime International (CMI) in 1990 adopted the CMI Uniform Rules for Electronic Bills of Lading (CMI Rules). However, these Rules which do not have the force of law on their own need to be incorporated into the contract between the parties.[23]

Mate Receipt

A mate's receipt is different from a bill of lading. It is a document which is used as a receipt in respect of goods, without being a document of title or evidence of the contract of carriage.[24] The mate's receipt is issued by the carrier after goods are loaded on board the ship. The holder of the mate's receipt can demand the issue of the bill of lading. Traditionally, it was issued by the ship's mate to acknowledge that the goods were received on the vessel.

Carrier

A carrier may be defined as any person including the ship-owner or charterer "who enters into contract of carriage with a shipper."[25] However, as will be seen below, the new trend is to draw a distinction between the actual or performing carrier, on the one hand, and the contractual carrier, on the other. Thus, apart from the ship-owner

---

[23] See Schnitzer (2006), p. 117; Beecher (2006), pp. 627–647; Carr (2014), pp. 192–93. The CMI Rules can be accessed from: http://www.comitemaritime.org/cmidocshules_idx.html.

[24] Aikens et al. (2006), p. 15.

[25] Hague-Visby Rules (cited below), Article 1(a). A similar definition is to be found in Hague Rules of 1924.

or charterer, other parties like a freight forwarder and a ship's manager may also be taken as included in the definition of a carrier.[26]

Common Law Duties of Carrier/Charterer in a Charterparty
Under common law, a carrier/ship-owner in addition to express terms of the contract has certain implied duties. These are: duty to provide a seaworthy ship; duty to proceed with due dispatch; duty to not deviate; and duty to use due care and skill.

Duty to Provide a Seaworthy Ship (Seaworthiness)
One of the most important duties of a carrier or ship-owner under the common law is to provide a seaworthy ship.[27] Under common law, a ship-owner's obligations in respect of seaworthiness are absolute. But as will be seen below, the modern, uniform law regimes adopt a different approach and a carrier is only liable if the loss is attributable to the failure to exercise due diligence in providing a seaworthy ship. Where the exercise of due diligence would not have prevented the ship being unseaworthy, the carrier is not liable.[28] This aspect is further discussed below, under the heading "seaworthiness."

Duty to Proceed with Due Dispatch
Under common law, the carrier is under the implied duty to ensure that the ship proceed on the voyage, load and discharge the goods in accordance with the contract of carriage.[29] The view has been expressed as the legal consequences of the breach of the duty and this will depend on the seriousness of the effects of the breach.[30] Further, duty to proceed with due dispatch is related to the duty not to deviate discussed below.

Duty Not to Deviate
The ship-owner/carrier, unless otherwise agreed upon, is under a duty to carry the goods to the destination without any deviation.[31] However, a departure from the deviation rule is possible in certain situations. These include: deviation for saving human life, for the safety of the adventure, and for effecting repairs.[32] However, under common law, deviation for the sole purpose of saving property is not allowed.[33] However, deviation, which is otherwise reasonable, does not become unreasonable if caused by the initial breach of the contract. In *Kish v Taylor*, Lord Atkinson held that "it is the presence of the peril and not its causes" which mattered in deciding whether deviation was justified or not.

The clauses excluding the liability of the ship-owner for deviation are valid but are to be construed strictly.[34] If a deviation clause is drawn too widely, it may be held

---

[26]Hamburg Rules (cited below), Article 1(2).

[27]Chorley and Giles (1970), p. 118.

[28]See the Yamatogawa [1990] Lloyd's Rep. 39.

[29]Chorley and Giles (1970), p. 191; Carr (2014), p. 203; Chuah (2009), pp. 223–24.

[30]See Chuah, ibid.

[31]See Chorley and Giles (1970), pp. 189–91; Carr (2014), pp. 203–06.

[32]In *Kish v Taylr, Sons & Co.* [1912] AC 604, deviation for effecting repairs was found excused.

[33]For further discussion, see Schnitzer (2006), pp. 125–26; Carr (2014), pp. 203–06.

[34]Chorley and Giles (1970), pp. 190–91.

void.[35] In *Stag Line v Foscolo, Mango & Co.*,[36] the bill of lading provided the master liberty "to call at any ports in any order, for bunkering or other purposes…." The ship in question sailed from Swansea but deviated to St. Ives to drop the engineers taken on board at Swansea to test certain newly installed machinery. But the Court found that the deviation was allowed under the Hague Rules. According to Lord Atkin, the use of the words, "other purposes" should be construed as business purposes which "would be contemplated by the parties as arising in carrying out the contemplated voyage of the ship."

Duty to Use Due Care

A carrier is under an implied duty to use due care in carrying the goods so that goods are not damaged for he is also a bailee of the goods. From the moment he receives the goods he is a "warehouseman" until he delivers them to the consignee.[37] Therefore, the ship-owner is under implied obligation to "use due care and skill in navigating the vessel and carrying the goods"[38] as well as the obligation "to take reasonable care of the goods" which is not limited to merely doing what is necessary to preserve them on board the ship "during the ordinary incidents of the voyage, but also in taking reasonable measures to check and arrest their loss, destruction or deterioration, by reason of accidents."[39]

Common Law Duties of Charterer

In relation to a ship-owner, a charterer is under the implied obligations to nominate a safe port; and to not ship dangerous goods without disclosure. A key issue in this context relates to the meaning of "safe port." A port will not be safe if the ship cannot reach it, and return from it safely.[40] Therefore, unpredictable weather and absence of weather reports[41] may render a port unsafe. It may further be noted that safety of the port in the context means prospective safety. In a leading case on the subject, *Kodros Shipping Corp. v Empresa Cubana de Fletes (The Evia) (No. 2)*,[42] the House of Lords took the view that a charterer's duty was not a continuing duty but relates to a prospectively safe port. According to the Court, if the characteristics of the port are such as make that port or place prospectively safe any "unexpected and abnormal event" making the port unsafe cannot make charterer liable for any resulting loss or damage.

As far as the meaning of dangerous goods is considered, it may be stated that dangerousness of the goods does not depend on their being listed as dangerous but on the surrounding circumstances.[43] In other words, what is important is not the

---

[35] Ibid.

[36] [1932] AC 328.

[37] Duncan (1917), p. 691.

[38] The Xantho, [1887] 12 AC 827.

[39] *Notara v Henderson* (1872) LR 7 QB 225.

[40] *Leeds Shipping v Societe Francaise Bunge (the Eastern City)* [1958] 2 Lloyd's Rep 127.

[41] *The Marinicki* [2003] 2 Lloyd's Rep. 655. For further discussion, see Carr (2014) pp. 156-61.

[42] [1982] 2 Lloyd's Rep 307.

[43] See Schnitzer (2006), p. 132; Chuah (2009), pp. 247–48.

"labeling in the abstract of goods as "dangerous" or "safe" but with the distribution of risk for the consequences of a dangerous situation arising during the voyage."[44]

Delivery Order

Since a bill of lading is used in respect of a fixed quantity of cargo, it cannot obviously be used where a whole consignment on board a ship is sold in parts to different buyers. In this case, it is the delivery order which is used in place of the bill of lading.[45] Delivery orders which contain instructions regarding the delivery of goods can be used to divide the whole consignment into different parts to deliver to individual buyers. But a delivery order is not a receipt for the goods nor is a document evidencing the contract of carriage.[46] S. 1(4) of COGSA 1992 defines a delivery order as "any document which is neither a bill of lading nor a sea waybill but contains an undertaking which—(a) is given under or for the purposes of a contract for the carriage by sea of the goods to which the document relates, or of goods which include those goods; and (b) is an undertaking by the carrier to a person identified in the document to deliver the goods to which the document relates to that person." Further, delivery orders may be either a ship's delivery order or a merchant's delivery order. The former are documents issued by or on behalf of a ship-owner/carrier while the goods are in its possession or control and which contain some form of undertaking that they will be delivered to the buyers.[47] But where documents contain instructions by the seller/shipper or consignee of the goods to his agent to deliver the goods to his buyer, the documents in question may be called merchant delivery orders.[48]

Freight

Freight is the reward or consideration payable by the shipper to the carrier for the carriage of the goods to the destination.[49] The freight may be due under the bill of lading or charterparty. Describing a freight in *Cho Yang Shipping Co. Ltd. V Coral (UK) Ltd*[50] it was stated that a shipper is personally liable to pay the reward, called freight, for the carriage of the goods. Under common law, freight is due to the carrier once the goods are delivered at the port of destination. However, the parties may agree that the freight will be payable according to the other terms.

Sea Waybill

Like a bill of lading, a sea waybill is a shipping document which is mainly used as evidencing the contract of carriage and a receipt of the goods. But unlike a bill of lading it is not a document of title and is non-transferable or "negotiable." The

---

[44] See *Athanasia Comninos* [1990] 1 Lloyd's Rep 277.

[45] Schnitzer (2006), p. 119; Aikens et al. (2006), p. 16.

[46] See Aikens et al., ibid.

[47] See *Waren Import Gesellschaft Krohn & Co. v Internationale Graanhandel Thegra NV* [1975] 1 Lloyd's Rep. 146.

[48] Aikens et al. (2006), p. 17.

[49] See Aikens et al. id, pp. 328–29; Schnitzer (2006), pp. 130–31.

[50] [1997] 2 Lloyd's Rep. 641.

advantage a waybill has over the bill of lading is that the former need not be transmitted to the consignee in order to enable him to receive the goods.[51] Thus, delivery of the goods is not delayed by a slow transmission of the transport documents to the consignee, as may happen in the case of a bill of lading. Where a shipper does not wish to sell the goods while in transit or he does not need a negotiable bill of lading, the sea waybill is considered sufficient.

Further, while Hamburg Rules apply to the sea waybill, Hague-Visby Rules do not.[52] Additionally, there are the CMI Uniform Rules for Sea Waybills adopted by the CMI in 1990, which may be voluntarily incorporated into the contract of carriage.[53]

Seaworthiness

Seaworthiness means the fitness of the ship for the purpose of carriage of goods.[54] As already stated, under a contract of shipment, the owner of the ship or the carrier undertakes a duty that the ship shall be fit for the purpose of receiving the goods as well as for the purpose of carrying the cargo safely to the destination.[55] Defining seaworthiness in the context of carriage of goods, Channel J in *McFadden v Blue Star Lane*[56] stated that to be a seaworthy a vessel "must have that degree of fitness which an ordinary, careful and prudent owner would require his vessel to have at the commencement of her voyage, having agreed to all the probable circumstances of it." In other words, where a ship has not the ability to encounter the ordinary perils of the sea it cannot be taken as a seaworthy ship. Seaworthiness, therefore, "expresses a relation between the state of the ship and the perils it has to meet in the situation it is in…"[57]

Further, seaworthiness not only refers to the physical fitness of the ship but also to a competent crew for undertaking the voyage.[58] If the master or the crew is inefficient, the ship will not be treated as seaworthy.

Under common law, a ship-owner's liability to provide seaworthy ship is absolute. But under the Hague and the Hague-Visby Rules the ship-owner is not liable for loss if it is proved that he exercised due diligence in providing seaworthy ship. In this background, in *Adamastos Shipping Company v. Anglo-Saxon Petroleum Company*,[59] a question arose were the owners liable under the charterparty for loss to the charterers which contained the paramount clause incorporating the 1924 Hague Rules. The owners in fact made every effort to engage a competent crew, but they failed because of the incompetent crew. The ship's engines frequently broke down resulting in the heavy loss to charterers. Although the Court of Appeal allowed the claim, but the

---

[51] Aikens et al. (2006), p. 15.

[52] Ibid, p. 16.

[53] CMI Uniform Rules can be found at http://www.comitemaritime.org/cmidocs/rulesidx.html.

[54] See Carr (2014), pp. 198–20; Chorley and Giles (1970), pp. 118–21.

[55] *Steel v State Line* [1877] 3 AC 72.

[56] [1905] 1 KB 697.

[57] *Gibson v Small* 10 All ER 499 [HL].

[58] *Rathbone v Maclver* [1903] 2 KB 378; *Standard Oil v Clan Line* [1924] AC 100.

[59] [1958] 2 W.L.R. 688; [1958] 1 All E.R. 725.

House of Lords reversed the decision concluding that since the ship-owners exercised due diligence they were not liable.[60]

Shipper

The term, "shipper" means a person who enters into a contract of carriage of goods by sea with a carrier/ship-owner. The term also includes a person by whom the goods are actually delivered to the carrier in relation to the contract of carriage by sea. Under common law, the shipper is under the duty to inform the carrier of the dangerous nature of the goods; not to engage in unlawful business; and the duty to pay freight.

10.2 International Liability Regime

10.2.1 Standardization of Sea-Carriers' Liability: Attempts to Balancing Ship-Owner and Cargo Interests

Under the (traditional) common law regime of liability, the ship-owner/carrier, because of its superior bargaining position, was able to insert a number of exemption clauses in the contracts of carriage enabling it to exclude its liability for loss or damage to the goods during their carriage. Thus, in order to strike a proper balance between the ship-owning interests and the cargo-interests, legislations were enacted in many countries including England, Australia, New Zealand, United States, and India.[61] This ultimately led to the several efforts to harmonize the domestic law regimes on the subject. The first such instrument was a convention, known as the Hague Rules of 1924. Although they were considerably successful, the need was soon felt to revise and update them. As a result, the Hague Rules were mainly amended by the Brussels Protocol of 1968 called, the Hague-Visby Rules. Further, in order to improve upon the scheme of liability of the Hague and the Hague-Visby Rules and to achieve increased uniformity, in 1978, the United Nations Convention on the Carriage of Goods by Sea 1978 (the Hamburg Rules) as prepared by the United Nations Commission on International Trade Law (UNCITRAL) was adopted. Finally, in December 2008 with a view to achieving more uniformity of the domestic legal regimes and to replace the existing regimes by a more balanced regime a new Convention, known as the Rotterdam Convention was adopted by the General Assembly.

---

[60] See Giles (1958), pp. 568–71.

[61] See Moens & Gillies (2006), pp. 165–67; O'Hare (1980), pp. 219–23; Aikens et al. (2006), pp. 11–12. Indian legislation on the subject (which corresponds to the COGSA 1992) is: Indian Carriage of Goods by Sea Act, 1925 enacted to give effect to the Hague and Hague-Visby Rules (the Hague Rules as amended by the Brussels Protocol of 1968 and 1979).

10.2.2 *"Hague Rules": Brief Overview*

The adoption in 1921 of the Hague Rules constitutes the first attempt to formulate a set of uniform rules governing the international carriage of goods by sea. The Rules impose upon the ship-owner/carrier a number of obligations in respect of carriage of goods (see Article III). Under the Rules, the carrier is liable for loss and damage to the goods during the period of carriage subject to certain exemptions contained therein (see Article IV). The Rules also contain provisions concerning a carrier's right to its liability and limit of the liability of the carrier. Further, the Hague Rules apply only to "contract of carriage covered by a bill of lading or any similar document of title, in so far as such document relates to the carriage of goods by sea" (Article I(b)).

Although the Hague Rules were generally considered successful but nearly after 40 years the need was felt to revise them. This ultimately led to the adoption in 1968 of the Hague-Visby Rules.[62]

10.2.3 *"Hague-Visby Rules"*

10.2.3.1 Scope of Application

Hague-Visby Rules, like Hague Rules, apply to a contract of carriage which is covered or evidenced by a bill of lading or similar documents of title.[63] Thus, they do not apply to charterparties. However, these Rules can be contractually incorporated into a charterparty with clauses paramount.[64]

According to Article 10, the Hague-Visby Rules apply to the carriage of goods between ports which are in two different countries if: (a) the bill of lading is issued in a contracting state, or (b) the carriage is from a port in a contracting state, or (c) the contract contained in or evidenced by the bill of lading provides that these Rules are to govern the contract. It may also be noted that for the purpose of applicability of the Rules, the nationality of the ship, the carrier, the shipper, the consignee, or any other interested person is not important.

10.2.3.2 Obligations of the Carrier

Obligations of a carrier are contained in Article III. According to Para 1, a carrier is under duty "before and at the beginning of the voyage" to exercise due diligence in order to make the ship seaworthy; properly man, equip, and supply the ship; and make the holds, refrigerating and cool chambers, and all other parts of the ship in which the goods are carried fit and safe for their reception, carriage, and preservation.

---

[62] See Aikens et al., id., p. 214.

[63] See *Pyrene v Scindia* [1954] 2 QB.

[64] See Aikens et al., p. 220; Carr (2014), p. 253.

The standard of due diligence obligation in respect of making a ship seaworthy is not absolute one. Further, the phrase "before and at the beginning of the voyage" means the period from at least the beginning of the loading until the ship started on her voyage.[65] Thus, where the carrier has exercised due diligence before the beginning of the voyage, the carrier will not be in breach of its due diligence obligation in respect of providing a seaworthy ship.[66]

Further, Para 2 provides that the carrier shall properly and carefully load, handle, stow, carry, keep, care for, and discharge the goods carried.

And thirdly, after receiving the goods into his charge "the carrier or the master or agent of the carrier shall, on demand of the shipper, issue to the shipper a bill of lading showing among other things":

(a) The leading marks necessary for identification of the goods as the same are furnished in writing by the shipper before the loading of such goods starts, provided such marks are stamped or otherwise shown clearly upon the goods if uncovered, or on the cases or coverings in which such goods are contained, in such a manner as should ordinarily remain legible until the end of the voyage.
(b) Either the number of packages or pieces, or the quantity, or weight, as the case may be, as furnished in writing by the shipper.
(c) The apparent order and condition of the goods.[67]

10.2.3.3 Immunities of the Carrier

In the first place, the carrier will not be liable for loss or damage resulting from the un seaworthiness of the ship so long as he has exercised due diligence in making the ship seaworthy. Article IV(1) provides:

> Neither the carrier nor the ship shall be liable for loss or damage arising or resulting from unseaworthiness unless caused by want of due diligence on the part of the carrier to make the ship seaworthy, and to secure that the ship is properly manned, equipped and supplied, and to make the holds, refrigerating and cool chambers and all other parts of the ship in which goods are carried fit and safe for their reception, carriage and preservation….

However, the burden of proving the exercise of due diligence in respect of claiming immunity from liability for loss or damage shall be on the carrier or other person claiming exemption under this article.

In addition, Para (2) contains a long list of exceptions from the liability for loss or damage. These are: "(a) Act, neglect, or default of the master, mariner, pilot, or the servants of the carrier in the navigation or in the management of the ship; (b) Fire, unless caused by the actual fault or privity of the carrier (c) Perils, dangers and accidents of the sea or other navigable waters; (d) Act of God; (e) Act of war; (f)

---

[65] *Maxine Footwear Co. Ltd. v Canadian Government Marine Ltd* [1959] AC 589.

[66] *Marc Rich and Co AG and Others v Bishop Rock Marine Co. Ltd.* (*The Nicholas H*) [1995] 3 All ER 307.

[67] Hague-Visby Rules, Article III(3). According to Article III(4), "such a bill of lading shall be prima facie evidence of the receipt by the carrier of the goods as therein described in accordance with para 3(a), (b) and (c)."

Act of public enemies; (g) Arrest or restraint of princes, rulers or people, or seizure under legal process; (h) Quarantine restrictions; (i) Act or omission of the shipper or owner of the goods, his agent or representative; (j) Strikes or lockouts or stoppage or restraint of labour from whatever cause, whether partial or general; (k) riots and civil commotions; (l) Saving or attempting to save life or property at sea; (m) Wastage in bulk of weight or any other loss or damage arising from inherent defect, quality or vice of the goods; (n) insufficiency of packing; (o) Insufficiency or inadequacy of marks; (p) Latent defects not discoverable by due diligence; (q) Any other cause arising without the actual fault or privity of the carrier, or without the fault or neglect of the agents or servants of the carrier…" Further, Para 4 clarifies that the carrier shall not be liable for any loss or damage resulting from any deviation in saving or attempting to save life or property at sea or any reasonable deviation.

10.2.3.4 Limits of Liability

Notably, the Hague Rules provide for financial limits of the carrier's liability. According to Article IV(5)(a), unless the value of the goods has been declared by the shipper before shipment and inserted in the bill of lading,

> neither the carrier nor the ship shall in any event be or become liable for any loss or damage to or in connection with the goods in an amount exceeding the equivalent of 666.67 units of account per package or unit or units of account per kilo of gross weight of the goods lost or damaged, whichever is the higher.

In addition, there is also a time limit on the liability of a carrier. According to Article III(6), the action against the carrier must be brought within one year from the date of delivery or the date when the goods should have been delivered. However, an action for indemnity against a third person may be brought even after the expiration of the year… if brought within the time allowed by the law of the law of Court seized of the case" (Para 6 *bis*).

10.2.3.5 Shipper's Duties and Immunities

The shipper is responsible for the accuracy of the marks, number, quantity, and weight provided by him to the carrier (Article III(5)). It then follows that where the carrier incurs loss or damage as a result of the inaccurate particulars about the goods provided by the shipper, he must indemnify the carrier for such loss.[68]

According to Article IV(6), where dangerous goods are shipped without the consent of the carrier, the master or the agent of the carrier, that is the shipper, will be liable for damage arising directly or indirectly as a result of such shipment.

[68] Carr (2014), p. 247.

10.2.4 UN Convention on the Carriage of Goods by Sea (the "Hamburg Rules")

10.2.4.1 Scope of Application

One of the most important features of the Hamburg Rules is that they, in contrast to the Hague-Visby Rules, cover the contract of carriage as such, that is to say, the charterparty as well as the contracts of carriage covered by the bill of lading.[69] The implication of this is that a shipper does not have to request a bill of lading in order to invoke the liability provisions of the Convention for the every contract of carriage attracts the mandatory provisions of the Convention into operation.[70]

Further, the criteria of internationality adopted by the Hamburg Rules are similar to those of the Hague-Visby Rules. Article 2(1) provides that the Convention shall apply to all contracts of carriage by sea between two different states, if: either the port of loading or the port of discharge as provided for in the contract of carriage by sea is located in a contracting state, or

one of the optional ports of discharge provided for in the contract of carriage by sea is the actual port of discharge and such port is located in a contracting state, or

the bill of lading or other document evidencing the contract of carriage is issued in a contracting state, or

the bill of lading or other document evidencing the contract of carriage provides that the "Convention or the legislation of any State giving effect to them are to govern the contract."

10.2.4.2 Actual and Contractual Carrier

One of the most striking features of the Hamburg Convention is that it draws a distinction between (a) the contractual carrier and the actual or performing carrier. The former denotes merely the person with whom the contract of carriage is entered into and who may or may not be the actual carrier. Actual carrier, on the other hand, is the person who actually performs the contract of carriage.[71] Hence, the phrase: "performing carrier." Article 1(2) provides:

> "Actual carrier" means any person to whom the performance of the carriage of the goods, or of part of the carriage, has been entrusted by the carrier, and includes any other person to whom such performance has been entrusted.

---

[69] Ramberg (1979), p. 391.

[70] Ibid.

[71] Id., p. 392.

10.2.4.3 Scheme of Liability

Notably, under the Hamburg Rules, the scheme of carrier's liability is strikingly different from the Hague-Visby Rules. Unlike the latter, Hamburg Rules adopt the scheme of liability based on presumed fault.[72] Article 5 which deals with the basis of liability provides that the carrier is liable for loss resulting from loss of or damage to the goods, as well as from delay in delivery… unless the carrier proves that he, his servants or agents took all measures that could reasonably be required to avoid the occurrence and its consequences.

Defences to liability are available to a carrier but in comparison to the Hague-Visby Rules these are limited in number.[73]

Like the Hague-Visby Rules, Hamburg Rules also place limit on the liability of the carrier. Article 6(1) provides:

(a) The liability of the carrier for loss resulting from loss of or damage to goods according to the provisions of Article 5 is limited to an amount equivalent to 835 units of account per package or other shipping unit or 2.5 units of account per kilogram of gross weight of the goods lost or damaged, whichever is the higher.
(b) The liability of the carrier for delay in delivery … is limited to an amount equivalent to two and a half times the freight payable for the goods delayed, but not exceeding the total freight payable under the contract of carriage of goods by sea.

Further, under the Hamburg Rules the limitation period for bringing an action against the carrier is two years (Article20(1)). "The limitation period commences on the day on which the carrier has delivered the goods or part thereof or, in cases where no goods have been delivered, on the last day on which the goods should have been delivered" (Article 20(2)).

10.2.5 2008 UN Convention on Contracts for the International Carriage of Goods Wholly or Partly by Sea (the "Rotterdam Rules")

10.2.5.1 General

The Rotterdam Convention was adopted by the General Assembly in December 2008 with a view to achieving more uniformity of the domestic laws on the subject.[74] The new Convention is intended to replace the earlier regimes established by the Hague Visby Rules of 1968, and the Hamburg Rules of 1978 by a new set of uniform rules

---

[72]See Carr (2014), pp.

[73]For defences, see Articles 5(5), (6) and (7).

[74]The text is available at: http://www.uncitral.org.

for carriage of goods by sea. As the General Assembly Resolution adopting the text of the Convention notes that a completely new and more balanced regime was needed because the existing regime on the international carriage of goods by sea "lacks uniformity and fails to adequately take into account modern transport practices, including containerization, door-to-door transport contracts and the use of electronic transport documents."[75] Some of the most striking features of the Convention relate to the provisions on transports ancillary to the maritime leg, the rules on the liability of the performing carrier and the limitation levels of the Hague-Visby Rules.[76]

10.2.5.2 Scope of Application

According to Article 5, the Convention applies to a contract of carriage in which the place of receipt/the port of loading and the place of delivery/the port of discharge are situated in different states, provided that any one of the following places is located in a contracting state: the place of receipt/the port of loading and the place of delivery/the port of discharge. Significantly, for the purpose of the applicability of Rotterdam Convention, the nationality of the vessel, the carrier, the performing parties, the shipper, the consignee, or any other interested parties is not important (Article 5(2)).

With respect to the scope of application, a further point to note is that the Convention applies also to transports ancillary to the maritime leg. According to Article 26, when loss of or damage to goods, or a delay in their delivery occurs during the carrier's period of responsibility but solely before their loading onto the ship or solely after their discharge from the ship, the provisions of this Convention do not prevail over those provisions of another international instrument that, at the time of such loss, damage or event or circumstance causing delay.

10.2.5.3 Identifying a Carrier

While the distinction between a carrier and actual carrier drawn in the previous Hamburg Rules is retained by the new Convention, it adopts a key concept of a "performing party." A performing party, as distinguished from a carrier, is defined as any person "other than the carrier that performs or undertakes to perform any of the carrier's obligations under a contract of carriage with respect to the receipt, loading, handling, stowage, carriage, keeping, care, unloading or delivery of the goods, to the extent that such person acts, either directly or indirectly, at the carrier's request or under the carrier's supervision or control" (Article 1(2)(6)). The purpose is to bring within the liability scheme of the Convention a broad range of actors who performs a range of services in connection with the carriage of goods.[77] The Convention further

[75] GA Res., A/Res/63/122 of 2 February 2009.

[76] See Schelin (2009), pp. 321–27.

[77] See Rotterdam Convention, Articles 18 and 19.

provides that a performing party will be treated as "maritime performing party" to the extent it undertakes to perform "any of the carrier's obligations during the period between the arrival of the goods at the port of loading of a ship and their departure from the port of discharge of a ship." For example, "an inland carrier is a maritime performing party only if it performs or undertakes to perform its services exclusively within a port area" (Article 1(2)(7)).

10.2.5.4 Obligations of Carrier

According to Article 11, the carrier shall carry the goods to the place of destination and deliver them to the consignee. So far as the period of responsibility of the carrier is concerned, it "begins when the carrier or a performing party receives the goods for carriage and ends when the goods are delivered" (Article 12). Further obligations of the carrier are provided for in Articles 13 and 14.

Article 13

1. The carrier shall during the period of its responsibility as defined in article 12, and subject to article 26, properly and carefully receive, load, handle, stow, carry, keep, care for, unload and deliver the goods.

Article 14

The carrier is bound before, at the beginning of, and during the voyage by sea to exercise due diligence to:

(a) Make and keep the ship seaworthy;

(b) Properly crew, equip and supply the ship and keep the ship so crewed, equipped and supplied throughout the voyage; and

(c) Make and keep the holds and all other parts of the ship in which the goods are carried, and any containers supplied by the carrier in or upon which the goods are carried, fit and safe for their reception, carriage and preservation.

10.2.5.5 Scheme of Liability and Defences

Regarding the nature of liability of a carrier, Article 17 provides that the carrier is liable for loss of or damage to the goods, as well as for delay in delivery, if it is proved that "the loss, damage, or delay, or the event or circumstance that caused or contributed to it took place during the period of the carrier's responsibility" (Para 1). However, the carrier will not be liable if it is proved that the cause of the loss, damage, or delay is not attributable to its fault or to the fault of any person referred to in Article 18. Further, the carrier is also relieved of its liability if, alternatively to proving the absence of fault as, it proves that the loss or delay was caused by one or more of the circumstances mentioned in Para (3) of Article 17. Para 3 mentions a long list of such events. These are act of God; perils, dangers, and accidents of the sea or other navigable waters; war, hostilities, armed conflict, piracy, terrorism, riots, and civil commotions; quarantine restrictions; interference by or impediments created by governments, public authorities, rulers, or people including detention, arrest, or seizure not attributable to the carrier; strikes, lockouts, stoppages, or restraints of labor; fire on the ship; latent defects not discoverable by due diligence; act or omission of the shipper, the documentary shipper, the controlling party, or any other person for whose acts the shipper or the documentary shipper is liable; loading, handling, stowing, or unloading of the goods performed unless the carrier or a performing party performs such activity on behalf of the shipper, the documentary shipper or the consignee; wastage in bulk or weight or any other loss or damage arising from inherent defect, quality, or vice of the goods; insufficiency or defective condition of packing or marking not performed by or on behalf of the carrier; saving or attempting to save life at sea; reasonable measures to save or attempt to save property at sea; reasonable measures to avoid or attempt to avoid damage to the environment; or acts of the carrier in pursuance of the powers conferred by Articles 15 and 16.[78]

10.2.5.6 Limit of Liability

The new Convention fixes a higher limit of liability than that fixed in the previous regimes. According to Article 59, "the carrier's liability is limited to 875 units of account per package or other shipping unit, or 3 units of account per kilogram of the gross weight of the goods that are the subject of the claim or dispute, whichever amount is the higher, except when the value of the goods has been declared by the shipper and included in the contract particulars, or when a higher amount than the amount of limitation of liability set out in this article has been agreed upon between the carrier and the shipper."[79]

The time limit for bringing an action against the carrier is, like the Hamburg Rules is two years (Article 62(1)).

References

Aikens, R., Lord, R., & Bools, M. (2006). *Bills of lading*. London: Informa Law.

Beecher, (2006). Can the electronic bill of lading go paperless? *International Lawyer, 40*(3), 627–647.

Carr, I. (2014). *International trade law*. London: Routledge.

Chorley & Giles. (1970). *Shipping law*. London: Pitman Publishing Ltd.

Chuah. (2009). *International trade law: Cross-border commercial transactions*. London: Sweet & Maxwell.

Duncan, C. S. (1917). The uniform bill of lading. *Journal of Political Economy, 25*(7), 67–97.

Giles, O. C. (1958). Bill of lading clause adapting to Charterparty. *Modern Law Review, 21*, 568–571.

[78] Articles 15 and 16 deal with the powers of a carrier to decline the goods that may become a danger and to sacrifice of the goods for common safety during the voyage by sea, respectively.

[79] For an account of the controversy surrounding the issue of the limit of liability, see Schelin (2009), p. 326.

Moens & Gillies. (2006). *International trade & business: Law, policy and ethics*. Oxon: Routledge, Cavendish.
O'Hare, C. W. (1980). Cargo dispute resolution and the Hamburg Rules. *International and Comparative Law Quarterly, 29*(2/3), 219–237.
Ramberg, J. (1979). The vanishing bill of lading & the "Hamburg Rules Carrier". *American Journal of Comparative Law, 27*(2/3), 391–406.
Schelin, J. (2009). The UNCITRAL convention on carriage of goods by sea: Harmonization or de-harmonization? *Texas International Law Journal, 44*, 321–327.
Schnitzer, S. (2006). *Understanding international trade law*. UK: Law Matters Publishing.

Online Resources

Comité Maritime International (CMI): http://www.comitemaritime.org/cmidocshules_idx.html.
United Nations Commission on International Trade Law (UNCITRAL).

Chapter 11
Carriage of Goods by Air

11.1 Key Terms

Air Waybill

Air waybill, which may be viewed as an air transport document, is of key significance in the context. In many respects, it is similar to a bill of lading discussed in the previous Chapter. However, the two are different in the sense that an air waybill does not serve the purpose of a document of title. It describes the goods shipped and constitutes prima face evidence of the carrier's receipt of those goods and the contract of carriage. But an air waybill is not a document of title, although it may be "negotiable" (or transferable).[1] It may be noted that all systems—whether the old Warsaw-Hague regime (cited below) or the new Montreal Convention—require the issue of an air waybill. Article 4 of Convention for the Unification of Certain Rules for International Carriage by Air (the Montreal Convention), adopted on May 28, 1999, specifically states that in respect of the carriage of cargo, an air waybill shall be delivered (Para1). However, the non-delivery of an air waybill or non-conformity with the Convention does not affect the validity of a contract of air carriage (Article 9).

Cargo Receipt

The Montreal Convention also provides for "the cargo receipt" which is an alternative to the air waybill. Article 4(2) provides that "any other means which preserves a record of the carriage to be performed may be substituted for the delivery of an air waybill." If such other means are used, the carrier shall, if so requested by the consignor, deliver to the consignor a cargo receipt identifying the cargo and consignment and "access to the information contained in the record preserved by such other means" (Article 4(2)). It may also be noted that the cargo receipt like an air waybill is *prima facie* evidence of the conclusion of the contract of carriage or the facts stated therein. Article 11 provides:

[1] Warsaw Convention as amended by the Hague protocol of 1955, Article 15(3). However, an air way bill is not negotiable in true sense of the term.

A. Srivastava, *Modern Law of International Trade*, International Law and the Global South, https://doi.org/10.1007/978-981-15-5475-9_11

1. The air waybill or the cargo receipt is *prima facie* evidence of the conclusion of the contract, of the acceptance of the cargo and of the conditions of carriage mentioned therein.
2. Any statements in the air waybill or the cargo receipt relating to the weight, dimensions and packing of the cargo, as well as those relating to the number of packages, are *prima facie* evidence of the facts stated; those relating to the quantity, volume and condition of the cargo do not constitute evidence against the carrier except so far as they both have been, and are stated in the air waybill or the cargo receipt to have been, checked by it in the presence of the consignor, or relate to the apparent condition of the cargo.

As regards the contents of air waybill or cargo receipt Article 5 provides that they shall include "(a) an indication of the places of departure and destination; and (b) if the places of departure and destination are within the territory of a single State Party, one or more agreed stopping places being within the territory of another State, an indication of at least one such stopping place; and (c) an indication of the weight of the consignment."

11.2 International Liability Regime[2]

11.2.1 Warsaw System and Background

The Warsaw System comprises the 1929 International Convention for the Unification of Certain Rules Relating to International Carriage by Air (the Warsaw convention) (which is the most important one in the System) and other related agreements containing a set of comprehensive and uniform rules governing international carriage by air of goods, baggage, and passengers. The other agreements adopted after the Warsaw Convention which have substantially amended and updated the legal regime of the Warsaw Convention from time to time include: the Hague Protocol of 1955 amending the Warsaw Convention (Hague Protocol),[3] 1961 Convention Supplementary to Warsaw convention (Guadalajara Convention), the Guatemala Protocol 1971, and four Protocols of 1975, namely Montreal Additional Protocol No 1 (MAP1), Montreal Additional Protocol No 2 (MAP2), Montreal Additional Protocol No 3 (MAP3), and Montreal Additional Protocol No 4 (MAP4). However, of these subsequent conventions, not all are relevant from the point of view of carriage of goods: the 1971 Guatemala City Protocol (officially known as the Warsaw Convention as amended at The Hague, 1955, and at Guatemala City, 1971) does not relate to carriage

[2]See D'Arcy et al. (2000), pp. 324–36; Chuah (2009), pp. 388–401; Carr (2014), pp. 309–35; Moens and Gillies (2006), pp. 229–43; Cheng (2004), pp. 833–59; Guest (2006).

[3]Protocol to Amend the Convention for the Unification of certain Rules relating to International Carriage by Air, in force 1963.

of goods at all and is outside the scope of our study.[4] Similarly, MAP1, MAP2, and MAP 3 make changes in respect of monetary unit for calculating damages. Now, monetary unit is fixed in terms of the Special Drawing Rights (SDR) as defined by the international monetary Fund (IMF).[5] Thus the only international agreements adopted after Warsaw convention which are important for our purpose are: the Hague Protocol of 1955, Guadalajara Convention and MAP4. Since these agreements make substantial modifications to the regime originally established by the Warsaw Convention, the discussion in this chapter will primarily refer to amended version of the legal regime and reference to the un-amended version will be made only when it is relevant to do so.

A further point to note is that although the Warsaw Convention is one of most ratified conventions, this is not the case with the subsequent conventions and not all states who ratified the Warsaw Convention have joined the subsequent conventions. The result is that the Warsaw System of treaties has become a "complex" web of legal rules applying differently to different states.[6]

Until 1999, the Warsaw System served as the only system of uniform rules governing international carriage by air of goods, baggage, and passengers at global level.[7] However, with the adoption of the Montreal Convention in 1999 (entry into force on June 28, 2004) which is intended to replace the conventions included in the Warsaw System and to "modernize and consolidate" the laws governing international carriage a new system of uniform rules was born.[8]

11.2.2 Warsaw System as Amended

As already indicated, the Warsaw System as amended applies to all international carriage by aircraft of persons, baggage, or goods for reward.[9] It sets out uniform rules on the carrier's liability including the issues related to jurisdictions. It thus establishes across the contracting states "a mandatory, exclusive, and uniform code on international carriage by air."[10]

---

[4] The Guatemala City Convention was later metamorphosed into the Montreal Additional Protocol No 3 (MAP3). Not yet in force.

[5] See Montreal Convention, Article 23.

[6] See Carr (2014), p. 310.

[7] Warsaw Convention as amended, Article 1(1).

[8] Cheng (2004), p. 833.

[9] Warsaw Convention as amended, Article 1(1).

[10] Cheng (2004), p. 834.

11.2.2.1 Scope of Application

Article 1(2) of the amended version defines an "international carriage" as a carriage in which, according to the agreement between the parties, "the place of departure and the place of destination, whether or not there be a break in the carriage or a transshipment, are situated either within the territories of two High Contracting Parties or within the territory of a single High Contracting Party if there is an agreed stopping place within the territory of another state, even if that state is not a High Contracting Party."

But the "[c]arriage between two points without an agreed stopping place within the territory of another state is not international carriage for the purposes of the convention."

Thus, under the Warsaw-Hague regime, a carriage is international if the places of departure and destination are in two, separate contracting states. A carriage from one place to another in the same contracting state or from a contracting state to a non-contracting state will not attract the provisions of the Warsaw Convention as amended by the Hague Protocol. However, a carriage will be international if the place of departure and destination are in the territory of the same contracting state, provided that "there is an agreed stopping place within the territory of another state." [11]

It may also be noted that a carriage will remain an international carriage even if it is broken into stages provided that the parties to the contract of carriage contemplate the carriage in question to be a single operation.[12]

11.2.2.2 Liability of the Carrier: Strict Liability Approach

Notably, the Warsaw-Hague regime adopts the strict liability approach in fixing the liability of the carrier. Article 18 provides that a carrier is *prima facie* liable for loss or damage to any registered baggage or cargo if this took place during the "carriage by air." Here, the term, "carriage by air" indicates the period during which the cargo was in charge of the carrier and is of key significance in determining the liability of the carrier. Para 2 of Article 18 provides that carriage by air comprises "the period during which the baggage or the cargo is in the charge of the carrier, whether in an aerodrome or on board an aircraft, or, in the case of a landing outside an aerodrome, in any place whatsoever."[13]

---

[11] Moens and Gillies (2006), p. 231; Carr (2014), pp. 315–16.

[12] Under the original version of the law as established by the Warsaw Convention, we find a similar definition of carriage. According to the Convention, a carriage was international if that begins and ends in territories of two states parties or in which the points of departure and destination are situated in the territory of one signatory and a stop is scheduled in another state, whether or not the latter is also a party to the Convention. Warsaw Convention, 1(2).

[13] See also *Swiss Bank Corp v Brink's Mat* [1986] 2 Lloyd's Rep 79.

Further, according to Article 19, the carrier is also presumptively liable for loss to the shipper resulting from delay in the carriage of goods. It is his duty to show that he or his agents took all necessary measures to avoid the damage or that it was impossible for him to take such measures.

11.2.2.3 Limits on Liability

Like the liability regime of other civil liability conventions, the Warsaw-Hague rules place upper limit on the liability of a carrier. According to Article 22 of the Warsaw Convention as amended, the limit of liability for loss or damage to the shipper is 17 SDRs per Kilogram (Para 2). In the cases of loss or damage of part of the cargo, the amount of liability is determined on the basis of the weight of the part lost or damaged. *Data Card Corp v Air Express International*[14] is a leading case on the point. In that case, it was held that in the case of the loss of the part of cargo, the amount of liability should be fixed by weight of the part of cargo lost.

11.2.2.4 Rights and Obligations of Consignor

First, the consignor is responsible for the correctness of the particulars relating to the cargo inserted by it or on its behalf in the air waybill. It shall be the duty of the consignor "to indemnify the carrier against all damage suffered by it, or by any other person to whom the carrier is liable, by reason of the irregularity, incorrectness or incompleteness of the particulars and statements furnished by the consignor or on its behalf" (Article 10(1)). Secondly, the consignor must also "furnish such information and such documents as are necessary to meet the formalities of customs, police and any other public authorities before the cargo can be delivered to the consignee." And if the carrier suffers any damage occasioned by the absence, insufficiency or irregularity of any such information or documents, unless the damage is due to the fault of the carrier, its servants or agents the consignor shall be liable (Article 16(1)).

As far as the rights of the consignor are concerned, Article 12(1) provides that the consignor has the right to dispose of the cargo by:

(a) withdrawing it at the airport of departure or of destination; or
(b) stopping it in the course of the journey; or
(c) calling for it to be delivered at the place of destination or in the course of the journey to a person other than the consignee originally designated; or
(d) requiring it to be returned to the airport of departure.

However, the consignor must not exercise the right of disposition in such a way as to prejudice the carrier or other consignors and must reimburse any expenses occasioned by the exercise of this right.

---

[14][1984] 1 WLR 198.

11.2.2.5 Rights and Duties of the Consignee

Article 13 provides as follows:

1. Except when the consignor has exercised its right under Article 12, the consignee is entitled, on arrival of the cargo at the place of destination, to require the carrier to deliver the cargo to it, on payment of the charges due and on complying with the conditions of carriage.
2. Unless it is otherwise agreed, it is the duty of the carrier to give notice to the consignee as soon as the cargo arrives.
3. If the carrier admits the loss of the cargo, or if the cargo has not arrived at the expiration of seven days after the date on which it ought to have arrived, the consignee is entitled to enforce against the carrier the rights which flow from the contract of carriage.

11.2.3 Montreal Convention

As already stated, the Montreal Convention seeks to modernize and consolidate the Warsaw Convention and its associated treaties. Since the Warsaw System combines a number of treaties it proved to be a highly complex system and the need was felt for a quite long time to revise and update the regime of liability for carriage by air of goods, baggage, and passengers. The entry into force in 2003 of the Montreal Convention is hailed as opening "a new era in the law on international carriage by air."[15] However, the new Convention is modeled on its precursor—the Warsaw System—and "largely takes over its basic philosophy, structure, and features."[16] Simply put, it retains the basic structure of its percurser and does not make any fundamental change in the system of liability established by the Warsaw-Hague regime of liability.[17]

Some of the most important changes introduced by the Montreal Convention are as follows: First, it inserts a provision recognizing the modern means of preserving a record of the carriage to replace a traditional air waybill (see above, Sect. 11.1). Secondly, it inserts a provision regarding the periodic review of the limit of liability. [18]

11.2.3.1 Scope of Application

As already indicated, the provision on scope of application under the new convention is not different from the one under the amended version of the Warsaw Convention (see Article 1).

[15]Cheng (2004), p. 844.

[16]Cheng (2004), p. 845.

[17]See Carr (2014), pp. 331–32.

[18]See Article 24.

11.2.3.2 Liability for Damage to Goods

Of particular relevance is the provision contained in Article 18 dealing with the issue of liability of the carrier in respect of loss or damage to goods or delay in carriage. Article 18 in respect of liability for damage provides:

1. The carrier is liable for damage sustained in the event of the destruction or loss of, or damage to, cargo upon condition only that the event which caused the damage so sustained took place during the carriage by air.
2. However, the carrier is not liable if and to the extent it proves that the destruction, or loss of, or damage to, the cargo resulted from one or more of the following:
   (a) inherent defect, quality or vice of that cargo;
   (b) defective packing of that cargo performed by a person other than the carrier or its servants or agents;
   (c) an act of war or an armed conflict;
   (d) an act of public authority carried out in connection with the entry, exit or transit of the cargo.
3. The carriage by air within the meaning of paragraph 1 of this Article comprises the period during which the cargo is in the charge of the carrier.

A carrier is also liable for damage caused by delay in the carriage of goods (Article 19). However, the carrier shall not be liable for damage caused by delay if it is proved that "it and its servants and agents took all measures that could reasonably be required to avoid the damage or that it was impossible for it or them to take such measures."

In addition to the defences specified above, the defence of contributory negligence is also available to a carrier. Article 20 provides:

If the carrier proves that the damage was caused or contributed to by the negligence or other wrongful act or omission of the person claiming compensation, or the person from whom he or she derives his or her rights, the carrier shall be wholly or partly exonerated from its liability to the claimant to the extent that such negligence or wrongful act or omission caused or contributed to the damage.

Further, following MP4, the basis of the carrier's liability for damage to cargo, except damage resulting from delay (Article 19), has been changed from presumed fault-based liability to absolute liability, apart from the exceptions specified in Article 18(2), such as inherent defect or war, and the defence of contributory negligence (Article 20).[19]

11.2.3.3 Limit of Liability

The Montreal Convention, like Warsaw Convention, puts financial limit on the liability of the carrier. Article 22(3) provides:

[19] See Cheng, p. 848.

In the carriage of cargo, the liability of the carrier in the case of destruction, loss, damage or delay is limited to a sum of 17 Special Drawing Rights per kilogramme, unless the consignor has made, at the time when the package was handed over to the carrier, a special declaration of interest in delivery at destination and has paid a supplementary sum if the case so requires. In that case the carrier will be liable to pay a sum not exceeding the declared sum, unless it proves that the sum is greater than the consignor's actual interest in delivery at destination.

References

Carr, Indira. (2014). *International trade law*. London: Routledge.

Cheng. (2004). A new era in the law of international carriage by air: From Warsaw (1929) to Montreal (1999). *International Comparative Law Quarterly, 53*(4), 833–59.

Chuah, J. C. T. (2009). *Law of international trade: Cross-border commercial trade transactions* (p. 2011). London: Sweet & Maxwell, South Asian Edition.

D'Arcy, L., Murray, C., & Cleave, B. (Eds.). (2000). *Schmitthoff's export trade: The law and practice of international trade*. London: Stevens.

Guest, A. G. (Ed.). (2006). *Benjamin*'s *sale of goods*. London: Sweet & Maxwell.

Moens & Gillies. (2006). *International trade and business: Law, policy and ethics*. Routledge Cavendish: New York.

Chapter 12
Carriage of Goods by Rail and Road

12.1 Key Terms

Carriage by Rail
According to Article 6(1) of the CIM Rules, a contract of carriage by rail is a contract in which the carrier undertakes the duty to carry the goods for reward to the place of destination and to deliver them to the consignee. Further, a contract thus concluded must be evidenced by the consignment note (Article 6(2)).

Consignment Note
In a carriage by rail and road, a consignment note plays a very significant role. It performs the functions of a transport document but it is not equivalent to a bill of lading. It only serves as the prima facie evidence of the (a) conclusion of contract of carriage; (b) the contents of such contract; and (c) the taking over of the goods by the carrier (CIM Rules, Article 12(1); CMR, Article 4). According to CIM Rules, Article 12(2), where the loading is carried out by the carrier, statements regarding the condition of the goods and packaging, number of packages, weight, marks and numbers are regarded as prima facie evidence. On the other hand, where loading is carried out by the consigner himself, statements regarding condition, packaging, marks, and so on will be regarded as prima facie evidence only if they have been examined by the carrier and recorded as such on the consignment note (CIM Rules, Article 12(3)).

Further, a consignment note in a carriage by rail and road must contain the particulars listed in Article 7 (CIM Rules) and Article 6 (CMR).

Carriage by Road
In a contract for the carriage of goods by road, the goods are transported in vehicles for reward. Like carriage of goods by rail, in such a carriage consignment note serves the purpose of a transport document. The consignment note is the prima facie evidence of the contract and certain other matters. Further, international carriage of goods

A. Srivastava, *Modern Law of International Trade*, International Law and the Global South, https://doi.org/10.1007/978-981-15-5475-9_12

by road is governed by the 1956 Convention for the Contract for the International Carriage of Goods by Road (CMR).[1]

Multimodal Transport

In a multimodal or combined transport, the contract of carriage is entered into between the operator of the transport in question and the shipper for carrying the goods to their destination by using two or more modes of transport, such as the rail and road. The transport operator may be a freight forwarder, container operator, or multimodal transport operator.[2] The United Nations Convention on International Multimodal Transport of Goods (MT Convention)[3] defines a multimodal transport as

> …the carriage of goods by at least two different modes of transport on the basis of a multimodal transport contract from a place in one country at which the goods are taken in charge by the multi modal transport operator to a place designated for delivery situated in a different country. The operations of pick-up and delivery of goods carried out in the performance of a unimodal transport contract, as defined in such contract, shall not be considered as international multi modal transport. (Article 1).

Further, a "multimodal transport operator" is defined by the MT Convention "as any person who on his own behalf or through another person acting on his behalf concludes a multimodal transport contract and who acts as a principal, not as an agent or on behalf of the consignor or of the carriers participating in the multi modal transport operations, and who assumes responsibility for the performance of the contract."

12.2 Liability Regime

12.2.1 Carriage by Rail: 1980 Convention concerning International Carriage by Rail (COTIF)

International carriage by rail of goods, baggage, and passengers is governed by the 1980 Convention Concerning International Carriage of Goods by Rail (COTIF)[4]. Included in its schedule (Appendix B) is the "Uniform Rules Concerning the Contract for International Carriage of Goods by Rail" (CIM).[5] COTIF also provides for the establishment of an intergovernmental organization—the Intergovernmental Organization for International Carriage by Rail (OTIF) which is aimed to promote, improve, and facilitate in all respects international traffic by rail. The 1980 COTIF was,

---

[1] Adopted on May 19, 1956.

[2] See Schnitzer, (Schnitzer 2006) p. 147; Carr (2014), p. 375.

[3] Adopted on May 24, 1980.

[4] May 9, 1980. The text is available at the official website of OTIF: www.otif.org/.

[5] There are seven Appendices to basic text of the COTIF setting out uniform railway law and appendix B containing CIM is one of them.

however, substantially revised by the Protocol for the Modification of the Convention concerning International Carriage by Rail (the Vilnius Protocol of 1999)[6] resulting in the 1999 COTIF. Similarly, a new version of CIM Rules appeared in 1999 which are appended to 1999 COTIF.

12.2.2 Uniform Rules Concerning the Contract for the International Carriage of Goods (CIM Rules)[7]

12.2.2.1 Scope of Application

CIM Rules are aimed to achieve harmonization of the laws governing the carriage by rail as well as to bring about harmony between these laws and the laws governing the other modes of transport, such as road.

According to Article 1(1), the CIM Rules "shall apply to every contract of carriage of goods by rail for reward when the place of taking over of the goods and the place designated for delivery are situated in two different Member States, irrespective of the place of business and the nationality of the parties to the contract of carriage." Further, these Rules "shall apply also to contracts of carriage of goods by rail for reward, when the place of taking over of the goods and the place designated for delivery are situated in two different States, of which at least one is a Member State and the parties to the contract agree that the contract is subject to these Uniform Rules" (Article 1(2)). However, CIM Rules "shall not apply to carriage performed between stations situated on the territory of neighbouring States, when the infrastructure of these stations is managed by one or more infrastructure managers subject to only one of those States" (Article 1(3)).

12.2.2.2 Basis of Liability of a Carrier

Article 23 fixes the liability of the carrier for loss or damage resulting from the loss or damage to the goods during their carriage. Para 21 provides:

> The carrier shall be liable for loss or damage resulting from the total or partial loss of, or damage to, the goods between the time of taking over of the goods and the time of delivery and for the loss or damage resulting from the transit period being exceeded, whatever the railway infrastructure used.

However, the carrier shall not be liable if certain circumstances mentioned in Article 23(2) and (3) exist. Article 23(2) provides that the carrier shall be relieved of the liability to the extent that the loss or damage or delay "was caused by the fault

---

[6]The text of the Vilnius Protocol of 1999 with subsequent modifications can be accessed from the official website of OTIF, supra note 1.

[7]See Guest (ed.) (2006), pp. 1805–14; Schnitzer (2006), pp. 146–47; D'Arcy et al. (2000), pp. 338–39; Chuah, (2009), pp. 388–96.

of the person entitled, by an order given by the person entitled other than as a result of the fault of the carrier, by an inherent defect in the goods (decay, wastage etc.) or by circumstances which the carrier could not avoid and the consequences of which he was unable to prevent."

Further, Article 23(3) provides that the carrier shall not be liable to the extent that the loss or damage arises from the special risks inherent in:

(a) carriage in open wagons pursuant to the General Conditions of Carriage or when it has been expressly agreed and entered in the consignment note; subject to damage sustained by the goods because of atmospheric influences, goods carried in intermodal transport units and in closed road vehicles carried on wagons shall not be considered as being carried in open wagons; if for the carriage of goods in open wagons, the consignor uses sheets, the carrier shall assume the same liability as falls to him for carriage in open wagons without sheeting, even in respect of goods which, according to the General Conditions of Carriage, are not carried in open wagons;
(b) absence or inadequacy of packaging in the case of goods which by their nature are liable to loss or damage when not packed or when not packed properly;
(c) loading of the goods by the consignor or unloading by the consignee;
(d) the nature of certain goods which particularly exposes them to total or partial loss or damage, especially through breakage, rust, interior and spontaneous decay, desiccation or wastage;
(e) irregular, incorrect or incomplete description or numbering of packages;
(f) carriage of live animals;
(g) carriage which, pursuant to applicable provisions or agreements made between the consignor and the carrier and entered on the consignment note, must be accompanied by an attendant, if the loss or damage results from a risk which the attendant was intended to avert.

Further, the duty of the carrier, according to Article 24, is strict as Para 1 clearly states that "the burden of proving that the loss, damage or exceeding of the transit period was due to one of the causes specified in Article 23 § 2 shall lie on the carrier."

However, where the carrier establishes that the loss or damage could have arisen from one or more of the special risks referred to in Para 3 of Article 23, "it shall be presumed that it did so arise. The person entitled shall, however, have the right to prove that the loss or damage was not attributable either wholly or in part to one of those risks."

12.2.3 Carriage of Goods by Road: 1956 Convention for the Contract for the International Carriage of Goods by Road (CMR)[8]

12.2.3.1 Scope of Application

According to Article 1(1), the CMR applies to every contract for the carriage of goods by road in vehicles for reward, when the place of taking over of the goods and the place designated for delivery, as specified in the contract, are situated in two different countries, of which at least one is a contracting country…

Further, in determining the applicability of the Convention, the place of residence and the nationality of the parties are not important.

Significantly, CMR may be stated to have adopted a novel approach in including the multimodal transport.[9] Article 2 provides:

Where the vehicle containing the goods is carried over part of the journey by sea, rail, inland waterways or air, and … the goods are not unloaded from the vehicle, this Convention shall nevertheless apply to the whole of the carriage. Provided that to the extent it is proved that any loss, damage or delay in delivery of the goods which occurs during the carriage by the other means of transport was not caused by act or omission of the carrier by road, but by some event which could only occurred in the course of and by reason of the carriage by that other means of transport, the liability of the carrier by road shall be determined not by this convention but in the manner in which the liability of the carrier by the other means of transport would have been determined if a contract for the carriage the goods alone had been made by the sender with the carrier by the other means of transport in accordance with the conditions prescribed by law for the carriage of goods by that means of transport.

12.2.3.2 Carrier's Liabilities

According to Article 17(1) of CMR, "the carrier shall be liable for the loss of the goods and for damage thereto occurring between the time when he takes over the goods and the time of delivery, as well as for any delay in delivery."

However, the carrier will not be liable if "the loss, damage or delay was caused by the wrongful act or neglect of the claimant, by the instructions of the claimant given otherwise than as the result of a wrongful act or neglect on the part of the carrier, by inherent vice of the goods or through circumstances which the carrier could not avoid and the consequences of which he was unable to prevent" Article 17(2).

Article 17(3) also provides that the carrier shall not be liable if the loss or damage results from the special risks inherent in

---

[8]Guest (ed.), id., pp. 1799–1804; Schnitzer (2006), pp. 145-46; D'Arcy et al. (2000), pp. 339–40; Chuah (2009), pp. 379–88; Carr (2014), pp. 354–55.

[9]Carr, id, pp. 354–55; Aikens et al. (2006), p. 324.

(a) use of open unsheeted vehicles, when their use has been expressly agreed and specified in the consignment note;
(b) the lack of, or defective condition of packing in the case of goods which, by their nature, are liable to wastage or to be damaged when not packed or when not properly packed;
(c) handling, loading, stowage or unloading of the goods by the sender, the consignee or person acting on behalf of the sender or the consignee;
(d) the nature of certain kinds of goods which particularly exposes them to total or partial loss or to damage, especially through breakage, rust, decay, desiccation, leakage, normal wastage, or the action of moth or vermin;
(e) insufficiency or inadequacy of marks or numbers on the packages;
(f) the carriage of livestock.

Further, the duty of the carrier is strict. Article 18 explicitly states that "the burden of proving that loss, damage or delay was due to one of the circumstances specified in Article 17, paragraph 2, shall rest upon the carrier."

12.2.4 Liability of Carrier under Multimodal Transport[10]: The United Nations Convention on International Multimodal Transport of Goods (MT Convention)

12.2.4.1 Scope of Application

According to Article 2, MT Convention applies to all contracts of multimodal transport between places in two states, if:

(a) The place for the taking in charge of the goods by the multimodal transport operator as provided for in the multi modal transport contract is located in a Contracting State, or
(b) The place for delivery of the goods by the multimodal transport operator as provided for in the multimodal transport contract is located in a Contracting State.

12.2.4.2 Basis of Liability

According to Article 16(1), the multimodal transport operator shall be liable for loss of or damage to the goods as well as from delay in delivery, "if the occurrence which caused the loss, damage or delay in delivery took place while the goods were in his charge, unless the multimodal transport operator proves that he, his servants or agents or any other person referred to in Article 15 took all measures that could reasonably be required to avoid the occurrence and its consequences."

---

[10]Guest (ed.) (2006), pp. 1814–19; Schnitzer (2006), pp. 147–48; Carr, id., pp. 386–88.

The wording suggests that the nature of a multimodal transport operator's liability under Article 16 is strict.

Article 16(2) explains the phrase, "Delay in delivery." It reads.

> Delay in delivery occurs when the goods have not been delivered within the time expressly agreed upon or, in the absence of such" agreement, within the time which it would be reasonable to require of a diligent multimodal transport operator, having regard to the circumstances of the case.

It may also be noted that Article 18, MT Convention, like other international instruments on the carriage of goods, imposes a ceiling on the financial liability of the multimodal transport operator. But the right to limit the liability will be lost if it is proved that the loss, damage, or delay in delivery resulted from an act or omission of the multimodal transport operator done with the intent to cause such loss, damage, or delay or recklessly and with knowledge that such loss, damage, or delay would probably result (Article 21).

References

Aikens, Richards, Lord, Richard, & Bools, Michael. (2006). *Bills of lading*. London: Informa Law.

Carr, Indira. (2014). *International trade law*. London: Routledge.

Chuah, J. C. T. (2009). *Law of international trade: Cross-border commercial transactions* (p. 2011). London: Sweet & Maxwell, South Asian Edition.

D"Arcy, L., Murray, C., Cleave, B. (Eds.). (2000). *Schmitthoff*'s *export trade: The law and practice of international trade*. London: Stevens.

Guest, A. G. (Ed.). (2006). *Benjamin*'s *sale of goods*. London: Sweet & Maxwell.

Moens, Gabriel, & Gillies, Peter. (2006). *International trade and business: Law, policy and ethics*. New York: Oxon Routledge-Cavendish.

Schnitzer, Simone. (2006). *Understanding international trade law*. UK: Law Matters Publishing.

Part V
Insurance and Finance

Chapter 13
Contracts of Marine Insurance

13.1 Nature of Marine Insurance Contract

13.1.1 Contract of Marine Insurance as a Contract of Indemnity

Section 1 of the Marine Insurance Act, 1906 (MIA 1906) [s. 3 of (Indian) Marine Insurance Act 1963 (MIA 1963) defines a marine insurance contract as "a contract whereby the insurer undertakes to indemnify the assured, in a manner and to the extent agreed, against marine losses… the losses incidental to marine adventure."[1] According to s. 3(2) [s. 2(d) of MIA 1963] there is a "marine adventure" where:

(a) Any ship goods or other moveables are exposed to maritime perils. Such property is in this Act referred to as "insurable property";

(b) The earning or acquisition of any freight, passage money, commission, profit, or other pecuniary benefit, or the security for any advances, loan, or disbursements, is endangered by the exposure of insurable property to maritime perils;

(c) Any liability to a third party may be incurred by the owner of, or other person interested in or responsible for, insurable property, by reason of maritime perils.

The term, "maritime perils" is defined as the perils consequent on, or incidental to, the navigation of the sea, that is to say, perils of the seas, fire, war, perils, pirates, rovers, thieves, captures, seizures, restraints, and detainments of princes and peoples, jettisons, barratry, and any other perils, either of the like kind or which may be designated by the policy.[2]

---

[1] A contract of insurance is understood as a contract whereby one party for some consideration, usually premiums, secures for him some benefit upon the happening of some event which is uncertain to happen and the insured has an insurable interest in the subject-matter of the contract. See *Prudential Insurance Co. v IRC* [1904] 2 KB 658; *Medical Defence Union Ltd v Department of Trade* [1980] Ch. 82.

[2] Section 3 (2) of MIA 1906.

A. Srivastava, *Modern Law of International Trade*, International Law and the Global South, https://doi.org/10.1007/978-981-15-5475-9_13

Thus, in a marine insurance what is actually insured is the risk associated with the adventure and not the property exposed to peril.[3]

Further, it is a fundamental rule of the law of insurance that a contract of marine insurance, unlike a life insurance, is a "contract of indemnity" whereby the insurer undertakes to indemnify the assured, in a manner and to the extent stated in the contract, against marine risks.[4] The Court of Appeal in *Castellain v Preston*[5] held:

> …the contract of insurance contained in a marine or fire policy is a contract of indemnity, and of indemnity only, and that this contract means that the assured, in case of a loss against which the policy has been made, shall be fully indemnified, but shall never be more than fully indemnified.

In a contract of indemnity, the promisor or insurer promises to indemnify a promissee (or assured) against a loss resulting from any cause such as fire or other accident. S. 124 of the Indian Contract Act provides:

> **124. "Contract of Indemnity" Defined**—A contract by which one party promises to save the other from loss caused to him by the conduct of the promisor himself, or by the conduct of any other person, is called a "contract of indemnity."

Illustration attached to s. 124 reads as follows:

> *A* contracts to indemnify *B* against the consequences of any proceedings which *C* may take against *B* in respect of a certain sum of 200 rupees. This is a contract of indemnity.

Further, dealing with the extent of liability of the promisor, s. 125 provides:

> **125 Rights of indemnity-holder when sued**—The promise in a contract of indemnity, acting within the scope of his authority, is entitled to recover from the promisor—
>
> (1) all damages which he may be compelled to pay in any suit in respect of any matter to which the promise to indemnify applies;
> (2) All costs which he may be compelled to pay in any such suit if, in bringing or defending it, he did not contravene the orders of the promisor, and acted as it would have been prudent for him to act in the absence of any contract of indemnity, or if the promisor authorized him to bring or defend the suit;
> (3) All sums which he may have paid under the terms of any compromise of any such suit, if the compromise was not contrary to the orders of the promisor; and was one which it would have been prudent for the promise to make in the absence of any contract of indemnity, or if the promisor authorized him to compromise the suit.

Since a marine insurance contract is a contract of indemnity, it follows that it does no more than indemnify the assured against losses.[6] As the Court of Appeal in *Castellain v Preston* (cited above) stated that since a marine insurance contract is a contract of indemnity "the assured, in case of a loss against which the policy has been made, shall be fully indemnified, but shall never be more than fully indemnified."

---

[3]Murthy and Sarma (1995), pp. 168–69.

[4]Legh-Jones and Nicholas (2002), p. 135; Jess (2001), pp. 452–53.

[5](1883) 11 QBD 380.

[6]See McGee (2011), p. 47; Jess (2001), pp. 452–53.

The rule that the assured shall be entitled to recover his losses and "no more than his losses" is of universal application.[7]

13.1.2 Insurable Interests

13.1.2.1 Wagering Contracts and Contracts of Indemnity Distinguished

Much like the contract of indemnity, the concept of insurable interest is central to a marine insurance contract. Since a contract of marine insurance is a contract of indemnity, it is necessary that the assured must have an insurable interest in the subject-matter of a contract of marine insurance to prevent it from becoming a wagering contract. In other words, insurable interest is required to prevent a contract of marine insurance from being considered to be a contract of wagering.[8] A wagering contract was defined in *Carlill v Carbolic Smoke Ball Company*[9] as a contract, whereby two persons mutually agree that upon the happenning of a future, uncertain event, one shall win and that other shall pay a sum of money.

13.1.2.2 Notion of Insurable Interest

Insurable interest means that the assured has some interest in the subject-matter of the insurance. Sections 4, 5, and 6 of MIA 1906 [ss. 6, 7, and 8 of MIA 1963] lay down the rules regarding the insurable interest. First, s. 4 provides that a marine insurance contract by way of wagering is void ab initio. It reads as follows:

Section 4

(1) Every contract of marine insurance by way of gaming or wagering is void.

(2) a contract of marine insurance is deemed to be a gaming or wagering contract—

(a) Where the assured has not an insurable interest as defined by this Act, and the contract is entered into with no expectation of acquiring such an interest; or

(b) Where the policy is made "interest or no interest," or without further proof of interest than the policy itself," or without benefit of salvage to the insurer" or subject to any other like term:

Provided that, where there is no possibility of salvage, a policy may be effected without benefit of salvage to the insurer.

Secondly, defining an insurable interest in the context of marine insurance, s. 5 (1) provides that a person who is interested in a marine adventure has an insurable

[7] Jess, id., p. 452.

[8] Legh-Jones and Nicholas (2002), p. 135.

[9] [1892] 2 QB 484 at pp. 490–91.

interest in the subject-matter of the insurance. And s. 5(2) provides that the assured must have a legal relationship to the subject-matter of the insurance.

Section 5

(1) Subject to the provisions of this Act, every person has an insurable interest who is interested in a marine adventure.

(2) In particular a person is interested in a marine adventure where he stands in any legal or equitable relation to the adventure or to any insurable property at risk therein, in consequence of which he may benefit by the safety or due arrival of insurable property or may be prejudiced by its loss, or by damage thereto, or by the detention thereof, or may incur liability in respect thereof.

Section 5 is based on the common law notion of insurable interest according to which an assured must have a legal relationship to the subject-matter of the insurance so that "he may benefit from its safety and suffer detriment from its loss."[10]

Further, s. 6 provides that the (insurable) interest must attach at the time of the loss, though he need not be interested when the insurance is effected. However, "where the assured has no interest at the time of the loss, he cannot acquire interest by any act or election after he is aware of the loss."

13.1.3 Parties to Insurance Contract and Formalities

Parties to a contract of insurance are: the assured or the proposer and the insurer. The provision contained in Section 23 of MIA 1963 is instructive:

When contract is deemed to be concluded.—A contract of marine insurance is deemed to be concluded when the proposal of the assured is accepted by the insurer, whether the policy be then issued or not; and for the purpose of showing when the proposal was accepted, reference may be made to the slip, covering note or other customary memorandum of the contract, although it be unstamped.

According to Sections. 23 and 24 of MIA 1906 [ss. 25 and 26 of MIA 1963] a marine insurance contract: "must specify the name of the assured, or of some person who effects the insurance on his behalf; and must be signed by or on behalf of the insurer." Further, "where a policy is subscribed by or on behalf of two or more insurers, each subscription, unless the contrary be expressed, constitutes a distinct contract with the assured."

Mention may also be made of s. 22 of MIA 1906 [s. 24 of MIA 1963] according to which a marine insurance contract is not admissible in evidence "unless it is embodied in a marine policy…The policy may be executed and issued either at the time when the contract is concluded, or afterwards."

---

[10]Legh-Jones and Nicholas (2002), p. 417.

13.2 Duty of Utmost Good Faith

A marine insurance contract, like other contracts of insurance, is a contract based upon the utmost good faith (or contract of *uberrimae fidei*).[11] According to the principle of utmost good faith, if utmost good faith is not observed by either party, the other party may rescind the contract.[12] S. 17 of MIA 1906 [s. 19 of MIA 1963] provides:

Insurance is uberrimae fidei

A contract of marine insurance is a contract based upon the utmost good faith, and, if the utmost good faith be not observed by either party, the contract may be avoided by the other party.

Doctrine of utmost good faith requires an assured (a) to disclose all material facts; and (b) not to make any misrepresentations. These "pre-contractual" obligations are essential part of every marine insurance contract.

13.2.1 Duty to Disclose All Material Facts: Doctrine of "Materiality"

The assured must disclose all facts that may be material in increasing the risks of the insurer.[13] Meaning of material facts in this context is clearly spelt out by s. 18 of MIA 1906:

Section 18. Disclosure by assured

(1) Subject to the provisions of this section, the assured must disclose to the insurer, before the contract is concluded, every material circumstance which is known to the assured, and the assured is deemed to know every circumstance which, in the ordinary course of business, ought to be known by him. If the assured fails to make such disclosure, the insurer may avoid the contract.
(2) Every circumstance is material which would influence the judgment of a prudent insurer in fixing the premium, or determining whether he will take the risk.

Certain facts, however, need not be disclosed. Subsection (3) provides:

(3) In the absence of inquiry the following circumstances need not be disclosed, namely:

(a) Any circumstance which diminishes the risk:

---

[11] As pointed out by Lord Chorley and Giles, although the principle of good faith is a common thread running through the whole law of contract, the insurance law requires the "utmost good faith" which is "an even higher standard of honesty than usual." See Chorley and Giles (1970), pp. 315–16.

[12] See D'Arcy et al. (2000), p. 363.

[13] See Carr (2014), pp. 408–12; Naidoo (2005), pp. 464–74; Huybrechts (2002), pp. 351–361.

(b) Any circumstance which is known or presumed to be known to the insurer. The insurer is presumed to know matters of common notoriety or knowledge, and matters which an insurer in the ordinary course of his business, as such, ought to know;

(c) Any circumstances as to which information is waived by the insurer;

(d) Any circumstance which it is superfluous to disclose by reason of any express or implied warranty.

As part of the duty of utmost good faith, the assured is subject to the duty of disclosure and representation.[14] Before the conclusion of a contract of insurance, the proposer or (the intending) insured is under the duty to disclose to the insurer all material information which is known to the assured regarding the nature of risk(s) involved.[15]

However, this duty is mutual or reciprocal and the assured can also expect the insurer to disclose all material facts known to him regarding the nature of the risk.[16] But disclosure by the insurer is rare. In *Banque keyser Ullman SA v Skandia (UK) Insurance Co. Ltd & Others*,[17] the Court of Appeal held:

> By the very nature of insurance cases allegations of non-disclosure of material facts are more likely to be made by the insurers than by the insured, in the ordinary course insurers will know of no material facts of which the insured himself is ignorant....
>
> In the rare case where there has been non-disclosure of a material fact by the insurer the position maybe rather different. Avoidance of the policy and the return of the premium may well constitute entirely sufficient relief for the insured if he becomes aware of the non-disclosure before the occurrence of the contingency against which he has intended to insure. If, however, he becomes aware of it only after the occurrence of the contingency, relief of this nature may be quite inadequate.

Where there is non-disclosure by either party, the other party is entitled to avoid the contract if it has been induced to enter into the policy on the relevant terms. In determining whether a fact is material, the question of whether the fact is one that would have an effect on the mind of the prudent insurer in estimating the risk is important.[18]

In a particularly instructive case on the point, *Manifest Shipping Co. Ltd v Uni-Polaris Insurance Co. Ltd (The Star Sea)*,[19] the House of Lords affirmed the view that although the duty of utmost good faith is basically a pre-contractual obligation, it continues to exist after the conclusion of the contract. However, according to the Court, the duty which continues post-contract does not require "a very high degree of openness." The degree of openness required by the duty of utmost good post contract is much lower than that required during the negotiation of a contract.

---

[14]Huybrechts, id., p. 351.

[15]See Beatson et al. (2010), pp. 334–36.

[16]Naidoo (2005), p. 465.

[17][1990] 1 QBD 723; [1991] 2 AC 249 (HL); Beatson et al. (2010), p. 334.

[18]*Pan Atlantic Insurance Co Ltd. v Pine Top Insurance Co. Ltd* [1995] 1 AC 501; *Marene Knitting Mills Pty Ltd v greater Pacific General Insurance Ltd* [1976] 2 Lloyd's Rep 631.

[19][2001] 1 All ER 743.

13.2.2 Duty Not to Make Any Misrepresentations

As part of the duty of utmost god faith, the assured is under the obligation not to make any material representation which is not true. Further, a representation is material which influences the judgment of a prudent insurer. Section 20 of MIA provides:

(1) Every material representation made by the assured or his agent to the insurer during the negotiations for the contract, and before the contract is concluded, must be true. If it be untrue the insurer may avoid the contract.

(2) A representation is material which would influence the judgment of a prudent insurer in fixing the premium, or determining whether he will take the risk.

(3) A representation may be either a representation as to a matter of fact, or as to a matter of expectation or belief.

(4) A representation as to a matter of fact is true, if it be substantially correct, that is to say, if the difference between what is represented and what is actually correct would not be considered material by a prudent insurer.

(5) A representation as to a matter of expectation or belief is true if it be made in good faith.

(6) A representation may be withdrawn or corrected before the contract is concluded.

(7) xxx.

13.3 Terms of Marine Insurance Contract

13.3.1 Warranty in Marine Insurance

The meaning of warranty in the context of the law of contract has already been noted (Chap. 6, Sect. 6.1.2). There it was noted that a warranty is a term of lesser significance; a breach of which only gives rise to the claim for damages but not a right to treat the contract as discharged. However, in the context of the insurance law, the term warranty is used in a "wholly different" sense to that understood in the contract law.[20] In the field of insurance law, where it has extremely important role to play in assessing the risk and performs a function similar to a "condition" under the contract law, the term warranty is clearly understood as not only giving rise the right to damages but also the right to terminate the contract for breach.[21] In insurance law, the term is used to determine the scope of a contract of insurance.[22] In other words, where a warranty is not complied with by the assured he cannot invoke the liability of the insurer in the event of the loss as the insurer is discharged from liability. Section 33 of MIA 1906 [35 of MIA 1963] which defines a warranty makes it succinct:

33.—(1) A warranty, in the following sections relating to warranties, means a promissory warranty, that is to say, a warranty by which by which the assured undertakes that

[20] See Hodges (2002), p. 202.

[21] The *Good Luck* [1991] 2 Lloyd's Rep. 191. See also Chuah (2009), pp. 466–67.

[22] See Soyer (2006), pp. 1–8.

some particular thing shall or shall not be done, or that some condition shall be fulfilled, or whereby he affirms or negatives the existence of a particular state of facts.

(2) A warranty may be express or implied.

(3) A warranty, as above defined, is a condition which must be exactly complied with, whether it be material to the risk or not. If it be not so complied with, then, subject to any express provision in the policy, the insurer is discharged from liability as from the date of the breach of warranty, but without prejudice to any liability incurred by him before that date.

Section 33 speaks of promissory warranties. In other words, a warranty is an undertaking by the assured that some particular thing shall be done.[23] However, it is not every contractual undertaking to do a particular thing that can be treated as a warranty. In order to be a warranty, the undertaking must relate to risk covred under the contract.[24]

There is also a second category of warranties which are not promissory in nature but describe the risk. A warranty of this kind merely implies that if the warranty is not complied with the risk will not attach.[25]

A further point to note is that the breach of a warranty cannot be remedied.[26] Section 34(2) provides:

Where a warranty is broken, the assured cannot avail himself of the defence that the breach has been remedied, and the warranty complied with, before loss.

13.3.2 Warranty Distinguished from Representation

Although there is a similarity between an express warranty and a representation made in the course of negotiations leading to a contract, there are some important differences between the two.[27] The first important difference between a warranty and a mere representation is that while a warranty is "a part of written policy," a representation "will seldom, if ever, be written in."[28] Secondly, an express warranty requires exact and literal performance of what has been promised, but a substantial compliance of a representation is sufficient. "A representation may be equitably or substantially answered; but a warranty must be strictly complied with."[29]

[23] See Derrington (2002), pp. 384–85; *Hales v Reliance Fire* [1960] 2 Lloyd's Rep. 391.

[24] Ibid.

[25] For further discussion, see McGee (2011), pp. 243–45.

[26] Soyer (2006), p. 137.

[27] Soyer (2006), pp. 4–5; Derrington (2002), p. 385.

[28] Ibid.

[29] Per Lord Mansfield in *De Hahn v Hartley* (1976) 1 TR 343 (cited in Soyer (2006), p. 5).

13.3.3 Express and Implied Warranties

As s. 33(2), MIA 1906 provides a warranty may be express or implied. Further, in order to create an express warranty no particular wording is required. It can be created by any kind of wording and the use of words like "warranty or warranted" is not required.[30] Section 35, MIA 1906 [s. 37 MIA 1963] provides:

> 35. (1) an express warranty may be in any form of words from which the intention to warrant is to be inferred.
> (2) An express warranty must be included in, or written upon, the policy, or must be contained in some document incorporated by reference into the policy.
> (3) An express warranty does not exclude an implied warranty, unless it be inconsistent therewith.

Under English law which applies to India and some other common law countries like Australia, an express warranty thus may come into existence in a number of ways. For example, a warranty may be created by the use of appropriate expression, such as, the word, "warranty" or a phrase like "condition precedent."[31]

13.3.4 Implied Warranties

13.3.4.1 General

While express warranties are part of the marine policy and are actually agreed upon by the parties to an insurance contract, implied warranties are implied by the law in every contract of marine insurance. It needs to be stressed that the concept of implied warranties is not known outside the area of the marine insurance law. In other areas of insurance law, we do not have a concept like implied warranties. The reason is that marine adventure is a quite unique feature of the marine insurance. It is to balance the conflicting interests of the contracting parties involved in a marine insurance that the law uses the device of implied warranties.[32]

In India and England, implied warranties are imposed by the respective statutes. Under MIA 1906 and MIA 1963, four warranties are implied. These are: (a) warranty of seaworthiness; (b) warranty of port-worthiness; (c) warranty of cargo-worthiness; and (d) warranty of legality. Here, a brief discussion of these implied terms is in order.

---

[30] Soyer, id., p. 10; Derrington (2002), p. 385.

[31] Derrington (2002), ibid.

[32] Soyer (2006), p. 47.

13.3.4.2 Warranty of Seaworthiness

Subsections (1), (3) & (4) of s. 39 of MIA 1906 which correspond to subsections (1), (3) & (4) of s. 41 of MIA 1906 deal with the implied warranty of seaworthiness.[33] To quote the text of s. 39:

> **39.—Warranty of seaworthiness of ship.**
>
> (1) In a voyage policy there is an implied warranty that at the commencement of the voyage the ship shall be seaworthy for the purpose of the particular adventure insured.
>
> (2) Where the policy attaches while the ship is in port, there is also an implied warranty that she shall, at the commencement of the risk, be reasonably fit to encounter the ordinary perils of the port.
>
> (3) Where the policy relates to a voyage which is performed in different stages, during which the ship requires different kinds of or further preparation or equipment, there is an implied warranty that at the commencement of each stage the ship is seaworthy in respect of such preparation or equipment for the purposes of that stage.
>
> (4) A ship deemed to be seaworthy when she is reasonably fit in all respects to encounter the ordinary perils of the sea of the adventure insured.
>
> (5) In a time policy there is no implied warranty that the ship shall be seaworthy at any stage of the adventure, but where, with the privity of the assured, the ship is sent to sea in an unseaworthy state, the insurer is not liable for any loss attributable to unseaworthiness.

Here, a few points may be noted. First, the Act implies a warranty of seaworthiness only in respect of a voyage policy, but not in a time policy.[34] Secondly, the law imposes the warranty of seaworthiness only "at the commencement" of voyage, that is to say, when the ship sets sail or when the ship leaves the port.[35] Therefore, once the ship has left the port in a seaworthy condition the policy will attach and there is no implied warranty that the ship shall be seaworthy during the entire voyage.[36] In other words, where a ship commences her voyage in a seaworthy state, the subsequent unseaworthiness shall not render the ship unseaworthy in the sense of s. 39 of MIA 1906.

13.3.4.3 Warranty of Portworthiness

Where a ship is insured for a voyage "at and from" as distinguished from a voyage "from" a particular place, there is an implied warranty that the ship is port-worthy. Portworthiness of a ship means that the ship in question is able "to encounter the perils of the port."[37] Subsection (2) of s. 39 MIA 1906 [Subsection (2) of s. 41 MIA

---

[33] For the meaning of "seaworthiness" see above, Chap. 10.

[34] For a discussion of the rationale for not implying the warranty of seaworthiness in a time policy, see Soyer (2006), pp. 81–82.

[35] Id., p. 74; Hodges (2002), p. 201.

[36] Hodges, ibid.

[37] Ibid.

1963] provides that "where the policy attaches while the ship is in port, there is also an implied warranty that she shall, at the commencement of the risk, be reasonably fit to encounter the ordinary perils of the port."

In may also be noted that under the maritime law, the idea of portworthiness is not treated as separate from that of seaworthiness.

13.3.4.4 Warranty of Cargo-Worthiness

Cargo-worthiness of a vessel means that the ship must not only be fit "to encounter the perils of sea" but also be able to carry the goods safely.[38] The implied warranty of cargo-worthiness requires the ship and her equipment to be fit for the purpose of carrying the goods safely to the port of destination. S. 40 (2) MIA 1906 provides:

> In a voyage policy on goods or other moveables there is an implied warranty that at the commencement of the voyage the ship is not only seaworthy as a ship, but also that she is reasonable fit to carry the goods or other moveables to the destination contemplated by the policy.

What is required is that the ship in question must also be fit and equipped to carry the particular kind of goods to be carried by the ship. However, there is no warranty that the goods shipped are seaworthy for s. 40 (1) MIA 1906 provides:

In a policy on goods or other moveables there is no implied warranty that the goods or moveables are seaworthy.

13.3.5 Warranty of Legality

It is a basic principle of the law of contract that a contract which is made for unlawful purpose cannot be enforced. This principle also applies to the field of insurance law. Accordingly, s. 41, MIA 1906 [s. 43 MIA 1963] provides:

> There is an implied warranty that the adventure insured is a lawful one, and that, so far as the assured can control the matter, the adventure shall be carried out in a lawful manner.

Notably, a marine insurance contract not only must be legal but the adventure insured must also be lawful.[39] Here reference may also be made to s. 3(1) of MIA 1906 which anticipates that the subject of a contract of marine insurance is the lawful marine adventure.

---

[38] See Soyer (2006), pp. 116–17; Chuah (2009), pp. 472–73. It may also be noted that ordinarily the scope of seaworthiness in the context of carriage by sea of goods is wide enough to cover within its ambit the idea of cargo-worthiness. Soyer (2006), ibid.; *Reed v Page* [1927] 1 KB 743.

[39] Soyer, id., p. 119.

13.4 Subrogation and Contribution

Where, in addition to the insurer, a third party is also liable for the loss, but the assured prefers to sue the insurer[40] under the policy and recovers the loss from the insurer, according to the principle of subrogation the insurer, upon paying the assured, steps into his shoes and becomes entitled to exercise all the rights of the assured against the third party.[41] The principle is recognized by s. 79 of MIA 1963 the wording of which is identical to that of s. 79 of MIA 1906.

79. Right of Subrogation

(1) Where the insurer pays for a total loss, either of the whole, or in the case of goods of any apportionable part, of the subject-matter insured, he thereupon becomes entitled to take over the interest of the assured in whatever may remain of the subject-matter so paid for and he is thereby subrogated to all rights and remedies of the assured in and in respect of that subject-matter as from the time of the casualty causing the loss.

(2) Subject to the foregoing provisions, where the insurer pays for a partial loss, he acquires no title to the subject-matter insured, or such part of it as may remain, but he is thereupon subrogated to all rights and remedies of the assured in and in respect of the subject-matter insured as from the time of the casualty causing the loss, in so far as the assured has been indemnified, according to this Act, by such payment for the loss.

Subrogation is a well-established principle of law based on the notion of equity recognized also by other branches of law, like the law of contract and property.

There is another relevant principle to note in the context. According to this principle, where there are two or more insurers, as it is the case with "double insurance," each insurer is under the duty to contribute "ratably to the loss in proportion to the amount for which he is liable." In other words, where one insurer pays for the total loss, that is to say, pays more than his proportion of liability, he is entitled to demand ratable contribution from the other insurer or insurers. Section 80 which recognizes the right of contribution reads as follows:

80. Right of Contribution

(1) Where the assured is over-insured by double insurance, each insurer is bound, as between himself and the other insurers, to contribute ratably to the loss in proportion to the amount for which he is liable under his contract.

(2) If any insurer pays more than his proportion of the loss, he is entitled to maintain a suit for contribution against the other insurers, and is entitled to the like remedies as a surety who has paid more than his proportion of the debt.

Double insurance is dealt with by s. 32 (1) of MIA 1906:

---

[40] In the case of double insurance, the assured has, unless the policy otherwise indicates, the right to claim for his loss from the insurers "in such order as he may think fit, provided that he is not entitled to receive any sum in excess of the indemnity allowed by this Act." Section 32 (2) of MIA 1906.

[41] See Bennett (2002), pp. 123–26.

32. Double insurance

(1) Where two or more policies are affected by or on behalf of the assured on the same adventure and interest or any part thereof, and the sums insured exceed the indemnity allowed by this Act, the assured is said to be over-insured by double insurance.

13.5 Types of Marine Policies

A policy can be classified as either valued or unvalued. Section 27(1) of MIA 1906 [s. 29 (1) of MI 1963]. A valued policy is defined as "a policy which specifies the agreed value of the subject-matter insured" (s. 27 (2) of MIA 1906 (corresponding to s. 29 (2) of MIA 1963). An unvalued policy, on the other hand, "is a policy which does not specify the value of the subject-matter insured, but subject to the limit of the sum insured, leaves the insurable value to be subsequently ascertained..." (s. 28 of MIA 1906).

A marine policy may further be classified as a voyage and time policy. According to s. 24 of MIA 1906, where the contract is to insure the subject-matter "at and from," or from one place to another or other, the policy is called a "voyage policy." But where the contract is to insure the subject-matter for a definite period of time the policy is called a "time policy." Section 24 also provides that a contract in respect of both, voyage and time policy may be included in the same policy.

13.6 Losses

13.6.1 Actual (Total or Partial) Loss

For the purpose of determining the liability of insurer the loss caused to the assured may be total (actual or constructive) or partial.[42] According to s. 57 of MIA 1963, "[w]here the subject-matter insured is destroyed, or so damaged as to cease to be a thing of the kind insured, or where the assured is irretrievably deprived thereof, there is an actual total loss." Thus, where a ship has sunk and lost or has ceased to be a ship, this is a case of a "total loss".[43] In the case of missing ship, s. 58 of MIA 1963 provides: Where the ship concerned in the adventure is missing, and after the lapse of a reasonable time no news of her has been received, an actual total loss may be presumed. As far as the goods are concerned, they are treated as actually lost when they cease to be the goods of the type "insured from a commercial point of

[42]MIA 1963, Section 56 [MIA1906, Section 56]. Section 56(3) reads as follows: "Unless a different intention appears from the terms of the policy, an insurance against total loss includes a constructive, as well as an actual, total loss."

[43]See Chorley and Giles (1970), p. 355; McGee (2011), p. 550.

view."[44] For example, where the goods in question cease to answer their description then there is an actual, total loss.[45]

13.6.2 Constructive (Total) Loss

Defining the constructive total loss, s. 60 (1) of MIA 1963 provides[46]:

> Subject to any express provision in the policy, there is a constructive total loss where the subject-matter insured is reasonably abandoned on account of its actual total loss appearing to be unavoidable, or because it could not be preserved from actual total loss without an expenditure which would exceed its value when the expenditure had been incurred.

Further, according to s. 60(2), the following situations in particular will be treated as a case of the constructive total loss:

(i) where the assured is deprived of the possession of his ship or goods by a peril insured against, and
   (a) it is unlikely that he can recover the ship or goods, as the case may be, or
   (b) the cost of recovering the ship or goods, as the case may be, would exceed their value when recovered; or

(i) in the case of damage to a ship, where she is so damaged by a peril insured against that the cost of repairing the damage would exceed the value of the ship when repaired. In estimating the cost of repairs, no deduction is to be made is respect of general average contributions to those repairs payable by other interests, but account is to be taken of the expense of future salvage operations and of any future general average contributions to which the ship would be liable if required; or

(ii) in the case of damage to goods, where the cost of repairing the damage and forwarding the goods to their destination would exceed their value on arrival.

References

Beatson, et al. (2010). *Anson's law of contract* (Beatson, Burrows, & Cartwright, eds.). Oxford: Oxford University Press.

Bennett, H. N. (2002). Valued policies. In Thomas (Ed.), *The modern law of marine insurance* (Vol. 2). London: LLP.

Carr, I. (2014). *International trade law*. London: Routledge.

Chorley, & Giles, O. C. (1970). *Shipping law*. London: Pitman Publishing Limited.

Chuah, J. C. T. (2009). *Law of international trade: Cross-border commercial trade transactions*. London: Sweet &Maxwell, South Asian Edition, 2011.

D'Arcy, L., Murray, C., & Cleave, B. (Eds.). (2000). *Schmitthoff's export trade: The law and practice of international trade*. London: Stevens.

---

[44]Chorley and Giles, id., p. 356.

[45]Ibid.

[46]The wording of s. 60 is almost identical to its English law counterpart (s. 60 of MIA 1906).

Derrington, S. (2002). Australia: perspectives and permutations on the law of marine insurance. In D. R. Thomas (ed.), *The modern law of marine insurance* (Vol. 2, pp. 363–403). London: LLP.

Hodges, S. (2002). The quest for seaworthiness: A study of US and English law of marine insurance. In D. R. Thomas (ed.), *The modern law of marine insurance* (Vol. 2, pp. 199–242). London: LLP.

Huybrechts. (2002). Marine insurance law: A san andreas fault between the Common law and civil law. In D. R. Thomas (ed.), *The modern law of marine insurance* (Vol. 2, pp. 335–61). London: LLP.

Jess, D. C. (2001). *The insurance of commercial risks: Law and practice* (pp. 452–53). London: Sweet & Maxwell.

Legh-Jones, Q. C., & Nicholas. (2002). The elements of insurance interest in marine insurance law. In D. R. Thomas (ed.), *The modern law of marine insurance* (Vol. 2, pp. 135–60). London: LLP.

McGee. (2011). *The modern law of insurance*. LexisNexis.

Murthy, & Sarma. (1995). *Modern law of insurance in India*. Bombay: NM Tripathi Private Limited.

Naidoo, A. (2005). Post-contractual good faith: A further change in judicial attitude. *Modern Law Review, 68*(3), 464–474.

Soyer, B. (2006). *Warranties in marine insurance* (pp. 1–8). London: Cavendish Publishing Limited.

Chapter 14
Export Finance

14.1 Direct Payment Methods

In addition to the commonly used payment methods in cross-border trade transactions such as documentary credit, also called, letter of credit, various collection arrangements, and forfaiting, attention will be paid to certain methods of payment which are less significant in the context but deserve mention here such as the bills of exchange and direct payment methods or methods based on "open account" terms. Since direct payment methods are the simplest methods of making payment, we will first turn our attention to these methods, albeit briefly.

In direct payment methods, the banker is making the payment directly to the seller at the instructions of the buyer.[1] Various terms may be used for this purpose. For example, in "sight" payment, the payment is made on sight of documents. The purchase price is remitted to the seller through cable, mail or by Society for Worldwide Inter-bank Financial Telecommunication (SWIFT) transfers.[2] Other similar methods include "cash with order" and "cash on delivery" terms. These are commonly used when the seller is not sure about the buyer's financial conditions.[3] In the latter, price of the goods is paid on delivery and is most suitable in an "ex works" contract.

[1]See Guest (ed.) (2006), p. 1869; D'Arcy et al. (2000), p. 146; Chuah (2009), pp. 500–01; Carr (2014), pp. 432–33.

[2]D'Arcy et al., ibid.; Chuah, ibid.

[3]Carr (2014), p. 432.

A. Srivastava, *Modern Law of International Trade*, International Law and the Global South, https://doi.org/10.1007/978-981-15-5475-9_14

14.2 Bill of Exchange

14.2.1 Nature of Bills of Exchange: Essential Characteristics

14.2.1.1 General

The "bill of exchange" is the most commonly used negotiable instrument in international trade.[4] It is defined by s. 5 of the Negotiable Instruments Act, 1881 (NIA 1881) as "an instrument in writing containing an unconditional order, signed by the maker, directing a certain person to pay a certain sum of money only to, or to the order of, a certain person or to the bearer of the instrument.[5] Examples include: cheques[6] and drafts drawn by one branch of a bank to another.

There are in general three parties to the bill of exchange: drawer, payee, and the drawee. The drawer is the person who makes the bill of exchange or gives the order to pay; drawee is the person to whom the order to pay is given; and payee is the person to whom the payment according to the order is to be made.[7] However, while a drawer and payee are different persons, a drawer and payee can be the same person. For example, a bill can be drawn in favor of the drawer himself. Further, as s. 13 (2) of NIA 1881 provides, "[a] negotiable instrument may be made payable to two or more payees jointly, or it may be made payable in the alternative to one of two, or one or some of several payees."

Further, bills of exchange are negotiable instruments, that is to say, they are freely transferable or transferable by delivery; and secondly, with their transfer all the rights of the transferor are transferred to the new transferee. But in order to have this effect, certain conditions must be met. First, the bill must be in the written form and must be signed by the party who is liable to pay under it; secondly, the obligations owed under the bill can be claimed only by the person who is the holder of the bill. The holder of the bill may be the payee, or indorsee, or bearer. Now these characteristics of the bill of exchange will be discussed below in some detail.

---

[4]Guest, (ed.) (2006), p. 1869. Besides a bill of exchange, the promissory note and cheques are also the negotiable instruments.

[5]This definition is similar to one provided by s. 3 of the (English) Bills of Exchange Act 1882 (BEA 1882). It reads as follows:

(1) A bill of exchange or draft is an unconditional order in writing, addressed by one person to another, signed by the person giving it, requiring the person to whom it is addressed to pay on demand or at fixed or determinable future time a sum certain in money to or to the order of a specified person, or to bearer.
(2) An instrument which does not comply with these conditions, or which orders any act to be done in addition to the payment of money, is not a bill of exchange.

[6]Section 6, NIA 1881.

[7]Section 7, ibid.

14.2.1.2 Unconditional Order to Pay

The first characteristic of the bill of exchange is that it is an unequivocal and unconditional order to pay.[8] This is evident from the use of words, "an instrument in writing containing an unconditional order..." (s. 5, NIA 1881). Section 5 further provides that "[a] promise or order to pay is not "conditional," within the meaning of this section and s. 4, by reason of the time for payment of the amount or any instalment thereof being expressed to be on the lapse of a certain period after the occurrence of a specified event which, according to the ordinary expectation of mankind, is certain to happen, although the time of its happening may be uncertain."

14.2.1.3 Parties Must Be Ascertainable

Secondly, the parties of a bill of exchange contract must be certain or ascertainable. Although, it may happen that the addressee of the bill "is mis-named or designated by description only" (s. 5, NIA 1881).[9] Thirdly, there should also not any uncertainty as to the sum payable. However, s. 5 provides that the sum payable may be certain, "although it includes future interest or is payable at an indicated rate of exchange, or is according to the course of exchange, and although the instrument provides that, on default of payment of an instalment, the balance unpaid shall become due."

14.2.1.4 Negotiability

According to the principle of negotiability as it applies to the negotiable instruments, a bill of exchange is transferable (or negotiable) by delivery. Explanation (i) attached to s. 5 reads:

> A promissory note, bill of exchange or cheque is payable to order which is expressed to be so payable or which is expressed to be payable to a particular person, and does not contain words prohibiting transfer or indicating an intention that it shall not be transferable.

Secondly, upon delivery of a bill of exchange, the rights of the transferor, under the bill of exchange, are transferred to the transferee or holder of the bill. In other words, if the transferee fits to the description of a bonafide transferee for value, that is to say, he has given consideration for the bill received by him and has no notice of any defects in the title of the transferor, his rights under the bill are not affected by any defects in the title of the transferor.[10] Section 14, NIA 1881 defines the term, "negotiation" as follows:

> When a promissory note, bill of exchange or cheque is transferred to any person, so as to constitute that person the holder thereof, the instrument is said to be negotiated.

---

[8] See *Hamilton v Spottiswoode* (1894) 4 Ex 200.

[9] In *Bird & Co. (London) Ltd v Thomas Cook & Son Ltd*, [1937] 2 All ER 227, the view was expressed that extrinsic evidence may be given to explain the ambiguity in the name of the payee.

[10] See further, Chuah (2009), pp. 509–12.

The corresponding provision contained in s. 31 (1) of BEA 1882 which is similarly worded. Further s. 31(2) provides that (a) a bill payable to bearer is negotiated by delivery; and (b) a bill payable to order is negotiated by the indorsement of the holder completed by delivery.

Here, mention may also be made of s. 43 of NIA 1881 which provides that

> **43. Negotiable instrument made, etc., without consideration**—A negotiable instrument made, drawn, accepted, indorsed or transferred without consideration, or for a consideration which fails, creates no obligation of payment between the parties to the transaction. But if any such party has transferred the instrument with or without indorsement to a holder for consideration, such holder, and every subsequent holder deriving title from him, may recover the amount due on such instrument from the transferor for consideration or any prior party thereto.

Holder in Due Course

In the context of the negotiability of a bill of exchange or cheque, a key concept to note is the "holder in due course." According to s. 9 of NIA 1881, the holder in due course is "any person who takes the bill of exchange or other negotiable instruments for consideration. Further he may be holding the bill as the bearer, or the payee or indorsee thereof, "before the amount mentioned in it became payable, and without having sufficient cause to believe that any defect existed in the title of the person from whom he derived his title."

The meaning is similar to that ascribed to the holder in due course under the BEA 1882. Section 29 of the Act of 1882 reads as follows:

(1) A holder in due course is a holder who has taken a bill, complete and regular on the face of it, under the following conditions; namely,

(a) That he became the holder of it before it was overdue, and without notice that it had been previously dishonoured, if such was the fact:

(b) That he took the bill in good faith and for value, and that at the time the bill was negotiated to him he had no notice of any defect in the title of the person who negotiated it.

(2) In particular the title of a person who negotiates a bill is defective within the meaning of this Act when he obtained the bill, or the acceptance thereof, by fraud, duress, or force and fear, or other unlawful means, or an illegal consideration, or when he negotiates it in breach of faith, or under such circumstances as amount to a fraud.

(3) A holder (whether for value or not), who derives his title to a bill through a holder in due course, and who is not himself a party to any fraud or illegality affecting it, has all the rights of that holder in due course as regards the acceptor and all parties to the bill prior to that holder.

Under the Convention, the transfer of an instrument by a protected holder vests in any subsequent holder the rights to and on the instrument that the protected holder had.

14.2.1.5 Payable on Demand

A further characteristic of a bill of exchange is that it is payable on demand or at a fixed or specified time. It is payable on demand when no time for payment is fixed (s. 19, NIA 1881) or when the expressions "at sight" and "on presentment" are used (s. 21, NIA 1881). In export trade, a bill is normally payable not on demand but either at a fixed period after the date of drawing or at a fixed date after "sight."[11] In fact, a bill remains valid even where it is payable at a future time which is determinable (see s. 11 of BEA 1882).[12]

14.2.2 1988 UN Convention on International Bills of Exchange and International Promissory Notes

14.2.2.1 General

The United Nations Convention on International Bills of Exchange and International Promissory Notes[13] is the result of the work of the United Nations Commission on International Trade Law (UNCITRAL) devoted to bringing out uniformity in the national laws governing bills of exchange with the overarching goal of "facilitating international trade and finance." It seeks to reconcile the Geneva System[14] which applies to the civil law countries and the Anglo-American System which applies to the United Kingdom and most countries of the Commonwealth.[15] The Convention contains the modern, comprehensive, and self-contained regime of legal rules governing international bills of exchange and international promissory notes that satisfy its requisites of form.[16] Further, these rules are not intended to replace the

---

[11] Guest (ed.) (2006), p. 1872.

[12] Section 11 of BEA 1882 provides:

A bill is payable at a determinable future time within the meaning of this Act which is expressed to be payable—

(1) At a fixed period after date or sight.
(2) On or at a fixed period after the occurrence of a specified event which is certain to happen, though the time of happening may be uncertain.

[13] Adopted on December 9, 1988. Not yet in force. The text can be accessed from the official website of UNCITRAL: www.uncitral.org.

[14] The Geneva System consists of the 1930 Geneva Convention on Uniform Law on Bills of Exchange and Promissory Notes; the 1930 Geneva Convention for the Settlement of Certain Conflicts of Laws in Connection with Bills of Exchange and Promissory Notes, the 1931 Geneva Convention on Uniform Law for Cheques, and the 1931 Convention for the Settlement of Certain Conflicts of Laws in Connection with Cheques.

[15] D'Arcy et al. (2010), p. 152; Guest (2008), p. 1867.

[16] See the Explanatory Note by the UNCITRAL Secretariat on the United Nations Convention on International Bills of Exchange and International Promissory Notes, at: www.uncitral.org.

domestic legislations on the subject, and the use of an instrument governed by the Convention is entirely optional. The Convention, in fact, offers an alternative regime to govern certain instruments covered by the Convention.[17]

14.2.2.2 Scope of Application

The Convention applies only to international bills of exchange and international promissory notes provided that they fulfill the requirements of form. In particular, the Convention applies only "to international instruments that bear in both their heading and their text the words "International bill of exchange (UNCITRAL Convention) or International promissory note (UNCITRAL Convention)."[18]

The terms, "bill of exchange" and "promissory note" are defined by the Convention in terms similar to those of the NIA 1881 and BEA 1882. According to Article 3(1) of the Convention, a bill of exchange is a written instrument which:

> a) contains an unconditional order whereby the drawer directs the drawee to pay a definite sum of money to the payee or to its order; b) is payable on demand or at a definite time; c) is dated; and d) is signed by the drawer.

And according to Article 3(2), a promissory note is a written instrument which:

> a) contains an unconditional promise whereby the maker undertakes to pay a definite sum of money to the payee or to its order; b) is payable on demand or at a definite time; c) is dated; d) is signed by the maker.

However, a bill of exchange and a promissory note will be governed by the Convention only if at least two of the places—the place where the bill is drawn, the place indicated next to the signature of the drawer, the place indicated next to the name of the drawee, the place indicated next to the name of the payee, and the place of payment—are situated in two different states "provided that either the place where the bill is drawn or the place of payment is specified on the bill and that such place is situated in a Contracting State" (Article 2).

14.2.2.3 Concepts of "Holder" and "Protected Holder"

Notably, the Convention seeks to reconcile the civil and common law approaches toward protecting the rights of the holder of an instrument. According to the Explanatory Note, the solution adopted was a "pragmatic two-tier system that distinguishes between a mere holder and a protected holder." Accordingly, in line with the civil law approach, under the Convention, a person in possession of an instrument is a holder of the instrument even if the instrument was obtained under circumstances, including incapacity or fraud, duress, or mistake of any kind.

---

[17] Ibid., Guest (2006), p. 1688.

[18] Ibid.

On the other hand, in introducing the concept of a "protected holder," the Convention adopts an approach similar in many respects to that adopted in the common-law-based systems. According to Article 29, a protected holder is the holder of an instrument who was in possession of a complete instrument; had no knowledge of any defect in the title of the transferor; the time limit for presentment of that instrument for payment had not expired, and did not obtain the instrument by fraud or theft. Significantly, the Convention omits any requirement that a protected holder has given value for the instrument. Moreover, every holder of an instrument is presumed to be a protected holder unless the contrary is proved.

14.2.3 New Developments: UNCITRAL's Draft Convention on International Cheques

It may also be noted that the 1988 Convention on International Bills of Exchange does not apply to international cheques. They are certainly bills of exchange and are covered by the domestic legal regimes established by the NIA 18881 and BEA 1882, and are nevertheless, subject of a separate project undertaken by UNCITRAL which is still in progress and has recently resulted in a Draft Convention on International Cheques.[19]

Under the draft convention, an international cheque is defined on the lines similar to an international bill of exchange. According to the draft Article 2, an international cheque will be treated as international one only if it contains, in the text thereof, the words "international cheque" (Convention of…). It further states that an international cheque is a written instrument, which contains an unconditional order whereby the drawer directs the drawee to pay a definite sum of money to the payee or to his order or to bearer; is drawn on a banker; (d) is dated; is signed by the drawer; shows that at least two of the following places are situated in different states. These places are: the place where the cheque is drawn; the place indicated next to the name or the signature of the drawer; the place indicated next to the name of the drawee; the place indicated next to the name of the payee; and the place of payment.

So far as the criterion of internationality is concerned, Article 2 states that the (draft) convention will apply without regard to whether the above-mentioned places indicated on an international cheque are situated in contracting states.

14.3 Collection Arrangements and ICC Uniform Rules for Collections (URC)

Sometimes, a bank or a third party is employed by the seller for collection of the payment in the buyer's country in order to minimize the risks associated with

[19]The text is available at https://uncitral.un.org/en/comm/sessions/15.

receiving payments abroad.[20] Under this arrangement, the third party is instructed by the seller to collect the payment at the buyer's place of residence. The collecting bank then presents the bill of exchange to the buyer/importer at his place of residence as advised by the remitting bank.

Since banking practices in regard to collection process are not uniform, the international chamber of commerce (ICC) has published a set of uniform rules, known as the ICC Uniform Rules for Collections (URC), ICC Publication No. 522. The URC is intended to aid bankers, buyers, and sellers in the collections process.[21] However, since the Uniform Rules merely codify *rules* of practice and are not legally binding, they need to be incorporated in the contracts to trigger their application.

14.4 Documentary Credit System: Letters of Credit

14.4.1 Nature and Characteristics

A "letter of credit" or "documentary credit" refers to an arrangement in which a banker, acting on behalf of its customer (the buyer), undertakes to pay the seller or the exporter against the presentation of the relevant documents. Further, payment to the seller by the bank may be direct; or by accepting and paying the bill of exchange drawn by the seller; or by authorizing another bank to pay.[22] The International Chamber of Commerce (ICC)—*the Uniform Customs and Practices for Documentary Credits* (UCP) defines a (an irrevocable) letter of credit as any arrangement whereby a "definite undertaking" is given by the issuing bank "to honour a complying presentation."[23] Where the contract of letter of credit so provides, the payment must be made on sight or on the date specified or "to accept a bill of exchange drawn by the beneficiary."[24] In other words, it is an undertaking by an issuing bank to the beneficiary that the provisions regarding payment contained in the credit, will be duly fulfilled provided that the documents comply with the terms and conditions of the credit. Article 15 of the UCP 600 states that where an issuing bank finds the presentation is complying, it must honor and where a confirming bank finds "that a presentation is complying, it must honour or negotiate and forward the documents to the issuing bank."

In comparison to a bill of exchange, the advantage with a letter of credit is that it promises a greater security to the seller/exporter.[25] As Cranston explains, in the case of a bill of exchange, by the time the buyer accepts the bill, the seller may

---

[20] See Schnitzer (2006), pp. 78–80; D'Arcy et al. (2000), pp. 161–65.

[21] Information is available at: https://iccwbo.org/. The URC can be purchased from the ICC.

[22] Cranston (2002), p. 385.

[23] See UCP 600, Article 2. The text is available for purchase from ICC: http://www.iccwbo.org. The text is reproduced in Bridge (2007), Appendix 7.

[24] For the definition of "honour," see UCP 600, s. 2.

[25] Carr (2005), p. 468.

have given up control of the goods. If the buyer then fails to accept the bill, the seller may be faced with considerable problems in correcting the situation. But the letter of credit considerably reduces the problem of uncertainty regarding payment as the seller receives payment from the banker as soon as he presents the relevant documents.[26] In view of this obvious advantage of the letter of credit over the bill of exchange that the former has become one of the most important method of making payment in international trade.[27]

Letters of credit are governed by the ICC-UCP, the latest version of which was published in 2007 as UCP 600.[28] As already noted (Chap. 2, Sect. 2.4.3), UCP is not a code of legally binding rules. Rather it codifies *rules* of practice which become binding only upon their incorporation into a contract of letter of credit. The UCP imposes a duty on both—the issuing and confirming banks to pay according to the provisions of the credit.[29]

14.4.2 Kinds of Letters of Credit

A letter of credit may be classified as the "revocable" and "irrevocable" letter of credit. However, UCP 600 does not recognize the former. Even under the previous version—UCP 500 a letter of credit was presumed to be an irrevocable one unless there is a clear indication that it is revocable.[30] The obligations promised by the issuing bank may take different forms depending on whether a credit is revocable or irrevocable. A revocable letter of credit, unlike an irrevocable credit, does not constitute a binding or definite undertaking by the issuing bank that the provisions of credit will be duly fulfilled.[31] In other words, a revocable credit can be canceled or amended by the issuing bank at any time and without notice to the beneficiary.[32]

Further, a credit may also be categorized as "confirmed or "unconfirmed." The categorization of a credit as confirmed or unconfirmed refers to the obligations of the advising bank to the beneficiary.[33] Once issued, the letters of credit become binding on the concerned bank. They can be neither amended nor canceled without the agreement of the beneficiary.[34]

---

[26]Ibid; Cranston (2002), p. 385.

[27]See D'arcy et al. (2010), p. 166; Kerr LJ in *RD Harbottle (Mercantile) Ltd v National Westminster Bank Ltd* [1978] QB 146; Donaldson LJ in *Intraco Ltd v Notis Shipping Corporation of Liberia: The Boja Tower* [1981] 2 Lloyd's Rep. 256.

[28]See at: http://www.iccwbo.org.

[29]Bridge (2007), p. 287.

[30]UCP 500, Article 6. See also Cranston (2002), p. 386.

[31]See Guest (2006), p. 1954; D'arcy et al. (2010), p. 194.

[32]UCP 500, Article 8.

[33]D'Arcy et al. (2010), ibid.

[34]Cranston (2002), p. 386; Moens and Peter (2006), pp. 304–05.

Here a brief reference may also be made of the "clean credits" or "open credits as opposed to documentary credits."[35] In a clean credit, a bank makes an unconditional offer to honor bills of exchange drawn on himself by the customer.[36]

14.4.3 Fundamental Principles

14.4.3.1 The Autonomy of the Credit

One of the most striking features of the letter of credit is that it is an autonomous or separate contract from the original contract between the seller and the buyer.[37] It contains an offer on the part of the issuing bank to pay the beneficiary once he presents all the relevant documents. As already indicated, it is a separate, binding agreement that may not be withdrawn when it is irrevocable. UCP, Article 5 states that "banks deal with documents and not with goods, services or performance…"

From the autonomous nature of the obligation undertaken by a banker, it follows that the obligation in a letter of credit is primary.[38] So long the relevant documents presented by a seller are conforming the payment, the seller cannot be denied payment on the ground that he has committed a breach of the terms of the underlying or original contract concluded between the seller and the buyer. Article 4(a) of the UCP 600 states that the obligations of the banks—whether the issuing, advising, or confirming bank—are separate from the respective obligations of the parties under the original, sale, or other contract on which the credit contract may be based and the undertaking of a bank under the credit is not subject to the conditions of the original contract between the parties.

14.4.3.2 Doctrine of "Strict Compliance"

A related principle in the context is the principle of strict compliance according to which when the relevant documents are presented by a beneficiary to the banks, acceptance of the document by the bank depends on whether or not the documents conform to the terms of the letter of credit.[39] The bank in question will accept the documents only when the documents are in strict conformity with the terms of the credit. According to Article 14(a) of the UCP 600, after the documents are presented, the banks—issuing bank or nominated bank or a confirming bank—must

---

[35] Guest (2006), p. 1953.

[36] See ibid.

[37] See UCP 600, Article 4(a). See also Bridge (2007), p. 296; Chuah (2009), pp. 534–35; Cranston (2002), p. 387; *Urquart Lindsay & Co. v Eastern Bank Ltd* [1922] 1 KB 318.

[38] Carr (2014), p. 442.

[39] See Chuah (2009), pp. 544–45; Cranston (2002), pp. 388. For requirements-related provisions, see UCP 600, Articles 19–28.

determine "on the basis of the documents alone, whether or not the documents appear on their face to constitute a complying presentation."[40] Even if the discrepancy is insignificant, the bank can rightly reject the documents.[41] However, Article 30 [Article 39, UCP 500] allows certain discrepancies in credit amount, quantity, and unit prices.

14.5 Stand-by Credit or Demand Guarantees

14.5.1 General

In a stand-by credit or demand guarantees, in contrast to a letter of credit, it is the buyer (beneficiary) who requires from the seller to provide guarantee to secure the performance of the obligation. In other words, they are intended to safeguard the buyer against non-performance by the seller.[42] As will be noted just below, demand guarantees or stand-by credits are the undertaking on the part of a bank to pay a beneficiary (the buyer in a sale contract), possibly on written demand or on presentation of a certificate by an independent third party or on submission of a court judgment.[43] Notably, like documentary credits, stand-by credits are treated as separate from the underlying or principal contract.[44]

14.5.2 1995 UNCITRAL Convention on Independent Guarantees and Stand-by Letters of Credit

Here mention may be made of the UN Convention on Independent Guarantees and Stand-by Letters of Credit which seeks to bring out uniformity in the laws and practice on international undertakings or guarantees. For the purpose of the Convention, an "international undertaking" is defined as:

> an independent commitment, known in international practice as an independent guarantee or as a stand-by letter of credit, given by a bank or other institution or person ("guarantor/issuer") to pay to the beneficiary a certain or determinable amount upon simple demand or upon demand accompanied by other documents, in conformity with the terms and any documentary conditions of the undertaking, indicating, or from which it is to be inferred, that payment is due because of a default in the performance of an obligation, or because of another

[40]See also *JH Rayner & Co. Ltd. v Hambro's Bank Ltd* [1943] KB 37; *Seconsar Far East Ltd v Bank Markazi Jomhouri Islami Iran* [1993] 3 WLR 756. However, the UCP rules themselves do not require that the compliance must be strict. See Bridge (2007), p. 277.

[41]*Seconsar Far East Ltd v Bank Markazi Jomhouri Islami Iran,* ibid.

[42]Cranston (2002), p. 390.

[43]Ibid.

[44]See below (Sect. 14.5.2); Bridge (2007), pp. 262–63; Cranston (2002), pp. 390–91.

contingency, or for money borrowed or advanced, or on account of any mature indebtedness undertaken by the principal/applicant or another person (Article 2(1)).

In determining the internationality of an undertaking, the Convention adopts the criterion of the location of the parties' places of business in different contracting states. Article 4 provides that an undertaking is international if the places of business of any two of the following persons are in different states: (a) guarantor/issuer, (b) beneficiary, (c) principal/applicant, (d) instructing party, and (e) confirmer.

Further, like a letter of credit, an undertaking is an autonomous or independent contract as the guarantor's obligation to the beneficiary is not dependent upon the existence or validity of any underlying or original contract, or upon any other undertaking or "any term or condition not appearing in the undertaking, or to any future, uncertain act or event except presentation of documents" (Article 3).

Regarding the applicability criteria, Article 1(1) specifies that the Convention will apply to an international undertaking only if the place at which the undertaking is issued is in a contracting state, or the rules of private international law lead to the application of the law of a contracting state, unless the undertaking excludes the application of the Convention. Further, Para 2 provides that the "Convention applies also to an international letter of credit not falling within Article 2 if it expressly states that it is subject to this Convention."

In respect of the rights and obligations of the beneficiary and the guarantee or issuer, a key rule is that they are determined by the terms and conditions set forth in the undertaking (Article 13). Further, in discharging its obligations under the undertaking, "the guarantor/issuer shall act in good faith and exercise reasonable care having due regard to generally accepted standards of international practice of independent guarantees or stand-by letters of credit" (Article 14(2)).

14.6 Other Export Financing Techniques

14.6.1 Factoring Contracts and 1988 UNIDROIT Convention on International Factoring

Sometimes, the banks or other financial companies purchase the debts of business companies at a discount and thus facilitates the financing of overseas transactions.[45] Under this type of arrangement, called factoring, the factor (the entity which offers such type of services) assumes control over the book-debts of its customer (the exporter) at a price and then collect the price from the buyer. In other words, the factoring company pays the exporter the price of goods and collects the price from

[45]See Guest (2006), pp. 2089–90; Chuah (2009), pp. 574–75; Cranston (2002), pp. 354–55; Goode (1995), pp. 800–19. Factoring facilities are also offered for the finance of the domestic commercial transactions. Guest, id., p. 2090.

the overseas buyers. In this way, the factor is also prepared to bear the risks of bad debts.

In order to standardize the laws governing international factoring contracts, the UNIDROIT in 1988 adopted the UNIDROIT Convention on International Factoring (the factoring Convention, also known as the "Ottawa Convention"). The Convention governs factoring contracts and assignments of the receivables and provide for a set of uniform rules "to facilitate international factoring, while maintaining a fair balance of interests between the different parties involved in factoring transactions."[46]

A "factoring contract" is defined by the Convention as a contract concluded between the supplier and the factor pursuant to which:

(a) the "supplier may or will assign to the factor receivables arising from contracts of sale of goods made between the supplier and its customers (debtors) other than those for the sale of goods bought primarily for their personal, family or household use;
(b) the factor is to perform at least two of the following functions

- finance for the supplier, including loans and advance payments;
- maintenance of accounts (ledgering) relating to the receivables;
- collection of receivables;
- protection against default in payment by debtors.

(c) notice of the assignment of the receivables is to be given to debtors (Article 1(2)).

According to Article 2 which deals with the scope of application, the Convention applies where the parties to a contract of sale of goods have their places of business in different states and those states and the state in which the factor has its place of business are contracting states; or both—the contract of sale and the factoring contract—are governed by the law of a contracting state. It may also be noted that the parties are free to exclude the application of the Factoring Convention. However, whenever the Convention is excluded by the parties to the contract of sale of goods, as regards receivables arising at or after the time when notice in writing of such exclusion must be given to the factor (Article 3).

So far as the rights and duties of the parties to a factoring contract are concerned, Article 7 provides that a factoring contract may validly provide between the parties thereto for the transfer of all or any of the supplier's rights deriving from the contract of sale of goods. Further, according to Article 8, a debtor is under an obligation to pay the factor. However, the debtor is obligated to do so "if, and only if, the debtor does not have knowledge of any other person's superior right to payment and notice in writing of the assignment:

(a) is given to the debtor by the supplier or by the factor with the supplier's authority;
(b) reasonably identifies the receivables which have been assigned and the factor to whom or for whose account the debtor is required to make payment; and
(c) relates to receivables arising under a contract of sale of goods made at or before the time the notice is given."

[46]Factoring Convention, Preamble.

14.6.2 *Forfaiting*

Finally, mention may be made of an important, modern technique of export financing, known as "forfaiting." Under this arrangement, the bankers or other financial institutions agree to collect payment under a negotiable instrument from the importer on a "non-recourse basis."[47] As pointed out by Dufey and Giddy, this technique was primarily evolved to finance the imports of capital goods by the state-owned enterprises mainly in socialist countries. Since the exporters from the industrialized countries are not generally willing to finance such transactions which are often very large also, the technique of forfaiting was evolved to address this problem. While factoring services are offered to finance small transactions, forfaiting is mostly used for large business transactions.

A forfaiting arrangement involves four parties: the exporter, the importer, the importer's bank, and the forfeiter (usually a bank in the exporter's country) which agrees to finance the transaction in question.[48] After the transaction is complete, a series of negotiable instruments are drawn by the exporter which are then accepted by the importer and backed or supported by the importer's bank. Thus, by indorsing the bill the importer's bank becomes liable to the exporter for the payment. The forfaiter purchases the negotiable instruments at a discount from the exporter without recourse. In this way, it bears the risks of obtaining payment from a bank in the importer's country without recourse to the exporter.[49] Obviously, this technique of export financing suits both the exporter and the importer. Not only importer benefits from the transaction, the exporter is also at the advantage. From the exporter's point of view, the risk of obtaining payment from a foreign enterprise is shifted to an entity which agrees to act as a forfeiter.

References

Bridge. (2007). *The international sale of goods*. Oxford: Oxford University Press.

Carr, I. (2005). *International trade law*. London, New York: Routledge-Cavendish.

Carr, I. (2014). *International trade law*. London, New York: Routledge-Cavendish.

Chuah, J. C. T. (2009). *Law of international trade: Cross-border commercial trade transactions*. London: Sweet &Maxwell, South Asian Edition, 2011.

Cranston, R. (2002). *Principles of banking law*. Oxford: Oxford University Press.

Dufey, G., & Giddy, I. H. (1981). Innovation in the international financial markets. *Journal of International Business Studies, 12*(2), 33–51.

D'Arcy, L., Murray, C., & Cleave, B., (Eds.). (2000). *Schmitthoff's export trade: The law and practice of international trade*. London: Stevens.

Goode, R. (1995). *Commercial law*. London: Penguin.

Guest, A. G. (Ed.). (2006). *Benjamin's sale of goods*. London: Sweet & Maxwell.

---

[47] See Chuah (2009), pp. 573–74; Schnitzer (2006), pp. 94–95; Dufey and Giddy (1981), pp. 37–38; Cranston (2002), pp. 382–84.

[48] Dufey and Giddy, id., p. 37.

[49] Id., pp. 37–38.

Moens, G., & Peter, G. (2006). *International trade & business: Law, policy and ethics*. Oxon: Routledge, Cavendish.
Schnitzer, S. (2006). *Understanding international trade law*. UK: Law Matters Publishing.

Online Resources

International Chamber of Commerce (ICC). http://www.iccwbo.org.
United Nations Commission on International Trade Law (UNCITRAL). http://www.uncitral.org.

Part VI
Trade Dispute Resolution

Chapter 15
International Cooperation in Dispute Settlement

15.1 General

For the parties to a cross-border, commercial transactions (who often trade from different parts of world and with conflicting legal systems) the issues of jurisdiction, the applicable law, and the enforcement of judgments, which relate to the private international law,[1] are a source of many difficulties. As already noted (see infra, Chap. 2, Sect. 2.3.1), in an international trade, the significance of these issues cannot be overstated and the need for the harmonization of the national laws concerning these aspects is widely recognized. In fact, unification of private international law rules offers an alternative to the unification of substantive laws and the difficulties caused by the presence of diverse national laws may be reduced to a considerable degree by unifying the private international law rules.

15.2 Jurisdiction in Private, Commercial Litigations

15.2.1 Traditional Principles

If any dispute arises between the parties to an international, commercial transaction issues related to jurisdiction, the applicable law and the recognition and enforcement of foreign judgments need to be settled. In this section an attempt is made to examine the different set of rules pertaining to jurisdiction which are the result of the harmonization of private international law rules by the European states. Attention will be paid, in particular, to the 2007 Lugarno Convention (OJ 1988 L 391/9), the 2001 Brussels I Regulation on Jurisdiction and the Recognition and Enforcement of Judgments in Civil and Commercial Matters (the Brussels I Regulation, OJ 2001 L

[1] As already noted in Chap. 2 (Sect. 2.3), private international law addresses the issues of jurisdiction, choice of law, and recognition of foreign judgments in cases in which a "foreign element" is involved.

A. Srivastava, *Modern Law of International Trade*, International Law and the Global South, https://doi.org/10.1007/978-981-15-5475-9_15

12/1) as updated by Regulation 1215/2012,[2] and the (Hague) Convention on Choice of Court Agreement.[3] But before we discuss these of harmonization a few words need to be stated about the general principles of jurisdiction.

In the present context, jurisdiction denotes a court's competence to hear actions and give decisions in matters submitted to it or in which it is called upon to do so.[4] Turning to the traditional principles of jurisdiction in respect of the actions in *personam* with which we are mainly concerned with in this book, some of the most important principles are as follows. First, the English courts have traditionally possessed a wide discretion in exercising jurisdiction. Secondly, under both the English common law and the Indian law the matter is simply a procedural one and a court can exercise jurisdiction if the defendant is served with the process or he voluntarily submits to the jurisdiction.[5] Under the "personal service" forum, an English court in a civil and commercial matter can automatically exercise jurisdiction where the defendant has been properly served with the process while he is present in England.[6] Thus, in common law countries it is simply the service of the process upon a defendant which confers jurisdiction upon a court. In fact, the issue of jurisdiction is treated as an issue concerning the procedural, private law[7] and the relevant question to be asked is: "Has the defendant been properly served?" If so, the court will have jurisdiction. If not, and the defendant does not submit to the jurisdiction voluntarily, the judgment rendered by the court will not be legally binding.[8]

A similar law is also applicable in India. Section 20 of the Code of Civil Procedure (CPC) 1908 provides:

> **20.**—Subject to the limitations aforesaid, every suit shall be instituted in a Court within the local limits of whose jurisdiction—
>
> (a) the defendant, or each of the defendants where there are more than one, at the time of the commencement of the suit, actually and voluntarily resides, or carries on business, or personally works for gain; or
>
> (b) any of the defendants, where there are more than one, at the time of the commencement of the suit, actually and voluntarily resides, or carries on business, or personally works for gain, provided that in such case either the leave of the Court is given, or the defendants who do not reside, or carry on business, or personally works for gain, as aforesaid, acquiesce in such institution; or
>
> (c) The cause of action, wholly or in part, arises.

Similarly, the courts also have wide discretionary in declining to exercise jurisdiction or staying the proceedings. A court, in the first place, can stay a proceeding

---

[2]The texts can be accessed from www.europa.eu.int.

[3]Adopted on June 30, 2005. For the text, see 44 ILM 1294, also available at the official website of the Hague Conference on Private International Law (HCCH): http://www.hcch.net.

[4]Diwan and Diwan (1998), p. 182; Fawcett and Carruthers (eds.) (2008), p. 199.

[5]Fawcett and Carruthers, id., p. 353.

[6]Verheul (1986), p. 413; Fawcett and Carruthers, ibid.

[7]Fawcett and Carruthers, id., p. 202.

[8]de Vries (1969), pp. 246–50.

"whenever it is necessary to prevent injustice" and secondly, where, subject to a relevant international convention, England is not an appropriate forum.[9] Therefore, before an English court the defendant, if properly served with a process, may apply for a stay of proceedings on the ground that a foreign court is a more appropriate than the English court in adjudicating the dispute.[10] The principle involved here is known as the *forum non conveniens*.

15.2.2 Lugano Convention

The 2007 Lugano Convention, which has replaced the old 1988 Convention, is not of much practical significance for two main reasons. First, the EU member states have a separate set of uniform rules contained in 2001 Brussels I Regulation on the same subject. Therefore, the new Lugano Convention practically applies only to three countries—Iceland, Norway, and Switzerland belonging to the European Free Trade Association (EFTA).[11] As far as the EU countries are concerned, the Lugano Convention will apply only when the defendant is domiciled in any of the three EFTA states or the Convention otherwise confers jurisdiction on the courts of these states. Secondly, the Lugano Convention is drawn on the lines similar or identical to the Brussels I Regulation.

Since there are no important differences between the Lugano Convention and the Brussels I Regulation from the point of view of international trade, we now turn our attention to the key provisions of the latter.

15.2.3 EC Regulations on Jurisdiction and the Recognition and Enforcement of Judgments in Civil and Commercial Matters (The Brussels I Regulation and Regulation 1215/2012)

The issues concerning jurisdiction and enforcement of judgments in civil and commercial matters were, untill recently, were governed by the 2001 Brussels I Regulation which modified and updated the earlier 1968 Brussels Convention on Jurisdiction and the Enforcement of Judgments in Civil and Commercial Matters. It entered into force in March 2002 and applied to all member states of the European Union except Denmark.[12] The Brussels I Regulation, however, is now updated and replaced by the Regulation 1215/2012. Broadly, both regualtions, namely the

[9]See Collins (ed.) (2006), pp. 461–63.

[10]See ibid.

[11]See Fawcett and Carruthers (eds.) (2008), pp. 342–43.

[12]See id., p. 204.

Brussels I Regulation and Regulation 1215/2012 applies to "civil and commercial" matters which definitely cover international trade transactions (Article 1). Definition of "civil and commercial matters" is neither provided by the Brussels Regulation I nor by the new Regulation. However, they clarify that the expression does not cover revenue, customs, and administrative matters.[13] Certain matters are specifically excluded from the scope of the both regulations.[14] Some of these matters include: the status or capacity of natural persons, rights in property arising out of a matrimonial relationship, wills and succession; bankruptcy, proceedings related to the winding up of insolvent companies; social security; and arbitration. Further, the Regulation applies to all courts and tribunals irrespective of their nature provided that the matter falls within the scope of the expression, "civil and commercial" matters.

So far as the basis of jurisdiction is concerned, it is generally required that the defendant must be domiciled in the member state. Only a defendant domiciled in a member state is subject to the jurisdiction of the courts of that member state (Article 2, Brussels I Regulation; Article 4, Regulation 1215/2012). Here, nationality of the person to be sued is not important.[15] However, an exception is provided there in both regulations. Articles 4 of Brussels I Regulation provides that if the defendant is not domiciled in a member state, the jurisdiction of the courts shall, subject to the provisions of Articles 22 and 23, be determined by the law of the relevant member state.[16]

15.2.4 (Hague) Convention on Choice of Court Agreement

The 2005 Hague Convention on Choice of Court Agreements (Choice of Court Convention) was adopted in providing to the parties of a trade dispute "an equal and viable alternative" to arbitration and is understood as laying down a parallel regime to the 1958 New York Convention on the Recognition and Enforcement of Foreign Arbitral Awards (the New York Convention) as discussed below.[17]

The purpose of the Choice of Court Convention is to enable the parties to the international commercial contracts to designate the courts of a contracting state as the "exclusive" courts to decide a dispute concerning such contracts. In other words, the courts of a contracting state designated by a choice of court agreement will have jurisdiction to decide the dispute arising between the parties to such an agreement (Article 5). Further, a court in a contracting state other than the court

---

[13]Brussels I Regulation, Article 1(1); Regulation 1215/2012, Article 1(1).

[14]Brussels I Regulation, Article 1(2); Regulation 1215/2012, Article 1(2).

[15]For the position under the Brussels I Regulation, see further, Fawcett and Carruthers (eds.), id., pp. 222–24; Schnitzer, id., p. 185; Carr (2014), pp. 487–88.

[16]Brussels I Regulation, Article 4(1); Regulation 1215/2012, Article 6(1).

[17]See Kruger (2006), pp. 447–455; Teitz (2005), pp. 543–558. Text of the Convention can be accessed from the official website of the Hague Conference on Private International Law (HCCH): hcch.net.

chosen by the parties is required to stay the related proceedings unless one of the following circumstances exist: (a) the agreement is void under the law of the state of the relevant court; or (b) a party lacked the legal capacity to conclude the choice of law agreement under the law of the state of the court; or (c) giving effect to such an agreement would result in manifest injustice or would be contrary to the public policy; or (d) for some exceptional reasons beyond the control of the parties, the agreement in question cannot be reasonably be performed; or (e) the chosen court has declined to exercise the jurisdiction (Article 6).

15.3 Choice of Law

15.3.1 General

In the context of an international commercial contract, the next issue that arises relates to the determination of the applicable law. Differently put, the question that assumes significance in the context is: which set of legal rules should govern the transaction in question? This leads us to the work on the harmonization of domestic laws in regard to the choice of law. The need for arriving at a set of uniform rules on the choice of law arises because the domestic laws on the subject are often conflicting and it is very likely that the question of the applicable law, like the question of jurisdiction, remains unpredictable until it is determined by the court.

As already noted in Chap. 2 (Sect. 2.1), where, on the basis of the choice of law rules, the parties to an international contract agree to elect a particular country's law, for example, the law of the seller's country, as the *law* applicable to their contract, the contract is governed by the law of that country. For this purpose, the parties normally insert a "choice of law clause" in their contract.[18] Where no such choice is made, the "applicable law" is ascertained on the basis of the private international law rules of the forum called the *lex fori.*[19]

But ascertaining the applicable law in the absence of the choice of law clause is a complex issue in view of the presence of a number of connecting factors.[20] And even if the applicable is ascertained in this way, the problem continues to arise because it is not unlikely that the parties are not familiar with the law so ascertained. In order to obtain a solution to this problem, states have preferred the approach of assimilating the (private international laws) laws of the countries belonging to a common group or having common commercial interests. For example, member states of the EU have

[18] A "choice of law" clause refers to an agreement that is normally contained in a contract of sale or service which makes the contract subject to the chosen law. On the "choice of law" clause and the issues pertaining to determination of the validity of the clause, see Symeonides (2013), pp. 888–91. See also Hayard (2006), p. 1; Becker (1989), p. 167.

[19] Opposed to the *lex fori* is the *lex causae.* The later expression refers to the law which governs the issue that has arisen. See Collins (ed.) (2006), pp. 33–34.

[20] See Fawcett and Carruthers (eds.) (2008), pp. 665–66.

adopted a number of uniform law instruments in all key areas. Of particular relevance are the international conventions laying down uniform rules in respect of jurisdiction, enforcement of judgments, and the choice of law issues to be applicable to international commercial transactions. As far as the issue of choice of law is concerned, two conventions are particularly notable: the 1980 Rome Convention on Contractual obligations and the 2008 Rome I Regulation (cited below). These conventions are intended to promote the principle of "party autonomy," a brief discussion of which is now in order.[21]

15.3.2 Rule of Party Autonomy[22]

15.3.2.1 Position in Common Law

According to the principle of "party autonomy" the parties to a contract have the freedom to choose the jurisdiction as well as the law.[23] In other words, the parties to a commercial contract can themselves determine which law is to govern their transaction and the court of which country shall have the jurisdiction.[24] Where parties to a contract express their preference for a particular country's law as the applicable law, the law so chosen becomes the "applicable law" or the "proper law of contract."[25] The effect of the applicable law is to replace the law that would otherwise have governed the contract.[26] The principle is intended to respect the free will of the parties which is the basis of the law of contract.[27] Choice of law may be expressed or implied.

---

[21] Also referred to as the doctrine of the "proper law of contract," especially in the judicial decisions of the courts of the common law countries, "party autonomy" is the basic principle of the law of international contracts and is accepted in most countries. See Verhagen (2002), p. 135.

[22] On the principle of "party autonomy," see Mann (1950), pp. 60–73; Verhagen (2002), pp. 135–54; Yntema (1952) 341–58, 350–52; de Szászy (1934), pp. 156–77; Baxter (1982), pp. 538–62; Atrill (2004), pp. 549–77; Fawcett and Carruthers (eds.) (2008), p. 690.

[23] See *Commentary to the Principles on Choice of Law in International Commercial Contract* (2015). The Hague Conference on Private International Law (p. 23), the text is available at: http://www.hcch.net; The 1980 Rome Convention on the Law Applicable to Contractual Obligations (the Rome Convention), [1980] OJ L266, Article 1(1). The 1980 Rome Convention is now replaced by the Rome I Regulation, Regulation No 593/2008, OJ 2008. In relation to jurisdiction, it is the Brussels I Regulation (discussed below) that incorporates the party autonomy principle.

[24] "Choice of law" and "choice of forum" clauses in international contracts are distinguishable from each other. The former determines the law (s) applicable to the contract whereas the latter determines the court or tribunal by which the contract is to be adjudicated. The jurisdiction or forum clauses are included in international contracts to avoid the uncertainty regarding jurisdiction much the same way a choice of law clause is inserted to do away the uncertainty regarding the law. See generally Becker (1989), pp. 167–75.

[25] See Mann (1950), supra note 22.

[26] Similar issue of the applicable law also arises in relation to tort, marriages, etc.

[27] See Jacobson (1954), p. 665.

The rule of party autonomy dates back to the fifteenth and sixteenth centuries[28] and has been used in international contracts to avoid "a court selection of a "proper" legal system."[29] It is accepted in most jurisdictions including the common and civil-law-based countries[30] and except in certain jurisdictions, the rule appears firmly established in civil law countries.[31] Further, the rule is accepted in all the Member States of the European Union.[32]

15.3.2.2 Rome Convention and EC Regulation on the Law Applicable to Contractual Obligations

The 1980 (EEC) Convention on the Law Applicable to Contractual Obligations (the Rome Convention) and the Regulation (EC) No. 593/2008 of June 17, 2008 on the Law Applicable to Contractual Obligations (the Rome I Regulation) adopted to create a uniform choice of law framework for the member states of the EU (earlier, the European Economic Community (EEC)) expressly recognizes the party autonomy rule.[33]

Where parties to a contract have expressed their choice, the contract, according to Article 3(1) of the Rome Convention, shall be governed by the law so determined by the parties. But where no such choice is expressed, a court can infer a choice if it is "demonstrated with reasonable certainty" either by the terms of the contract or the circumstances of the case. The rule is retained by the Regulation (EC) No. 593/2008 of June 17, 2008 on the Law Applicable to Contractual Obligations (the Rome I Regulation) which has now modified the Rome Convention. Here certain important changes in regard to the inferred choice of law introduced by the Rome I Regulation are noticeable.[34] It provides that such a choice must be "clearly demonstrated" instead of "demonstrated with reasonable certainty." Further, the Regulation provides for a rule of presumption in this regard. Where there is an agreement between the parties to confer on courts of a member state exclusive jurisdiction to determine disputes, this should be taken as "one of the factors to be taken into account in determining whether or not a choice has been clearly demonstrated."[35] This clearly shows that conferring on courts of a member state exclusive jurisdiction does not necessarily

---

[28]Baxter (1982), p. 541.

[29]Ibid.

[30]Verhagen (2002) supra note 22; Jacobson (1954), p. 665; Yntema (1952), p. 345.

[31]Yntema, id., pp. 350–52. See Symeonides (2013), p. 876.

[32]Fawcett and Carruthers (ed.) (2008), p. 690.

[33]See the Rome Convention, Article 3 (1) ("a contract shall be governed by the law chosen by the parties.").

[34]It may be noted that the Rome I Regulation seeks to clarify certain provisions of the Rome Convention and makes improvement over the latter in certain important respects. It was made part of the English law following entry into force of the Law Applicable to Contractual Obligations (England and Wales and Northern Ireland) Regulations 2009 on December 17, 2009.

[35]Rome I Regulation, Recital 12 of the Preamble ("An agreement between the parties to confer on one or more courts or tribunals of a Member State exclusive jurisdiction to determine disputes

mean that the law of the country of the court or tribunal is impliedly chosen as the "applicable law."

15.3.2.3 The "Closest Connection" Rule and Limitations of the Party Autonomy Rule

Further, where no such express choice has been made nor a choice can be inferred, the applicable law is determined on the basis of Article 4 of the Rome Convention, according to which, the applicable law shall be the law of a *country* with which the contract in question is most closely connected.[36] Here an important difference between the common law rule of party autonomy and the rule embodied in the Rome Convention is noticeable. Under the former, the applicable law is the law or legal system with which the contract is most closely connected, whereas under the Convention it is instead the law of the *country* with which the contract is most closely related.

It may be noted that the law so determined, according to the Rome Convention, can also replace certain mandatory rules of the forum.[37] But it cannot be applied if incompatible with public order[38]; consumer contracts[39]; and employment contracts.[40] However, in the case of a domestic contract,[41] the law so chosen cannot affect the applicability of any mandatory rule of the country with which the contract is objectively connected.[42] It may further be noted that the Rome Convention has "universal" application in the sense that it applies to all contracts whether or not having connection with an EU member state.[43] In other words, it is not required that either party to a contract be domiciled in a contracting state. What is required is that the court of a contracting state is seized with a dispute involving a "choice of

---

under the contract should be one of the factors to be taken into account in determining whether a choice of law has been clearly demonstrated.").

[36]Id., Article 4(1) ("To the extent that the law applicable to the contract has not been chosen in accordance with Article 3, the contract shall be governed by the law of the *country* with which it is most closely connected.") Emphasis added. This position may be contrasted with the doctrine of the proper law of contract in the common law countries including England and India. Under the traditional proper law of contract theory, a contract is governed by its proper law, i.e., the *law* (not the law of the country) by reference to which it was made or with which is most closely related. One implication of this rule is that it rules out the applicability of non-state law or law contained in international conventions or model laws. However, the Rome I Regulation allows the parties to a contract to select non-state law provided that it fulfils the requirement of certainty. Rome I Regulation, id, Recital 12.

[37]Rome I Regulation, Article 3(2).

[38]Id., Article 16.

[39]Id., Article 5.

[40]Id., Article 6.

[41]The "choice of law" issue is raised in an otherwise domestic contract where parties to such a contract agree to choose a foreign law as the law applicable to their contract.

[42]Id., Article 3(3).

[43]Fawcett and Carruthers (ed.) (2008), p. 677.

law" situation. The Rome I Regulation adopts a similar approach. Article 2 of the Regulation provides that "[a]ny law specified by [the] Regulation shall be applied whether or not it is the law of a Member State."[44]

15.3.2.4 Contracts (Applicable Law) Act 1990 and Law Applicable to Contractual Obligations (England and Wales and Northern Ireland) Regulations 2009

In England, the party autonomy rule, which had traditionally been part of the common law, was given statutory recognition by the Contracts (Applicable Law) Act 1990 implementing the 1980 EEC Convention which is now modified by the Law Applicable to Contractual Obligations (England and Wales and Northern Ireland) Regulations 2009. According to the Act of 1990, the applicable law is determined by reference to the provisions of Articles 3 and 4 of the Rome Convention referred to above. Under the traditional rule of the "proper law of contract," parties to a contract have the freedom to choose their law provided that the intention expressed is bonafide, legal and not opposed to the public policy.[45] The Rome Convention retained the rule that a contract is to be governed by the law chosen by the parties provided that the choice is expressed or "demonstrated with reasonable certainty by the terms of the contract or the circumstances of the case."[46] As stated above, in the absence of any such choice the applicable law is to be ascertained by reference to the law of the *country* with which the contract has the closest connection.

15.3.2.5 Position in India

In India, unlike England, no statute except the Arbitration and Conciliation Act, 1996 (discussed below) which is also applied to international commercial arbitrations,[47]

---

[44]In the context of jurisdiction, Brussels I Regulation, Article 23 succinctly recognizes the party autonomy rule. It, inter alia, provides that where the parties to a contract, one or more of whom is domiciled in a Member State of the European Union, have agreed that a court of a Member State is to have jurisdiction to settle any disputes which have arisen or which may arise in connection with a particular legal relationship, that court shall have jurisdiction.

[45]See, in particular, *Vita Food Products Inc v Unus Shipping Co. Ltd.* [1939] AC 277 (As per Lord Wright, "[W]here there is an express statement by the parties of their intention select the law of the contract, it is difficult to see what qualifications possible, provided the intention expressed is bona fide and provided there is no reason for avoiding the choice on the public policy." Id., p. 277. See also *Spurrier v La Cloche* [1902] AC 446 p. 450; *R v International Trustee* [1937] AC 500, p. 529; *Hamlyn & Co. v Talisker Distillery* [1894] AC 202 p. 208. On this principle, see Fawcett and Carruthers (ed.) (2008), pp. 666–67.

[46]Rome Convention, Article 3(1). But see Rome I Regulation which now requires that such a choice must be "clearly demonstrated." It may also be noted that according to Article 3(1), the parties can choose different laws to govern different parts of the contract. This provision explicitly recognizes "depecage" which allows severance of a contract between different laws.

[47]Arbitration and Conciliation Act, 1996, s. 28(6)(i).

expressly recognizes the party autonomy or the proper law of contract rule. But there is the long line of judicial authorities clearly supporting the principle that the parties to an international contract have freedom to decide which law will govern their contract.[48] It seems that in the absence of the statutory recognition the rule is applicable to this country as part of the common law doctrine of the proper law of the contract. In *National Thermal Power Corporation v Singer* the Supreme Court expressed the view that "The parties have the freedom to choose the law governing an international commercial arbitration agreement...." "...where the proper law of the contract is expressly chosen by the parties, as in the present case, such law must, in the absence of an unmistakable intention to the contrary, govern the arbitration agreement which, though collateral or ancillary to the main contract, is nevertheless a part of such contract."

But application of the rules evolved to deal with the choice of law problem is beset with difficulties. The principle of party autonomy is not a universally accepted rule and where parties to a contract have the freedom to choose the law they may, out of ignorance or for the reason that they cannot agree on the choice of a particular country's law as the applicable law or for some other reason, omit to insert a choice of law clause. As stated above, in the absence of a choice of law clause in the contract, the applicable law is determined on the basis of the private international law rules of the forum. But these (choice of law) rules differ from country to country and in certain cases, the difference is so substantial to affect the outcome of the case.[49] For example, there does exist a great deal of difference between the common law and the civil law countries in respects of contracts, marriage, and succession to moveable or immovable property.[50] Even among the countries of similar legal background, significant differences are noticeable in certain respects.

[48]See, in particular, *Modi Entertainment Network v WSG Cricket Pvt. Ltd.* AIR 2003 SC 1177 ("Normally, the court will give effect to the intention of the parties as expressed in the agreement entered into by them except when strong reasons justify disregard of the contractual obligations of the parties.") Ibid.; *National Thermal Power Corporation v Singer*, AIR 1993 SC 998; *Konkan Railway Corpn. Ltd. & Ors. v. Mehul Construction Co.* (2000) 7 SCC 201 (even where the arbitration is held in India, the parties to the contract would be free to designate the law applicable to the substance of the dispute) Ibid.; *Shin-Estu Chemical Company Limited v M/s. Akash Optifibre Limited and Another, AIR 2005 SC 3766*; *Dhanrajmal Govindram v Shamji Kalidas* AIR 1961 SC 1285 ("Where the parties have expressed themselves, the intention so expressed overrides any presumption. Where there is no expressed intention, then the rule to apply is to infer the intention from the terms and nature of the contract and from the general circumstances of the case.") Ibid.

[49]See supra, Chap. 2, Sect. 2.3.1.

[50] Fawcett and Carruthers (eds.) (2008), pp. 11–12.

15.3.3 Hague Principles on Choice of Law for International Commercial Contracts

As already noted (Chap. 8, Sect. 8.2), the 2015 Hague Principles on Choice of Law for International Commercial Contracts ("Hague Principles") were adopted to promote the principle of party autonomy in countries where the principle is not yet firmly established. Since these Principles have already been discussed in Chap. 8 in some detail, no further discussion is required here.

15.4 Enforcement of Foreign Judgments and Arbitral Awards

15.4.1 Enforcement of Foreign Judgments

15.4.1.1 Principles of "Comity" and Obligation

In common law countries, it has long been established that the judgment of a competent, foreign court can be enforced provided that certain conditions are met.[51] Traditionally, such judgments were enforceable on the basis of the principle of comity. The term, "comity" is generally used in the sense of courtesy and also as a synonym for public international law or the respect for the territorial jurisdiction of other states.[52]

But recently the courts in England have adopted a new doctrine, known as the doctrine of obligation. According to this doctrine, the judgment of a court of competent jurisdiction imposes a duty on the defendant/debtor to pay which the courts are under the obligation to enforce.[53]

15.4.1.2 EU Regulation 1215/2012 and Brussels I Regulation

EU Regulation 1215/2012, like the Brussels I Regulation, seeks to establish a uniform law regime on recognition and enforcement of foreign judgments in civil and commercial matters for the member states of European Union and simplifies the procedural requirements of the common law rules in this respect. Article 33 of Brussels I Regulation [Article 36 of Regulation 1215/2012 provides that a judgment in a member state shall be recognized in the other member states without any requirement of special procedure. Similarly, a judgment given in a member state is automatically enforceable

---

[51] For a discussion of these conditions, see Fawcett and Carruthers (eds.), id., Chap. 15.

[52] Fawcett and Carruthers (eds.), id., pp. 514–15; Collins (2006), pp. 5–6.

[53] See Fawcett and Carruthers (eds.), ibid.

in other member states on the fulfillment of certain formal or procedural requirements (Article 38 of Brussels I Regulation; Article 39 of Regulation 1215/2012).

Significantly, in order to achieve the objective of the free movement of judgments, both regulations introduce a number of important changes in the traditional common law rules on the subject. The effect of these changes is to considerably reduce the formal requirements regarding recognition and enforcement of judgments. As noted in *Chesire, North and Fawcett Private International Law*, the changes introduced by the Brussels I Regulation are: first, the recognition of judgments is "automatic," that is to say, in recognizing judgments, unlike common law, no special procedure is required; secondly, enforcement of judgment is largely a procedural matter and "follows on from recognition;" and finally, the defences available under the Regulation are limited.[54] The recognition and enforcement of judgments is dealt with by Chapter III (Articles 32–56) of the Brussels I Regulation and Chapter III (Articles 36–57) of Regulation 1215/2012 which only apply to the international recognition and enforcement of judgments.

In respect of the enforcement of judgments also, the Brussels I Regulation establishes a similar, efficient, and simplified procedure and the declaration of enforceability is practically automatic.[55] Article 38 of the Brussels I Regulation provides:

> A judgment given in a Member State and enforceable in that State shall be enforced in another Member State when, on the application of any interested a party, it has been declared enforceable there.

Where a declaration of enforceability is granted the defendant is notified and he has the right to appeal. Similarly, where such a declaration is refused, the applicant may also appeal against the declaration.

Defences

The Brussels I Regulation (Articles 34 and 35) also provides for certain defences to be taken by the defendant against recognition and enforcement of judgments. Defences available under Article 34 are: (1) public policy; (2) natural justice; (3) irreconcilability with a judgment in respect of the same parties given in the member state in which the declaration of recognition is sought; and (4) irreconcilability with an earlier judgment given in another member state or in third state having the same cause of action and between the same parties. Additionally, Article 35 provides for defences applicable in two situations. First, where a judgment conflicts with the jurisdictional provisions related to insurance and consumer contracts, and exclusive jurisdiction. Secondly, where the judgment conflicts with the duty of a member state vis-á-vis a non-member state to not recognize judgments given against the residents of that state (these provisions are similar to those contained in Articles 45 and 46 of Regulation 1215/ 2012).[56]

---

[54] Id., pp. 596–97. These observations also apply in respect of the new Regulation.

[55] Id., p. 607. Fawcett and Carruthers (eds.), ibid.

[56] Under Article 59 of the Regulation, a contracting state can enter into an agreement with a non-Ccntracting state under which the former agrees to not recognize "exorbitant" judgments rendered

15.4.1.3 Lugano Convention

The Convention applies to the European Union member states and the EFTA countries. As already stated, the 2007 Lugano Convention is closely based on the Brussels I Regulation, and in matters of recognition and enforcement of foreign judgments also it closely follows the Regulation. However, there are also certain differences between the two. One of the most important differences is that under the Lugano Convention an additional defence is given to the defendant. A Court has the discretion to refuse to recognize or enforce a judgment where the ground of jurisdiction on which the judgment is based "differs from that resulting from this (Lugano) Convention."[57]

15.4.1.4 The HCCH "Judgments Project"

In the early 1990s, the HCCH began work (Judgments Project) on the harmonization or unification of the private international law rules in two key areas: the international jurisdiction of courts; and the recognition and enforcement of foreign judgments.[58] This resulted in landmark conventions, namely the 2005 Convention on the *Choice of Court Agreements* and the 2019 Convention on the Recognition and Enforcement of Foreign Judgments in Civil or Commercial Matters. While the 2005 Convention has already been discussed in the context of the convention-based regime on international jurisdiction of courts the latter—2019 Convention—will be discussed just below. The 2019 Judgment Convention establishes a general legal regime on recognition and enforcement of foreign judgments and recognizes a wider set of bases for enforcement of foreign judgments among contracting states.

15.4.1.5 2019 Convention on the Recognition and Enforcement of Foreign Judgments

On July 2, 2019, the HCCH adopted the landmark Convention on the Recognition and Enforcement of Foreign Judgments in Civil or Commercial Matters[59] with a view to providing "greater predictability and certainty in relation to the global circulation of foreign judgments." The 2019 Convention is intended to complement the regime on the choice of court established by the 2005 Convention on Choice of Court Agreements (see supra).

---

against persons domiciled or resident in the latter. For further discussion, see id, pp. 610–27; Collins (ed.) (2006), pp. 661–67.

[57] For further discussion, see Fawcett and Carruthers (eds.) (2008), pp. 639–40.

[58] The information is available at the official website of HCCH: https://www.hcch.net.

[59] Adopted on July 2, 2019, not yet in force. The text is available at https://www.hcch.net/en/instruments/conventions. The Convention does not apply to arbitration and related proceedings (Article 2(3)).

According to Article 1 (scope of Convention) the Convention shall apply to the recognition and enforcement of judgments in civil or commercial matters. The expression does not cover revenue, customs, or administrative matters. In addition, certain matters are expressly excluded from the purview of the Convention (Article 2). These matters include but are not limited to: the status and legal capacity; maintenance obligations and other family law matters; wills and succession; insolvency, composition, the carriage of passengers and goods; transboundary marine pollution, liability for nuclear damage; defamation; privacy; intellectual property; activities of armed forces, including the activities of their personnel in the exercise of their official duties; law enforcement activities, including the activities of law enforcement personnel in the exercise of their official duties; and anti-trust (competition) matters.

Under this Convention, the judgment rendered in one contracting state subject to certain conditions can be recognized and enforced in the court of another contracting state. According to Article 4, which contains the general principles of recognition and enforcement of foreign judgments, "a judgment given by a court of a Contracting State (State of origin) shall be recognized and enforced in another Contracting State (requested State)" provided that necessary conditions are met (Para 1). A fundamental feature of the Convention is that, like the Brussels I Regulation and Regulation 1215/2012 (discussed above), it departs from the discretion-based approach of the common law in respect of the jurisdiction, recognition, or enforcement of foreign judgments. Significantly, enforcement of a judgment may be refused only on the grounds specified in the Convention. Article 4 further states that there shall be no review of the merits of the judgment in the requested State (Para 2); and a judgment shall be recognized only if it has effect in the State of origin, and shall be enforced only if it is enforceable in the State of origin (Para 3).

Further, conditions required to be fulfilled before a foreign judgment is treated eligible for recognition and enforcement are set out in Article 5. Some of the most important bases or conditions for the purpose are the habitual residence or the location of the principal place of business in the State of origin of the person against whom enforcement is sought.

15.4.1.6 Enforcement of Foreign Judgments Under the UK and Indian Law

Position under English Law

A foreign judgment cannot be directly enforced at common law.[60] The party wishing to enforce a foreign judgment has to bring a civil action on the judgment. Notably, the common law establishes a simplified procedure in this regard and recognizes only a limited number of defences.[61] Since a detailed discussion of the common law rules will be outside the scope of this book, only a few fundamental points may be

[60] Collins (ed.) (2006), pp. 570.

[61] For further discussion, see Collins, ibid.

made here. First, a foreign judgment involving a right in *personam* can be enforced only when the relevant foreign court had jurisdiction according to the English law. Secondly, for the purpose of deciding the question whether or not a foreign court had jurisdiction, the presence of the defendant is the sufficient basis of jurisdiction.[62]

Turning to the statutory regime for enforcement of foreign judgment, it may be stated that it is based on a multiple statutes. These are: the Civil Jurisdiction and Judgments Act, 1982; the Foreign Judgments (Reciprocal Enforcement) Act 1933. Further, while the regime establishes a more direct and simplified procedure, at the same time, it has "limited geographical application." It mainly applies to certain European countries and the countries of the Commonwealth.[63]

Under the Foreign Judgments (Reciprocal Enforcement) Act 1933, a foreign judgment of particular countries can be introduced in England on the basis of reciprocity.[64] Under the Act the registration of judgments of courts of (foreign) countries to which it applies may be made within a period of six months.

Position in India

The legal position in India is similar in many respects to the position at common law. Here a few rules which are also to be found in English common law may be stated. First, a foreign judgment involving a right in *personam* cannot be enforced when the relevant foreign court had no jurisdiction to decide the case. Secondly, as provided by Section 13 of the Code of Civil Procedure (CPC), a foreign judgment is conclusive if: (a) it is pronounced by a court of competent jurisdiction (b) has been given on the merits of the case; (c) it is not based on an incorrect view of international law or a refusal to recognize the law of India in cases in which such law is applicable; (d) the proceedings in which the judgment was obtained are not opposed to natural justice; (e) it has not been obtained by fraud; and (f) it does not sustain a claim founded on a breach of any law in force in India. Thirdly, a foreign judgment cannot be enforced if it does not determine the matter at issue conclusively. And finally, a foreign judgment is not subject to review.[65]

15.4.2 Enforcement of Foreign Arbitral Awards

15.4.2.1 General

[62] See Collins, id., pp. 591–92.

[63] Id., p. 573. For a list of the countries to which the regime applies, see Collins (ed.), id, pp. 571–72; Fawcett and Carruthers, id., p. 587.

[64] See Collins (ed.) ibid.; Fawcett and Carruthers (eds.) (2008), pp. 578–86; Schnitzer (2006), p. 196.

[65] See Diwan and Diwan (1998), p. 617.

Like a judgment, an arbitral award made in a foreign country may also be enforced at the domestic law. The question of the recognition and enforcement of the award is mainly governed by the principles similar to those which govern a foreign judgment.[66] In England, such an award may be enforced at common law as well as under the statutory law. However, with the enactment of the statutes on the subject, the significance of the traditional principles related to the enforcement of foreign awards has declined. Significantly, in 1958, the New York Convention on the Recognition and Enforcement of Foreign Arbitral Awards[67] was adopted to modernize and harmonize the rules and procedures for recognition and enforcement of foreign awards under the domestic laws.[68] The statutory laws on the recognition and enforcement of foreign arbitral awards in India and UK are based on the provisions of the Convention.

15.4.2.2 1958 New York Convention on the Recognition and Enforcement of Foreign Arbitral Awards

The Convention applies to a foreign or non-domestic[69] award. Article I states that "the Convention shall apply to the recognition and enforcement of arbitral awards made in any State other than the State in which recognition and enforcement is sought." For example, where an arbitral award is made outside India, it is treated as binding and enforceable in this country provided that it meet the requirements of the Convention or the Chapter II of the Act of 1996. Thus, the scope of the Convention is considerably wide as the award made in any state—not just a state which is party to the Convention—is covered.

Under the Convention, it is a "central obligation of the Parties to recognize all arbitral awards within the scheme as binding and enforce them…" Further, the Convention is based on this fundamental principle that foreign arbitral awards will not be discriminated against the domestic awards. Therefore, it obliges states parties to ensure that such awards are recognized and generally capable of enforcement in their jurisdiction in the same way as domestic awards. Article III provides:

---

[66] See Fawcett and Carruthers (eds.) (2008), pp. 651–52.

[67] Entry into force: June 7, 1959. Currently 161 states including India are parties. The text of the Final Act of the United Nations Conference on International Commercial Arbitration, New York, May 20 to June 10, 1958 embodying the text of the Convention is available at: http://www.uncitral.org.

[68] See Objectives of the Convention, ibid. (The Convention seeks "to provide common legislative standards for the recognition of arbitration agreements and court recognition and enforcement of foreign and nondomestic arbitral awards"). See also the Excerpts from the Final Act of the United Nations Conference on International Commercial Arbitration, New York, May 20 to June 10, 1958 ("5. It considers that greater uniformity of national laws on arbitration would further the effectiveness of arbitration in the settlement of private law disputes …") ibid. The text is available at http://www.uncitral.org.

[69] The term "non-domestic" awards refer to awards which, although made in the state of enforcement are treated as "foreign" under its law because of some foreign element in the proceedings is involved. See Introduction to the Convention, ibid.

> Each Contracting State shall recognize arbitral awards as binding and enforce them in accordance with the rules of procedure of the territory where the award is relied upon, under the conditions laid down in the following articles. There shall not be imposed substantially more onerous conditions or higher fees or charges on the recognition or enforcement of arbitral awards.

One of the key provisions relate to the grounds for refusal of arbitral awards. According to Article V, there are five grounds upon which recognition and enforcement may be refused. These are:

(a) Incapacity of the parties, or invalidity of the arbitration agreement under the law to which the parties have subjected it or, failing any indication thereon, under the law of the country where the award was made; or
(b) Lack of proper notice of the appointment of the arbitrator or of the arbitration proceedings to the party against whom the award is invoked; or
(c) The award falls outside the scope of the arbitration agreement; or
(d) the arbitral procedure was not in line with the arbitration agreement; or
(e) The award has not yet become binding on the parties, or has been set aside or suspended by a competent authority of the country in which, or under the law of which, that award was made.

The Convention sets out two additional grounds upon which the enforcement of an award may be refused: (1) the dispute is not capable of settlement by arbitration under the law of the country where the enforcement is sought; or (2) recognition or enforcement of the award is contrary to the public policy of that country.

15.4.3 Enforcement of Arbitral Awards Under the UK and Indian Law

The recognition and enforcement of foreign arbitral awards are governed in India and England, respectively, by the Arbitration and Conciliation Act, 1996 (Part III) and the Arbitration and Conciliation Act, 1996 (Part II and Part III). The respective parts of the two statutes dealing with the foreign or non-domestic awards (see infra, Sect. 15.6.5) make provision for the enforcement of awards given under the Geneva Convention for the Execution of Foreign Arbitral Awards and the New York Convention.

According to s. 101 of the (English) Arbitration Act 1996, awards under the New York Convention may be enforced like a judgment or order of the court. Further, an arbitral award may be refused recognition on the grounds mentioned in s. 103 of the Act. These are similar to those provided for in the New York Convention (see supra, Sect. 15.4.2) and need no further elaboration.

Under the Indian Arbitration Act, a similar scheme is adopted. In virtue of s. 46, a foreign award (award subject to the New York Convention[70]) may be enforced

[70] Awards to which Geneva Convention applies are enforceable under Chapter II of Part II of the Act.

provided that certain conditions given under s. 47 are met. Further, s. 49 provides that if a foreign award is enforceable, it "shall be deemed to be a decree of that Court." It may also be noted that a foreign award may be refused recognition on the grounds mentioned in s. 48 of the Act. But these are similar to those provided for in the New York Convention.

15.5 Alternative Dispute Resolution (ADR) Procedures

15.5.1 Mediation and Conciliation in General

It is widely accepted that litigation through court is often costly and time-consuming. Further, the intricacies involved in the national legal procedures may be unknown to the parties.[71] This led to the development of several techniques of dispute resolution, called alternative dispute resolution (ADR) procedures.

ADR procedures mainly include: mediation and conciliation. "Mediation" refers to a process whereby a third party, called mediator, works with the parties to a dispute and seeks to resolve their dispute by agreement. Conciliation is an essentially similar procedure but differs from the mediation in that in the latter, the third party, called mediator has "a more proactive role to play" and it is a less formal procedure.[72] Mediation is "a flexible and consensual technique" in which a neutral party helps the parties reaching a settlement of the dispute. The parties have control over the process of settling the dispute. Settlements thus reached are legally binding on the parties.[73] On conciliation, on the other hand, the third party assumes a more formal role, investigates the details underlying the dispute, and comes out with formal, albeit non-binding proposals for the resolution of disputes.[74] Mediation and conciliation have become increasingly institutionalized in recent years and offer an effective alternative to the contentious, adversarial techniques of arbitration and judicial settlement.[75]

15.5.2 1980 UNCITRAL Conciliation Rules

The increasing significance of ADR processes in settling international trade disputes led the UNCITRAL to prepare a set of Conciliation Rules which were adopted by the General Assembly on December 4, 1980.[76] The Resolution adopting the Rules

---

[71] See McLaughlin (1979), p. 212.

[72] Lew et al. (2003), pp. 13–14; Sands and Klein (2001), p. 350.

[73] Information is available at: ICC https://iccwbo.oservices/mediation/rg/dispute-resolution.

[74] Sands, Philippe and Klein, supra note 72.

[75] Id., p. 351.

[76] Resolution No. 35/52. The texts of the Resolution and the Conciliation Rules can be accessed from the web site of UNCITRAL: https://uncitral.un.org/.

recommends the use of these Rules "in cases where a dispute arises in the context of international commercial relations and the parties seek an amicable settlement of that dispute by recourse to conciliation." UNCITRAL's Conciliation Rules will apply only if the parties to a dispute have agreed that their dispute be resolved through these Rules (Article 1).

The conciliation proceedings begin when a written invitation to conciliate under these Rules is accepted by the other party. But where the other party rejects the invitation, there will be no conciliation proceedings (Article 2). According to the Rules, there shall be one conciliator but if the parties agree there may be two or three conciliators (Article 3). The role of the conciliator is limited to assisting the parties in reaching an amicable settlement of their dispute (Article 7(1)). In carrying out his duties the conciliator will act in "an independent and impartial manner" and "will be guided by principles of objectivity, fairness and justice, giving consideration to, among other things, the rights and obligations of the parties, the usages of the trade concerned and the circumstances surrounding the dispute, including any previous business practices between the parties" (Article 7(1) and (2)). Further, there is no fixed procedure for conducting the proceedings and "the conciliator may conduct the conciliation proceedings in such a manner as he considers appropriate, taking into account the circumstances of the case…" (Article 7(3)). During the conciliation proceedings, the parties may not initiate any arbitral or judicial proceedings in respect of a dispute that is the subject of the conciliation proceedings, except where a party thinks that such proceedings are necessary for preserving his rights (Article 14). Finally, if the parties reach a settlement of the dispute, they will draw up and sign a written settlement agreement and where requested by the parties, the conciliator will draw up, or assist the parties in drawing up, the settlement agreement. The settlement agreement thus signed will be binding on the parties (Article 13).

15.6 Arbitration

15.6.1 General Characteristics

Arbitration differs from non-judicial or ADR methods described above in one important respect. It implies a duty on the part of a party to a dispute that it will be abide by the award of the arbitral tribunal.[77] In this way, arbitration which is "a definite legal process" is generally not treated as an ADR technique. Rather it is more likely to be treated as a judicial method of dispute settlement.[78] In fact, "the former (arbitration) is only a species of the latter."[79] But at the same time, arbitration differs from a judicial method. First, in arbitration, the parties retain the right to choose the arbitrators

[77]See Article 37 of the 1907 The Hague Convention on Peaceful Settlement of Disputes.

[78]See Waldock (1963), p. 347.

[79]Ibid.

whereas in a pure judicial settlement, the parties do not have any say in the process of the appointment of a Judge.[80]

Arbitration is defined by *New International Webster's Comprehensive Dictionary* as "[t]he hearing and settlement of a dispute between two parties by the decision of a third party or court to which the matter is referred..."[81] In the context of settlement of inter-state disputes, Article 37 of the 1907 the Hague Convention on Peaceful Settlement of Disputes, defines an (international) arbitration as the method of "the settlement of disputes between States by Judges of their own choice and on the basis of respect for law."

Arbitration is understood as a simple, flexible, consensual, and informal process as it is not burdened with the complex legal rules related to evidence and procedures. The judges, called arbitrators are often chosen by the parties themselves. Further, the arbitration offers a neutral forum as neither party is placed at a disadvantage; is confidential and cost-effective.[82] Since it is simple and offers speedy resolution of a dispute by a neutral third who is often well versed in the customs of the particular industry, it has been very popular among the business community and has long been used as a preferred mode of dispute resolution and has indeed been very popular among the business community.[83]

15.6.2 Institutional and Ad Hoc Arbitration

There are two types of arbitration—institutional and ad hoc. The former is administered under the aegis of an institution such as the ICC and London Court of Arbitration (LCA).[84] The institutions which provide the forum for arbitration generally have their own rules of arbitration based on practices between business people that establish a "procedural framework" for conducting arbitral proceedings.[85] As will be seen below, some institutions also supervise the arbitral proceedings. In ad hoc arbitration, on the other hand, parties themselves establish the framework of procedure on the basis of the arbitration agreement.[86] The main advantage of the institutional arbitration is that it offers the parties a wide range of arbitrators and laws to be selected

---

[80]Ibid; Sands and Klein (2001), pp. 352–53.

[81]*New International Webster's Comprehensive Dictionary* (2006). Trident Press International, p. 74. On the other hand, "conciliation" is defined as "the settlement or attempt to settle a labour dispute by the proposal of measures acceptable to the disputants." *New International Webster's Comprehensive Dictionary*, id., p. 271.

[82]McLaughlin (1979), p. 212; Allen (2000), pp. 57–60.

[83]O'Hare (1980), p. 228.

[84]See Allen, id., p. 59; Park (1984), p. 1784. Other institutions that offer the forum and the legal framework for arbitration include: the American Arbitration Association (AAA), the Nederland Arbitrage Instituut (NAI) and the Stockholm Chamber of Commerce (SCC). See Carr (2014), p. 590.

[85]See Allen, id., p. 59.

[86]Ibid.

by them. Further, it is the arbitration clauses which generally provide either for ad hoc arbitration or for arbitration conducted under the aegis of an institution.[87] An arbitrator's jurisdiction normally is created by inserting an arbitration clause in the main contract, drafted well before the dispute.[88]

15.6.3 International Court of Arbitration

The International Court of Arbitration (ICA) is the arbitration body of the International Chamber of Commerce (ICC). It was established in 1923 to offer an institutional framework for conducting arbitration through duly constituted arbitral tribunals. The statutes of the ICA are set forth in Appendix I.[89]

The ICA monitors the functioning of these arbitral tribunals; organize and supervise arbitrations held under Rules of Arbitration framed by the ICC. According to Article 1(1), "the function of the ICA is to provide for the settlement by arbitration of business disputes of an international character in accordance with the Rules of Arbitration…." In fact, the ICA does not itself settle a dispute. It only ensures the conduct of arbitral proceedings in accordance with the Rules (Article 1(2). Notably, although the ICC Rules of Arbitration have been especially created for arbitrations in an international context, they may also be used for non-international cases and where so empowered by an arbitration agreement, "the ICA shall also provide for the settlement by arbitration in accordance with these Rules disputes not of an international character" (Article 1(1)).

An arbitral proceeding under the Rules commences with the submission of the request for arbitration to the Secretariat by the claimant (Article 4). The respondent is required to file the answer within 30 days from the receipt of the Request. The answer shall contain such particulars as are required by Article 5. The place of arbitration shall be decided by the ICA unless otherwise agreed upon by the parties (Article 13). Further, all proceedings before the Arbitral Tribunal constituted for the purpose shall be conducted in accordance with the Rules (Article 15).

15.6.4 Substantive Law Applicable to the Dispute: The "Applicable Law"

According to the principle of party autonomy the parties to arbitration have the right not only to choose the procedure for conduct of the proceedings but also have the right to choose the substantive law. This aspect of the matter has already been discussed

[87] Park (1984), p. 1784.

[88] Ibid.

[89] See the text of the ICC Rules of Arbitration in 36 ILM 1604 (1997). The current Rules of Arbitration entered into force on January 1, 1998.

in some detail above (see supra, Sect. 15.3.2). Suffices to say that the substantive law so chosen by the parties, called the applicable law, becomes the source of the right and duties of the parties and applies to the merits of the dispute. It would be relevant here to quote the text of Article 17 of the ICC-ICA Rules of business which expressly state that the parties are free to agree upon the rules of law to be applied in their case.

Article 17 Applicable Rules of Law

1. The parties shall be free to agree upon the rules of law to be applied by the Arbitral Tribunal to the merits of the dispute. In the absence of any such agreement, the Arbitral Tribunal shall apply the rules of law which it determines to be appropriate.
2. In all cases the Arbitral Tribunal shall take account of the provisions of the contract and the relevant trade usages.
3. The Arbitral Tribunal shall assume the powers of an *amiable compositeur* or decide *ex aequo et bono* only if the parties have agreed to give it such power.

For the purpose of choosing the applicable law, the parties often insert a choice of law clause in their agreement of arbitration. A choice of law clause generally is respected by arbitrators. However, the substantive law agreed upon by the parties should not be contrary to public policy norms of the law that would otherwise govern the contract.[90] It may also be noted that the parties may, instead of the national law, choose the *lex mercatoria* as the applicable law. In fact, there is nothing in the law to prevent the parties from choosing the non-state norms or law such as the UNIDROIT Principles or Principles of European Contract Law (PECL).[91]

Further, in the absence of any agreement between the parties about the applicable law, an arbitrator can apply the law or *rules* of law which he considers appropriate in the case.[92]

15.6.5 UNCITRAL Model Laws on Commercial Arbitration: Overview

The 1985 UNCITRAL Model Law on International Commercial Arbitration ("MLICA")[93] (as amended in 2006) was adopted with a view to bringing out uniformity in the domestic laws of arbitration including international commercial arbitration. The Model Law was promulgated to address "considerable disparities in national laws on arbitration."[94] According to the Explanatory Note, it covers all stages of the

[90] Park (1984), p. 1787.

[91] See Symeonides (2006), p. 211.

[92] ICC Rules of Arbitration provides that, in the absence of a choice-of-law clause, "the Arbitral Tribunal shall apply the law(s) or rules of law which it considers appropriate." Id., p. 213.

[93] Adopted on June 21, 1985. The text with the Explanatory Note by the UNCITRAL Secretariat on the Model Law is available at: https://uncitral.un.org/.

[94] Ibid.

arbitral process from the arbitration agreement to the recognition and enforcement of the arbitral award and reflects a worldwide consensus on the principles and important issues of international arbitration practice.[95] While the Model Law was drafted with international commercial arbitration in mind, a set of basic rules it contains are not, "in and of themselves, unsuitable to any other type of arbitration."[96]

According to Article 1(3), an arbitration will be treated international if: (a) "the parties to an arbitration agreement have, at the time of the conclusion of that agreement, their places of business in different States"; or (b) where the places of arbitration, the contract performance, or the subject-matter of the dispute is situated outside the state where the parties have their place of business; or (c) "where the parties have expressly agreed that the subject-matter of the arbitration agreement relates to more than one country." Another key term which is important to note in the context is arbitration agreement which is also defined broadly under the Model Law. It is defined as "an agreement by the parties to submit to arbitration all or certain disputes which have arisen or which may arise between them in respect of a defined legal relationship, whether contractual or not" (Article 7).

Significantly, according to Article 16(1), the arbitral tribunal has the right to rule on its own jurisdiction, "including any objections with respect to the existence or validity of the arbitration agreement." As the Explanatory Note states, Article 16(1) adopts the principle of "*Kompetenz-Kompetenz*" according to which an arbitral tribunal may independently rule on the question of its jurisdiction.

Further, the MLICA is based on the principle of equality (Article 18); respects the parties' freedom to choose the procedure according to which the proceedings are to be conducted, subject to a few mandatory provisions (Article 19), and the freedom to choose the substantive, "rules of law" to be applied to the dispute (Article 28).

References

Allen, T. I. A. (2000). In Zylva & Harrison (Eds.), *International commercial arbitration: Developing rules for the new millennium* (pp. 57–60). Bristol: Jordan Publishing Limited.

Atrill, S. (2004). Choice of law in contract: The missing pieces of the Article 4 jigsaw? *International and Comparative Law Quarterly, 53,* 549–577.

Baxter, I. F. (1982). International conflict of laws and international business. *International and Comparative Law Quarterly, 34,* 538–562.

Becker, J. D. (1989). Choice-of-law and choice-of-forum clauses in New York. *International and Comparative Law Quarterly, 38,* 167–175.

Carr, I. (2014). *International trade law*. Oxon: Routledge.

Collins, S. L. (Ed.). (2006). *Dicey, Morris and Collins on conflict of laws*. London: Sweet & Maxwell.

de Szászy, S. (1934). Choice of law by the parties to a contract with principal reference to the English and American law. *Transactions of the Grotius Society, 20,* 156–177.

de Vries, H. P. (1969). Jurisdiction in civil law countries. *American Bar Association Journal, 55*(3), 246–250.

[95] Ibid.

[96] Ibid.

Diwan & Diwan. (1998). *Private international law*. New Delhi: Deep & Deep Publications.
Fawcett & Carruthers. (Eds.). (2008). *Chesire, North & Fawcett: Private international law*.
Hayard, R. (2006). *Conflict of laws* (p. 1). London: Cavendish Publishing Limited.
Jacobson, D. (1954). International sale of goods. *International and Comparative Law Quarterly, 3*, 659–673.
Kruger, T. (2006). The 20th session of the Hague conference: A new choice of court convention and the issue of EC membership. *International and Comparative Law Quarterly, 55*(2), 447–455.
Lew, J. D. M., Mistelis, L. A., & Kroll, S. M. (2003). *Comparative international commercial arbitration*. Kluwer Law International (First Indian Reprint (2007)).
Mann, F. A. (1950). The proper law of the contract. *International and Comparative Law Quarterly, 3*, 60–73.
McLaughlin, J. T. (1979). Arbitration and developing countries. *International Lawyer, 13*(2), 211–232.
O'Hare, C. W. (1980). Cargo dispute resolution and the Hamburg rules. *International and Comparative Law Quarterly, 29*(2/3), 219–237.
Park, W. W. (1984). Arbitration of international contract disputes. *Business Lawyer, 39*(4), 1783–1799.
Sands, P. Q. C., & Kliein, P. (2001). *Bowett's law of international institutions* (South Asian Edition). London: Sweet & Maxwell.
Schnitzer, S. (2006). *Understanding international trade law*. Law Matters Publishing.
Symeonides, S. C. (2006). Contracts subject to non-state norms. *American Journal of Comparative Law, 54*, 209–231.
Symeonides, S. C. (2013). The Hague principles on choice of law for international contracts: Some preliminary comments. *American Journal of Comparative Law, 61*, 873–899, 888–891.
Teitz, L. E. (2005). The Hague choice of court convention: Validating party autonomy and providing an alternative to arbitration. *American Journal of Comparative Law, 53*(3) (Summer, 2005), 543–558.
Verhagen, H. L. E. (2002). The tension between party autonomy and European Union law: Some observations on Ingmar GB Ltd v Eaton Leonard Technologies Inc. *International and Comparative Law Quarterly, 51*, 135–154.
Verheul, J. P. (1986). The forum (non) conveniens in English and Dutch law and under some international conventions. *International and Comparative Law Quarterly, 35*(2), 413–423.
Waldock, (Ed.). (1963). *JL Brierly The law of nations: An introduction to the international law of peace*. Oxford: Clarendon Press.
Yntema, H. E. (1952). Autonomy in choice of law. *American Journal of Comparative Law, 1*(341–58), 350–352.

Online Resources

European Union (EU): www.europa.eu.int.
Hague Conference on Private International Law (HCCH): http://www.hcch.net.
United Nations Commission on International Trade Law (UNCITRAL): https://uncitral.un.org/.

The manufacturer's authorised representative in the EU is Springer
Nature Customer Service Centre GmbH, Europaplatz 3, 69115 Heidelberg,
Germany. If you have any concerns regarding our products, please
contact ProductSafety@springernature.com

Printed and bound by CPI Group (UK) Ltd, Croydon, CR0 4YY
30/09/2026
02225325-0013